# FIGHTING CHURCHILL, APPEASING HITLER

# FIGHTING CHURCHILL, APPEASING HITLER

NEVILLE CHAMBERLAIN, SIR HORACE WILSON, &
BRITAIN'S PLIGHT OF APPEASEMENT: 1937–1939

## ADRIAN PHILLIPS

PEGASUS BOOKS
NEW YORK  LONDON

Fighting Churchill, Appeasing Hitler

Pegasus Books, Ltd.
148 West 37th Street, 13th Floor
New York, NY 10018

Set in Adobe Garamond Pro

First Pegasus Books hardcover edition December 2019

ISBN: 978-1-64313-221-1

10  9  8  7  6  5  4  3  2  1

Printed in the United States of America
Distributed by W. W. Norton & Company

*For Sheila*

# CONTENTS

Preface      ix

Dramatis Personae and Explanatory Notes      xvii

| | | |
|---|---|---|
| Prologue | A Man I Can Do Business With | 1 |
| Chapter One | Personal Discourtesy Is His Chief Weapon | 11 |
| Chapter Two | Winston's Power for Mischief | 27 |
| Chapter Three | My Master Is Lonely Just Now | 37 |
| Chapter Four | Taking Personal Charge | 57 |
| Chapter Five | Woolly Rubbish | 69 |
| Chapter Six | Getting on Terms with the Germans | 79 |
| Chapter Seven | A New Chapter in the History of African Colonial Development | 87 |
| Chapter Eight | All That Is Well Sewn Up | 97 |
| Chapter Nine | The Central Weakness | 113 |
| Chapter Ten | Every Effort to Bring About Appeasement | 127 |
| Chapter Eleven | A Nice Fraudulent Balance Sheet | 147 |
| Chapter Twelve | A Wise British Subject | 157 |
| Chapter Thirteen | The Best the English Can Do | 169 |
| Chapter Fourteen | Their Just Demands Had Been Fairly Met | 181 |
| Chapter Fifteen | Clearly Marked Out for the Post | 191 |
| Chapter Sixteen | The Appalling Sums It Is Proposed to Spend | 197 |
| Chapter Seventeen | Well Anchored | 203 |
| Chapter Eighteen | Abandonment and Ruin | 213 |
| Chapter Nineteen | Riding the Tiger | 219 |
| Chapter Twenty | The Right Line About Things | 227 |

| Chapter Twenty-One | Advice from the Devil | 233 |
| Chapter Twenty-Two | The Mountebank | 239 |
| Chapter Twenty-Three | Combating Hoare's Heresies | 247 |
| Chapter Twenty-Four | The End of the Rainbow | 253 |
| Chapter Twenty-Five | Pay Whatever Price May Be Necessary | 267 |
| Chapter Twenty-Six | Catching the Mugwumps | 273 |
| Chapter Twenty-Seven | Talking Appeasement Again | 283 |
| Chapter Twenty-Eight | More Ways of Killing a Cat | 291 |
| Chapter Twenty-Nine | Mr Boothby Expects a Rake-Off | 301 |
| Chapter Thirty | Too Many People at the Job | 307 |
| Chapter Thirty-One | Entitled to Demand Concessions | 319 |
| Chapter Thirty-Two | Pathetic Little Worms | 329 |
| Chapter Thirty-Three | A Potato War | 341 |
| Chapter Thirty-Four | A Civil Servant with a Political Sense | 353 |
| Chapter Thirty-Five | Minister to Iceland | 365 |
| Chapter Thirty-Six | A Guilty Man in the Realm of King Zog | 377 |
| Chapter Thirty-Seven | He Has Returned to Bournemouth | 385 |
| | | |
| Endnotes | | 389 |
| Select Bibliography | | 413 |
| Acknowledgements | | 435 |
| Index | | 437 |

# PREFACE

*'Appeasement', now a 'dirty' word, was once quite respectable.*
– LORD STRANG, *BRITAIN IN WORLD AFFAIRS*

In 1941, as his time in office drew to a close, the head of the British Civil Service, Sir Horace Wilson, sat down to write an account of the government policy with which he had been most closely associated. It was also the defining policy of Neville Chamberlain, the Prime Minister whom Wilson had served as his closest adviser throughout his time in office. It had brought Chamberlain immense prestige, but this had been followed very shortly afterwards by near-universal criticism. Under the title 'Munich, 1938', Wilson gave his version of the events leading up to the Munich conference of 30 September 1938, which had prevented – or, as proved to be the case, delayed – the outbreak of another world war at the cost of the dismemberment of Czechoslovakia. By then the word 'appeasement' had acquired a thoroughly derogatory meaning. Chamberlain had died in 1940, leaving Wilson to defend their joint reputation. Both men had been driven by the highest of motivations: the desire to prevent war. Both had been completely convinced that their policy was the correct one at the time and neither ever admitted afterwards that they might have been wrong.

After he had completed his draft, Wilson spotted that he could lay the blame for appeasement on someone else's shoulders. Better still, it was someone who now passed as an opponent of appeasement. In an amendment to the typescript, he pointed out that in 1936, well before Chamberlain became Prime Minister, Anthony Eden, the then Foreign

Secretary, had stated publicly that appeasement was the government's policy. The point seemed all the more telling as Eden had been edged out of government by Chamberlain and Wilson in early 1938 after a disagreement over foreign policy. Eden had gone on to become a poster-boy for the opponents of appeasement, reaping his reward in 1940 when Chamberlain fell. Chamberlain's successor, Winston Churchill, had appointed Eden once again as Foreign Secretary. Wilson was so pleased to have found reason to blame appeasement on Eden that he pointed it out a few years later to the first of Chamberlain's Cabinet colleagues to write his memoirs.[1]

Wilson's statement was perfectly accurate, but it entirely distorted the truth, because it ignored how rapidly and completely the meaning of the word 'appeasement' had changed. When Eden first used the word, it had no hostile sense. It meant simply bringing peace and was in common use this way. 'Appease' also meant to calm someone who was angry, again as a positive act, but Eden never said that Britain's policy was to 'appease' Hitler, Nazi Germany, Mussolini or Fascist Italy. Nor, for that matter, did Chamberlain use the word in that way. The hostile sense of the word only developed in late 1938 or 1939, blending these two uses of the word to create the modern sense of making shameful concessions to someone who is behaving unacceptably. The word 'appeasement' has also become a shorthand for any aspect of British foreign policy of the 1930s that did not amount to resistance to the dictator states. This is a very broad definition, and it should not mask the fact that the word is being used here in its modern and not its contemporary sense. The foreign policy that gave the term a bad name was a distinct and clearly identifiable strategy that was consciously pursued by Chamberlain and Wilson.

When Chamberlain became Prime Minister in May 1937, he was confronted by a dilemma. The peace of Europe was threatened by the ambitions of the two aggressive fascist dictators, Hitler in Germany and Mussolini in Italy. Britain did not have the military strength to face Germany down; it had only just begun to rearm after cutting its armed forces to the bone in the wake of the First World War and was at the last gasp of strategic over-reach with its vast global empire. Chamberlain chose to solve the problem by setting out to develop a constructive dialogue with Hitler and Mussolini. He hoped to build a relationship of trust which would allow the grievances of the dictator states to be settled by negotiation and to avoid the nightmare of another war. In other words, Chamberlain sought to appease Europe through discussion and engagement. In Chamberlain's eyes this was a positive policy and quite distinct from what he castigated as the policy of 'drift' that his predecessors in office, Ramsay MacDonald and Stanley Baldwin, had pursued. Under their control, progressive stages in aggression by the dictators had been met with nothing more than ineffectual protests, which had antagonised them without deterring them.

Chamberlain's positive approach to policy was the hallmark of his diplomacy. He wanted to take the initiative at every turn, most famously in his decision to fly to see Hitler at the height of the Sudeten crisis. Often his initiatives rested on quite false analyses; quite often the dictators pre-empted him. But Chamberlain was determined that no opportunity for him to do good should be allowed to escape. The gravest sin possible was the sin of omission. At first his moves were overwhelmingly aimed at satisfying the dictators. Only after Hitler's seizure of Prague in March 1939 did deterring them from further aggression become a major policy goal. Here, external pressures drove him to make moves that ran counter to his instincts, but they were still usually his active choices. Moreover, the deterrent moves were balanced in a dual policy in which Hitler was repeatedly given fresh opportunities to negotiate a settlement of his claims, implicitly on generous terms.

Appeasement reached its apogee in the seizure of Prague in 1939. Chamberlain was the driving force behind the peaceful settlement of German claims on the Sudetenland. He was rewarded with great, albeit short-lived, kudos for having prevented a war that had seemed almost inevitable. He also secured an entirely illusory reward, when he tried to transform the pragmatic and unattractive diplomatic achievement of buying peace with the independence of the Sudetenland into something far more idealistic. Chamberlain bounced Hitler into signing a bilateral Anglo-German declaration that the two countries would never go to war. Chamberlain saw this as the first building block in creating a lasting relationship of trust between the two countries. It was this declaration, rather than the dismemberment of Czechoslovakia under the four-power treaty signed by Britain, France, Germany and Italy, that Chamberlain believed would bring 'peace for our time', the true appeasement of Europe. At the start of his premiership, Chamberlain had yearned to get 'on terms with the Germans'; he thought that he had done just that.

Appeasing Europe through friendship with the dictators also required the rejection of anything that threatened this friendship. One of the most conspicuous threats was a single individual: Winston Churchill. Almost from the beginning of Hitler's dictatorship Churchill had argued that it was vital to Britain's interests to oppose Nazi Germany by force, chiefly by rearming. Unlike most other British statesmen, Churchill recognised in Hitler an implacable enemy and he deployed the formidable power of his rhetoric to bring this home in Parliament and in the press. But Churchill was a lone voice. When he had opposed granting India a small measure of autonomy in the early 1930s, he had moved into internal opposition to the Conservative Party. Only a handful of MPs remained loyal to him. Churchill was also handicapped by a widespread bad reputation that sprang from numerous examples of his poor judgement and political opportunism.

Chamberlain was determined on a policy utterly opposed to Churchill's view of the world. He enjoyed a very large majority in Parliament and faced no serious challenge in his own Cabinet. Chamberlain and Wilson were so convinced that their policy was correct that they saw opposition as dangerously irresponsible and had no hesitation in using the full powers at their disposal to crush it. Churchill never had a real chance of altering this policy. It would have sent a signal of resolve to Hitler to bring him back into the Cabinet, but this was precisely the kind of gesture that Chamberlain was desperate to avoid. Moreover, Chamberlain and Wilson each had personal reasons to be suspicious of Churchill as well as sharing the prevalent hostile view of him that dominated the political classes. Wilson and Churchill had clashed at a very early stage in their careers and Chamberlain had had a miserable time as Churchill's Cabinet colleague under Prime Minister

Stanley Baldwin. Chamberlain and Wilson had worked closely to fight a – largely imaginary and wildly exaggerated – threat from Churchill's support for Edward VIII in the abdication crisis of 1936.

Churchill was right about Hitler and Chamberlain was wrong. The history of appeasement is intertwined with the history of Churchill. According to legend Churchill said, 'Alas, poor Chamberlain. History will not be kind to him. And I shall make sure of that, for I shall write that history.' Whatever Churchill might actually have said on the point barely matters; the witticism expresses a mindset that some subsequent historians have striven to reverse. The low opinion of Chamberlain is the mirror image of the near idolatry of Churchill. In some cases, historians appear to have been motivated as much by dislike of Churchill – and he had many flaws – as by positive enthusiasm for Chamberlain. Steering the historical debate away from contemporary polemic and later hagiography has sometimes had the perverse effect of polarising the discussion rather than shifting it onto emotionally neutral territory. Defending appeasement provides perfect material for the ebb and flow of academic debate, often focused on narrow aspects of the question. At the last count, the school of 'counter-revisionism' was being challenged by a more sympathetic view of Chamberlain.

Chamberlain's policy failed from the start. The dictators were happy to take what was on offer, but gave as good as nothing in return. Chamberlain entirely failed to build worthwhile relationships. Chamberlain's advocates face the challenge that his policy failed entirely. Chamberlain's defenders advance variants of the thesis that Wilson embodied in 'Munich, 1938': that there was no realistic alternative to appeasement given British military weakness. This argument masks the fact that it is practically impossible to imagine a worse situation than the one that confronted Churchill, when he succeeded Chamberlain as Prime Minister in May 1940. The German land attack in the west was poised to destroy France, exposing Britain to a German invasion. It also ducks the fact that securing peace by seeking friendship with the dictators was an active policy, pursued as a conscious choice and not imposed by circumstances.

Chamberlain's foreign policy is by far the most important aspect of his premiership and the attention that it demands has rather crowded out the examination of other aspects of his time at Downing Street. Discussion of his style of government has focused on the accusation that he imposed his view of appeasement on a reluctant Cabinet, which has been debated with nearly the same vigour as the merits or otherwise of the policy itself. In the midst of this, little attention has been paid to Wilson, even though Chamberlain's latest major biographer – who is broadly favourable to his subject – concedes he was 'the éminence grise of the Chamberlain regime ... gatekeeper, fixer and trusted sounding board'.[2] Martin Gilbert, one of Chamberlain's most trenchant critics, made a start on uncovering Wilson's full role in 1982 with an article in *History Today*, but few have followed him. There has been an academic examination of his Civil Service career and an academic defence of his involvement in appeasement.[3] Otherwise, writers across the spectrum of opinions on appeasement have contented themselves with the unsupported assertion that Wilson was no more than a civil servant.[4] Wilson does, though, appear as a prominent villain along with Chamberlain's shadowy political adviser, Sir Joseph Ball, in Michael Dobbs's novel about appeasement, *Winston's War*.

Dismissing Wilson as merely a civil servant begs a number of questions. The British Civil Service has a proud tradition and ethos of political neutrality, but it strains credulity to expect that this has invariably been fully respected. Moreover, at the period when Wilson was active, the top level of the Civil Service was still evolving, with many of its tasks and responsibilities being fixed by accident of personality or initiative from the Civil Service side. Wilson's own position as adviser to the Prime Minister with no formal job title or remit was unprecedented and has never been repeated. Chamberlain valued his political sense highly and Wilson did not believe that his position as a civil servant should restrict what he advised on political tactics or appointments. Even leaving the debate over appeasement aside, Wilson deserves attention.

This book attempts to fill this gap. Wilson was so close to Chamberlain that it is impossible to understand Chamberlain's premiership fully without looking at what Wilson did. The two men functioned as a partnership, practically as a unit. Even under the extreme analysis of the 'mere civil servant' school whereby Wilson was never more than an obedient, unreflecting executor of Chamberlain's wishes, his acts should be treated as Chamberlain's own acts and thus as part of the story of his premiership. It is practically impossible to measure Wilson's own autonomous and distinctive input compared to Chamberlain's, but there can be no argument that he represented the topmost level of government.

Wilson's hand is visible in every major aspect of Chamberlain's premiership and examining what he did throws new light almost everywhere. Wilson's influence on preparations for war – in rearming the Royal Air Force and developing a propaganda machine – makes plain that neither he nor Chamberlain truly expected war to break out. One of the most shameful aspects of appeasement was the measures willingly undertaken to avoid offending the dictators, either by government action or by comment in the media; Wilson carries a heavy responsibility here.

Above all it was Wilson's role in foreign policy that defined his partnership with Chamberlain and the Chamberlain premiership as a whole. He was also the key figure in the back-channel diplomacy pursued with Germany that showed the true face of appeasement. Wilson carries much of the responsibility for the estrangement between Chamberlain and the Foreign Office, which was only temporarily checked when its political and professional leaderships were changed. Chamberlain and Wilson shared almost to the end a golden vision of an appeased Europe, anchored on friendship between Britain and Germany, which was increasingly at odds with the brutal reality of conducting diplomacy with Hitler. The shift to a two-man foreign policy machine culminated in the back-channel attempts in the summer of 1939 intended to keep the door open to a negotiated settlement of the Polish crisis with Hitler, but which served merely to convince him that the British feared war so much that they would not stand by Poland. Chamberlain and Wilson had aimed to prevent war entirely; instead they made it almost inevitable. This book is the story of that failure.

# DRAMATIS PERSONAE AND EXPLANATORY NOTES

The names, titles, descriptions and positions of the individuals are shown as they were at the time they feature in the narrative. No attempt is made to provide other biographical information.

---

AMERY, LEOPOLD
Conservative MP and passionate imperialist

ANDERSON, SIR JOHN
Civil servant turned MP and minister responsible for air raid precautions

ASHTON-GWATKIN, FRANK
Head of economics section, Foreign Office; number two on Lord Runciman's mission to Czechoslovakia; extensive contacts in Germany. Supported German ambitions in Balkans

ATHOLL, DUCHESS OF
Conservative MP

ATTLEE, CLEMENT
Labour leader 1935–55; War Cabinet 1940 onwards; Prime Minister 1945–51

BALDWIN, STANLEY
British Prime Minister 1923–24, 1924–29, 1935–37

BALL, SIR JOSEPH
Conservative Party propagandist; former MI5 officer; friend of Chamberlain

BASTIANINI, GIUSEPPE
Italian ambassador to London 1939–40

BEAVERBROOK, LORD
Press baron; personal friend of Churchill but favoured appeasement

BECK, JÓZEF
Foreign minister of Poland 1932–39

BENEŠ, EDVARD
President of Czechoslovakia 1935–38

BOCCHINI, ARTURO
Mussolini's chief of police

BONNET, GEORGES
Foreign minister of France 1938–39

BOOTHBY, BOB
MP; one of Churchill's few loyal supporters; heavy and unsuccessful stock market speculator; involved in second-tier financial market businesses; junior food minister 1940

BRACKEN, BRENDAN
Conservative MP; newspaper executive; ally of Churchill

BRIDGES, EDWARD
Cabinet Secretary 1938–46; Treasury representation on Air Ministry

Supply Committee 1938–39; permanent secretary to Treasury and head of Civil Service 1945–56

BROCKET, LORD
Chairman of Anglo-German Fellowship; Nazi supporter; social ties to Chamberlain

BRUCE-GARDNER, SIR CHARLES
Industrialist; close associate of Montagu Norman; appointed chairman of Society of British Aircraft Contractors in January 1938 to act as link between Downing Street and aircraft industry at a point when rearming RAF was in trouble

BRYANT, ARTHUR
Successful British popular historian

BUCCLEUCH, DUKE OF
Lord Steward of Britain; close to Hitler's deputy Rudolf Hess; pro-appeasement

BURGIN, LESLIE
Minister of Supply 1939–40

BUTLER, RICHARD 'RAB'
Junior Foreign Office minister but had responsibility of presenting policy in House of Commons; pro-appeasement

CADOGAN, SIR ALEXANDER 'ALEC'
Permanent secretary to Foreign Office 1938–46

CAMROSE, LORD
Proprietor of *Daily Telegraph*; brother of Lord Kemsley

CHAMBERLAIN, AUSTEN
Half-brother of Neville Chamberlain; died in 1937

CHAMBERLAIN, NEVILLE
Chancellor of Exchequer 1931–37; Prime Minister 1937–40; Lord President of the Council 1940

CHANNON, HENRY ('CHIPS')
Conservative MP; PPS to Rab Butler; strong supporter of appeasement. Socialite and diarist

CHATFIELD, ADMIRAL LORD
First Sea Lord 1933–38; Minister of Defence Coordination 1939–40

CHURCHILL, WINSTON
President of Board of Trade 1908–10; Home Secretary 1910–11; First Lord of the Admiralty 1911–15; combat service on the Western Front 1915–16; Minister of Munitions 1917–19; Secretary of State for War and Secretary of State for Air 1919–21; Secretary of State for the Colonies 1921–22; Chancellor of Exchequer 1924–29; backbench MP 1929–39; First Lord of the Admiralty 1939–40; Prime Minister 1940–45, 1951–55

CIANO, COUNT GALEAZZO
Foreign minister of Italy 1936–43; married to Mussolini's daughter Edda

COLVILLE, JOHN 'JOCK'
Junior personal secretary to Chamberlain (1939–40) then to Churchill (1940–41, 1943–45)

CONWELL-EVANS, PHILIP
Secretary of the Anglo-German Fellowship; former professor at Königsberg University; close ties to Ribbentrop and active in unofficial contacts between Britain and Germany; began as supporter of appeasement but turned against it after Munich

COOPER, ALFRED DUFF
Conservative MP; First Lord of the Admiralty 1937–38. Resigned in protest at Munich agreement

DALADIER, ÉDOUARD
Prime Minister of France 1933, 1934, 1938–40

DALTON, HUGH
Labour MP; chairman of Labour Party 1936–37

DAVIDSON, J. C. C.
Chairman of Conservative Party 1926–30

DAWSON, GEOFFREY
Editor of *The Times* 1912–19, 1923–41

DIETRICH, OTTO
Hitler's press secretary

DINGLI, ADRIAN
Legal adviser to Italian embassy, London

DIRKSEN, HERBERT VON
German ambassador to London 1938–39

DRUMMOND WOLFF, HENRY
Former far-right Conservative MP; associate of Sir Joseph Ball and Duke of Westminster

DUGDALE, TOMMY
Conservative MP; PPS to Stanley Baldwin 1935–37; friend of Wilson

DUNCAN, ANDREW
President of Board of Trade 1940, 1941–42; associate of Montagu Norman

DUNGLASS, LORD (ALEC)
Conservative MP; parliamentary private secretary to Chamberlain 1936–40; Prime Minister 1963–64 (as Sir Alec Douglas-Home)

EDEN, ANTHONY
Foreign Secretary 1935–38, 1940–45; Prime Minister 1955–57

FASS, SIR ERNEST
Public Trustee; director general designate, Ministry of Information

FISHER, SIR WARREN
Permanent secretary to Treasury and head of Civil Service 1919–39

FREEMAN, SIR WILFRID
Air marshal 1937; air chief marshal 1940

GEYR VON SCHWEPPENBURG, LEO
German military attaché in London 1933–37, then on Ribbentrop's
personal staff in Berlin

GOEBBELS, JOSEPH
German minister for propaganda and public enlightenment 1933–45

GOERING, HERMANN
Senior Nazi politician; no formal role in foreign policy but had ambitions in this direction

GRANDI, COUNT DINO
Italian Fascist politician; ambassador to London 1932–39

GREENWOOD, ARTHUR
Deputy leader of Labour Party 1935–45

HALIFAX, LORD
Foreign Secretary 1938–40

HANKEY, SIR MAURICE
Cabinet Secretary 1916–38; director of Suez Canal Company 1938–39;
War Cabinet 1939–41

HARVEY, OLIVER
Foreign Office official; private secretary to Eden then Halifax; personally close to Eden

HENDERSON, SIR NEVILE
British ambassador to Berlin 1937–39

HENLEIN, KONRAD
Leader of the Sudetendeutsche Partei, representing German speakers in Czechoslovakia

HESSE, FRITZ
Press adviser to German embassy in London; worked closely with Ribbentrop when he was ambassador to London and when he became foreign minister

HEWEL, WALTHER
Friend of Hitler; tasked with liaison between Hitler and Ribbentrop

HITLER, ADOLF
German dictator

HOARE, SIR SAMUEL
Home Secretary 1937–39; Lord Privy Seal 1939–40

HORE-BELISHA, LESLIE
National Liberal MP; War Secretary 1937–40

HUDSON, ROB
Conservative junior trade minister 1937–40

INFIELD, LOUIS
Junior civil servant, Ministry of Health

INSKIP, SIR THOMAS
Minister for Defence Coordination 1936–39, Dominions Secretary 1939, 1940

JEBB, GLADWYN
British diplomat, private secretary to Sir Alexander Cadogan

JONES, SIR RODERICK
Chairman of Reuters news agency; supporter of appeasement

KEARLEY, HUDSON
Parliamentary Secretary of Board of Trade 1905–09

KEMSLEY, LORD
Press baron, owner of *Sunday Times* and *Daily Sketch*; consistent supporter of Chamberlain and appeasement

KENNEDY, JOSEPH
US ambassador to London 1938–40

KIRKPATRICK, IVONE
Official, British embassy, Berlin; member of British delegation to Bad Godesberg and Munich conferences; accompanied Wilson on his solo visits to Hitler during the Sudeten crisis

KORDT, ERICH
German diplomat; counsellor (number two) at German embassy in London until March 1938 when he returned to Berlin as head of Ribbentrop's private office; close to Ernst von Weizsäcker

KORDT, THEODOR
German diplomat; joined embassy in London when his brother returned to Berlin; chargé d'affaires there during Sudetenland crisis

LEEPER, REX
Foreign Office official; head of press department until 1939; opponent of appeasement

LINDEMANN, PROFESSOR FREDERICK
Churchill's science and aviation adviser

LLOYD GEORGE, DAVID
Former Prime Minister (1916–22); still held great ambitions; persistent critic of successive governments

LONDONDERRY, LORD
Air Secretary 1931–35

MACDONALD, JAMES RAMSAY
Prime Minister 1924, 1929–35

MACMILLAN, LORD
Minister of Information 1939–40

MAISKY, IVAN
Soviet ambassador to London 1932–43

MANENTI, MARIO
Italian sculptor and property developer, supposedly linked to Arturo Bocchini

MARGESSON, CAPTAIN DAVID
Conservative MP and chief whip 1931–40

MASARYK, JAN
Czech ambassador to London 1925–38

MILCH, ERHARD
Luftwaffe field marshal

MOLOTOV, VYACHESLAV
Soviet foreign minister 1939–49

MORRISON, WILLIAM 'SHAKES'
Conservative MP; Minister of Agriculture 1936–39; Minister of Food
1939–1940

MUSSOLINI, BENITO
Italian dictator

NEURATH, KONSTANTIN VON
German foreign minister 1932–38

NICOLSON, HAROLD
National Labour MP so theoretically a government supporter but opposed to appeasement

NICOLSON, NIGEL
Conservative MP; son of Harold

NORMAN, MONTAGU
Governor of the Bank of England 1920–44; close associate of Wilson

NUFFIELD, LORD
Industrialist, car-maker

PETSCHEK, PAUL
Émigré Czech businessman

PHIPPS, SIR ERIC
British ambassador to Berlin 1933–37; British ambassador to Paris 1937–39

REITH, SIR JOHN
Director general of BBC 1927–38; chairman of Imperial Airways 1938–
39; Minister of Information 1940

RIBBENTROP, JOACHIM VON
Negotiated Anglo-German Naval Agreement 1935; German ambassador to London 1936–38; foreign minister 1938–45

ROOSEVELT, FRANKLIN D.
US President 1933–45

ROOTHAM, JASPER
Junior private secretary to Chamberlain

ROTHERMERE, LORD
Press baron

RUNCIMAN, LORD
British politician; headed British mission to Czechoslovakia July–September 1938

SANDYS, DUNCAN
Conservative MP; married to Churchill's daughter Diana

SCHACHT, HJALMAR HORACE GREELY
President of Reichsbank, German central bank; close associate of Montagu Norman

SCHMIDT, PAUL
Auswärtiges Amt interpreter

SIMON, SIR JOHN
National Liberal MP; Foreign Secretary 1931–35; Home Secretary 1935–37; Chancellor of Exchequer 1937–40

SINCLAIR, SIR ARCHIBALD
Leader of the opposition Liberal Party 1935–45; close to Churchill, whose adjutant he had been during the First World War when Churchill commanded a battalion in combat on Western Front

SPEARS, EDWARD
Conservative MP and businessman

STALIN, JOSEF
Soviet dictator

STAMP, LORD
Statistician and senior railway company executive; close associate of
Montagu Norman

STANLEY, OLIVER
Conservative MP; President of the Board of Trade 1937–40

STEWARD, GEORGE
Press officer at 10 Downing Street

STRANG, WILLIAM
Foreign Office official; accompanied Chamberlain on all his visits to
Germany

STUART, SIR CAMPBELL
Chairman of Cable & Wireless; head of Department of Enemy Propaganda 1938–40

STUART, JAMES
Conservative MP; deputy chief whip

SWINTON, LORD
(formerly Sir Philip Cunliffe-Lister) Air Secretary 1935–38

TALLENTS, SIR STEPHEN
Director general designate of Ministry of Information 1936–39

TENNANT, ERNEST
Founder of Anglo-German Fellowship; wealthy City businessman; constituent of Butler; close friend of Ribbentrop when he was ambassador to Britain

THOMAS, J. P. L.
Conservative MP; parliamentary private secretary to Jimmy Thomas 1932–35; parliamentary private secretary to Eden 1937–38

THOMAS, JIMMY
Labour politician; given task of finding solutions to unemployment with Wilson as his civil servant 1929–31

THORNTON-KEMSLEY, COLIN
Conservative Party activist in Churchill's Epping constituency; organised attempts to undermine Churchill

VANSITTART, SIR ROBERT
Permanent secretary to Foreign Office 1930–38; chief diplomatic adviser 1938–41

WEININGER, RICHARD
Émigré Czech businessman; business partner and friend of Bob Boothby

WEIR, LORD
Industrialist; unofficial adviser to Lord Swinton; associate of Wilson

WEIZSÄCKER, ERNST VON
Professional head of the Auswärtiges Amt 1938–43

WESTMINSTER, DUKE OF, 'BENDOR'
Aristocrat; friend of Churchill but pro-German

WILSON, SIR HORACE
British civil servant; chief industrial adviser 1932–35, seconded for service to Downing Street 1935–39, permanent secretary to Treasury and head of Civil Service 1939–42

WINTERTON, LORD
Conservative MP 1904–51; Commons spokesman for Air Secretary 1938

WOHLTHAT, HELMUT
Businessman and economic adviser to Goering

WOOD, SIR KINGSLEY
Conservative MP; Minister of Health 1935–38; Air Secretary 1938–40

WOOLTON, LORD
Businessman; friend of Wilson; Minister of Food 1940–43

YOUNG, GORDON
Associate editor, Reuters

---

## EXPLANATORY NOTES

Between 1924 and 1929 Stanley Baldwin was Prime Minister in a purely Conservative government. Baldwin lost the 1929 election and was replaced by Ramsay MacDonald in a purely Labour minority government. In 1931 the Labour government split over MacDonald's austerity proposals and was replaced by a 'National Government' coalition of Conservatives, Liberals and a small number of Labour MPs. The general election of 1931 gave the Conservatives a large parliamentary majority in their own right but they continued to support the National Government, with MacDonald remaining as Prime Minister. The Liberals split, with some MPs joining Labour in opposition. MacDonald stepped down as Prime Minister in June 1935 to be replaced by Baldwin. The Conservative majority was reduced in the general election of November 1935. Baldwin's was still a National Government, although the Liberal and Labour components were small and lacked influence. Baldwin voluntarily stepped down in Chamberlain's favour in May 1937. Chamberlain maintained the façade of National Government and invited Labour to enter government when war broke out in September 1939, but the Labour leaders declined. Chamberlain's National (*de facto* Conservative) Government was replaced by a coalition of all main parties under Winston Churchill in May 1940.

*British Secretaries*

The word secretary appears in a number of different British political and Civil Service titles, sometimes confusingly:

- Secretary of State: a senior government minister. The foreign and home affairs ministers are always the Foreign Secretary and the Home Secretary.
- Under-Secretary of State: a junior minister.
- Permanent secretary (or Under-Secretary): a senior civil servant in charge of a ministry.
- Parliamentary private secretary (often known as a PPS): an MP who assists a minister who sits as an MP. There was no corresponding support for a minister who sat in the House of Lords.
- Private secretary: a civil servant who assists either a minister or a permanent secretary.

Lord Halifax as Secretary of State for Foreign Affairs, or Foreign Secretary, was thus assisted by Oliver Harvey, a civil servant, as his private secretary. Halifax was politically responsible for the Foreign Office, which was run by Sir Alexander Cadogan, a civil servant, its permanent secretary. Cadogan was assisted by Gladwyn Jebb, a civil servant, his private secretary. Halifax was politically senior to Rab Butler, the Under-Secretary of State for Foreign Affairs, who was supported by Henry 'Chips' Channon MP as parliamentary private secretary and Peter Loxley, a civil servant, as private secretary. All of these left memoirs or diaries except for Loxley, who was killed in a wartime plane crash.

# A MAN I CAN DO
# BUSINESS WITH

*If Hitler had been a British nobleman and Chamberlain*
*a British working man with an inferiority complex,*
*the thing could not have been better done.*
– HUGH DALTON

When Neville Chamberlain flew to Munich to meet Adolf Hitler on 15 September 1938 he was trying to save Europe from war. This was the mission that had dominated his time as Prime Minister, which had begun in May 1937, when Chamberlain had set out with the broad intention to 'get on terms with the Germans'. This had narrowed to the specific goal of finding a peaceful resolution to Germany's claims against Czechoslovakia, which had provoked a crisis that had been growing in intensity through the summer. France was treaty-bound to defend Czechoslovakia and Britain was loosely allied to France so a German attack would trigger a broad European war. A German attack was looking ever likelier and as a last-ditch move to ward one off, Chamberlain had proposed coming to Germany for a personal discussion with Hitler. Chamberlain was driven by a strong sense of personal mission. In an era long before summit diplomacy and international travel by air had become routine, his move was a dramatic intervention in the fullest sense, attracting widespread surprise and admiration.

Such was the amazement that greeted Chamberlain's decision to fly to Germany that comparatively little attention was paid to the man who accompanied him on his journey, or why he should have been chosen: Sir Horace Wilson, GCB, GCMG, CBE. Wilson was a very senior civil servant, who acted as personal adviser to the Prime Minister. The string of initials after his name meant that not only was he a knight twice over, but he also held the top grade in the two most highly ranked orders of chivalry that someone not born into the aristocracy was ever likely to attain. He was Britain's most powerful civil servant but, far more important, Wilson was Chamberlain's closest confidant and one of his few personal friends. Even before Chamberlain became Prime Minister, he and Wilson had been allies in a well-hidden but deep-seated struggle over how to handle the crisis that led to the abdication of Edward VIII, the gravest threat to Britain's constitutional stability for a generation. The flight to Munich was also, in part, Wilson's project. He and Chamberlain had thought up the idea of a summit meeting with Hitler in the course of one of the late-night private conversations that characterised their relationship. They had given it the suitably melodramatic codename of 'Plan Z'.

Wilson fully appreciated the loneliness of Chamberlain's position, especially as he struggled with questions of war or peace. He saw that part of his job lay in keeping up Chamberlain's morale when faced with the risks of his work and the criticism inevitable for any politician. As the plane droned on its five-hour flight from Heston aerodrome to Munich through turbulent weather, Wilson read out to Chamberlain a selection of the letters that had poured into Downing Street praising the Prime Minister's courage and initiative in undertaking the mission to preserve peace.[1] Chamberlain and Wilson had already spent long hours poring over detailed maps showing the boundaries between Czech- and German-speaking areas. Moreover, Chamberlain saw the purpose of the mission as, above all, to establish a personal dialogue with the German leader rather than detailed negotiation.

The third and most junior member of the party was William Strang, the head of the Foreign Office's Central Department, which handled the London end of relations with Germany, although he was far from an expert on the details of the regime. At Munich they were joined by

Sir Nevile Henderson, the strongly pro-appeasement British ambassador to Berlin. Together they travelled to Hitler's mountain retreat, the Berghof at Berchtesgaden.

There were good reasons to query why Chamberlain had chosen Wilson for the mission. Wilson had very little experience of diplomatic negotiations and no direct knowledge of the Nazi regime, and he spoke no German. Few insiders, however, were surprised that Wilson had been chosen and not a professional diplomat. Relations between Downing Street and the Foreign Office had deteriorated over the previous year. Chamberlain and Wilson had come to lose confidence in both its political master, Lord Halifax, and the professional diplomats. They saw the diplomats' willingness to take a harder line with Hitler as a risky approach that might provoke him into precipitate action. A number of members of the Foreign Office, most notably Sir Robert Vansittart, its former permanent secretary, were violently opposed to Chamberlain's policy and behaved as a form of opposition party. Downing Street, in particular Wilson, was aware that it could not count on the normal professional loyalty of every member of the Foreign Office. Strang was a forbidding and disciplined figure whose private reservations about appeasement remained well enough hidden for him still to be acceptable. Wilson shared Chamberlain's utter confidence that the policy of appeasing Hitler was the only possible way to avert war. He had been deeply involved in the British attempts to find a basis for agreement between Germany and Czechoslovakia over the summer. These had focused on establishing a formula for surrender, which the Czechs could be forced to accept. Wilson had a low opinion of the Czechs and feared they might threaten peace by holding out against the Germans.

When the British party arrived at the Berghof, the substantial business of the mission began almost immediately: a private conversation between Hitler and Chamberlain. It had been agreed beforehand to exclude Germany's ferociously anti-British foreign minister, Joachim von Ribbentrop. Ribbentrop had been the German ambassador to London from 1936 to 1938, but had failed to build a good, lasting relationship between the countries, which had embittered him against the British. Chamberlain wanted to have a direct man-to-man conversation with

Hitler. The only other person present was Paul Schmidt, the chief interpreter for the Auswärtiges Amt, the German foreign ministry, whom Hitler passed off as a neutral figure. Afterwards there was an unseemly wrangle when the Germans refused to give the British Schmidt's note of the meeting, because it was a 'personal' conversation. This left Chamberlain to reconstruct the conversation from memory. The British choice for the structure of the meeting had already put them at a disadvantage.

The conversation between Hitler and Chamberlain lasted three hours. Hitler was still in the state of exaltation brought on by addressing the faithful at the Nazi Party rally in Nuremberg a few days before, and he began with a tirade against the supposed iniquities of the Czech government and attacked Britain for interfering in an area of purely German interests. Somewhere along the way he brought up the naval agreement signed between Britain and Germany in 1935 and said it proved that he would never be at war with England. Even though in the next breath, Hitler threatened to denounce the agreement, Chamberlain still latched on to this as a hopeful sign. Hitler over-reached himself by stating bluntly that he would settle the Sudeten question 'one way or another' ('*so oder so*'), implicitly by force. This gave Chamberlain the opening to ask why Hitler had then accepted the offer of talks at all and the conversation ended with Hitler agreeing to negotiate a solution.

The other members of the British party did not play a substantive part in the discussions. Wilson did, though, speak informally to a number of the Germans after Chamberlain's conversation with Hitler and what he was told greatly influenced how the British – above all Chamberlain – thought that the meeting with Hitler had gone. What Wilson heard gave him the impression that Chamberlain's initiative had been 'a bold master-stroke in diplomacy'.[2] He first spoke to Ernst von Weizsäcker, the professional head of the Auswärtiges Amt. Weizsäcker worked for Ribbentrop but was an old-style professional diplomat, who despised his upstart, incompetent politicised boss and strove for friendly relations between Britain and Germany. He told Wilson that Chamberlain had 'made just the right impression' on Hitler. According to Schmidt and Herbert von Dirksen, the German ambassador to London, Hitler had been 'impressed' by Chamberlain, appreciating his 'directness ... and the rapidity with which he grasped the essentials of the situation'. Wilson next spoke to Walther Hewel, whom he described simply as Ribbentrop's personal secretary, thus accidentally letting slip how poorly briefed he was about the German side at the Berghof. Hewel was much more than a foreign ministry official. He was a long-standing friend of Hitler, who had been imprisoned with him following the attempted Beer Hall Putsch of 1923, as well as being one of the very few people in Hitler's inner circle who could pass as a decent human being. This might explain why he had the unenviable task of liaising between Hitler and Ribbentrop, who was a byword for cravenness and treachery as well as stupidity. Hewel told Wilson that Hitler felt he was dealing with 'a man' ... '& one with whom I can do business'.³ The only German who did not sing Hitler's praises of Chamberlain to Wilson was Ribbentrop himself.

Wilson took all these honeyed words at face value and passed them on to Chamberlain and, later, the Cabinet uncritically. He took Ribbentrop's failure to say anything about Hitler's 'favourable view' of Chamberlain as merely 'characteristic'. Wilson recognised that different camps of opinion existed on the German side, but did not attempt any deeper analysis of how this might affect what each group said or did. Over the preceding months he had immersed himself in the minutiae of population distribution in the Sudetenland but not in how the Germans' foreign policy machine worked. The German side presented almost a precise mirror image of the British one: the German professional diplomats were anxious for peace, whilst the political leaders – Hitler and Ribbentrop – were indifferent to the risk of war; the British leaders – Chamberlain with Wilson in support – were desperate for peace, whilst large sections of the Foreign Office were prepared to risk war. Before the talks Weizsäcker had told Wilson, 'This visit must succeed.'⁴ Wilson missed the logical consequence of this: that Weizsäcker and his colleagues would do whatever was necessary to ensure that the visit did succeed. Keeping up Chamberlain's commitment to the negotiations with some well-placed encouragement was an obvious starting point. Weizsäcker was aware of the rift within the British camp and knew that

Chamberlain and Wilson were much more committed to the search for a peaceful solution than some members of the Foreign Office.

Chamberlain's most recent biographer describes this blizzard of praise as 'flattery cynically calculated to exploit Chamberlain's vanity and it more than succeeded'.[5] Chamberlain's vanity was one of his most regrettable features. It was not just a character flaw; it was a professional weakness. He was quite incapable of spotting even the most transparent flattery. Like Wilson he took the Germans' comments at face value and they deeply influenced him. He was particularly taken with Hewel's claim that the Führer had been impressed by his manliness. He quoted it to his sister in an infamous letter which also described Hitler as 'a man who could be relied upon when he had given his word'.[6] Chamberlain's grotesque misreading of Hitler and their mutual relationship led him to declare to the Cabinet on his return to London 'that the Führer had been most favourably impressed [by him]. This was of the utmost importance, since the future conduct of these negotiations depended mainly upon personal contacts.'[7]

Chamberlain's belief that he had developed a viable rapport with Hitler survived the gruelling negotiations during the fortnight after his first visit to Germany. It held the hope of ultimate success. The detailed discussions promised at the Berghof took place a few days later at Bad Godesberg on the Rhine. Here Hitler began by accepting one deal, then back-tracked and pushed up his demands against the Czechs. Even after this Chamberlain claimed to the Cabinet that 'he had now established an influence over Herr Hitler, and that the latter trusted him and was willing to work with him'.[8] A Cabinet revolt was only averted by a solo mission to Berlin by Wilson, ostensibly to present a firm line, but in reality to ram home the fact that he and his master were willing to force the Czechs to accept a deal. Conflict was averted at the last moment, when Hitler blinked and accepted the intervention of Benito Mussolini, the Italian Fascist dictator, who proposed four-power talks to settle Czechoslovakia's fate. At the ensuing conference in Munich – another long flight for Chamberlain and Wilson followed by a draining late-night session – Britain, France, Germany and Italy duly dismembered Czechoslovakia without reference to that country's democratic government. The Munich agreement was a piece of brutal realpolitik but it averted war. It did not, though, satisfy Chamberlain's ambitions to dispel the risk of war entirely and he set out to improve on this harsh piece of diplomatic pragmatism by securing a lasting guarantee of peace that went far beyond the removal of a single potential conflict. Immediately after the agreement had been signed Chamberlain sought a private meeting with Hitler. He wanted him to sign a brief Anglo-German declaration that Strang had drafted for him. The declaration read:

> We ... are agreed in recognising that the question of Anglo-German relations is of the first importance for the two countries and for Europe.
>
> We regard the agreement signed last night and the Anglo-German Naval Agreement as symbolic of the desire of our two peoples never to go to war again.
>
> We are resolved that the method of consultation shall be the method adopted to deal with any other questions that may concern our two countries, and we are determined to continue our efforts to remove possible sources of difference and thus to contribute to assure the peace of Europe.

Chamberlain had added the reference to the Naval Agreement to the first draft against the objections of Strang, who felt the agreement was actually something to be ashamed of.[9] Strang was probably right. The most important result of the Naval Agreement was to make the French believe that the British were prepared to cut side-deals with Hitler to protect their own interests. As an exercise in arms limitation it was a near-total failure: the Germans disregarded its restrictions on the expansion of their navy from the start. The only reason to bring it into the declaration was that Chamberlain took at face value Hitler's claim that the agreement meant there would be no war between Germany and Britain. Chamberlain was trying to mine an illusory seam of goodwill that he thought he had glimpsed at the Berghof.

Chamberlain presented the declaration to Hitler at his modest flat in Munich the morning after the agreement had been signed. Hitler signed it without modification or serious discussion. Almost everyone involved gave a conflicting account of the meeting. Perhaps predictably, Chamberlain believed that Hitler had signed the Anglo-German Declaration with enthusiasm after 'a very friendly and pleasant talk'.[10] His was the only unequivocally optimistic and positive account of the meeting; the others make plain that the whole proceeding fell well short of the basic requirements of a piece of serious diplomacy. Strang commented in his memoirs, 'Never was a diplomatic document so summarily agreed upon.'[11] Chamberlain's parliamentary private secretary, Lord Dunglass (later Prime Minister under the name Sir Alec Douglas-Home), who was the only member of the British delegation to accompany Chamberlain to Hitler's flat, wrote later that Hitler signed 'almost perfunctorily'.[12] Schmidt, the interpreter, found Hitler ill disposed and absent-minded during the conversation and hesitant over signing the declaration.[13]

To Chamberlain the declaration was his true achievement at Munich. It was the piece of paper that he read and then held up to the crowds at Heston aerodrome on his return to London. It was the declaration that Chamberlain proclaimed in Downing Street brought 'peace for our time'. It was the document that Chamberlain believed was 'only a prelude to a larger settlement in which all of Europe may find peace'.[14] The four-power Munich agreement that had dismembered Czechoslovakia was mentioned only in passing. Chamberlain uncritically lapped up the praise lavished on him as the man who saved Europe's peace; he believed that he had achieved something that would last – a true revolution in the diplomacy of Europe – and not merely that he had resolved one especially dangerous crisis. The Anglo-German Declaration was the result of Chamberlain's deluded belief that he had established a relationship of trust and respect with Hitler that he could use to pursue his policy of rapprochement.

Chamberlain's confidence in his relationship with Hitler rested on illusion. There was at least one senior British diplomat who could have given Chamberlain a far more accurate account of what the Führer thought of him and his efforts. Ivone Kirkpatrick, the head of chancery, in effect number two at the British embassy, had been there since 1933.

He spoke German fluently and had built up an extensive network of well-informed German contacts. In the First World War he had been an intelligence officer, running agents behind German lines. He was not a promising target for the efforts of the German diplomats. Hewel attempted precisely the same soft soap on Kirkpatrick as he had on Wilson: '[Hewel] was at pains to persuade me that Mr Chamberlain's visit had been worthwhile. It was an excellent thing, he said, that the two men should have become acquainted, and he could tell me that Hitler had acquired a high regard for Mr Chamberlain...'[15] He found, however, that he was dealing with someone far better briefed. Kirkpatrick was already well informed as to Hitler's true opinion of Chamberlain and that it was entirely different to the story that Hewel was peddling.

> I knew this was bunkum and said so to Hewel. My reliable informants in the German camp had already made it clear to me that Hitler regarded the Prime Minister as an impertinent busybody who spoke the outmoded jargon of an out-moded democracy. The umbrella, which to the ordinary German was the symbol of peace, was in Hitler's view only a subject of derision.

It is unlikely that Kirkpatrick had any opportunity to correct Wilson's naive acceptance of German flattery, still less to counteract its effect on Chamberlain. As far as Wilson was concerned, Kirkpatrick could be tolerated as an interpreter and minute-taker. Serious advice was not required from anyone who did not share the view that Hitler should be trusted.

The version of the Berghof conversation that the Germans had fed Wilson was a fabrication. Hitler described Chamberlain to Joseph Goebbels, the propaganda minister, who was closest to him of all the senior Nazis, as an 'ice-cold Englishman'.[16] That was the most complimentary he got. Immediately after the meeting Hitler claimed to Ribbentrop and Weizsäcker that he had manoeuvred Chamberlain into a corner and gave no hint of any admiration for him at any level.[17] Moreover, Hitler had in fact taken a particular personal dislike to the British Prime

Minister. The record abounds with tales of the vulgar abuse Hitler applied to Chamberlain in the aftermath of Munich. One, in particular, gives the lie to the story which Hewel had tried to sell – successfully to Wilson, unsuccessfully to Kirkpatrick – that Hitler had been impressed by Chamberlain's masculinity. A few weeks later Hitler was boasting to German journalists that his strong nerves had enabled him to out-bluff Édouard Daladier, the French Prime Minister, and Chamberlain, whom he described respectively as 'quaking in his trousers' and as a 'miserable floppy-cock' (*jämmerlicher Schlappschwanz*).[18]

# CHAPTER ONE

# PERSONAL DISCOURTESY
# IS HIS CHIEF WEAPON

*Lloyd George and Churchill have a good case, but personal discourtesy*
*will not help them, and that is C's chief weapon.*
– Charles Hobhouse, fellow member
of the Asquith Cabinet

In 1908, Winston Churchill was a golden boy in British politics. His ascent of the greasy pole had been so breathtakingly rapid that it gave him the air of someone irresistibly destined for the greatest prizes. Everything seemed to be on Churchill's side. He was the grandson of a duke in an era when such things still mattered and his father had been a glamorous politician who had reached the rank of Chancellor of the Exchequer at the youthful age of thirty-seven. His widowed mother remained one of the high-society beauties of her day and a regular feature at the most distinguished dinner tables. Churchill had had a spectacular career in Britain's imperial wars as a cavalry officer and journalist, culminating in a heroic escape from a Boer prison. He had been elected as a Conservative Member of Parliament and then defected to the Liberals through a mixture of opportunism and an objection on principle to the Conservatives' turn away from free trade. He had come under the wing of the Liberals' rising star, the charismatic and radical David Lloyd George, who was also moving up rapidly through the ranks of British politics. Herbert Asquith had become Prime Minister that year and promoted Lloyd George to Chancellor of the Exchequer, creating a vacancy at the Cabinet table into which Churchill moved as though by right.

Then as now, a seat in Cabinet was the vital career stepping stone for a politician who aimed for the top. Churchill achieved it at the age of only thirty-three, making him the youngest man to enter the Cabinet in over forty years. His ministerial job brimmed with promise. He replaced Lloyd George as President of the Board of Trade, which Lloyd George had transformed from its dusty legacy as the seventeenth-century body set up to organise the development of Britain's colonies. Lloyd George had made the Board of Trade the nerve centre of his schemes to modernise British society, industry and commerce. His measures had touched a swathe of different shipping, patent and industrial statistics. He proved an adept arbitrator in tense industrial negotiations in the rail, cotton and coal industries. Churchill succeeded him with a brief to drive Lloyd George's working of modernisation even further forward. It was the start of a powerful, volatile and often uneasy relationship between the radical Welsh solicitor and the Duke's grandson, both ultimately outsiders, both supremely self-confident.[1] Churchill was to introduce huge social reforms, embracing minimum wages, labour exchanges and compulsory unemployment insurance. Churchill was the architect of the National Insurance Act of 1911, which set the groundwork for a cornerstone of Britain's structure of social security that endures today.

Churchill's rapid rise through the ranks provoked the inevitable crop of jealous denigration, but some of it had the ring of truth; there were deep flaws in his character. He was the archetypal young man in a hurry. The story ran that the fairy who had been assigned responsibility for him at birth was overly generous in giving him every talent available. When this was reported to her line manager, she was instructed to remove one of the talents. It was the talent of judgement that she chose. He was also a notably abrasive personality, which he tried to rationalise away by splitting his life into separate compartments: the one of work, where frank and brutal dialogue was the norm but implied no ill will, and the one of social life, where everyone was friendly. It was the spirit embodied in the rule of the 'Other Club', a prestigious and secretive dining group of which Churchill was a founder, that 'nothing in the Rules of Intercourse of the club shall interfere with the rancour or asperity of party politics'. Not everyone swallowed Churchill's light-heartedness or his ingenious system of distinctions. One of his Cabinet colleagues complained that 'personal discourtesy' was Churchill's 'chief weapon'.[2]

Churchill ran the Board of Trade with his usual flair and dynamism, but with minimal interest in the happiness or otherwise of the people who worked for him. Churchill wanted to achieve goals, not build happy organisations. He did not make the Board of Trade a happy place to be. Churchill lacked the interpersonal skills of Lloyd George and it showed. Lloyd George had adroitly managed his junior minister at the Board of Trade, Hudson Kearley, already a successful and well-established businessman in his own right. He had left Kearley in sole charge of his own areas of the ministry whilst Lloyd George attended to matters of high policy.[3] Churchill reversed this practice and, true to his later habits, began to intervene directly in every aspect of the Board of Trade's activities. Kearley had hoped vainly for a seat in Cabinet himself and did not take kindly to being subordinated to a far younger and less experienced man who had been promoted over him. Churchill was not noted for his tact with anyone, least of all people who worked for him. Kearley's interest in the Board of Trade began to tail away.

Within a few months, the unhappy state of affairs became painfully obvious at one meeting chaired by Churchill.[4] A very junior member of Kearley's team in his mid-twenties found himself with a huge challenge to surmount. His minister was ill, perhaps diplomatically, and not present at the meeting, so the junior had to speak on his behalf. There was no guarantee that Churchill would agree with him. The young man was Horace Wilson, and he had none of Churchill's advantages in life. He had been raised on the fringes of the working class at the then dowdy seaside resort of Bournemouth. He had received no more than a basic education and had entered the Civil Service as a boy clerk, the lowest form of life. But he was ambitious, dedicated, intelligent and competent. He took a degree in economics at night school. In 1908, Wilson had just been advanced to the rank of assistant for special enquiries in the statistical department of the ministry, the first step up from humble clerkship towards responsibility and influence. It was a tribute to the social inclusiveness of the Civil Service that someone of his age and background should have had his feet on even this lowly rung in the ladder. The Civil Service was a generation ahead of the armed services and the other bodies at the top of British society. Under Queen Victoria, the state had begun to regulate vast swathes of society and industry, creating the need for a larger and more professional Civil Service to superintend it all. Previously heretical ideas of recruitment and promotion on merit had become accepted.

Wilson had a job to do that would have been daunting for anyone of his age and standing in the friendliest of environments; the atmosphere that day became anything but friendly. Churchill objected strongly to the case that Wilson presented on behalf of his minister and made this brutally plain. Churchill's rejection of what Wilson said went far beyond annoyance at being contradicted and spilled over into the violent abuse of a man who was only doing a job he was duty-bound to do. Churchill insulted Wilson personally – 'overbearingly', in Wilson's account – and told him to get back to his job as a junior civil servant. It was a tirade that would have been painful to hear had it been directed at a fellow minister of equal standing in the rough and tumble of political argument, but here it was a toe-curling ordeal for Wilson's professional equals and superiors who had to listen. The yawning social and hierarchical gap between Churchill and the target of his abuse meant that Wilson had practically no means of defence or retaliation.

Churchill did make a perfunctory attempt at an apology a few days later, but it was a small drop of balm on an open wound. Turning on all his boyish charm, he admitted to Wilson, 'I'm afraid I was rather hard on you at that Committee the other day', or something to that effect. Churchill's charm was strong enough for Wilson to label the performance 'irresistible', but it did not undo the damage. It was feeble and a lame trivialisation of a piece of grotesquely unfair behaviour. It was all very well for the high-flying politicians and establishment figures of the Other Club to socialise amicably over dinner in the Pinafore Room of the Savoy Hotel, setting aside their daytime arguments, and quite another thing for someone of their standing to pour out his 'asperity and rancour' on a defenceless junior and expect him to take it all in good spirit.

The episode did not damage Wilson's career. Churchill was hot-tempered, but rarely bore grudges and anyway moved on to another, even more important job less than two years later. It was almost twenty years until their paths crossed again, but the event was still fresh in Wilson's mind for many more years than that. Well into his retirement, it was the anecdote he used to capture Churchill's essential nature. Even after a long career that had given him every opportunity to see the best and worst of the way senior figures in public life behaved, he still saw fit to label Churchill's behaviour at the Board of Trade meeting as 'most offensive and ungentlemanly'. His verdict at the time can only be imagined. By any standard, Churchill had behaved with a shocking lack of professionalism, to say nothing of his personal arrogance and petulance.

Churchill had also sinned against one of the unwritten rules for someone starting out on almost any career: 'Be nice to people when you're on your way up as you'll meet them again when you're on your way down.' In the narrow world of Westminster and Whitehall, the memory of a single piece of thoughtless behaviour can linger for a long time. The professional acquaintanceship of Churchill and Wilson had got off on the wrong foot and was doomed to stay there. No one could have predicted accurately what the coming decades would bring to Wilson, the newly promoted Civil Service clerk. But Churchill was never a man for regretful hindsight.

\*　　\*　　\*

Over the next two decades, Wilson enjoyed a stellar ascent through the ranks of the Civil Service whilst Churchill's career moved far more erratically. Wilson was the right man, in the right place, at the right time. He had a calm, unruffled and patient personality that translated into exceptional skills as a mediator in industrial disputes, and this was just what was required at that time. Since the turn of the century, labour disputes had often been poisonous and violent. When the First World War imposed a total war economy on Britain, the tone softened but the need for good labour relations was as urgent as before. Labour was a resource that required adroit management, and the relevant parts of the Board of Trade provided the nucleus of a separate, full-scale Ministry of Labour in 1916. In 1921, Wilson became the ministry's chief civil servant before he had even reached the age of forty.

Twenty years after the fateful Board of Trade committee, Churchill was again a prominent government minister, but one who was starting to look like a man with a great future behind him. Much of it was due to Churchill's own misjudgements. Seven years after the Board of Trade incident, Churchill as First Lord of the Admiralty had carried the can for his own many mistakes and those of others in the naval and military attacks on Turkey through the Dardanelles, which culminated in the futile bloodbath of Gallipoli. He had been edged out of government and had bolted from Westminster to serve on the Western Front, leaving a growing reputation for poor judgement and impulsiveness. When Lloyd George became Prime Minister in a coalition government in 1917, it was only with the greatest difficulty that he overcame the hostility and suspicion of his Conservative allies towards Churchill as a defector and brought him back into the Cabinet. This effect was magnified by growing mainstream Conservative hatred of Lloyd George and his coalition government. After Lloyd George was unseated by the coup mounted by Conservative back-benchers gathered at Carlton House in 1922, Churchill lost his seat in Parliament at the ensuing general election. Churchill returned to the Conservative fold and won a new seat in Parliament under their new leader, Stanley Baldwin, in 1924. To near-universal amazement (including his own) he was made Chancellor of the Exchequer. But he was there on sufferance. The mood in the party had swung firmly against the men of Lloyd George's coalition and Churchill had no local or sectional power base to set against this. Lloyd George himself, Churchill's patron and early supporter, had been firmly pushed into the wilderness, from which he would never return. Churchill's future prospects were not bright.

In the early months of Churchill's time as Chancellor of the Exchequer, he returned to the happy hunting ground of his Board of Trade days, strengthening social reform through enhanced national insurance, and he was able to score a victory over Sir Horace Wilson's more conservative instincts. Churchill's scheme featured a sharp rise in the contributions to be paid by agricultural workers, which Wilson opposed as too radical. Churchill won the battle although Wilson sniped back in a rearguard action fought over the civil servant's preferred battlefield, the minutiae of policies, when they actually had to be transformed into practical measures. Churchill might have had his small victory, but it was a false dawn. The remainder of Churchill's time as Chancellor was a disappointment. If, as is sometimes theorised, Baldwin had given Churchill this big job in the knowledge that he was unsuited to it and that he would suffer thereby, he had achieved his goal. Churchill was on the down escalator of politics; Wilson was on the up escalator of bureaucracy.

Wilson had already achieved much for someone of his background, but he was now poised to enter the inner sanctums. The General Strike of 1926 brought Wilson into the heart of government. In any crisis, formal job titles and descriptions count for little. What matters is how close you are to the seat of power, how often your advice is called for by the people at the top, and how much your judgement is trusted. The ordinary calculations of routine politics are suspended. Wilson was one of the handful of close advisers who helped Baldwin tackle one of the country's most threatening internal crises ever, which many feared – and some hoped – would trigger a revolution. He had the advantage of technical knowledge; his familiarity with the trade unions and their leaders was far more detailed and extensive than practically any minister's. More importantly, he was a man who inspired confidence and, confronted with the enormous risks involved, that was a prize quality for the government. As the crisis unfolded, Wilson helped make the key decisions taken at Downing Street. Baldwin was a man of great patience and even temper, who did not deal in provocation, but he could be far more brutal than his avuncular image led people to expect. When the strike finally collapsed, Baldwin chose Wilson to deliver the *coup de grâce* to the Trades Union Congress (TUC) leaders, telling them that only unconditional surrender was acceptable.[5] Baldwin had decided that the moment had arrived to tell the unions unequivocally that it was the government that ruled the country and not them. The handling of the General Strike is usually considered to be one of Baldwin's greatest successes – if not his greatest success – as Prime Minister, and Wilson shared fully in the achievement. But it earned Wilson undying hatred from the union leaders.

As Wilson sat firmly at the centre of the government's handling of the General Strike, Churchill was held on the periphery. He was allocated the minor job of editing the *British Gazette*, the government's strike-breaking newspaper. Churchill fumed that Wilson should be entrusted with conversations with the miners whilst he was left 'meandering all over the place'.[6] Baldwin was aware that subtler negotiating abilities than Churchill had at his command were needed. Churchill fared no better in the aftermath. As the miners fought on alone, Churchill pleaded for a conciliatory approach, but the hardliners, with Wilson to the fore, set the policy of facing the miners down to abject surrender.

*      *      *

Churchill could at least take consolation from his waning political career in his private passions: his house Chartwell in Kent, writing history (which was also vital to funding his extravagant lifestyle), painting and, his most recent and quirkiest hobby, brick-laying. In 1928, Churchill's brick-laying triggered a bizarre episode that saw him flirt with the world of unionised labour, when he found himself in the highly unaccustomed position of seeking the advice of Horace Wilson on a most sensitive topic. Churchill's new hobby caught the eye of a journalist who gleefully reported to the country that it had a Chancellor of the Exchequer who laid bricks for relaxation. The story unleashed the usual flood of correspondence. Some of the letters criticised – fairly – Churchill's strictly amateur technique in the work, but there was one more kindly disposed from Alderman James Lane, Labour Mayor of Battersea, who suggested that Churchill might wish to join his union, the Amalgamated Union of Building Trade Workers (AUBTW), if he wished to pursue his involvement in this 'honourable occupation' and, in time, to improve his skills. Membership would offer Churchill advantages such as one shilling (5p) a day in strike pay and extra unemployment benefit.[7] It would have been a gentle and undemanding stunt that could have softened Churchill's aristocratic and anti-union image; Churchill was inclined to accept.

Before he committed himself, Churchill took the precaution of seeking the advice of Wilson, then still the country's chief Civil Service expert on trade union matters, on whether he might be letting himself in for 'wrangles'.[8] Wilson replied genially but with the faintest hint of irony that 'it would be pleasing to know you had joined. The trade is well paid and you could always earn a living at it.'[9] Wilson's levity and superficial geniality towards Churchill was doubly out of character; he was usually conservative and highly averse to risk. He normally reserved his understated but acerbic sense of humour for those he trusted. The suggestion that Churchill might find himself in search of alternative employment to politics was not calculated to appeal. On a more practical level, Wilson assured Churchill that he would be within his rights to opt out of the political levy, the portion of the union membership fee that went to fund the Labour Party. He concluded with another light-hearted note, confessing uncertainty as to what should be done if the AUBTW nominated Churchill as a delegate to the TUC.

With a green light from the head civil servant at the Ministry of Labour, Churchill applied to join and was inducted into membership by a delighted Alderman Lane in the august surroundings of Churchill's own office at the Treasury. His membership card read, 'Winston S. Churchill, Westerham, Kent. Occupation, bricklayer.' Churchill's arrival in the ranks of organised labour attracted even more press coverage than the news that he had taken up brick-laying, with headlines such as 'New Role for Versatile Winston'. The cheery mood, though, was doomed to be short-lived as Churchill was beset by the 'wrangles' of which he had expected Wilson would be able to warn him.

Churchill was not the only one to spot the opportunity for a little cheap publicity. The AUBTW had a distinct political bent to the left – it recently had voted to campaign against the government's rearmament measures – and there were plenty of members ready to make capital out of an easy target. A flood of protests flowed in and the union's executive council voted that Churchill had been ineligible for membership on the pernickety pretexts that he had failed to state how long he had been laying bricks and that his cheque for the membership fee had not been cashed. Churchill publicly challenged this decision, but there the matter rested: a light-hearted, well-meant gesture transformed into a futile squabble. At fault was political miscalculation. Churchill had not sought Wilson's advice on this aspect of the matter and, strictly speaking, it was not Wilson's job to volunteer such advice to someone who was not a minister in his department, but it is hard to imagine that Churchill was pleased with the outcome.

\*   \*   \*

The following year, the political wheel of fortune began to turn far against Churchill. The Conservatives lost the 1929 general election, so Churchill ceased to be Chancellor of the Exchequer. More fatefully for him, the Labour government that took over initiated a policy that immediately inspired him to passionate opposition. In the face of growing Indian nationalism, the Labour government launched a series of round-table discussions that embraced Britain's major parties to identify ways in which India might move towards some form of autonomous rule with dominion status as the ultimate goal. From the start Churchill fought this bitterly and continued to do so after the Labour government was replaced by a 'National' coalition government in the wake of the economic crisis in 1931. This put him immediately at odds with the leaders of the Conservative Party, the dominant element in the new government, who took over the Labour government's India policy. Churchill was not offered a post in the National Government either when it was formed or when a general election later in 1931 confirmed it in office with an overwhelming majority in the House of Commons.

The search for a reform of Britain's relationship with India ground on and ultimately led to the India Act of 1935. The measures in the Act were limited, ambiguous and so heavily compromised that it was never possible to implement it in any meaningful sense. It dwindled into irrelevancy and was entirely forgotten as the changed world after 1945 swept India to full independence, but it still caused one of the most venomous internecine rifts the Conservative Party suffered in the twentieth century. A large group of Conservatives – the 'diehards' – were violently opposed to anything but a continuation of the British Raj with no reform whatsoever and fought a long and often bitter rearguard action against the Act.

With his habitual blend of passionate conviction and political opportunism, Churchill was the leading figure amongst the diehards, but they did not fully trust him.[10]. He committed a major tactical blunder in instigating the 'Committee of Privileges' affair and confusing the India campaign with personal loyalty to himself.[11] If Churchill ever intended opposing the India Act to build a significant personal following amongst Conservative MPs, it was a resounding failure. The exercise gave Churchill the opportunity to display his oratorical talents, but little more. It confirmed his status as a trouble-maker and left Baldwin with little inclination to bring him back into government. The India Act campaign marked the start of Churchill's 'wilderness years', when he spent ten years out of office, on the fringes of mainstream politics and with apparently shrivelling prospects of returning to power.

Churchill was an exile but not a rebel. He maintained an outward show of loyalty to Baldwin's government and still nourished hopes of returning to the Cabinet. Baldwin was willing to dangle hopes of office, however faint, in front of Churchill to soften his criticism of the government. This process reached its peak in March 1936, when Baldwin bowed to complaints at the slow pace of rearmament and created the post of Minister of Defence Coordination, as a token that he was taking the question seriously. The new job would have provided an appropriate platform from which Churchill could have driven rearmament forward, but this was not Baldwin's intention at all. The job was given to Sir Thomas Inskip, an Anglican evangelical lawyer, whose political moment of glory had been to talk down moves to reform the Church of England's prayer book. Chamberlain had advised Baldwin to reject Churchill, for the 'excellent reason ... that [his] known opinions & history might well embarrass any Govt which they joined at this moment'.[12] Inskip's appointment is one of the many routinely described as the worst or most extraordinary since Caligula made his horse a consul. In reality, he proved a low-key but effective chairman in discussions amongst the armed services on priorities.

*　　*　　*

With an odd symmetry, Wilson's career went through a rocky patch in the early 1930s but not remotely as severe as Churchill's. In 1929, he had moved from the Ministry of Labour to act as the chief civil servant to the Labour minister Jimmy Thomas, who had been tasked with finding a solution to the surge in Britain's unemployment during the slump. It was a challenging if not impossible job, and the experiment soon collapsed ignominiously. Wilson was out of a job, but he was far too valuable a man for the Civil Service to dispense with lightly. Unlike Churchill, his technical abilities and unchallenging conformity were widely recognised. A job was invented for him to keep him on the Civil Service payroll. He became chief industrial adviser, with no specific remit or department attached. In practice, he operated as the very senior odd-job man for economic matters that did not neatly fall into anyone else's sphere. He organised and ran the British Civil Service group that went to the Imperial Conference at Ottawa in 1932. The conference failed completely to mobilise the resources and trade of the Empire to counteract the slump, but it was universally recognised that the support provided to the British delegation was far superior to any other country's, and Wilson was justly credited with this. Ottawa cemented his high standing in the eyes of both Stanley Baldwin and Neville Chamberlain, who provided the backbone of the National Government's domestic policy as Chancellor of the Exchequer.

This all served as the springboard to Wilson's next career step, which was to take him to the heights of power and, finally, to public disgrace and obscurity. His career became intertwined with the schemes of his ultimate boss, Sir Warren Fisher, the head of the Civil Service. Fisher had immense ambitions for his own job and the Civil Service as a whole. By dint of some far-fetched constitutional theorising, he believed that his job entitled him to be the Prime Minister's chief adviser. Fisher had a double job title: permanent secretary of His Majesty's Treasury and official head of His Majesty's Civil Service. The head of the Treasury had always been recognised as Britain's most senior civil servant but it was only when Lloyd George promoted Fisher to the post in 1919 that he had been explicitly given the job of managing the entire Civil Service. In Fisher's eyes, the fact that the Prime Minister's official job title was First Lord of the Treasury (the plate on the black door of 10 Downing Street still carries the title) meant that he, as the head of the Treasury, was automatically the Prime Minister's chief civil servant.[13] Fisher entirely ignored the fact that generations of his predecessors had been content to work for the Chancellor of the Exchequer (nominally the Second Lord of the Treasury) as their head of department. As part of this project, he had set his heart on transforming the Prime Minister's private office at 10 Downing Street into the exclusive preserve of the Civil Service and to erode the support available to the Prime Minister from any other resource. Hitherto, the Downing Street private office had operated as a low-key extension of the Prime Minister of the day's political allies, friends and family.

Fisher's moment came in 1935 when Baldwin replaced Ramsay Mac-Donald as Prime Minister. Fisher was able to take a radical step towards creating a perfect Civil Service cocoon around the Prime Minister. The signs were propitious. At the age of sixty-seven, Baldwin was tired and he knew it. As deputy Prime Minister in MacDonald's coalition government and leader of the dominant Conservative Party, he had borne much of the political burden since 1931. Stepping up to the official top job meant an enormous increase in his workload. The Prime Minister bore a massive administrative burden and Baldwin had neither the skills nor the taste to bear it alone. Baldwin's heart lay in the House of Commons and not in the meeting rooms of Whitehall. Fisher came up with a remarkably simple solution. A top-level civil servant whom Baldwin already knew and trusted would be attached to the staff at 10 Downing Street: '[E]xperience had shown … the need of an experienced official at No 10 on the PM's Staff who knew the machine of government. The burden on the PM was such that he needed this help more and more.'[14] He would have no official job title, defined remit or set term of office. He would just help the Prime Minister however he could and however the Prime Minister thought he could. The man who was chosen – according to one account, specifically asked for by Baldwin – was Sir Horace Wilson.

Whilst Wilson was an anomaly on the organisation chart, he was given one priceless advantage in the mechanics of bureaucratic power: a small office immediately next to the Cabinet Room overlooking Horse Guards Parade. As one later Downing Street insider has said, 'It was seen as the key room because of its access. ... The point was its location with access to all ministers coming to wait in the lobby outside the cabinet room and knowing when cabinet meetings were ending and [the] Prime Minister [was] free. Access equals power.'[15]

Later occupants included Brendan Bracken and Marcia Williams, virtuosi of translating access to the Prime Minister into power and influence far beyond that of their official jobs. A muted but sustained struggle amongst the members of the entourage of incoming Prime Ministers to be the one to occupy the room has been a regular feature of changes of government. Baldwin preferred to work in the intimacy of his library upstairs at No. 10, which somewhat diluted the tactical value of Wilson's office, but it was a formidable location nonetheless.

Wilson was formally attached to the Treasury for service at Downing Street, but he remained on the books of the Civil Service as chief industrial adviser. He no longer did the job. The title lingered on and has caused limitless confusion as to who and what he was. It was all very nebulous and uncertain, which naturally fuelled the reputation that grew up around Wilson as some kind of éminence grise operating in the shadows. In reality what he did was very similar to what a modern British Cabinet Secretary or the chief of staff to a US President does. Wilson himself recognised that a similar post already existed in France, the head of government's *chef de cabinet*.[16] By any standards it was an immensely powerful job, and part of the explanation for the vagueness with which it was surrounded was to mitigate the suspicion and jealousy of Civil Service colleagues and ministers who would understand immediately that their own power and access was being diluted.

One accidental outgrowth of Wilson's informal status was that he worked on his own in a Downing Street staff that was anyway minuscule by today's standards. Lloyd George had aroused immense suspicion and hostility when he had created a sizeable personal secretariat as Prime Minister during the First World War, which acted as a powerful deterrent here. Until Wilson became permanent secretary to the Treasury in September 1939, he did not even have a private secretary, a highly rated young civil servant who acts as personal assistant to Civil Service heads of department. Naturally Wilson had access to government papers, but he had no research capacity under his direct control. The nature of the relationship between Chamberlain and Wilson also precluded open debate. This was in notable contrast to Churchill's methods as Prime Minister, in which comparatively junior figures were listened to, albeit under gladiatorial conditions. As was to become painfully apparent, Wilson and Chamberlain sometimes formed opinions on the basis of decidedly limited data.

During the battle over the India Act, there was little cause for Churchill and Wilson to have any contact. Senior civil servants, even if their positions are somewhat ambiguous, have little call to become involved with rebellious back-benchers. But the year Wilson was appointed to Downing Street and the India Act was finally passed, something occurred that threw the two into a ferocious conflict that was shaped by the heights to which Wilson had risen and the depths to which Churchill had sunk.

# CHAPTER TWO

# WINSTON'S POWER
# FOR MISCHIEF

*A third gain is, I hope, that power for mischief
in Winston and his like has now been killed.*
– LORD TWEEDSMUIR (JOHN BUCHAN) TO BALDWIN

The 1935 election set the seal on Churchill's fall from grace. Baldwin did not bring Churchill into the National Government when he became Prime Minister. The following year he was asked to advise on a pressing political issue by one of the key players but what ensued was a disaster for him. It helped lead him into a series of catastrophic misjudgements that appeared to confirm Wilson's low opinion of him and pushed him deeper into the wilderness.

In January 1936 Edward VIII succeeded to the throne on the death of his father, George V. Churchill had a long and friendly relationship with Edward, going back to 1911 when he had been Home Secretary and organised Edward's inauguration as Prince of Wales at Caernarfon Castle. The friendship resumed after Edward's accession when they met at a house party at Blenheim Palace, the ancestral home of Churchill's family, in June. The host was Churchill's cousin the Duke of Marlborough, and the other guests were the standard fare of a high-society weekend party: another duke and duchess, a Cabinet minister and a high-society hostess. The only exception was Mrs Wallis Simpson, the scandalous love of the King's life, discreetly chaperoned by her complaisant husband, Ernest. Edward VIII relished Churchill's powers of oratory and asked Churchill to write him a speech to deliver to the Brigade of Guards when he presented them with colours a few weeks later. He was so pleased with the result that Churchill was charged with an even higher-profile speech by the King, to 6,000 Canadian veterans at the inauguration of the national monument to Canada's war dead at Vimy Ridge, the site of their most famous victory.

The King moved on from the routine business of monarchy and sought Churchill's advice on a topic of the utmost sensitivity. His relationship with Mrs Simpson, an American of fairly modest social standing who had been divorced once before, was already considered deeply shocking in the highest circles of government even though the British press kept a total and respectful silence about it. In deepest secrecy Edward planned to go even further and to marry her. He was already mapping out the next steps to take and sought Churchill's opinion.[1] He wanted Mrs Simpson to divorce her husband and to accompany him on holiday to Balmoral Castle. The first would give Edward exclusive rights to her and the second would advertise unmistakably to the world that she was entirely fit to be part of the royal court. Churchill advised firmly against both proposals: divorce would take the affair out of the trivial realm of 'gossip' and open the King to public accusations of stealing the wife of an innocent man, whilst Balmoral was both an official and a sacred place, Churchill strongly implying that Mrs Simpson would besmirch it by her presence. Unsurprisingly a chill descended on the relationship. Mrs Simpson was taken aback to find that Churchill was 'against her' and the King broke off contact with him until the height of the abdication crisis some months later when the situation had changed radically.

Churchill had been entirely correct to foresee difficulties with a divorce and they went far further than he had imagined. The news of the divorce case became public in mid-October and marked the start of the crisis proper. Wilson and Fisher, the country's two top civil servants, had been fuming for months at Baldwin's failure to tackle the problem of the relationship, that the Prime Minister was being 'too lazy' on a question that involved the 'fate of the Empire'.[2] They now leaped into action. Wilson went to Chequers with the stark message that Baldwin was to see the King to tell him that the divorce proceedings should be stopped. The civil servants' call to action was just one of those with which Baldwin was bombarded at a very grand house party at Cumberland Lodge in Windsor Great Park. Baldwin caved in and sought an audience with the King, who was politely attentive but flatly refused to get involved in Mrs Simpson's divorce. Wilson and Fisher also went to work on Mrs Simpson via her solicitor and extracted a vague undertaking to 'fade away'.

Baldwin was conciliatory towards the King, but Wilson was confrontational and fully prepared to take desperate measures. Even before Baldwin was told about Mrs Simpson's divorce proceedings, Wilson persuaded the Prime Minister to task Britain's domestic security agency, MI5, with investigating the King.[3] It is often assumed that this was because of the King's supposed sympathy for Nazi Germany, but MI5's own internal history tells a quite different story: its task was 'very far removed from any question of guarding the King's realm from penetration by external enemies or of rebellion by a section of the King's subjects'.[4] The target was the King himself and his supporters. He was driving the country towards a constitutional crisis. Even before the Prime Minister had spoken to him on the topic, the King was being treated as a rebel against Parliament. In Wilson's eyes, his actions alone were sufficient to convict him – he and anyone who helped him threatened national stability. The head of state had become the enemy of the state.

The King's behaviour got worse and Mrs Simpson conspicuously failed to 'fade away'. To the horror of Fisher and Wilson, the King cheerfully defied convention and the strictures of the laws of the day which practically forbade contact between anyone in the process of obtaining a divorce and a new lover. Edward went around for dinner twice in Mrs Simpson's first week at the luxurious house on Cumberland Terrace in Regent's Park where he had installed her. Radical action was called for and Fisher and Wilson launched a dual-track strategy to inject the handling of the King with the uncompromising ruthlessness that they wanted. The first prong of the attack was to enlist a senior politician who could be trusted to push for the kind of action that Baldwin fought shy of. Neville Chamberlain, the Chancellor of the Exchequer, was in practice Baldwin's deputy as Prime Minister and widely regarded as the man who would take over when Baldwin retired. Since the start of the National Government in 1931 they had operated as a double act in which Baldwin handled the vulgar side of parliamentary and party politics and Chamberlain applied his energy and phenomenal attention to detail to the nitty-gritty of detailed policy measures. Whilst Baldwin schmoozed in the smoking room of the Palace of Westminster, Chamberlain laboured over the files and committees. He was rather aggrieved at the disparity in workload and was inclined to put Baldwin's reluctance to take action down to idleness rather than anything else.

It took little effort by Fisher and Wilson to win Chamberlain over to their programme.[5] After a quick appeal to Chamberlain's enormous vanity by telling him that he was the only man the King would listen to, Fisher and Wilson persuaded him that the King should be instructed bluntly that his misconduct should cease. The King was to be advised formally by the government that he should send Mrs Simpson out of the country. This went far further than anything that Baldwin had contemplated and ruled out any possibility that the King could defuse the issue by behaving discreetly with Mrs Simpson, treating her, as Baldwin had put it, as a 'respectable whore'.[6] Fisher and Chamberlain drafted letters to the King which were so abrupt that they verged on the insulting. The kindest verdict is that they were intended to be rejected as part of a process to force the King's abdication. Chamberlain convened a meeting of ministers to bounce the Prime Minister into action and handed the letters to Baldwin. Baldwin simply pocketed the letters, supposedly to consider them at Chequers, but really to consign them to oblivion. Baldwin knew full well what an appalling impression the letters would make if they were made public. The constitutional decencies, the King's obstinacy and simple judgement of what the public would tolerate all argued for a more subtle and patient approach, which Baldwin was determined to pursue.

The civil servants had had better luck with the other arm of their pincer, alerting the King to the gravity of the situation through his private secretary, Alex Hardinge. Here they received some discreet support from Baldwin himself and Hardinge sent the King a blunt warning that he was running the risk of a constitutional crisis. The King objected violently to this and raised the stakes even further by saying outright that he was determined to marry Mrs Simpson and would abdicate unless he was allowed to do so. There was no witness to the conversation between the King and Baldwin, and their versions of it cannot be reconciled. Afterwards, Baldwin told anyone who would listen that the King had told him that he was definitely leaving the throne, but the Duke of Windsor (as he had become) claimed that he had told the Prime Minister that he was willing to leave the throne only if he was barred from marrying. In fact, the King still hoped that he would be able to get away with marrying Mrs Simpson and remaining on the throne. One draft of his memoirs went so far as to state, 'But of course I was not going to accept without a challenge his bold statement that the Cabinet and the country would not stand for the marriage.'[7] The crisis had started in earnest with a direct confrontation between the King and his government. As the King set out to find allies for the battle, it looked as though Wilson had been right to prepare for the worst.

\* \* \*

With the help of some shaky intelligence from MI5 and a bit of paranoia, Wilson put together a dark scenario of what the government had to contend with. He was one of the first to coin the phrase 'the King's Party' as a label for Edward's supporters. The term had come into being as a term of abuse (and, very occasionally, praise) for those who had backed Charles I against Parliament in the run-up to the English Civil War. It reeked of self-interest and irresponsibility. These were men who had to be opposed. It summed up the explicitly confrontational view that Wilson took of anyone who supported Edward VIII.

In Wilson's eyes, the head of the King's Party was Churchill. At 10 Downing Street, Churchill was a 'possible snake in the grass ... whose very freedom from loyalties makes him a "dark horse in a loose box"'. His breach with the King over his advice against Mrs Simpson's divorce and the Balmoral visit had not registered in Downing Street. Churchill was already bad, but some of the potential allies were almost in Churchill's league of wickedness: the press barons the Harmsworth family and Lord Beaverbrook. A few years before Baldwin had denounced them for trying to exercise 'the prerogative of the harlot ... power without responsibility'.

According to Downing Street's information they had been conspiring since the early days of the crisis with the King as their pawn. Their schemes revolved around the idea dreamed up by Churchill that Edward should marry Mrs Simpson morganatically – that is, without her becoming Queen. They had persuaded the King that he could get away with this and he had gone back on his supposed promise to Baldwin to abdicate. The press barons used their newspapers to push the morganatic marriage once the crisis had broken publicly. When the morganatic proposal hit difficulties, they egged him on to push for the right to put his case directly to the British people by a radio broadcast in defiance of the constitution. Their goal was to trigger a constitutional crisis that would force Baldwin from office.

Wilson's analysis found a ready market fuelled by suspicion of Churchill's political ambition. The King's relationship with Mrs Simpson had created an unprecedented and entirely unsettling world of frightening possibilities. Churchill was perfectly cast as an all-purpose bogeyman and the crisis became an outright battle with the 'underworld gangster element'.[8] Fears of a coup were in the air. Even before the morganatic scheme was floated, Leslie Hore-Belisha, the lightweight careerist Secretary of State for War, was babbling drunkenly to the guests at a dinner party that 'the Conservatives will resign, and that the premiership will be hawked about to anyone who will take it and that Winston Churchill will summon a party meeting, create a new party and rule the country!'[9] Sir John Reith, head of the BBC and a firm ally of Fisher and Wilson, was looking at the bleak prospect of 'the King as a kind of dictator, or ... Churchill as PM, which is presumably what that worthy is working for'.[10]

The intelligence picture built up at Downing Street of the King's Party was incomplete and sometimes downright false. The picture wildly exaggerated the threat that the King's Party posed. It overstated how closely in touch its members were. There is no sign that there was any significant contact between the Churchill/Beaverbrook faction and the Harmsworths. Churchill and Beaverbrook were certainly in constant contact but there were deep differences in what they were trying to achieve: only Beaverbrook wanted to unseat Baldwin, Churchill just wanted to keep the King on the throne. The King refused to allow Beaverbrook to launch an all-out press campaign in his favour. The morganatic-marriage plan was far less important than Downing Street imagined, although here Beaverbrook was accidentally to blame because for some private motive of his own he told the King that Churchill was the true author of the plan.[11] In reality, Churchill only fleetingly considered a morganatic marriage, but the King believed Beaverbrook and the story fed back to Downing Street through intelligence channels. It was enough to cement the belief that Churchill was the head of the King's Party and Churchill himself did nothing to weaken this belief.

Downing Street had a seriously garbled picture of what Churchill was doing but was correct on the essential question that he was not backing their approach. Had Churchill intentionally set out to inspire suspicion at Downing Street of what he was up to he could hardly have done better. He succumbed to a fatal blend of quite genuine romantic attachment to the King and an opportunistic readiness to fish in troubled waters. He had taken the first step on his path to disaster at an early stage in the crisis when Baldwin sounded him out as to whether he would back the government. Churchill had reserved his position, unlike the official leaders of the opposition, who had recognised there was no dividend in supporting the King. In the final days of the crisis, Churchill went even further and obliged his detractors with a display of support for Edward that broke with the solid mass of reputable politicians who had closed ranks against the King. His actions had no prospect of achieving anything and merely served to damage his reputation further.

Churchill's passionate devotion to the King's cause blinded him to just how hopeless it had become and how slim the King's chance of survival was. Once the government had vetoed in quick succession both a morganatic marriage and his scheme to broadcast over its head, even the King himself had come to recognise this. Fatally for Churchill, though, the King was still willing to make one last roll of the dice, with the shreds of Churchill's political credibility as the stake. He was driven by petulance, desperation and obstinacy, which reached a flashpoint on the afternoon of Friday 4 December 1936. With no warning, the government had issued a public ultimatum to the King when Baldwin announced to the House of Commons that the morganatic plan was unacceptable, which meant that the King had to choose between the throne and Mrs Simpson. He had been told two days before that he could not get away with a morganatic marriage, but the unheralded public announcement of the fact came as a slap in the face and he responded with an act of almost childish defiance: he told Baldwin that he was going to consult Churchill, giving him minimal opportunity to object. Up until then, Baldwin had forbidden Churchill to contact the King. It was a piece of futile and quite token self-assertion on Edward's part. The King had little realistic prospect of survival but he had nothing to lose by finding out whether Churchill might save him at the last moment.

The King and Churchill duly met for dinner, but the only positive outcome was to lift the King's morale briefly. He ignored Churchill's advice to stonewall against the government, although he did follow up Churchill's suggestion that he try to get his doctors to certify that he was under excessive strain. This idea fed the same vein of self-pity and stress that led to the abortive plan to flee Britain for Switzerland. It did not go far, but far enough for a garbled version to feed back to Wilson at Downing Street, which further hurt Churchill's already poor reputation in that quarter.

Churchill completed his work of self-immolation on the afternoon of Monday 7 December, with a performance in the House of Commons that must rate as one of the most disastrous ever by a major statesman. He utterly misjudged the mood of the House with his plea for patience. All the tension that had been building up through the crisis boiled over and Churchill was the perfect target given the long-standing suspicions held about him by members of all parties. He was shouted down and no one came to his aid; it was an ugly display of the House of Commons at its most vengeful, with no pretence at consideration or mercy.

Revealingly, the insults directed at him included 'twister', testimony to his reputation as disloyal and unreliable. Humiliatingly for a politician who set great store by the rules of the House, he was called to order by the Speaker for persisting. Immediately afterwards, he was shaken enough to tell a fellow member that his career was over and for weeks afterwards he was in a subdued mood.

The abdication crisis was a triumph for the forces of conservatism. A loose-cannon King had been edged off the throne with a minimum of fuss. Baldwin crowned his adroit handling of the crisis with a well-received speech to Parliament, which promoted an entirely false but comforting version of the crisis as a calm and reasoned dialogue between himself and Edward. Baldwin allowed himself a side-swipe – elegantly placed in the mouth of the ex-King – at the 'abhorrent' notion of a King's Party. The defeat of the King's Party could be woven into the triumphant narrative of how well the crisis had been handled. Hidden from the general public but understood in the rarefied upper levels of politics and bureaucracy, it served to prove how right the civil servants Wilson and Fisher, together with their stooge in Cabinet, Neville Chamberlain, had been to push for a hard line of action. The humiliation of Churchill was welcomed with savage relish in the broad circle of his enemies. The governor general of Canada, Lord Tweedsmuir (the novelist John Buchan in another incarnation), wrote gloatingly to Baldwin enumerating the compensatory benefits of the crisis: '[A] third gain is, I hope, that power for mischief in Winston and his like has now been killed.'[12]

After some weeks of deep depression, Churchill's legendary resilience enabled him to bounce back, but the memory of his blunder continued to dog him. Almost three years later, as Britain stood on the verge of war with Germany, Hitler reminded an ally of Chamberlain's, who was visiting him in a vain attempt to preserve peace, of Churchill's misjudgement in supporting Edward VIII. Reminding the government of Churchill's misjudgement in 1936 was a tool to undercut Churchill's correct judgement in 1939 that Hitler had to be opposed.

# CHAPTER THREE

# MY MASTER IS LONELY
# JUST NOW

*I must go and look after my master; he's feeling very lonely just now.*
– Sir Horace Wilson to Lord Woolton

Neville Chamberlain took over from Stanley Baldwin as Prime Minister in May 1937, days after the coronation of King George VI, which each had done so much to bring about in their different ways. The two men had entered the top level of politics relatively late in life but otherwise it is difficult to find two Prime Ministers who were less similar.

Chamberlain's first serious public service job had been as lord mayor of Birmingham, the family fiefdom, where the Chamberlains had made their mark as progressive and efficient managers of the city's mushroom expansion to become England's second largest. It was more like running a business than politics. Chamberlain's natural territory was the implementation of projects such as town planning, expanding Birmingham University, creating a municipal savings bank, establishing a top-class symphony orchestra and rationalising utilities. This kind of work had an automatic consensus in its favour and did not demand the intricate balancing acts required to build support for politically contentious measures and mitigate opposition to them. Chamberlain's long-standing and bitter opponent Lloyd George castigated him for 'looking at things through the wrong end of the municipal drainpipe'. When Chamberlain moved on to national politics for the first time as director of National Service, he took with him as his assistant Ernest Hiley, his trusted lieutenant from Birmingham. It was a telling mistake. Chamberlain imagined that he had been called upon to perform a clear task in the national interest at a time of crisis. In reality, he had been drafted in as window-dressing for a tokenistic project that had already been sabotaged by Lloyd George's side-deals with the labour leaders. Chamberlain survived a few miserable months before leaving with a lifelong loathing of Lloyd George and his methods.

Despite his punishing stint as director of National Service, Chamberlain persevered with national-level politics and successfully stood for Parliament in 1918. He found himself on the right side of the vast political schism triggered by the Carlton House coup of 1922 and he could begin to exact his long-drawn-out revenge on Lloyd George. Discontent amongst the more traditional Conservatives had been building up for years against governing in coalition with Lloyd George and they found an opportunity to destroy the coalition in its aggressive handling of a diplomatic crisis in Turkey. The perpetrators put back into power far more orthodox politicians who set out to restore decency to Westminster after the suspect and often corrupt adventures of the glamorous figures who had clustered around Lloyd George. Lloyd George was despatched into the political wilderness, from which he never returned, and his allies, including Churchill, into temporary disgrace. Chamberlain was firmly amongst the new men and rose spectacularly fast, peaking in a brief stint as Chancellor of the Exchequer before the Conservative government lost the general election of 1923.

When Stanley Baldwin led the Conservatives back to victory in 1924, Chamberlain was far better prepared for a top-level political career. He had Baldwin's support and the benefit of intense apprenticeship in the brutal realities of Cabinet politics, and he needed every bit of this. For the five years that Baldwin's second government lasted, Chamberlain was bogged down in a murderous Cabinet battle. His opponent was Winston Churchill, whom Baldwin had astonishingly brought back into government as Chancellor of the Exchequer – to the horror of Chamberlain. Chamberlain had himself been offered the job but had preferred to become Minister of Health. The name of the ministry was misleading as it was responsible for a wide range of social policy and local government affairs. Chamberlain saw the chance to drive through at national levels the kind of modernising reforms with which he had made his name in Birmingham. Unhappily for him, Churchill had similar ideas but on a much grander scale. The centrepiece of Churchill's vision was to remove the burden on business of local taxes. Churchill tried to bully Chamberlain into supporting his own schemes (and doing much of the hard work) as the price of Treasury support for Chamberlain's reforms. Ahead of one crucial session in Parliament, Chamberlain pessimistically captured the difference in their approaches to the question: 'Winston will do all the prancing and I shall do all the drudgery.'[1] In the end the Local Government Act of 1929 was one of Chamberlain's finest political achievements, bringing into the modern world the jumble of overlapping, often centuries-old rules, structures and social care. Chamberlain triumphed but Churchill did not. Economics were never Churchill's strong point and his scheme for reducing local taxes on business for which he fought so hard failed to kickstart the national economy. The help to business from these local tax cuts was far outweighed by the damage done by one of Churchill's early acts as Chancellor of the Exchequer. His decision to put Britain back on the Gold Standard had hammered the final nail into the coffin of international competitiveness for British exports.

Chamberlain reaped his reward when the Conservatives returned to power in 1931 after the interregnum of Ramsay MacDonald's second Labour government. Chamberlain had led the assault on the government's desperate and doomed struggle to balance the Budget. When the ensuing general election made the Conservatives the dominant element of the supposedly national coalition government under the token prime ministership of MacDonald, Chamberlain was the almost automatic choice as Chancellor of the Exchequer. He became Baldwin's deputy in all but name and the dominant figure in practically every aspect of policy. Baldwin had no ministerial responsibility and was happy to work at the more substantial issue of keeping Conservative MPs aligned to support the façade of government in the national interest. His main difficulty was the historic Conservative suspicion of ruling in coalition, which was deepened by the simple fact that the Conservatives held a commanding majority in Parliament after the election of 1931 and had no need for allies. Chamberlain became Baldwin's sounding board when he was trying policy options for size, as well as undertaking the hard labour of translating policies into legislation. Baldwin's style was to hold himself back from the nitty-gritty work of the government. The division of labour reflected the individual styles of the two men and it worked in practice, although Chamberlain became increasingly resentful at what seemed to be an uneven share of the workload.

\*    \*    \*

Under the National Government, Chamberlain far outstripped Churchill as Churchill's own miscalculations took him into the wilderness years of the 1930s. Churchill hastened his own exile from the Conservative mainstream by picking as the platform for his political relaunch the only issue that seriously divided the Conservative Party: autonomy for India. The issue inspired him to great but futile flights of rhetoric. From his eminence at the heart of the National Government, Chamberlain could smugly observe Churchill's sustained exercise in self-destruction:

> As for Winston he makes a good many speeches, considerably fortified by cocktails & old brandies. Some of them are very good speeches in the old style, but they no longer convince. His following tends to shrink rather than to increase and I have no reason to believe that the passage of the [India] Bill will be delayed.[2]

Chamberlain reached the summit of joy as Churchill rounded off his work of self-destruction during the abdication crisis, relishing his defeat in the House of Commons as 'Winston['s] ... gorgeous vision of a clash between the Sovereign & his Cabinet ... faded like an unsubstantial pageant'.[3] He took equal pleasure in briefing journalists against Churchill's disastrous press release against the possibility of abdication. The abdication crisis was the last hurrah of Baldwin's premiership.

He could leave Downing Street on a note of triumph and hand over to Chamberlain, who had been his deputy for so many years, when George VI was safely crowned in May 1937. The new King was a radical change from his elder brother and Chamberlain was a radical change from Baldwin. Chamberlain was untroubled by self-doubt in any form when he took over from Baldwin. The long years of waiting in growing frustration at Baldwin's apparent inaction were over. Chamberlain would replace Baldwin's drift and inertia with positive and resolute action. He was determined to be 'a new style of Prime Minister' and he also had his eye on his future reputation: 'I hope to leave my mark behind me as PM.'[4] Chamberlain had come to despise Baldwin's passive approach of watching a problem unfold and postponing difficult decisions. To Chamberlain, this was idleness and cowardice; the job of the Prime Minister was to set out and take the active steps demanded by the problem. This divide between the two men had surfaced during the abdication crisis, when Chamberlain had yearned to tackle the scandal of the King's relationship with Mrs Simpson by peremptorily telling him to behave himself.[5] Chamberlain did not pause to reflect that his approach might have been wrong when Baldwin's patience achieved a brutal but clean resolution. He merely grumbled that Baldwin did not deserve all the praise that was showered on him.

Baldwin and Chamberlain were very different personalities with almost totally different approaches to their tasks. Chamberlain had a firm idea of the things he wanted to achieve as Prime Minister and worked unswervingly to achieve them. There was a correct answer to any problem and it could be discovered by hard work and application. It only remained to apply the solution. Chamberlain never doubted that he would be able to find the right answer and never flinched from putting it into effect. If difficulties arose, it was because other people were too stupid, perverse or self-interested to recognise that the solution was correct. He never showed the slightest sign of doubt or regret.

Anything that stood in the way of him doing the right thing was 'humbug' or 'sentimentality'. The solutions were self-evident once the work had been done to identify them. The notion of persuading anyone else or winning them over to his decisions was utterly alien. Ministers were selected and judged on their ability to execute the policies that Chamberlain set down for them. They were mere subordinates. He had nothing but utter contempt for opposition political parties. This fed an impression of patronising arrogance to the outside world. By a weird process, Chamberlain converted this into a virtue. He would have been false to his own personality if he softened his conviction that he was in the right.

Chamberlain projected a glacial and forbidding image. His half-brother lamented that 'N[eville]'s manner freezes people'.[6] His demeanour was compared to that of a 'provincial undertaker'. Whilst Baldwin was in his element with MPs in the smoking room of the House of Commons, Chamberlain's natural environment was in the committee rooms of Whitehall. He had no friends or even cronies amongst his fellow politicians. He was devoted to his wife Annie and wrote long and confiding letters to his sisters, which discussed in detail his political doings, but otherwise there was as good as no intimacy in his private life. He was entirely focused on his work and seldom discussed anything not strictly related to business with his staff. He never invited them to social meals.

Lurking beneath Chamberlain's forbidding exterior was an acute preoccupation with what other people thought about him. His conviction of his own superior ability as a problem-solver was a facet of a more alarming flaw in his personality and one that was to lead him into a catastrophic misjudgement: vanity. Chamberlain appeared to be pathologically incapable of making a balanced judgement about anything that he did. Everything he did was a triumph. His self-view was entirely unclouded by doubt or irony. His overweening vanity left him vulnerable to even the most transparently dishonest flattery, which he lapped up entirely uncritically, taking anything positive as truth. Chamberlain's vanity was both strong and childlike; his letters to his sisters are full of accounts of his delight at other people recognising his skills at, to cite a few examples, diplomacy, fishing or shooting. Almost invariably, he reported that his public speeches were triumphs. He genuinely believed it when he was told by professionals at a film studio that his acting skills were better than those of 'eminent Actors'.[7]

He divided journalists into the wise and perceptive who praised him and the irresponsible and foolish who questioned his policies.

*   *   *

Chamberlain wanted to change the style of government, but he was happy to keep Baldwin's old guard. He did not need new allies in the Cabinet – the rightness of his policies should be apparent to everyone, and nobody had any favours to call in; he had risen to the job entirely on his merits. To fill his slot as Chancellor of the Exchequer, Chamberlain promoted Sir John Simon, a lawyer who had never held a financial or economic portfolio before and who had no pretensions to understanding the topic. Chamberlain would continue to set economic policy himself. The rest of his appointments merely filled the gaps created by promotions with a nod to maintaining the balance amongst the parties in what still claimed with ever-diminishing credibility to be a 'National' government.

Continuity was also the watchword for the Civil Service presence at 10 Downing Street. Sir Horace Wilson remained in the same ill-defined job he had held under Baldwin. There was little doubt that Chamberlain would want to keep him on. He had been impressed by Wilson's work organising the British delegation to the Imperial Conference in Ottawa of 1932 but, above all, he had demonstrated his soundness to Chamberlain by driving a hard line towards Edward VIII during the abdication crisis. He also shared Chamberlain's work ethic. On the fateful last Saturday night of Edward VIII's reign, Wilson had been one of the tiny group of insiders chaired by Chamberlain who had laboured past midnight in a state of near exhaustion to find a solution to the conundrum of how to guarantee that Mrs Simpson's divorce would be finalised whilst Baldwin slept soundly upstairs.[8] If the divorce failed, Edward would have abdicated for nothing. Wilson was fully in tune with Chamberlain's style of government and set for a major place in the new premiership.

Wilson hesitated fractionally in deciding to continue with Chamberlain. One of his friends, the businessman Lord Woolton, was aware of the risks that Wilson was running and advised him against staying

on. Woolton understood that civil servants must tread a fine line between professional loyalty to their political masters and becoming their
outright political allies.[9] Woolton saw the danger that Wilson would
step onto the wrong side of the line, albeit with the best of motives.
Woolton knew that a civil servant should not become the confidant of
the Prime Minister, abandoning the distance that should exist between
a senior politician and an official. He appreciated the danger that lay
in Wilson's sympathy for the Prime Minister amidst the huge pressures
of his job. He recognised that Wilson was driven in part by affection
and sympathy for Chamberlain, but he also saw that Wilson relished
the immense power that his position gave him and was reluctant to
abandon it. Wilson turned down Woolton's advice.

Chamberlain's top policy priority as Prime Minister was foreign affairs.
The British economy was slowly and steadily recovering from the ravages
of the slump, and the abdication of Edward VIII had removed one great
potentially damaging domestic issue. By contrast, danger lurked everywhere abroad. The reoccupation of the Rhineland a year before in March
1936 was manifestly only the start of Hitler's drive to rebuild Germany's
strength and prestige from the humiliations of the Treaty of Versailles.
Relations between Mussolini and the democratic powers were still overshadowed by their compromised and bungling reaction to Fascist Italy's
invasion of Ethiopia, which marked a new stage in external aggression
and self-confidence. A full-scale civil war had been raging in Spain since
the summer of 1936, which had already drawn in Hitler and Mussolini,
as allies of Franco's insurgent nationalists, and the Soviet Union, which
was driving Communist control of the Republican government. Europe
faced a grave danger of war, but France was hamstrung by internal political instability. Britain offered Europe's best chance of peace.

Even before he took over as Prime Minister, Chamberlain's analysis
of the foreign policy problems facing Britain was defined by his certainty that Churchill was wrong:

If the menace of attack from Germany is as imminent as Winston
would have us believe, there is nothing we could do which would
make us ready to meet it. But I do not believe that it *is* imminent. By

careful diplomacy I believe we can stave it off, perhaps indefinitely, but if we were now to follow Winston's advice and sacrifice our commerce to the manufacture of arms we should inflict a certain injury upon our trade from which it would take generations to recover, we should destroy the confidence which now happily exists and we should cripple the revenue.[10]

Almost since Hitler had become the Chancellor of Germany, Churchill had recognised the danger that he posed. This had spurred Churchill to call for Britain to rearm, above all in the air, where he explicitly focused on Germany's lead over Britain as an urgent problem. As Chancellor of the Exchequer Chamberlain had fought a long rearguard action against the scale of spending on rearmament. He believed – largely correctly – that his economic policies had rescued the British economy from the ravages of the Great Slump and he resisted anything that might compromise this achievement.

Chamberlain accepted the need for rearmament, but he saw it as his duty to keep spending to a minimum. Even the imminent switch from being Chancellor of the Exchequer to taking over as Prime Minister did not change his priorities. In April 1937, just before he became Prime Minister, Chamberlain boasted of the 'constant & harassing rearguard action that I am fighting against the Services all the time'.[11] The armed forces were just another set of spending ministries, who could 'see … how good the going is now and … want to be 100% or 200% safe on everything'. Chamberlain was entirely correct about the huge economic cost that any confrontation with Germany required; the flaw lay in the 'careful diplomacy' he pursued to ward one off. He defined his diplomatic plan as a contrast to what he saw as Baldwin's reactive policies. To Chamberlain, these had been 'drift' and he was determined to undertake a 'positive' policy; in simple terms, to do something.[12] Fatefully, what Chamberlain decided to do was not to try to face down the dictators, but to build bridges to them. Appeasement was anything but a cautious policy forced on Chamberlain by circumstance; it was an all-out, positive pursuit of friendship with Hitler and Mussolini that was actively chosen as a policy and conducted accordingly.

Churchill's instinctive desire to face up to the dictators was the anti-thesis of Chamberlain's policy. He had already proved himself danger-ous in Chamberlain's eyes by advocating costly rearmament. He now appeared as an outright opponent.

According to J. P. L. Thomas, an MP who had extensive dealings with Wilson and was also deeply involved in foreign affairs as parliamentary private secretary to Foreign Secretary Anthony Eden, it was actually Horace Wilson who shaped Chamberlain's policy of appeasement from the outset:

> He [Wilson] told me that he had been somewhat nervous about Mr Chamberlain as PM, but it was up to him, Sir Horace, to make this Premiership outstanding. Mr Baldwin had shone in home affairs so there were no laurels to be had in that quarter. Sir Horace had, therefore, decided that Mr Chamberlain would have to be a 'Foreign Affairs' Prime Minister and that his first step must be to start to build up this reputation by an attempt to break down the hostilities of the Dictators towards this country.[13]

Thomas's story is dubious for a number of reasons, but Wilson was certainly very close to the shift in priorities at Downing Street. He was fully involved in Chamberlain's moves in foreign policy from the start and approved of them entirely. Unless Thomas's account is a complete fiction, it shows us the dawn of what was to become a very powerful partnership indeed, which drove one of Britain's most controversial exercises in diplomacy ever.

Wilson feared the prospect of war. He was dogged by the common nightmare vision of modern air warfare, which was at the top of the list of the topics that he knew Chamberlain would have to address.[14] Wilson was singularly unqualified to advise the Prime Minister on diplomacy. His only serious exposure to international affairs had been the Ottawa Conference, which had ultimately amounted to little more than a series of bilateral trade negotiations amongst fundamentally similar British do-minions. There is no evidence that he spoke any foreign language or had travelled in Europe. His mental template for diplomacy came from his experience as a labour negotiator. Here he had great success, but as a mediator and not a principal. W. J. Brown, the Civil Service trade unionist and later politician, had ample opportunity to see Wilson in action.

> The essence of settling such disputes is for the Conciliator to meet each side separately. Then he drafts a formula, which each side will interpret in its own way, and persuades each side that it really gives them the essentials of what it wants ... Now such a training is first-class for dealing with all sorts of people. But not, unfortunately, for dealing with a Hitler! Therein lay the secret of the badness of Wilson's influence. In all the critical years, when swift, bold, strong action could have served our need, Wilson's temporising, 'play for safety', formula-evolving mind reinforced and emphasised the weakness of the Prime Minister.[15]

Wilson's influence was all the greater because of the small number of people that surrounded a Prime Minister in those days. His staff was barely bigger than that of a provincial bishop. Wilson was by far the most senior of them and a consummate insider. He had spent more than twenty years at the highest level of the Civil Service and so knew intimately the mechanism and the individuals that helped shape and implement policies. As gatekeeper and sifter of correspondence alone, he controlled a large slice of the Prime Minister's working life. Chamberlain spent far less time and effort on the purely political side of the job and spent a minimum of time in the Houses of Parliament. It was the administrative side of the job that appealed to him and here Wilson was in his element.

Insiders recognised how much power Wilson held. To Sir John Reith he was 'a great power in the land'.[16] Rab Butler, Chamberlain's junior Foreign Office minister who worked very closely with him on foreign affairs, went even further: 'Sir Horace Wilson's power is very great. He is the Burleigh* of the present age' and even 'the uncrowned ruler of England'.[17] Woolton, a personal friend of Wilson as well as Chamberlain, and later a government minister, ranked him only second to

---

\* William Cecil, Lord Burghley, Elizabeth I's chief minister.

Chamberlain: '[T]remendous power ... unequalled by any member of the Cabinet except the Prime Minister.'[18]

Who was in the driving seat in the relationship? Outwardly, Wilson never flaunted his position, maintaining the traditional reserved discretion of the senior civil servant. Even when he wrote detailed accounts of the great crises in which he had been involved to be read many years later, Wilson air-brushed himself out of his own history. Informed contemporaries close to the relationship told a different story as to who was the dominant partner. At one extreme was Butler: '[H]is influence over Chamberlain is something extraordinary[; he] simply cannot move without him.'[19] Butler saw Wilson as 'the real PM' and painted a sinister picture of him in operation on Chamberlain: he 'moves in a mysterious way his wonders to perform'.[20] Butler remained a close ally of Chamberlain and Wilson in pursuing appeasement to the bitter end, so had little motive to blacken the picture. Two of Chamberlain's junior private secretaries believed the Prime Minister depended on Wilson. Jasper Rootham, who did the job in 1938 and 1939, believed this strongly;[21] whilst John ('Jock') Colville, who took over from Rootham, wrote that Chamberlain 'did little without [Wilson's] advice' to the extent that he would ask Colville to submit his own (Chamberlain's) decisions (on presumably relatively minor matters) to Wilson for approval.[22] Sir Alexander Cadogan, a senior Foreign Office civil servant, also ranked Wilson's position within the relationship highly: 'in [Wilson] he had complete confidence, and was not unnaturally inclined to turn to him for advice and suggestions.'[23] Chamberlain enthused openly to a passing visitor, 'He is the most remarkable man in England. I couldn't live a day without him.'[24] By contrast one of Chamberlain's principal private secretaries was more guarded: 'NC needed someone who agreed with him to try out his views.'[25]

J. P. L. Thomas had an extreme view, but it is beyond argument that Wilson was uniquely placed to work on Chamberlain. Wilson's relationship with Chamberlain was entirely in a league of its own; there is no account of any other senior figure enjoying this level of access to Chamberlain during his premiership. Wilson was certainly the only person who might have shaped seriously the decisions Chamberlain took. Chamberlain was used to giving instructions from authority and not gently manoeuvring people to do what he wanted. He was poorly equipped to detect attempts by other people to bend him to their will unless they were entirely unsubtle. During the abdication crisis, Wilson and Sir Warren Fisher had found Chamberlain an easy target for manipulation when they needed a senior ally in Cabinet to push for ruthless measures against Edward VIII.[26] Wilson had the people skills that Chamberlain patently lacked. The art historian Kenneth Clark, who visited Downing Street on a number of occasions, remarked:

> Mr Chamberlain was not an imaginative man and was singularly devoid of 'antennae'. Decisions involving these qualities were made for him by an extraordinary character called Sir Horace Wilson. He sat in a small office outside the Prime Minister's room … and everyone with an appointment had to pass through this office and have a few minutes' conversation with Sir Horace. He was a fascinating contrast to his chief, very feminine, with a supple and what used to be called Jesuitical turn of mind.[27]

In contrast to his master, Wilson had a welcoming personality. He made many friends amongst the people he dealt with. He had a gentle, understated but teasing sense of humour. Wilson's low-key exterior masked the force of his personality. His instinctive self-effacement was so strong that a German diplomat had to brief his chief in Berlin on his true importance:

> Horace Wilson is generally considered to be one of the most influential men in the British Government. He does not like to appear in the limelight. It is an established fact Neville Chamberlain asks for his advice on all matters. This man, who is opposed to all outward show, commands respect from all those who come in contact with him. He is an embodiment of Moltke's idea: 'To be more than you appear to be.'[28]

Wilson hid from attention but he enjoyed his power. Woolton believed that this was the decisive reason why Wilson rejected his advice and accepted Chamberlain's invitation to continue at Downing Street:

[H]e found himself enjoying tremendous power – in fact with a power unequalled by any member of the Cabinet except the Prime Minister, and few people who have ever had power will be prepared to make a harsh judgement about a man who did not find it easy to give up.[29]

Butler echoed Woolton, but in far more hostile tones: 'Horace Wilson has, however, tasted blood and likes power.'[30]

Chamberlain and Wilson trusted each other completely. The strength of the relationship excluded other people and their points of view. Irrespective of whether he was an éminence grise or merely a deferential assistant, Wilson reinforced one of Chamberlain's characteristics that was to prove fatally damaging. Both men were completely convinced of the accuracy of their own judgement: '[Wilson] had come to believe himself as infallible as Chamberlain considered him to be.'[31] Chamberlain and Wilson were utterly convinced that the policy of appeasement was right and never weakened despite the growing evidence of its flaws. Wilson was not so much a sounding board as an echo chamber.

Both men believed passionately that theirs was the correct policy but their views were not necessarily identical. Wilson was obsessively cautious and desperate to avoid anything that might provoke the dictators. His voice was constantly in Chamberlain's ear advising against firmness, and he can fairly be blamed for the flavour of grovelling submissiveness that made appeasement so shameful.

Whatever the balance of power might have been in the relationship, Chamberlain and Wilson functioned as a unit. It was soon understood that Wilson spoke with the full authority of the Prime Minister and that anything he said came from the very top. Wilson was far more influential than he had been under Baldwin. Practically all correspondence with Downing Street passed across his desk and Chamberlain almost always accepted Wilson's decision on how to handle questions as they arose. When he had first been appointed to Downing Street, Wilson had been confident that he could read Baldwin's mind and Chamberlain presented far less of a challenge. Eventually ministers gave up the pretence of having direct access to the Prime Minister and wrote directly to Wilson, entirely abandoning the established protocol.

Wilson was Chamberlain's dominant official adviser and he was Chamberlain's only real friend. This gave him a position that went far beyond anything that he had enjoyed with Baldwin. Chamberlain's need for friendship was accentuated by his fundamentally solitary character. The job of head of government is a lonely one under any circumstances; he or she can only give his or her confidence very sparingly. Chamberlain's parliamentary private secretary, Lord Dunglass, knew from later personal experience what drove the relationship between Chamberlain and Wilson:

> It is useless, too, resenting the choice by a Prime Minister of a confidant who acquires a position of intimacy with him ... The office of Prime Minister is a solitary tenancy and it is natural to choose someone of trust to be always on call and to ease the burden with advice and company.[32]

After the day's business was done, Wilson offered Chamberlain a chance to unwind that was all the more vital if he was under pressure. Wilson knew full well how important this psychological support was and treated it as part of his duties as an official and a friend, albeit with a touch of cynicism. He excused himself for leaving a dinner with Woolton by saying, 'I must go and look after my master; he's feeling very lonely just now.'[33]

\* \* \*

Only one other man came near to winning Chamberlain's confidence to the same extent as Wilson. Sir Joseph Ball offered him professional support as a party politician, matching Wilson's work with the civil servant. They both operated well out of the public eye. Whilst Wilson was cloaked in the traditional anonymity of a civil servant, Ball operated in even deeper shadows. He had trained as a barrister and spent ten years in the Metropolitan Police dealing with foreign nationals in Britain before finding his true vocation during the First World War when he moved to MI5. Here he became an interrogator covering the whole gamut of potentially interesting individuals that the security services thought might be enemy agents or useful sources of information. He stayed on at MI5 after the Armistice working for B Branch, responsible for 'investigations and inquiries'. By then, Imperial Germany was no longer the chief threat to national security – a position now held by international communism following its triumph in the Russian Revolution.

Somewhere along the way, Ball acquired an army rank, and was almost invariably known as Major Ball until he stepped up to become Sir Joseph Ball. Many men who had served in the war continued to use their ranks, but Ball had never undergone military training or seen combat. Ball rarely missed an opportunity to remind people with whom he was dealing of his senior-level ties to the world of intelligence, even long after he had left government service.

In 1927, Ball was lured away from the poor pay and prospects of MI5 by J. C. C. Davidson, a crony of Baldwin who was then chairman of the Conservative Party and was in the process of putting the organisation on a professional footing. Ostensibly, Ball was in charge of 'Information', but his deeper role was far more interesting and firmly rooted in his skills and experience at MI5. Davidson later wrote:

> With Joseph Ball I ran a little intelligence service of our own, quite separate from the Party organization. We had agents actually in the Labour Party headquarters, with the result that we got their reports on political feeling in the country as well as our own. We also got advance 'pulls' of their literature. This we arranged with Odhams Press, who did most of the Labour Party printing, with the result that we frequently received copies of their leaflets and pamphlets before they reached Transport House [Labour Party headquarters]. This was of enormous value to us [as] we were able to study Labour Party policy in advance, and in the case of leaflets we could produce a reply to appear simultaneously.[34]

Ball's network eventually extended to agents at the Trades Union Congress headquarters. It seems that his agents were corrupt and worked for money rather than ideology. He was certainly at home in this kind of environment and his subsequent business career in the City of London showed a familiarity with and tolerance of financial corruption, remarkable even by the lax standards of the 1950s, but for the next decade and a half he was firmly entrenched at the highest levels of the Conservative Party.[35] In 1955, Davidson wrote:

> Joseph Ball and I have been associated for a great many years, and still are; he is undoubtedly tough and has looked after his own interests. On the other hand, he is steeped in [presumably Secret] Service tradition, and has as much experience as anyone I know on the seamy side of life and the handling of crooks...[36]

The 1920s were a golden age for private venture espionage under the spur of the fight against Bolshevism and its threat to the established order. The line between communism and the labour movement was blurred and the security services were suspicious of Britain's parliamentary Labour Party as a potential Soviet tool. There were close ties between MI5 and the Industrial Intelligence Bureau, organised by the ferociously anti-trade-union industrialist Sir George Makgill and financed by a variety of business groups, notably the Federation of British Industries, ancestor of today's CBI. Suspicion of socialism was strong enough to serve as a justification for extreme measures of dubious legality. The episode of the Zinoviev letter came perilously close to casting the intelligence services as allies of the Conservative Party. Grigori Zinoviev headed the Communist International and the letter instructed the British Communist Party to launch a campaign of subversion, implying that Ramsay MacDonald's Labour-led government presented an opportunity for communism. The letter was obtained by British intelligence, leaked to the Conservative Party and splashed in the right-wing *Daily Mail* just before the 1924 general election, which brought down Britain's first Labour government under MacDonald. Many years later, the letter itself was shown to be a blatant forgery, but it accurately embodied Soviet intentions. Ball is one of a number of suspects as prime mover of the original operation, and he was deeply

involved in deciding how Baldwin's government should handle the disclosure of how the leak occurred.

In 1930, Davidson was squeezed out of the chairmanship of the
party, but Ball stayed on and thrived. He was promoted to be director of a newly created Conservative Research Department, giving an
official dimension to his unofficial information-gathering activities. It
also brought him close to the formulation of party policy. From the
outset, Chamberlain was closely involved with the new department and
developed a close relationship with Ball, lubricated by Ball's outrageous
flattery. Chamberlain briefly replaced Davidson as party chairman,
but when he stepped down from the job in 1931, he kept control of
the Conservative Research Department. Under Ball's stewardship the
department became Chamberlain's private army. Chamberlain even
considered adding propaganda to Ball's remit, which would have
shifted a vital operation away from the Conservative Party proper. Ball
somehow held control of the fleet of mobile cinema vans which toured
the country providing free entertainment laced with party propaganda.
Chamberlain relished the prominence that Ball gave to films in which
he featured.

Ball's involvement in back-channel contacts with Italy mirrored Wilson's with Germany. He, too, was a man whom Chamberlain trusted
completely to implement his desires, in contrast to the reservations he
entertained about his Foreign Secretaries and the Foreign Office itself.

Wilson gave Chamberlain the comfort of having a friendly and discreet confidant, and Ball gave him outright relaxation. The two men
had a common passion in the sport of fly-fishing. Ball claimed that
he had taught Chamberlain the sport, and the latter was often a guest
at Ball's cottage on the River Test, one of Britain's most prestigious
fly-fishing locations.[37] It became one of Chamberlain's great relaxations
and passions. The only thing that Chamberlain mentioned about Lord
Dunglass on his appointment as parliamentary private secretary was
that his family owned some excellent salmon fishing.[38] On one occasion, Chamberlain whiled away the time during a tedious speech in the
House of Commons by making notes on angling for the benefit of a
fellow MP who was writing a book.[39] The sport matched Chamberlain's

solitary and reflective approach to life and he analysed political decision-making in angling terms.

Chamberlain was passionate enough about the sport to build it into his public persona. There were photo opportunities with Ball at his angling cottage. Once, Chamberlain squeezed a speech to the Birmingham Anglers' Association into an over-loaded diary.[40] Admittedly he claimed the speech would bring a propaganda benefit, but this was in marked and revealing contrast to his attitude to other sports. He refused point blank to work up any interest in the visiting Australian Test cricket team and he, only reluctantly and barely successfully, underwent a crash course in football to prepare him for the visit to 10 Downing Street by the FA Cup finalists, which was a ritual social event in those days.[41] Showing some interest in popular sports like tennis, horse-racing, cricket or football might have offered easy dividends in terms of public recognition and support, but Chamberlain's personality revolted against anything that he thought false or artificial; 'it would be humbug and I won't be party to it'.[42]

# CHAPTER FOUR

# TAKING PERSONAL CHARGE

*The prime minister has now got in his own hands the direction of foreign policy. Whilst he is not interfering in the normal work of the Foreign Office he personally takes every decision of importance. This is a radical change from what happened during the Baldwin era.*

Dino Grandi, Italian ambassador to London

From the moment he became Prime Minister Chamberlain was determined to change the way that foreign policy was conducted. He 'meant to be his own foreign minister'.[1] Soon after he had taken over the Italians were informed that '[t]he prime minister has now got in his own hands the direction of foreign policy. Whilst he is not interfering in the normal work of the Foreign Office he personally takes every decision of importance. This is a radical change from what happened during the Baldwin era.'[2]

Chamberlain also had a clear idea of how he wanted to use his power. The drift and passivity of his predecessor's foreign policy was to be replaced by a clearly thought-out and resolutely executed scheme. Henceforth Britain was to pursue a 'double policy of rearmament & better relations with Germany & Italy [which I believe] will carry us through the danger period if only the FO will play up'.[3] The search for rapprochement with the dictator states was to become the overriding mission of Chamberlain's government. Having built his political career up until then on domestic achievements Chamberlain now looked abroad for his place in history. He declared, 'I hope to leave my mark behind me as PM.'[4]

Chamberlain was determined to revolutionise foreign policy but he did not see any need to renew the colleagues who were to help him in this new era of British diplomacy. The changes he made to his first Cabinet were minimal. Predictably, there was no serious thought of including Churchill. Chamberlain's step up to the premiership created a vacancy as Chancellor of the Exchequer which he filled with Sir John Simon, one of the fixtures of National Government Cabinets. Simon was replaced as Home Secretary by another stock character of National Governments, Sir Samuel Hoare. Chamberlain kept Baldwin's team of ministers at the Foreign Office unaltered. Above all this meant that he made the fateful decision to keep Anthony Eden on as his Foreign Secretary. It would have been a brave and risky step for Chamberlain to remove Eden, not least because he was a considerable electoral asset. Few of his Cabinet colleagues could remotely have been classed as big vote-winners. Simon and Hoare, his two leading ministers, had especially dowdy reputations. Both had been unsuccessful Foreign Secretaries. Neither inspired trust. Simon was an extremely successful barrister and retained an aggressive courtroom manner. He was known as 'Sir John Snake'. Hoare was especially distrusted; at the time, there was a popular card game, 'slippery Sam', which gave him an instant and irresistible nickname.

Eden was one of the more glamorous and publicly appealing politicians of the era. He was young, handsome and stylish. His passion for homburg hats led to them being known as Eden hats, making Eden and the Duke of Wellington the only British Prime Ministers to give their names to an item of dress. Born into the upper reaches of the landed gentry, he had gone to fight in the trenches straight from Eton. He had been a courageous and a highly competent soldier, decorated with the Military Cross and, at the age of twenty, the youngest brigade-major in the British army. Out of uniform, he had taken a first-class degree in oriental languages from Oxford. He already spoke French and German. He then entered politics and almost inevitably graduated into foreign affairs as parliamentary private secretary to the then Foreign Secretary, Chamberlain's half-brother Sir Austen Chamberlain. Diplomacy became Eden's life, doubtless fed by the overwhelmingly Etonian ambiance of the Foreign Office. Eden was either a junior Foreign Office minister or a roving ambassador during the first National Government. Compared to his successive ministerial seniors, the dowdy and vacillating Simon and the devious and widely distrusted Hoare, he was a perfect embodiment of forthright and determined British diplomacy. Eden' s activities were closely tied to the League of Nations, which was at the height of its prestige amongst the British public as the forum for dealing with international issues. Eden had extensive experience of negotiating with Mussolini after handling much of the negotiation around the Ethiopian invasion. He was perfectly aware of the Italian dictator's brutality and duplicity. He entered Baldwin's third and final Cabinet as minister with a special brief for League of Nations affairs and he stepped up to the top job at the Foreign Office when Hoare was forced into resignation by the furore over the cynical scheme he devised with Pierre Laval, the French Prime Minister, to acquiesce in Italy's invasion of Ethiopia. At the age of thirty-eight he was the youngest Foreign Secretary since 1851 and he seemed marked for great things. Personally, Eden had great charm, inspiring affection and loyalty in many people who worked closely with him, but he was subject to bad temper and was very touchy. Rab Butler quipped that he was 'half mad baronet, half beautiful woman'.[5]

From almost the moment that he became Foreign Secretary, Eden had had to fight off moves to encroach on his powers but they came from Treasury Chambers, the headquarters of the Civil Service, and not Downing Street. Sir Warren Fisher had become the head of the Civil Service in 1919 and established a firm control over the domestic ministries but the Foreign Office had eluded his repeated attempts to subordinate it, thanks to the protection of successive Foreign Secretaries. As was his wont, Fisher tried to exploit the change in political incumbent to bluff Eden into accepting an expansion in his powers. He pretended that as head of the Civil Service he already controlled the key responsibility of recommending ambassadors to the Prime Minister. Eden faced him down but Fisher's next move was not long coming and he made it in partnership with Sir Horace Wilson, which gave it formidable momentum in Whitehall's corridors of power.

No figure embodied the Foreign Office's autonomy and sense of its own uniqueness than Sir Robert Vansittart, its permanent secretary or professional head. Vansittart appeared to have stepped out of an earlier age. As a young attaché at the embassy in Paris he had written a play in French which had been performed at the prestigious Théâtre Molière for six weeks and he still entertained literary ambitions. He cut a grand figure with a large house in Mayfair, a magnificent country house at Denham and a lavish lifestyle funded by marriage to a wealthy woman. In common with the majority of Foreign Office officials of the day he was an Etonian. Fisher had initially been greatly impressed by Vansittart, whom he had parachuted into Downing Street as private secretary to the Prime Minister and then engineered his appointment as the head of the Foreign Office in 1930. Fisher soon repented of this enthusiasm as it became apparent that Vansittart had serious professional weaknesses. His entire senior-level career had been in London so he lacked experience of high-level foreign service and he operated by long, verbose and rambling memoranda. Wilson, too, disliked Vansittart's style: 'he was a poet. He spoke in adjectives.'[6] He had come to symbolise to Chamberlain all that was objectionable at the Foreign Office as an institution and a drag on his policy of appeasement. Vansittart was ferociously anti-German although he failed to appreciate that the Nazi regime was unique. He viewed an aggressive German foreign policy as simply a continuance of the old tradition of Prussian expansionism. With the full approval of Eden, who was then still Foreign Secretary, Vansittart was kicked sideways at the end of 1937 to the newly created, and largely meaningless, post of chief diplomatic adviser and replaced by a far calmer and more pragmatic diplomat, Sir Alexander ('Alec') Cadogan.

Cadogan was a far more hard-headed individual, who had headed the British delegation to the League of Nations and been ambassador to China. He was fully at home in the gritty detail of day-to-day diplomacy and carried no baggage of theory or prejudice. He had none of Vansittart's grandiose style but as the son of an earl from a family that had provided distinguished public servants for centuries he could move with complete self-assurance. Chamberlain rejoiced that 'the change will make a great difference in the FO and that when Anthony can work out his ideas with a slow sane man like Alick [*sic*] Cadogan he will be much steadier'.[7] In common with almost all of Chamberlain's optimistic forecasts this proved entirely wrong and Cadogan's first weeks in the job gave him a baptism of fire as they coincided with the agony of the end of Eden's departure.

The manner of Vansittart's effective demotion succeeded in masking what had actually gone on. The Germans were initially inclined to see it as a promotion and were accordingly nervous.[8] Churchill by contrast instantly recognised its potential ill-effects. He knew it might be seen as a victory for pro-German forces in Britain, as he told Sir Eric Phipps, the British ambassador to Paris, with whom he was staying at the time.[9] Perversely, the French press read Vansittart's move as a significant promotion, but Phipps still blamed Churchill for this.

Just before Chamberlain took over as Prime Minister, Eden's parliamentary private secretary moved on to greater things and Wilson knew just the man to replace him. J. P. L. (Jim) Thomas was a promising young MP who had lost his first minister – also called Jimmy Thomas – the year before when an insider dealing scandal had forced his resignation. Thomas and Wilson had come to know each other well from their time on the British delegation to Ottawa and the ultra-delicate financial arrangements over Jimmy Thomas's resignation. Eden was willing to take him on and J. P. L. Thomas accepted the post. Shortly afterwards Fisher called Thomas into tea with Wilson and tried to recruit him as his personal mole ('bridge between 10 Downing Street and the Foreign Office') to undermine Vansittart's position. Fisher and Wilson claimed Vansittart was an 'alarmist' who exercised a malign influence over Eden and used his power to block contacts with the dictators. This was not the end of Fisher's plans, as Thomas explained:

> Sir Warren Fisher then became very expansive and told me exactly how low was his opinion of Eden, but as Mr Baldwin was determined to leave him where he was, Sir Warren would have to help him by weeding out the weaker or more dangerous elements in the Foreign Office, and that my help in this direction would enable him and Sir Horace to compile their list.[10]

Thomas refused emphatically to take any part in this and the tea party broke up abruptly. Wilson recognised that Fisher had misread Thomas's character and apologised the next day for Fisher's 'impulsive' nature. Thomas went on to become a devoted adherent of Eden in and out of office.

Chamberlain shared the civil servants' suspicions of Vansittart and the Foreign Office as a whole, saying, 'FO who seem to me to have no imagination and no courage ... persist in seeing Mussolini as a sort of Machiavelli putting on a false mask of friendship in order to further nefarious ambitions' or 'But really, that FO! I am only waiting for my opportunity to stir it up with a long pole.'[11] Patronisingly Chamberlain imagined that Eden required his 'support and guidance' to make good the deficiencies in what the Foreign Office could provide.[12] 'Van had the effect of multiplying the extent of Anthony's natural vibrations and I am afraid his instincts were all against my policy though he told me the other day that he had always been in favour of it but had been obstructed by others!'[13]

Reforming the Foreign Office would require time and effort but Chamberlain was in a hurry to put his new policy into effect. He chose a strategy that set the pattern for his whole foreign policy. Chamberlain opted to signal his new policy direct to the Italians, bypassing Eden entirely using a covert back channel that cut out Britain's existing foreign policy establishment, but that he could trust to do exactly as he wished. This set the pattern for the furtive parallel diplomacy that was to become the hallmark of Chamberlain's appeasement policy, back-channel contacts handled by the two men in whom he had utter confidence, Sir Horace Wilson and Sir Joseph Ball.

Ball had come to know Adrian Dingli, the legal adviser to the Italian embassy in London, some while before. They were both members of Gray's Inn and Dingli belonged to the Carlton Club, *de facto* the Conservative gentlemen's club. Dingli had rather divided loyalties. He came from the colonial establishment on Malta where his father was a distinguished judge, but he worked hard there for the interests of the Italian-speaking community, which became embroiled in a political dispute over language education in the 1930s. He had been honoured for his services as a British officer during the First World War. He worked simultaneously for the Italian embassy and the War Office until his British Civil Service boss forced him to choose between the two; he chose to continue working for the Italians.[14] Whilst Britain was working with the League of Nations to impose sanctions on Italy for the invasion of Ethiopia in 1935 he had rendered 'useful' services in taking soundings and gathering information. He was now set to be given far greater tasks. For a ruthless spotter of potential double agents like Ball he was perfect material.

Ball sent Dingli to Count Dino Grandi, the Italian ambassador in London, with the task of laying the groundwork for Chamberlain's planned charm offensive. Grandi was not a professional diplomat but a Fascist politician, who rapidly got the measure of Chamberlain's policy. Dingli was to go to Rome to speak to Count Galeazzo Ciano, Mussolini's foreign minister and son-in-law, to find potential topics on which to build a rapprochement between Italy and Britain. Ball dangled before the Italians the prize of *de jure* recognition by Britain of Italy's conquest of Ethiopia, or, in Mussolini's terms, the 'recognition of the Italian Empire'. It was of no practical significance but Mussolini craved the symbolic validation it would give his imperial neo-Roman project. To begin with Grandi was sceptical of any such unofficial contacts. He also questioned how much weight Ball carried in government circles, compared with the network of personal contacts he had built up since arriving in London in 1932. He did, though, think that the exercise might be useful, spotting the potential to drive a wedge between Chamberlain and Eden. Dingli was duly granted two interviews with Ciano.[15] The message was passed loud and clear to the Italian foreign policy establishment that Chamberlain wanted to rebuild friendly relations.

Having prepared his ground surreptitiously, Chamberlain moved into the open and arranged to meet Grandi for an official conversation. Eden and the Foreign Office saw an opportunity to pursue their own agenda and not the Prime Minister's. They jumped at the chance to turn the conversation in a direction that brought Britain something concrete in the immediate future. For some months, worries had been growing at the build-up of Italian forces in the Mediterranean, especially army units in Libya, which posed a potential threat to British control of neighbouring Egypt. Alarmists even voiced fears that Mussolini would launch a 'mad dog' attack on Britain's Mediterranean possessions if he were provoked too far. Eden endorsed a briefing paper for the Prime Minister which detailed the expansion of Italy's land forces in Libya and recommended asking Grandi to persuade Mussolini to scale this back as a proof of Italy's commitment to normalise the relationship with Britain.[16] Wilson was appalled at the idea and was determined to prevent the Foreign Office hijacking Chamberlain's initiative: 'This is not my idea of a basis for a genial conversation.'[17] Instead he advised Chamberlain to pass a personal message to Mussolini via Grandi asking him to tell Britain want he wanted to be done to bring a rapprochement:

> Desire earnestly to see opinion in both countries return to its traditional state of cordial friendliness and if there is anything in our action or policy that you feel is in any way inimical to the interests of Italy, I should welcome an opportunity of learning what it is and of doing all in my power to arrive at a proper understanding.

Both Chamberlain and Grandi wrote accounts of their conversation when it took place and they provide remarkably different pictures of what was said.[18] Grandi produced a near-verbatim minute but Chamberlain's was an edited summary, making play of an 'extremely frank' discussion of Libya. Grandi reported a very genial conversation indeed in which Chamberlain downplayed the Libyan build-up as part of a 'vicious circle' in which British moves also played a part. Chamberlain did not challenge Grandi when he claimed the Italian move was purely defensive and emphasised the need to break the circle. The contrast between the two is even more striking on the question of *de jure* recognition, which the Chamberlain version insisted would require a general settlement of all questions including Libya. In Grandi's minute, Chamberlain insisted that Ethiopia was firmly in the past and that there was no difference between *de facto* recognition of Italy's conquest, which Britain had already conceded, and *de jure* recognition. Chamberlain's account was for the official record and available to the Foreign Office, who would have been horrified at the conversation reported by Grandi. Chamberlain closed the meeting by following Wilson's recommendation with a small *coup de théâtre* and wrote out a note to *il Duce*. This had the added appeal to Wilson that the personal note did not have to be shown to Eden as Foreign Secretary before it was sent.[19] It began by recalling 'my happiest holidays in Italy' and continued, 'I wish to assure you that this Government is actuated only by the most friendly feelings towards Italy and will be ready at any time to enter upon conversations with a view to clarifying the whole situation and removing all causes of suspicion or misunderstanding.'

Chamberlain was delighted when the Italians disclosed publicly that he had sent the note and relished Grandi's description of Britain and Italy as a couple who were remarrying after being divorced for two years.[20] He was further rewarded with a personal reply from *il Duce*, which in turn created the opportunity for another friendly chat with Grandi when it was delivered. Chamberlain went into ecstasies when Grandi let it be known that 90 per cent of the relaxation of tension between Britain and Italy was due to Chamberlain himself: 'It gives one a sense of the wonderful power that the Premiership gives you. As Ch. of Ex. I could hardly have moved a pebble; now I have only to raise a finger and the whole face of Europe is changed!'[21]

He even allowed himself a moment to wag his finger at the Foreign Office, 'which left to themselves would be in danger of their letting pass the critical moment'. Chamberlain's impatience was fed by his assessment that 'these dictators are men of moods. Catch them in the right mood and they will give you anything you ask for.'[22] On the basis of scant experience Chamberlain imagined he could read these moods, which usually corresponded to his own urgent desire to act. The fantasy that two insubstantial conversations had genuinely rebuilt diplomacy was the high point of appeasement as Chamberlain conceived it. The harsh reality of international relations could not be magicked away by a light scattering of goodwill. Chamberlain would have been well advised to pay more attention to the rest of the note in which Vansittart had informed Chamberlain that the Italians were saying that marital harmony had been restored.[23] Underlying Chamberlain's overtures to the Italians had been the hope that this would wean them away from friendship with Germany and into friendship with Britain. Vansittart sceptically observed that the dictators were firmly set against the benign institution (in international relations) of 'polygamy', so 'concentrated bigamy' was the most that could be hoped for.

*De jure* recognition would have been a hard sell both at home and abroad anyway, but Italian involvement in the Spanish Civil War was expanding in a way that hurt British interests in a very conspicuous fashion. This made a mockery of Mussolini's protestations of goodwill. Italian submarines were sent to help Franco enforce a naval blockade of the Republican ports and they attacked merchant ships, including British ones, indiscriminately. A Royal Navy destroyer was also torpedoed. Led by Britain, an international conference to address the question was called at Nyon, a suburb of Geneva. Geneva itself would have confronted Italy with the much-hated League of Nations. Diplomatic euphemism went even further in blaming the attacks on 'piracy'. Nyon came up with a formula which was widely hailed as a success even though it had only a modest effect in restraining Italian attacks. Chamberlain relished the accolades but bemoaned the fact that these had been won at the expense of Anglo-Italian relations.[24]

The big picture of diplomacy was increasingly one in which the instinctive mutual sympathies of the dictatorships and militarist powers was a key driving force. In late September 1937 Mussolini paid a high-profile state visit to Germany and a few weeks later Italy joined the Anti-Comintern Pact, originally agreed a year before between Germany and Japan. The moves were symbolic but made clear that the militarist, nationalist states were coming ever closer. At a diplomatic level Britain was facing the nightmare of opposing these three states simultaneously. In Chamberlain's eyes this meant that rapprochement with Italy should be pursued as hard as possible.

The secret back channel to the Italian embassy in London went into overdrive. In mid-October 1937 Grandi was reporting he had met Ball four times in a fortnight and Ball had made clear that Chamberlain wanted to maintain his contact but hidden away from Eden.[25] Grandi was overcoming his initial sniffiness at Ball's standing, admitting that he was important enough and firmly in Chamberlain's confidence. Chamberlain and Ball's furtiveness led Ball to an indiscretion astonishing in a former professional intelligence officer and one that bordered on the treasonable. Ball insisted to Grandi that reports on the conversations should only be passed to Rome by courier and not by cypher telegram. This practically disclosed to the Italians that Britain's GC&S code-breakers were reading Italian diplomatic codes and Downing Street attached greater priority to hiding Chamberlain's covert diplomacy from the Foreign Office than to protecting British code-breaking success. Ball's indiscretion was all the more culpable, as this was Britain's most important cryptological insight into the Axis.[26]

Grandi next played a game with Ball in which he was manipulated into giving further confirmation that some Italian cyphers were compromised and of the splits in British foreign policy. Grandi mischievously telegraphed Ciano with his thoughts on a proposal that a British minister should visit Germany, in a cypher that he was certain the British could read.[27] The telegram was stuffed with red rags waved in front of Chamberlain: the British foreign policy establishment had succeeded in transforming Chamberlain's avowed policy of resuming parallel contacts with Rome and Berlin into the exact opposite. Their goal was to weaken the Rome–Berlin axis. Chamberlain and Ball fell firmly into the trap. The following day Ball telephoned the Italian embassy seeking an urgent appointment. Ball expressed his concern that Grandi should have shared pessimistic comments about British intention towards Italy with 'friends in common (!?)'. Grandi was clearly taken aback that Ball either took it as common ground that the cypher was compromised or could not be bothered to invent an adequate pretext. Ball harangued the ambassador on Chamberlain's continuing desire for good relations between Britain and Italy. What Chamberlain had said at the embassy in July still held good. Ball denied that the start of formal talks between the British ambassador to Italy and Ciano were subject to an agreement over Spain. He was angry that the Foreign Office was trying to obstruct the Prime Minister's intentions. Grandi replied with a direct and brutal complaint that Chamberlain had not followed up his promises with any concrete action. That very evening Chamberlain bumped into Grandi at a banquet at Buckingham Palace and confirmed to him what Ball had said. At no cost whatever Grandi had used the mere suggestion that Italy doubted Britain's intentions to panic Chamberlain into renewing his commitment to appeasement as well as confirming the weakness of Italy's code.

Chance then put another unofficial line to the Italian government, albeit a vastly more open one than Ball's furtive contacts. Ivy, Lady Chamberlain, the widow of Chamberlain's half-brother, was an enthusiast for Fascist Italy, one of *il Duce*'s elderly British fangirls mocked in the movie *Tea with Mussolini*. She was spending a few weeks in Rome and was regularly calling on Ciano. Even he thought that it was excessive of her to wear a Fascist badge in her lapel. Chamberlain saw the opportunity to send another signal to Rome that he wanted to begin formal negotiations with Italy and wrote to his sister-in-law that he expected these to start imminently. The British embassy was informed of this and Eden protested to Chamberlain that the letter would almost certainly have been read by the Italian secret services. Chamberlain affected to doubt this but it hardly mattered as Lady Chamberlain read out the letter to Ciano. She also wrote back to Chamberlain, urging him to take action as Mussolini was at the right 'psychological moment' and the opportunity might be missed. This fitted perfectly Chamberlain's impatience to put his plans into effect and Lady Chamberlain's letters were read out at the Cabinet Foreign Policy Committee to support his case.[28] Alec Cadogan described Lady Chamberlain's activities as 'very dubious'.[29]

# CHAPTER FIVE

# WOOLLY RUBBISH

*On January 19th I had another interview with Horace Wilson who dismissed all the American suggestions as 'woolly rubbish' and made it perfectly plain to me that he was using all his powers to persuade the Prime Minister to pour cold water on America and to go on with his plans to appease the Dictators.*
– J. P. L. THOMAS

The stage had been set for the final struggle amongst the British politicians over the crucial question of formal talks which might bring Mussolini *de jure* recognition but, before it could be fought out, a wholly unexpected development distracted the opposing sides with a new issue that sharpened their differences. On the evening of 11 January 1938, the US President, Franklin D. Roosevelt, sprang on the British a plan to deploy US mediation to bring peace to the world including Europe. The process was to start with a conference of ambassadors in Washington on 22 January. This was the first sign of significant US interest in the affairs of Europe apart from the grinding, futile and divisive wrangle over war debt since the First World War. The US had famously failed to join the League of Nations even though it had been initiated by President Woodrow Wilson. Roosevelt's scheme was flawed in a number of ways. Above all it was imprecise. He would not launch it without British support and set a deadline of 17 January for Britain to decide. The ground had not been prepared. Eden was on holiday in the south of France, which would have hampered a British response at the best of times. Roosevelt did not assess the state of internal British politics and failed to realise that Eden was his best potential ally.

Chamberlain and Wilson detested the move from the start. To them it presented a threat to their schemes to appease Italy and Germany by bilateral deals with Britain, which they expected to bear fruit rapidly. Chamberlain was instinctively anti-American and suspected a trap in which Britain would find itself locked in an initiative which Roosevelt could then abandon. Relations between Britain and the US were uneasy already; the question of how to confront growing Japanese aggression in the Far East was bedevilled by uncertainty over whether the two nations were fellow defenders of democracy or still imperial rivals. In Chamberlain's eyes Roosevelt's idea was a bomb that had to be disposed of safely and nothing else.[1] He saw nothing good in it. To Wilson, the plan was 'woolly rubbish'.[2] What mattered to Wilson was to push ahead with the talks with Germany and Italy. If these progressed, 'the effect here would be a considerable revival of confidence'.[3] The President's initiative was only a temporary interruption; 'Roosevelt may have obscured the horizon by another cloud of words, but it should clear off after a bit'. Sir Alexander Cadogan analysed Chamberlain's response in damning terms: 'It may sound to you incredible but I really believe that he was annoyed by the Roosevelt message because it suddenly cut across his pet plan of an agreement with Italy.'[4]

The British response was decided by a conflict between amateurs in diplomacy and the professionals, to whom any friendly move by a major state deserves to be nurtured. The Foreign Office recognised full well the problems with Roosevelt's plan but immediately knew that there was considerable value in the simple fact of the US taking an interest in Europe. There was no risk that Roosevelt would support the dictators and a real prospect that he could be used as a lever on them. Both the British ambassador in Washington and Cadogan, who had taken over from Vansittart as permanent secretary at the Foreign Office at the start of the year, desperately wanted to encourage Roosevelt. When Eden got back to London having been recalled from his holiday and was briefed by Cadogan, he went even further than the diplomats. Cadogan found himself caught unwillingly in the conflict between Foreign Secretary and Prime Minister. '[Eden] wants to let the President go ahead and doesn't believe a bit in the PM's initiatives regarding Italy and Germany. I think he exaggerates as much one way as the PM does on the other!'[5]

Eden's subsequent conversations with Downing Street made it clear that conflict was brewing. As he and Chamberlain talked over the holding replies that had already been sent Eden sensed that '[f]or the first time our relations were seriously at odds'.[6] The following day he argued with Wilson and refused point blank to discuss foreign affairs with him:

> If it ever fell to my lot to have to cross the road to Downing Street, and I had there to deal with an industrial problem, I would send for him and almost certainly take his advice, for I knew that he understood industrial affairs but I asked him to believe me that he did not understand foreign affairs.[7]

After prolonged and acrimonious debate, a final reply was sent that was an unhappy compromise between the two camps within British foreign policy. It effectively killed off Roosevelt's plan and the US remained a spectator of European affairs for the next four years. An anonymous diplomat tore into Chamberlain's decisions:

> **Rebuff administered by Mr Chamberlain to the President's overture**
> That Mr NC, with his limited outlook and inexperience, should have possessed the self-sufficiency to wave away the proffered hand stretched out across the Atlantic, leaves one, even at this date, breathless with amazement. The lack of all sense of proportion, even of self-preservation, which this episode reveals in an upright, competent and well-meaning man charged with the destinies of our country and all who depend on it, is appalling.[8]

The office dynamics of the manoeuvres over the Roosevelt plan made plain just how important Wilson had become. He was practically the deputy to the Prime Minister and no longer merely his adviser. To all intents and purposes Wilson had crossed the line into politics but still thought of himself as a civil servant, with all the anonymity and unaccountability that this brought. Before Eden's return to the UK Cadogan found himself talking to Wilson as much as, if not more than, to the Prime Minister himself. Cadogan spotted the disagreement between Chamberlain and Eden but resisted Wilson's urgings to mediate between the two men. Cadogan had a clear sense of what was proper for a civil servant and knew that this was work for a politician. His task was to advise his minister in his area of expertise and to the best of his ability. He was taken aback to find Wilson attending a meeting of the Cabinet's Foreign Policy Committee.

Whilst the British thrashed out their response to Roosevelt, Chamberlain pursued his goal of beginning formal talks with the Italians. The interplay between Downing Street's unofficial diplomacy, the open and formal diplomatic steps involved, the steady breakdown in relations between Chamberlain and Eden and events elsewhere in Europe created an intricate, multi-layered chessboard. Chamberlain haggled with Eden over the process for the move with Cadogan running between the two but, far more important, used his secret channels to tell the Italians that the ball was rolling.[9] Sir Joseph Ball sent Adrian Dingli to tell Dino Grandi that Chamberlain wanted to begin conversations as soon as possible, covering all topics including Ethiopia (implicitly *de jure* recognition) and leaving aside any prior conditions.[10] Eden was to be held back from setting any preconditions on the Italians such as trying to force them to agree to troop withdrawals from Spain or anything else before talks could begin. Grandi accordingly asked to speak to Eden and Chamberlain but followed normal diplomatic practice of writing to the Foreign Secretary.[11] This gave Eden, already unsettled by Downing Street's hijacking of the British response to Roosevelt, the opening to call Grandi into the Foreign Office and talk to him without Chamberlain's presence.

The pattern was set for an occasionally ludicrous three-way struggle in which Chamberlain tried to bring Eden behind his drive for formal negotiations. Eden resisted petulantly but the ground was cut from his feet by near-daily contacts between Chamberlain and Grandi via the Ball–Dingli back channel, which made clear Chamberlain's determination to proceed. Ball emphasised that Eden's value lay in his electoral appeal, implying that his contribution to policy was unimportant. As Grandi pressed ever harder for Chamberlain to deliver on his promise of talks, Eden threw another bout of Italian submarine attacks and a trivial border dispute in Kenya into the fray. The crucial issue came down to Eden's unwillingness for Chamberlain to meet Grandi himself. Grandi resisted Eden's repeated invitations for talks on his own, at one point pleading that he wanted to play golf. Grandi cheerfully admitted to Galeazzo Ciano, a notorious golf fiend, that he detested the game but had needed a pretext. Ball finally outflanked Eden by telling Grandi that Chamberlain would simply gatecrash a two-way conversation between him and Eden; Grandi should thus accept Eden's invitation. Scenting victory, Grandi saw that he could go one better than simply talking to Chamberlain and insisted that the British would have to invite him to do so. Above all he wanted to deprive Eden of any grounds for a semi-public claim that Britain and Italy were 'consulting' over the crisis brewing in Austria, where Hitler was preparing the ground to incorporate it into Germany. Downing Street meekly complied and at 8 p.m. telephoned the Italian embassy asking for a conversation the following day.

Grandi came to Downing Street on 19 February 1938 and his conversation with the Prime Minister and the Foreign Secretary has gone down in legend as one of the most bizarre high-level diplomatic discussions ever. Grandi described it as a confrontation between two fighting cocks rather than the discussion of a delicate situation between a head of government, his foreign minister and a foreign ambassador.[12] The two Englishmen sometimes behaved as though the Italian was just not there. Chamberlain struggled openly with Eden to control the conversation. Every time Eden challenged Grandi on a point Chamberlain gave the Italian a way out. Eden attempted to get Grandi to acknowledge that the terms of the Stresa agreement of 1935 obliged Italy to consult with Britain over Austria but Grandi was too skilled a diplomat to allow himself to be trapped. Chamberlain was manifestly seeking 'ammunition' against Eden and Grandi was happy to supply it.

Both sides were delighted with the fruits of their covert diplomacy.

After the meeting Chamberlain sent Ball to thank Grandi personally for his 'statements which had been very useful to him, and [to say] that he was confident that everything would go very well next day' at a crucial Cabinet meeting called to discuss the question of opening formal negotiations. Chamberlain had tasted the blood of success and the price had not even registered. Henceforth secret channels were the way forward. On the Italian side Grandi was emphatic that Ball, who had been the 'direct and secret link between myself and Chamberlain' since the previous October, had been very valuable in the whole episode. He had enabled Grandi to wring the utmost from Chamberlain's precipitate determination to make friends with Italy and to marginalise the Foreign Office, who were far more cautious.

The Cabinet meeting the following day duly followed the Prime Minister's wishes to start negotiations, with a provision inserted as a last-minute face-saver by Lord Halifax that the Italians should make some progress on withdrawing troops from Spain before proceeding. This provoked a flurry of pleas from Downing Street, by way of Ball, that the Italians provide Chamberlain with the cover he needed ahead of a second Cabinet meeting called for 3 p.m. the following day.[13] Grandi passed the word to Downing Street that he could give his 'formal assurance' that his government would accept the condition. This was enough for Chamberlain to be able to tell Eden that the Italians had accepted the Eden formula for withdrawing troops, although Eden skewered the Prime Minister by affecting astonishment that he had not heard of this as Foreign Secretary.[14] Chamberlain miserably confessed that he could not tell Eden how he had come to know. Eden knew that his fate was sealed; the outcome of the Cabinet meeting was a foregone conclusion and he told Chamberlain bluntly that the Italians were being given his 'head on a charger'.[15]

The possibility that Eden might resign had been in the air for days and each side was manoeuvring to secure advantage or minimise damage. J. P. L. Thomas threatened Wilson with the possibility that the story of the Roosevelt plan might leak and 'the country would then know that the PM preferred to turn down the help of a democracy in order that he might pursue his flirtation with the Dictators untrammelled'.[16] This threw Wilson into a 'towering rage' and he countered Thomas's threat with one of his own: 'He would use the full power of the Government machine in an attack on AE's past record with regards to the Dictators and the shameful obstruction by FO of the PM's attempts to save the peace of the world'. In a final rearguard action, the core members of the government worked up a story that Eden was resigning on grounds of ill-health. Thomas asked why Eden should do so as he was perfectly fit, whereupon Wilson launched into further dark menaces: 'Because it would be better for him. And it would be better for you if you persuaded him to do so.'

The Italians were naturally delighted at Eden's removal, but he was also unpopular with the German leadership. Goebbels's diaries are copiously littered with personal abuse of him, which provides the reader with a small consolation for the depressing business of reading them: 'England's misfortune', 'not clever and on top of that has no luck', 'incompetent', 'spoils everything for England', 'stupid and childish' (of one of his speeches), 'England lost its mind choosing him', 'elephant in a china shop', 'an unhappy figure as a foreign minister', 'grossly tactless', 'singularly useless and dangerous as a foreign minister', 'hypocritical', 'travelling salesman for Bolshevism', 'a fool', 'truly a rogue', 'it would be a blessing if he resigned' and, very best of all, 'a bare-faced conniving piglet' (*freches Intrigantenschweinchen*).

Eden's resignation was the first major upset for Chamberlain's government and he was deeply unsettled. He had misread the extent of Eden's suspicion of Mussolini and his opposition to his, Chamberlain's, approach to appeasement. Eden was not, though, a rabid anti-fascist and Chamberlain genuinely seemed to think that he had swung behind the idea of talking to the Italians.[17] Possibly the most accurate summary of the affair came from Cabinet minister Lord Swinton, who saw it as a clash between 'a headstrong old man and a headstrong young man [who] could not get on terms of mutual trust and goodwill'.[18] Wilson was not sorry to see him go and did not think he was up to the job. When Wilson heard a rumour that Eden was to leave the Foreign Office ministerial position in Churchill's government in 1944, Wilson claimed that both he and Chamberlain were aware of flaws in his character: 'I have always shared Neville's opinion about his [Eden's] deficiencies.'[19] Eden certainly blamed Wilson for his departure from the Foreign Office.[20]

To replace Eden as Foreign Secretary Chamberlain was not spoiled for choice. His two closest Cabinet allies, Sir John Simon and Sir Samuel Hoare, had both held the office before and had been considered failures. Chamberlain had little alternative but Halifax, a shining example of the all-purpose British grandee. Halifax was not a special ally of Chamberlain. He had attained the most imposing job in the British Empire as Viceroy of India before returning to mainstream politics as the most senior non-departmental minister, the Lord Privy Seal. He had often deputised for Eden on foreign affairs matters during the Foreign Secretary's absences abroad or on sick leave.

Halifax is one of the most intriguing and ambivalent figures in the story of appeasement. Churchill once said, 'Halifax's virtues have done more harm in the world that the vices of hundreds of other people.'[21] Tellingly, two politicians who strongly supported appeasement and worked closely with Halifax arrived at radically different views of his attitude. The ferociously unreflecting appeaser Henry 'Chips' Channon, who was parliamentary private secretary to Rab Butler, Halifax's junior minister, for more than two years, was reserved in his judgement of 'Halifax's extraordinary character; his high principles, his engaging charm and grand manner ... his eel-like qualities and, above all, his sublime treachery which is never deliberate, and, always to him, a necessity dictated by a situation. Means are nothing to him, only ends. He is insinuating, but unlovable.'[22] Channon saw a growing estrangement between the two: 'Halifax is weaned away from Neville now on many points.'[23] By contrast, Butler himself believed that Halifax entirely shared the faith that he and Chamberlain had in appeasement. As he wrote at almost the same time as Channon's comments:

> Looking back upon the last eighteen months it is possible to say that any difference of opinion between the Foreign Office and No. 10 has been so considerably reduced as to be almost imperceptible. There remains the difference of character between the two principal personalities concerned, but barely any difference in design.[24]

Halifax was a hereditary aristocrat, who could approach his work with a serene sense of superiority and a genuine commitment to public service. He had none of Eden's obsessive touchiness. He combined high-minded Anglicanism with a passion for fox-hunting. Halifax's own comments and writings demonstrate well-bred reluctance to allow a breath of criticism of the people with whom he worked to escape. He had none of Eden's protective territoriality about the workings of the Foreign Office. The incursions of Wilson into foreign affairs certainly registered on him but never to an extent that his self-control was seriously tested. Butler told Halifax's biographer that he 'thought he was frequently irritated at Wilson's interference. Sometimes indeed, but seldom, he uttered a mild protest, but only if the provocation was too great to be ignored.'[25] Cadogan judged that Halifax took the same pragmatic approach towards Wilson as he himself.[26] One of Cadogan's successors was taken aback that Halifax 'acquiesced in the Prime Minister's conduct of important business that was proper to the Foreign Office through channels outside the Foreign Office'.[27] For public consumption Halifax asserted that Wilson 'was extremely helpful, when the pressure of work was heavy, in ensuring that I was fully acquainted with the thought of the Prime Minister's and vice versa'.[28] Chamberlain was never concerned to hide his true opinions, but some of his actions he kept closely concealed.

Halifax displayed perfect loyalty towards his Prime Minister although there would be significant divergences over policy. Halifax is often bracketed with Chamberlain as a committed appeaser, but he consistently argued for a firmer line with the dictators. When outright disagreements arose, Halifax won his point more often than not. The insidious dimension to disputes between Downing Street and the Foreign Office came when the former avoided debate by conducting secret, parallel diplomacy. Afterwards Halifax would allow himself to be drawn into only gentle criticisms of Chamberlain's more egregious foreign policy blunders: 'He acted irresponsibly in one or two speeches and in the Munich declaration.'[29] Halifax also labelled the latter 'amateur and unconvincing'.[30] A pointless and unproductive visit to Rome to visit Mussolini, which served merely to nourish Chamberlain's vanity, was 'in H.'s view unsatisfactory'.[31]

# CHAPTER SIX

# GETTING ON TERMS WITH THE GERMANS

*If only we could get on terms with the Germans
I would not care a rap for Musso.*
– NEVILLE CHAMBERLAIN TO HIS SISTER

Chamberlain knew full well that Hitler's Germany was the key to the balance of power in Europe and he clearly recognised that Germany was by far the more important of the two fascist powers. He had a reason that went beyond the crude facts of German military and economic strength. Chamberlain was suffused by a positive vision of the benefits that would flow from a harmonious relationship between Britain and Germany. Appeasing Germany was not just a question of restraining Hitler's dreams of expansion and warding off war, it had an optimistic and constructive goal as well.

The first step in Chamberlain's moves to get on friendly terms with Germany began even before he had formally become Prime Minister, when the need arose to find a new British ambassador to Germany to replace Sir Eric Phipps. Phipps was a traditional Foreign Office grandee, who had warned consistently of the dangers of Nazi ambitions and saw through the hollowness of Hitler's desire for friendship with Britain. He had nothing but personal contempt for the Nazi leadership. Phipps was moving on to the blue riband of the Foreign Office overseas postings, the ambassadorship in Paris. This presented a golden opportunity to place a man in Berlin who would support Chamberlain's policy to the hilt. The man chosen was Sir Nevile Henderson and the move represented a considerable step up from his previous ambassadorships: Yugoslavia, where he had become a close friend of King Alexander, assassinated in 1934; and then Argentina, which had come as a bitter disappointment to him. He had served little time at the Foreign Office in London and was suspicious of the French, both strong recommendations for Chamberlain. Henderson's success in developing close ties to the autocratic King Alexander – largely cemented on the hunting field – demonstrated that he had the abilities to get on terms with non-democratic statesmen. Henderson took the job as a personal mission from the Prime Minister and exercised his ambassador's prerogative to communicate with him directly. He also, and more debatably, began an extensive direct correspondence with Wilson. He was passionately committed to the cause of appeasement.

Henderson had a number of weaknesses. He had only been in place since May 1937 and had not built up an extensive network of senior German contacts. He never seemed to grasp the convoluted and savage way in which the internal politicking at the top of the Nazi government operated. Like many British people, Henderson was taken in by Hermann Goering's bluff, military persona. In the alien world of the blood-soaked and chaotic tyranny of Nazi Germany, Goering came closest to an individual whom the British ambassador thought he could understand and empathise with. This was a telling contrast to Phipps, whose despatch sneering at Goering's bison-rearing activities has gone down in legend. Goering might have been the easiest to talk to of the Nazi leaders, but it was a false conclusion that he was a pragmatist. Henderson's knowledge of German was patchy although he could display an impressive familiarity with specialised hunting vocabulary, which provided another delusive bond with Goering. He was an upper-class Englishman who communicated in the lapidary, non-committal style of British diplomacy in which everything was hedged about with impenetrable conditionality. The Nazi leadership simply failed to appreciate how good a friend they had in him.

Downing Street also developed its own sources of unofficial information on Germany. Philip Conwell-Evans, the secretary of the

Anglo-German Fellowship, had long promoted informal contacts between the higher reaches of the British establishment and Nazi Germany. He had lectured at Königsberg University and was a genuinely idealistic advocate of friendship between the two countries.[1] He had played a leading part in organising the visit by David Lloyd George to Hitler at the Berghof in 1936. The advent of Chamberlain as Prime Minister gave Conwell-Evans his chance to move close to the summit of power. By November 1937 he was acting as Downing Street's 'unofficial sleuth' and one of Geoffrey Dawson's pro-appeasement henchmen at *The Times* rated him a good man for the job.[2] There was no doubt of Conwell-Evans's idealism, but the accuracy of his reports from Germany was another matter. He saw German public opinion moving against Hitler and in favour of Chamberlain. His principal contact was Joachim von Ribbentrop, Hitler's supposed expert on foreign affairs, with whom he had a good relationship, but he fell into the common trap of exaggerating Ribbentrop's standing with Hitler.[3] Members of the Anglo-German Fellowship were to figure largely in Downing Street's contacts with Germany over the next two years.

Chamberlain was determined to 'get on terms' with Hitler, but it was far from obvious how he was to go about this. There seemed to be more obstacles than avenues to contact. There were no live negotiations on serious topics. In stark contrast to Mussolini's ambassador, Dino Grandi, who played up to Downing Street's overtures, Ribbentrop, after he had become the German ambassador to London, stood as a bar to friendly relations in almost every respect. He had become increasingly anti-British as his early hopes for his mission had been dashed. He had been sent to London to build on his supposed triumph in securing the signature of the Anglo-German Naval Agreement in 1935, but he had failed. He had followed a strategy of cultivating members of the aristocracy and high society, above all Edward VIII's mistress Wallis Simpson, rather than truly influential figures. Ribbentrop had deluded himself that Edward would be able to open a new era of friendly relations with Germany and took his abdication as a manoeuvre designed to frustrate this. The one senior politician with whom he established friendly relations was Lord Londonderry, who was hardly a prize. Londonderry had only thrived thanks to Ramsay MacDonald's snobbish adoration of the aristocracy and he had been a failure as Air Secretary. Apart from his personal hostility towards Britain, Ribbentrop was a bad ambassador. He was famous for the length of his absences from London. He was reluctant to spend too much time away from Hitler's court in Berlin or Bavaria, well aware that the career of any Nazi leader would be decided there. Above all he was stupid, rude, gauche and quite unable to learn anything useful about Britain or how its politics functioned.

In May 1937 Chamberlain was presented with what seemed to be a break in the logjam, a perfect opportunity to start up a dialogue or simply provide ideas for a way in which such a dialogue might begin with Nazi Germany. Lord Halifax was invited to Berlin to attend the International Hunting Exhibition, supposedly in his capacity as a master of foxhounds. Halifax was one of Chamberlain's most senior ministers, at that point in the non-departmental position of Lord President of the Council. Chamberlain was especially enthusiastic at the idea that Halifax might meet Hitler personally and urged him to arrange a meeting. Nevile Henderson enthusiastically endorsed the plan for the visit to Horace Wilson, to whom he wrote directly in his own hand.[4] The British went to great lengths to mask their determination that Halifax should meet Hitler but, just as had happened with Mussolini, the initiative came overwhelmingly from the British side. Eden, then still Foreign Secretary, made no objection to the visit.

An invitation was secured for Halifax to visit Hitler at his mountain retreat, the Berghof in Bavaria. It was a meeting of two worlds that were quite alien to each other. From his seat in the half-track Mercedes limousine that had collected him from the station Halifax spotted the black trousers and patent leather pumps of the Führer, who had courteously come down the steps to meet him as he arrived, and assumed that he was a footman.[5] His conversation with Hitler seemed uneasy and fruitless – socially and diplomatically – to the other listeners on both the British and the German sides.[6] Hitler appeared to make a pointed criticism of Halifax when he expressed bewilderment at the mild treatment that the imperial authorities handed out to Mahatma Gandhi. As the Viceroy of India at the height of Gandhi's campaign, Halifax had been responsible for British moderation towards someone whom Hitler saw merely as a native agitator. Hitler had little interest in Halifax's verbose exposition of British considerations and was far more interested in the nitty-gritty of Britain's likely reaction to aggressive moves that he was planning in eastern Europe, on Austria and Czechoslovakia. Here he was able to take great comfort from Halifax's failure to send him any clear signal that Britain would oppose German expansion in the east.[7] Halifax merely repeated the British mantra that Germany should not use violence to achieve its ends that was to endure until the end of appeasement. This was enough for Hitler to decide that 'Halifax was a clever politician who fully supported Germany's claims' and to defend him from criticism by Eva Braun's slutty friends from Munich, who had derided the visitor for his thin frame and for wearing two pullovers to ward off the mountain cold.[8] The Germans were anyway accustomed to sartorial malapropisms by potentially useful British visitors. George Lansbury, former Labour Party leader and fervent pacifist, had disgusted Goebbels by wearing a knitted cardigan.[9]

Hitler was, though, concerned that the conversation had made little positive impression and he ensured that Halifax had a more fulsome experience with Goering and Goebbels when he returned to Berlin.[10] Halifax thus had more engaging conversations in Berlin and he took to both of the Nazi ministers, in Goebbels's case with a degree of shamed embarrassment. Halifax was impressed by Goering's magnificent country home, Carinhall, with its liveried servants, without reflecting that this was all funded by milking the Nazi state. Goering was more to his tastes as a 'composite personality, film star, great landowner interested in his estate, prime minister, party-manager, head gamekeeper at Chatsworth'.[11] The conversation also ran far more amicably, with Goering dangling a glorious prospect that good relations would soon be established between Britain and Germany. The visit to Carinhall helped overcome the disappointment of the visit to the Berghof and allowed Halifax to return to London with a moderately optimistic account of the journey. Goering also seemed to open an avenue towards a definite goal in getting on terms with Germany with one of the ideas that he tossed into the conversation: a deal over colonies in Africa which deserves a chapter to itself.

The path towards establishing good relations with Germany was further smoothed at the end of 1937 by the replacement of Sir Robert Vansittart as permanent secretary of the Foreign Office by Sir Alec Cadogan, who did not share Vansittart's obsessive hostility to Germany. Unlike Vansittart, who bitterly resented Wilson, Cadogan was sufficiently pragmatic to accept the strength of his position and work with him as well as he could. Cadogan instantly recognised Wilson's importance in foreign policy and the influence that he exercised. He stopped short of denouncing him as a malign force but was alert to his encroachments on the turf of the Foreign Office. In contrast to Vansittart, Cadogan fended off his complaints about what he was up to: 'We can't stop it and we'd better nobble him.'[12] Looking at the whole relationship in retrospect, he was milder but was entirely realistic as to the human dynamics and the balance of forces that he faced:

Chamberlain was bitterly criticized in some quarters for being unorthodox in the choice of his advisers. I think that came in part from his comparative inexperience in Foreign affairs. He thought he saw that everything had not always been right in the conduct of British Foreign Policy, and he seemed to share Horace Wilson's belief that the conduct of foreign relations was very much the same as the handling of trade disputes ...

[The relationship with Eden] tended to create in Chamberlain a certain feeling of isolation. Horace Wilson had been for long in many ways his right-hand man, in whom he had complete confidence, and he was not unnaturally inclined to turn to him for advice and suggestions.

Horace Wilson had become an institution, for good or for evil, but there he was like the wind or the rain, and I came to the conclusion that we must make the best of him – for which I was doubtless criticized by members of my own Service. If I had tried to fight against him, I should only have been removed.

... The best thing to do was to watch out carefully and, where possible, correct any mistake that he seemed likely to make.[13]

On another occasion Cadogan stated bluntly that Wilson was 'out of his depth'.[14] Cadogan was caught between Eden's extreme touchiness and the peremptory directives from Downing Street, which often went against his own judgement of diplomatic realities. He was confronted with what must have been a severely testing level of interference but behaved entirely professionally. He advised in favour of following up Roosevelt's approach, for all its flaws ('we mustn't snub him'), but knew that Wilson's hatred of the proposal counted for far more. Cadogan also found that the Foreign Office's information was being jobbed against that of Philip Conwell-Evans, Wilson's own tame amateur 'expert' on Germany: that Goering was pushing Ribbentrop to be 'forthcoming' in London.[15] Cadogan could only bite his lip. The disintegrating relationship between Eden and Downing Street added another layer of complexity to the situation he faced. On principle he saw that the failure in the relationship between Chamberlain and Eden was something that the two politicians would have to sort out between themselves and declined Wilson's suggestion that he step in as an intermediary between them. Unlike Wilson, Cadogan had a firm idea of how ministers and their professional advisers should interact, above all that a civil servant's primary job was to advise his minister and to execute the policy that was decided after the advice had been given.

Wilson was prone to attempt to blur lines of accountability and tried to make Cadogan serve Downing Street as much as the Foreign Office. As Downing Street mulled how to follow up Halifax's visit to Germany, he instructed Cadogan in the Prime Minister's name to prepare what seems to have been a combination of a shopping list of concessions to ask of the Germans and a prospectus for an appeased Europe if the plan succeeded: 'a sort of picture might emerge … if those concerned put their heads together and tried to make the most of the material that is available'.[16] Wilson was labouring under the delusion that Hitler might ever be willing to seek out ways in which he could help the appeasement of Europe. He threw out a number of suggested 'contributions' including, as a manuscript but significant afterthought, 'no use of force' on Austria or Czechoslovakia. Wilson was consistently willing for Hitler to get what he wanted in the east provided that there was no obvious resort to violence to obtain it. In Chamberlain's vision appeasement was to be reached by everyone forgoing calculated bargaining in favour of each making a 'contribution' to the ultimate goal.

The task that Wilson had set verged on being a loyalty test for the Foreign Office under its new professional head, aimed at assessing whether they were true believers in Downing Street's vision of appeasement. Very gently, Wilson was sounding Cadogan out as to whether he would serve Prime Minister and Foreign Secretary as equal masters. Cadogan's response was a disappointment. He came up with a list of open questions together with the obstacles that stood in the way of agreeing them, prompting Wilson to suspect that the Foreign Office had not fully bought into appeasement as a practical and achievable goal: 'I do not think the FO have yet worked out (very likely there has not been time since my minute of the 14th) the possible "picture" on the assumption that we really do want to get an agreement if we can.'[17] The Foreign Office lacked Downing Street's commitment and faith in success.

# CHAPTER SEVEN

# A NEW CHAPTER IN THE HISTORY OF AFRICAN COLONIAL DEVELOPMENT

*The notion which had been developing in his [the Prime Minister's] mind was the possibility of a solution by the adoption of an entirely new method of presenting the problem. His suggestion was that the matter should not be treated as a restoration to Germany of territory of which she had been deprived, but the opening of an entirely new chapter in the history of African colonial development.*

– CABINET FOREIGN POLICY COMMITTEE MINUTES

The Nazis had long demanded publicly that Britain surrender to Germany the colonies in Africa that Britain had taken from it after the First World War. The most famous expression came in October 1936 when in a speech at Berlin's Sportpalast to assembled Nazi dignitaries, Hermann Goering coined a phrase that was to echo down the years in the course of an impassioned plea for Germany to attain self-sufficiency in raw materials. This would reverse the theft of Germany's colonies by Britain. The world – Britain to the fore of course – grudged Germany her 'place in the sun'. The fiction that Nazi Germany was remotely interested in colonies was to dog British notions of how to deal with Hitler almost until war broke out. Goering, whose father had been the Governor of German South West Africa before the First World War, blended self-pity with aggression. Germany was asked to pay for raw materials with gold, but the British had stolen her gold.

In the final days of Baldwin's premiership in April 1937 Hjalmar Horace Greely Schacht, president of the German central bank, the Reichsbank, had floated unofficially the idea of a colonial rejig to Sir Frederick Leith-Ross, a British Treasury official. This got as far as the Cabinet Foreign Policy Committee, where it was pointed out that it would cause 'moral outrage' to hand Africans over to Nazi rule. The proposal was put on hold, but the use of colonies to appease Hitler did not go away and was revived in November by what might have been no more than a throwaway remark to Lord Halifax on his German visit. In the course of their discussion at Carinhall, Goering had assured Halifax 'that that seemed to him to be the only direct issue between us and he was optimistic enough to believe that, recognising that the only Colonies we had were Togoland and Cameroons, and Tanganyika,* and recognising our special difficulties about the latter, it could be solved without too much difficulty.'[1]

This was precisely the sort of message of which Chamberlain had dreamed and he latched on to the German shopping list for African colonies as a concrete basis on which negotiations could be launched. He did not consider the possibility that Goering mentioned these two colonies precisely because France had interests in them as well, aiming to stir difficulties between Britain and France. General complaints at Germany's lack of colonies had long been a routine stock-in-trade of Nazi speechifying, but this looked like an opening for a practical conversation. It looked precise, deliverable and not too costly. The price would be well worth paying for 'getting on terms' with Germany. Chamberlain thought he had a bargaining chip comparable to the *de jure* recognition which had nurtured his approaches to Mussolini, which he could use to make Hitler negotiate in a civilised fashion. He had to surmount two immediate obstacles. Firstly, he had to persuade France to endorse the scheme as the German list featured zones of French interest. By coincidence the French prime and foreign ministers were visiting London soon after Halifax's mission. Chamberlain boasted that his personal handling of the French visitors won their approval for a formula under

---

* Goering was referring to formerly German colonies held directly by Britain.

which the two governments were prepared to discuss colonies as part of a general settlement.[2] The public announcement of this new direction for policy attracted broadly favourable press comment but Chamberlain knew that his next job would be to win over his senior Cabinet colleagues to the idea of giving back to Germany possessions that had been won in the First World War. Over the next few weeks he began the softening-up process to build a consensus in favour of a plan, which he could roll out at a Cabinet committee.

In the next stage in translating the colonies project into policy, Sir Alexander Cadogan was confronted with a startling demonstration of just how firmly Sir Horace Wilson had become installed in the inner mechanism of the government's foreign policy machine, but he was powerless to do anything about it. After talking individually to his ministers Chamberlain formally presented his scheme for meeting Germany's colonial ambitions at a meeting of the Cabinet's Foreign Policy Committee (FPC) on 24 January 1938. Cadogan was taken aback to find Wilson attending the meeting along with the government ministers. Cadogan appears not to have been aware that Wilson had been attending FPC meetings since Chamberlain became Prime Minister the previous May, whilst he was still ambassador to China. Civil servants, military officers and other experts commonly attend Cabinet and Cabinet committee meetings when they have specific news or professional advice in their fields that can help the discussion – as head of the Foreign Office it was natural for Cadogan to be there – but this did not apply to Wilson, who did not speak. The ministers and Cadogan knew that what they said about the Prime Minister's pet project was being silently appraised and potentially weighed in the balance against them by his closest adviser.

If ever a Prime Minister's initiative deserved to be subjected to critical scrutiny, this was one. It had all the appearances of having been thought up at the last moment and was severely lacking in detail, as well as being morally dubious. At the last moment Chamberlain had dreamed up a scheme 'which does seem to me to open up a hopeful prospect' and he sprang it on the committee unprepared.[3] Chamberlain's project had expanded into a far-reaching plan that would 'open an

entirely new chapter in the history of African colonial development'.[4]
His father, Joseph Chamberlain, had been one of the architects of the
British Empire in southern Africa as Colonial Secretary and the idea of
extending his work appealed to his son's sense of destiny. A vast new
territorial unit was to be created including British, French, Belgian and
Portuguese possessions stretching from the Sahara to South Africa. The
administration of distinct parts of this was to be split between individual countries, including Germany. Quite which ones were to be handed
over to Germany did not appear to have been settled; Togoland and
the Cameroons had been divided between Britain and France. Chamberlain's plan offered an elegant but quite impractical way to bring
Germany back into Africa whilst providing some 'safeguard for native
rights'. Given that the Germans' record before the First World War
was conspicuously atrocious, even by the standards of colonial Africa,
the Colonial Office was sensible to anticipate some desire to protect
the inhabitants from them. The total population of Togoland was one
million people and the Cameroons over three million, each split roughly one quarter in British hands and the rest in French. Chamberlain
himself was alert to the risk that there might 'be widespread opposition
to proposals involving the handing over of from one Power to another
of native populations as though they were mere chattels'.[5] This objection would have sounded quaint and probably incomprehensible to the
Nazis. Sir Nevile Henderson, the ambassador to Berlin, who was attending the meeting, doubted that it would be acceptable to Germany,
and Chamberlain conceded that it might be necessary to give Germany
full sovereignty over the territories handed back. Chamberlain's scheme
was not merely dishonest, but expendable as well.

The Colonial Office official handed the unappealing task of composing a paper exploring the detailed options allowed himself the desperate
suggestion that the Africans handed over to Germany might become
enthusiastic Nazi supporters themselves: 'It may of course be found
that the natives are no less susceptible to German propaganda than
the German people themselves and that they may develop a pride and
keenness in the achievements of their German masters.'[6] The whole
scheme had been cooked up in such haste that the Colonial Office

made a crass error of calculation and initially gave the area involved as 5¾ million square miles ('the same size as India and China together') rather than the actual 4.4 million square miles ('nearly three times the size of India') later specified in its briefing paper.[7] Anthony Eden already had enough on his plate fighting Chamberlain and Wilson over Italy and Roosevelt's approach and perhaps wisely he did not bother to criticise the scheme beyond insisting that it should only be considered as part of a general settlement. Cadogan shared Henderson's doubts and his inward scepticism went further: 'quite good, as *presentation*, but it won't satisfy the Germans'.[8] The committee approved and the luckless ambassador was tasked with sounding out the Nazi government.

Some of the preparation of the scheme was manifestly over-hasty, but Wilson's media management operation was fully behind it. Just before Henderson's meeting with Hitler the BBC was instructed to cancel a series of talks that had already been scheduled on the proposal to return colonies to Germany.[9] One of the speakers was to have been Leo Amery from the imperialist wing of the Conservative Party. Amery would not have been friendly to anything that reduced the surface area of the globe coloured in British red.[10] The reason the BBC gave was that the talks would have been 'possibly distracting to discussions with Germany'. Amery ruefully commented, 'Just as well perhaps for though the discussions have disappeared my remarks would have been unnecessarily mild in view of subsequent events.'

Chamberlain's Africa plan was ill-omened from the start. It was not just badly flawed in its own right, but the timing of its launch was abominable. Chamberlain was constitutionally impatient and always anxious to set something in hand. Just as the proposal was being approved Hitler and his close circle eliminated the last significant pools of non-Nazi influence from serious power in Germany. In the space of two weeks beginning at the end of January 1938 the war minister, General Werner von Blomberg, was removed for marrying an ex-prostitute and the foreign minister, Konstantin von Neurath, was replaced by Ribbentrop. Neither Blomberg nor Neurath had opposed Hitler but mere help and compliance was no longer sufficient. Germany's leaders now had to support Hitler's plans to the hilt. Any professional inclination to argue against the Führer's judgements was unacceptable. Neurath had been neutral towards Britain but Ribbentrop was anything but a friend. Hitler had nothing but contempt for Ribbentrop's abilities; his appeal was that he was a weak yes-man. With the decks cleared of politically unreliable elements, Hitler could begin to put his desire for eastern expansion into effect. In mid-February 1938 the crisis over Austrian independence was triggered which led to the incorporation of Austria into the Reich – the *Anschluß* – a month later on 12 March. Compared to the hard reality of bringing all of Greater Germany into his Reich and grabbing the *Lebensraum* he craved, Hitler had little attention to spare for nebulous ideas for restricted colonial expansion.

The ructions at the top of the German leadership meant that it took more than a month after the FPC had approved the Africa plan for Henderson to launch it in Berlin. He was not going to have an easy job. Henderson's instructions from London expose fully the incoherence in Downing Street's thinking at the time and the imperfect grasp as to what mattered in Germany at that time. Initially he was told not to bring up the questions of Austria or Czechoslovakia other than in the context of a vague general appeasement.[11] London could not decide what attitude to take on the topic and it was to be left aside in the hope that the Germans would be happy with a deafening silence. Another paragraph was devoted to trying to follow up one of Hitler's recurrent (and wholly meaningless) platitudes about the desirability of abolishing bombing aircraft. The nub was to set out the Africa scheme in its full complexity and to present it as a viable solution. Just to make sure that the Germans did not feel that the deal had already been stitched up behind their back, Henderson was to tell Hitler that it was being sprung simultaneously on the French. A fortnight later as the Austrian crisis intensified Henderson was given supplementary instructions to raise the matter as 'recent events had aroused apprehension in many quarters which must inevitably render more difficult the negotiation of a general settlement'.[12] It was perfectly calculated to cause Hitler the maximum irritation at British interference in a zone of purely German interest with the minimum prospect of deterring him.

The Germans quickly got wind of what was afoot and were able to prepare in advance for Chamberlain's colonies project. Somehow the story leaked to the German embassy in London and the Auswärtiges Amt passed this on to Hitler.[13] They knew in advance that the former German South West Africa was not to be included and that the package would mainly include Portuguese territories. The *quid pro quo* was that Germany would return to a reformed League of Nations. Armed with this information Ribbentrop could go straight onto the counter-offensive, when Henderson called on him in his new capacity as Foreign Minister to put in the formal request for a conversation with Hitler on 3 March 1938.[14] Ribbentrop told him blankly that Germany's claim to colonies could not be bargained over as it was a legal one, in effect declaring that the Versailles Treaty no longer applied here either.

Despite Ribbentrop's hostile preliminaries, Henderson's conversation with the Führer took place at his office in the Reichskanzlei on 5 March 1938. It must rate as one of the most unpleasant and taxing discussions that any ambassador has experienced with the government to whom he or she was accredited.[15] He faced both Hitler and Ribbentrop, who worked actively to make it as nasty as possible by egging Hitler on whenever the moment arose to be hostile. Henderson contributed by his own ineptitude that began with his opening declaration that he was not there to engage in a *Kuhhandel* (cattle trade).[16] He made no attempt to sell Chamberlain's colonial plan to Hitler and explained it with so many reservations that he might as well have been advising against it. He began by saying that the other colonial powers had not been seriously consulted about the plan. He also admitted that the plan foresaw limitations on raising armed forces locally and would include protection for African rights.[17] Predictably Hitler's already peevish mood deepened into outright hostility and he poured cold water on the plan, claiming that it would take some years for it to be appropriate to discuss Africa seriously. Hitler launched into a tirade on his favourite subject, the iniquitous abuse that he suffered in the British press and the interference of British bishops in purely German affairs. The mood lightened only at the end of the meeting when Henderson produced a pencil sketch of Hitler by a Miss Colley from New Zealand and asked him to sign it. Ever willing to sign stray pieces of paper and susceptible to flattery, the Führer obliged. He also promised Henderson a written answer to the proposals, contradicting his own claim that the time was not ripe.

Henderson's despatch to Halifax reporting the conversation verged on despair. For all his determination to help in appeasement the ambassador had been fully confronted by the difficulties he faced. His chief impression was

> the difficulty of finding a common basis for reasonable discussion. Hitler's sense of values is so abnormal that argument seems powerless. The ordinary rules of the game seem to have no meaning for him … His capacity for self-deception and his incapacity to see any point which does not meet his own case are fantastic, and no perversion of the truth seems too great for him to accept as the gospel of Hitler and of Germany. It is that his influence over his own countrymen is based on these very characteristics.[18]

Today none of this reads as at all surprising or controversial but it is striking that the one professional diplomat amongst the small group of individuals charged with 'getting on terms' with Germany should be so emphatic at a relatively early stage in the process, especially as he was personally convinced that the policy was correct. It is a tribute to Henderson's sense of duty that he was willing to soldier on against these odds but it casts a remarkable light on the mentality of his masters in London that they did not try to analyse how they should be dealing with Hitler. A more forthright personality than Henderson might have told Downing Street outright that its approach was fundamentally flawed.

Hitler did give the plan some serious consideration and seems to have relished the hypocrisy of Britain trying to buy him off with territory that belonged to another country.[19] He was unsure whether to trust the offer but did not want to stiffen Britain's attitude towards Germany with his own eastern projects still far from accomplished. He was still mulling a full reply when the Austrian crisis burst a few days later. From then on it was eastern Europe that dominated relations between Britain and Germany. At the far right of the Conservative Party, Kenneth de Courcy of the Imperial Policy Group rejoiced ('Thank God for it!') that the colonial question had been removed from the table as a piece of practical diplomacy.[20] Henderson never received the written answer that he had been promised during the remaining eighteen months of his ambassadorship.

The notion of a colonial settlement lingered on until 1939. Colonies continued to feature in Nazi speech-making. In the aftermath of the Munich settlement in the autumn of 1938 the topic seemed to come back on the agenda. An article that Churchill had prepared opposing the return of German colonies when the plan first arose was eventually published.

Sandwiched as it was between the high drama of Eden's resignation on 20 February 1938 and the *Anschluß* on 12 March, Chamberlain's Africa scheme has attracted comparatively little attention. It certainly led nowhere, but that does not mean that it was unimportant. It shows how actively Chamberlain sought friendship with Germany, which was to become a source of potential embarrassment as appeasement failed. Just as *de jure* recognition of the Italian 'empire' in Abyssinia had been dangled in front of Mussolini, Hitler was offered African territory as a bribe to win his friendship. The importance of the scheme can be read back from subsequent attempts by the appeasers to minimise the record of it. When Henderson was writing his bluntly titled memoir *Failure of a Mission* in the early months of the war whilst Chamberlain and Wilson were still in charge, the men who were censoring his draft eliminated all but passing references to the scheme.[21] In Wilson's own account of appeasement it appears merely as a 'test [of] the possibility of some understanding with Germany'.[22] To his credit the plan shows that Chamberlain was willing to take the domestic political risk of pushing what would in some quarters at least have been a deeply unpopular policy. But it also shows that Chamberlain and Wilson could be amateurish and ill prepared in how they attempted to execute appeasement. They failed to grasp the true intentions of the Nazi leadership and imposed on them a false template that conformed to their own projects. The Foreign Office and the Colonial Office were there to put into effect whatever plans they came up with and not to shape them. The levers of British foreign policy had been dangerously concentrated in the hands of Chamberlain and Wilson.

The attempt to interest Hitler in colonies marked a watershed in Chamberlain's policy towards Germany until the end of the year. It was the last proactive step that Britain took before it lost the initiative to Hitler's relentless drive towards the east. A policy of actively seeking Germany's friendship dwindled into one of not offending the Nazi regime whilst yet trying to formulate a response to ever more outrageous moves.

# CHAPTER EIGHT

# ALL THAT IS WELL SEWN UP

*If we could get access to the broadcast some progress could
be made. All that is very carefully sewn up over here.*
– WINSTON CHURCHILL

In 1937 a middle-ranking civil servant at 10 Downing Street was given
a grander job title. George Steward had been working there since 1931
without any specific job title but with the change of Prime Minister his
function was formalised. Steward's initial appointment and his work
before Chamberlain had attracted little attention, but he marked in
a small way a significant step in the development of modern politics.
He was the first person ever to be given a full-time job as the Prime
Minister's press officer. Steward's career up until then had been un-
distinguished: after a low-key start in journalism he had switched to
government service, supporting the travelling circus of international
diplomacy after the First World War. The appointment cannot have
been considered as one of major importance and Steward left almost
no mark at first. One of his professional rivals sneered that he was 'a
cheap journalist who told lavatory jokes'.[1] But he successfully made
the transition from the era of Ramsay MacDonald to that of Baldwin
then Chamberlain as Prime Ministers, with Wilson as the dominant
civil servant of the – by today's standards tiny – staff around the Prime
Minister at Downing Street. His masters were happy with his work
and in 1937 he was promoted to Chief Press Liaison Officer, HM Government.[2] Steward was the only person ever to hold that particular
title and its creation marked a sharp turn in top-level policy towards

relations with the press under the new Prime Minister. His day-to-day work was unchanged and he continued to be the only individual on the Downing Street press desk. His tasks had just become more important.

All politicians down the ages have tried to influence the public's perception of them and their work, but Neville Chamberlain has been described as 'the first prime minister to employ news management on a grand scale'.[3] The accidents of individual personality and the demands of the policies that Chamberlain pursued added new dimensions to the way government and press interacted. From a minor aspect of the machinery of government, press relations took on a central role.

News management fitted with Chamberlain's character and style of politics. He was vain and deeply preoccupied by what other people thought of him. Like many politicians he developed a near obsession with what the newspapers wrote about him. It was one of the least balanced features of his personality. His letters to his sisters abound with gloating references to favourable press coverage of his acts and speeches, which to him bore out his own superior abilities. He was correspondingly hostile to any references that were anything less than complimentary. As often as not he saw these as evidence of sinister plots by his political rivals.

Chamberlain's obsession with press coverage went even further. At his worst he analysed politics as a competition for flattering press articles. When he was edging Eden out of any serious role in foreign policy during the early months of his premiership he assumed that Eden was driven by the same forces:

[I]f only the FO will play up. I see indications that they are inclined to be jealous, but though it is natural that they should be annoyed at press headlines about the 'Chamberlain touch' instead of the 'Eden touch' there is no desire on my part to take credit away from the FS [Foreign Secretary] and I shall try now to put him in the foreground again.[4]

The real issue was not who was to reap adulation for the imagined benefits of rapprochement with Mussolini but whether the rapprochement should be pursued with the blind enthusiasm that Chamberlain wanted. Of course, the 'Chamberlain touch' was the most promising way to achieve this and Chamberlain never questioned for a second whether the goal that it might achieve was the correct one. Still less did it occur to him that press praise for his work might be ill founded. In Chamberlain's mind his policies were correct and bound to succeed and this should be recognised by the press. It would be no sin to help them towards this conclusion.

The dictators with whom Chamberlain was negotiating to attain appeasement diplomacy were also deeply preoccupied with press coverage, although calculation played a far greater part than personal conviction. Comprehensive news management was an integral part of the methods of totalitarian dictators and both Hitler and Mussolini were fully attuned to the question. In the democracies news management was something of a necessary evil, but it was the life blood of dictators. As a one-time corrupt journalist, Mussolini well understood the mechanisms involved. Control of the media was just one part of Goebbels's work as Hitler's propaganda supremo and, by some measures, his most intimate and unconditional ally. Neither Hitler nor Mussolini had any reason to be concerned about the output of the media in their own countries but they were both acutely sensitive about how they personally and their regimes were covered in foreign media. Any voice that contradicted the 'big lie' of fascist propaganda was unacceptable. If nothing else it was a potential source of criticism that could find its way across borders that were still relatively open into Germany or Italy. Hostile British and French newspaper articles on these topics were routine fodder for complaint by the Führer and *il Duce* in their contacts with the diplomats of the democracies.

The difference between the presses in the dictatorships and the democracies posed a dilemma for the statesmen in the democracies who wanted to pursue good relations with the dictators. The dictators could turn off the tap of media criticism of the democracies at will if it suited their policy to oblige western statesmen. Mussolini earned great kudos with Chamberlain by silencing broadcasts into the Arab world from a radio transmitter at Bari, which the British blamed for fomenting riots in Palestine. Western statesmen could not reciprocate as effectively and were left with the question of how to respond to the dictators' complaints at the comments of the free press. The British appeasers chose to apologise lamely and make a great parade of what they were able to achieve in imposing their will on their own newspapers and broadcasters.

Complaining about western media was a handy stand-by when the dictators wanted to distract western statesmen from their own iniquities. When Lord Halifax had visited Hitler at the Berghof in November 1937 Hitler had delivered a manifesto for the control of the press as a necessary step to remove tension from Europe:

> It was only the part played by the press which was sinister. Nine-tenths of all tension was produced simply and solely by it. The Spanish crisis and the alleged occupation of Morocco by German troops were typical examples which clearly showed the dangers of irresponsible journalism. A first condition of calming international relations was therefore the co-operation of all peoples to make an end of journalistic free-booting.[5]

When Hitler granted an interview to Sir Nevile Henderson, Britain's enthusiastically pro-appeasement ambassador in Berlin, in the midst of the Austria crisis in March 1938, he did more than wave aside the offer of African colonies that Chamberlain hoped would persuade him of the benefits of friendship with Britain. Hitler repeated in even more direct terms the complaints he had made to Halifax at the Berghof the previous November. He railed against the 'British press ... [which] opposed Germany everywhere and conducted a campaign of slander against this country', in the face of which 'Germany had remained absolutely silent for ... 3 years'. Henderson had been braced for this and was able to assure the Führer that active measures had been undertaken already to address his concerns.[6]

After his conversation at the Berghof Halifax had thrown himself into the task of bringing the press under control. In contrast to his far more nuanced approach when he later became responsible for British diplomatic operations, he worked unreservedly in support of appeasement. He spoke to the main newspaper editors, the newspaper trade association and senior officials of the BBC to stress the 'responsibilities of these authorities for peace'. In other words, the British government was firmly endorsing the view that criticism of Germany in British media risked war and that it was willing to do the maximum to head off this danger. Hitler had not even complained about the BBC but it was the one major outlet that exercised sufficient control to make it the poster child of this thrust in media manipulation. Halifax did not limit his campaign to the great and good of the media world. He called in David Low, the New Zealander who was arguably the most influential cartoonist of the period.[7] Low was resolutely anti-dictator and his depictions of Hitler and Mussolini caused particular offence to their targets. Halifax asked Low directly, 'Do you want to make things more difficult for this country?' Low relented far enough to create a cartoon composite of the two dictators, Muzzler, which avoided a direct lampoon of either.

A few days later Wilson followed up Henderson's efforts to persuade the Germans that the government was doing its utmost to deal with Britain's lamentably free press in a conversation with a German diplomat in London. Wilson treated the German to an imaginative, incoherent, self-contradictory and quite weird analysis of how British society worked.[8] 'British freedom was counter-balanced by a certain self-imposed discipline' which was based on the membership of some big organisation in most spheres of life; this relieved the individual of the task of making choices and prevented them from taking 'extreme decisions'. Only in the field of the press did this not operate. Chamberlain, of course, did what he could to minimise the harm this might cause, considering that the only resource available to him was 'personal influence'. Wilson illustrated how this worked with the example of how Chamberlain had exploited the narrative of Eden's resignation to convince influential journalists at the time that his (Chamberlain's) policy was to 'achieve general appeasement'. The nearest Wilson came to defending press freedom was to remind the German that British statesmen suffered as well. They had to bear stoically 'violent attacks' and caricatures, but they understood that the best way to counter them was by ignoring them as they were not very important: 'It's just pouring water on a duck's tail.'* What Wilson did not state openly was that criticism of the dictators in the press was also criticism of Chamberlain himself in his attempts to make friends with them.

The day-to-day contact with journalists fell to 10 Downing Street's press officer, George Steward, but Chamberlain had even heavier guns available for high-level tasks. Under Chamberlain relations with the newspapers became increasingly politicised. Sir Joseph Ball took over the briefing of the parliamentary lobby correspondents at St Stephen's Club, his unofficial headquarters. It was understood that he was acting as Chamberlain's spokesman in this respect, but he was also an official of the Conservative Party. Inevitably this fused Chamberlain's status as Prime Minister with his position as a party politician. Silently he had forfeited the claim that his predecessor Stanley Baldwin had sedulously built up as a Prime Minister in the national interest. The British parliamentary lobby has always functioned on an anonymous basis, however feeble the pretence might have become. As someone lurking in a no-man's land between party politics, government service and acting as the Prime Minister's personal emissary, Ball was perfectly placed to serve as the unattributable and untraceable source of stories in Chamberlain's interest.

The work of handling the British newspapers was spread amongst the members of Chamberlain's inner circle. Chamberlain gave interviews but the most active minister in press contact was Halifax. As Foreign Secretary he was the most directly interested in the important issues and also knew well how to deploy establishment flattery on senior newspaper executives to persuade them of their high responsibilities as contributors to British diplomatic efforts for peace. Halifax's greatest contribution to the government press campaign was with Geoffrey Dawson, editor of *The Times*. They were both fellows of All Souls College in Oxford, the exclusive preserve of the most intellectual members of the British establishment. Dawson was also acutely aware of his paper's near-universal reputation as the mouthpiece of informed

---

* The idiom may have changed over time or the diplomat may have invented his own.

and responsible opinion in Britain and this shaped his editorial policy. Combined with Halifax's guidance, this meant that *The Times* became an uncritical and unconditional supporter of appeasement. At one crucial moment *The Times* appeared to anticipate Nazi wishes favourably. As the Czechs vainly tried to find a formula that would satisfy the Sudeten Germans (with Nazi Germany lurking in the background) a leader in the paper even recommended that Czechoslovakia abandon the Sudetenland in its entirety, cutting the ground from under the feet of Lord Runciman's mediation mission. The official disclaimer issued the following day that this was the view of the British government merely underscored just how much *The Times* was seen as an official media outlet. It is often claimed that Dawson transformed *The Times* into a government mouthpiece for its policy of appeasement, but the truth is more subtle. Dawson saw himself and his paper as part of the fabric of British society, which conferred a higher duty on him than on a normal editor.

Wilson was often accused of planting stories or letters in *The Times*, but this may be an instance of opponents of appeasement succumbing to a false sense of Wilson's omnipotence. He was certainly close enough to Dawson to find time for lunch with him at the height of the Munich crisis, but Dawson records how discreet he was on this occasion.[9] Otherwise, hard evidence of Wilson's influence over Dawson is absent.

*The Times* was the most important press champion of appeasement but most national newspapers – at least to begin with – shared the broadly anti-war sentiment of the public. The Kemsley papers, above all the *Sunday Times*, were Chamberlain's most slavishly loyal allies. The *Daily Telegraph* under Lord Kemsley's brother Lord Camrose gradually moved away from its customary uncritical support of a Conservative government. The Nazis saw Lord Rothermere and his *Daily Mail* as their most reliable allies, helped by their legacy of support for fascism and the paper's foreign editor, George Ward-Price, a committed fanboy of dictatorship. The other dominant proprietor of popular newspapers, Lord Beaverbrook, played a more ambiguous role. His editorial line was also solidly anti-war despite his personal friendship with Churchill. Nevertheless he was still viewed with deep suspicion by mainstream

Conservatives. The suspicion was if anything deepened by Beaverbrook's close ties to Sir Samuel Hoare, whom he was paying secretly. Hoare was an unchallenging supporter of Chamberlain but was distrusted across the political spectrum. The only newspapers to oppose fascism consistently were left of centre: the *Daily Herald*, practically a Labour Party organ, and the Nonconformist *News Chronicle*.

Beaverbrook was willing to give a platform to opponents of appeasement if they helped sell newspapers. The cartoonist David Low, who excoriated the dictators and appeasement, was a striking example. Beaverbrook's *Evening Standard* carried Churchill's main regular press column until March 1938, when it decided that the divergence between their political views was too great in the wake of a speech Churchill gave castigating Hitler's seizure of Austria.[10] Churchill did not remain without a forum for long and in April he was signed by the *Daily Telegraph* in one of its first moves away from government loyalism.

The bureaucratic battle between Downing Street and the Foreign Office complicated the question of government press relations still further, opening a new battleground between appeasers and their opponents.[11] The Foreign Office's press officer since 1935, Rex Leeper, was one of the most determined opponents of appeasement. He had built an extensive coterie of friendly journalists whom he briefed without reference to Downing Street. The collegial ways of the Baldwin years provided a perfect environment for Leeper's style of private venture operation, but this was to change under Chamberlain, whose centralising instincts were resolutely opposed to rival and unfriendly voices of foreign policy. Leeper was a particular bugbear of Wilson. It is testimony to the Foreign Office's ability to operate autonomously that Leeper survived in his job as long as he did. Sir Alec Cadogan represented a great improvement on Sir Robert Vansittart in Downing Street's eyes but his commitment to supporting appeasement did not extend as far as eliminating Leeper. Leeper overstepped the mark when he issued a communiqué stating that the Soviet Union was prepared to back Britain and France in military action to support Czechoslovakia at the height of the Sudeten crisis – even though it had been sanctioned by Halifax. Wilson treated him to a furious phone call claiming that members of the Cabinet thought he was disloyal and would be better posted abroad. *The Times* declined to mention Leeper's inflammatory communiqué, which was a much more potent denial. Even though the story was an official one *The Times* could deprive it of much of its force.

Downing Street and the Foreign Office were rivals in news management, with Leeper fighting appeasement and Steward promoting it. This was not the only way that Downing Street could promote friendly press coverage. When journalist Fritz Hesse arrived in London with the dual job of embassy press adviser and London correspondent of the Deutsches Nachrichten Büro news agency, he soon encountered Leeper's hostility, which he ascribed to anti-German rather than anti-Nazi sentiment, but found a far more congenial contact in Steward at Downing Street, who peddled the government's far more emollient line.[12] Hesse and Steward established a strong and enduring relationship. In turn this led to a series of direct contacts between Hesse and Wilson, which went far beyond journalism.

The government made full use of the tools to hand to control the newspapers, but it had to rely on well-established patterns of influence, with the uniquely British establishment dimension provided by Dawson and *The Times*. It had an even stronger hand to play with the BBC, with whom it had a far more ambiguous relationship. Joseph Ball could boast to the Italian embassy that the government had far greater means of 'persuasion' on the BBC than on the press.[13] The BBC's status as a *de facto* monopoly broadcaster meant that it was an even more effective tool than influencing newspapers. Radio was on its way to becoming the most important mass channel of communication and the BBC was the only broadcaster likely to influence public opinion. Radio Luxembourg did broadcast to Britain but solely light entertainment on a purely commercial basis. Part of the foundation myth of the BBC as an independent non-political public service is what happened during the General Strike of 1926. It was then a private venture company but Winston Churchill, then Chancellor of the Exchequer, wanted to bring it under government control as an organ for propaganda against the strikers. The BBC's managing director, John Reith, resisted vigorously and the Prime Minister, Stanley Baldwin, allowed the BBC to function independently. Escaping direct government control did, though, come at a price. The BBC did not become a mouthpiece for the government but it gave no airtime to the strike leaders or Labour politicians. By default it pushed the status quo. The BBC passed unmistakably into the state sphere in 1927 but its autonomy was recognised in the royal charter by which it ceased to be a private company.

By the mid-1930s the BBC was a crucial part of the media landscape and it stood at a crossroads in deciding how it operated. With opinions on public affairs diverging ever more violently it had a choice between informing its listeners of voices across the political spectrum and opting for a middle way of broadcasting a bland consensus. The traditional pattern of politics had fractured with the formation of the National Government in 1931, and the rise of extremism at both ends of the spectrum complicated things yet further. Growing international tensions added another layer of complexity and the BBC's comments on foreign affairs became the subject of acute concern in political circles. The negotiations over renewal of the BBC's charter, due in 1937, left it vulnerable to government influence. The question of finance and control of commercial rivals gave Whitehall substantial leverage. Matters came to a head in 1935–36 when the government compelled the BBC to cancel a series of broadcasts which gave airtime to the Communist Party of Great Britain and the British Union of Fascists.[14] The BBC was even prevented from explaining that the government had forced the cancellation. Restricting the BBC to providing a platform for the established parts of the political landscape inevitably drove it in a conservative direction. By early 1936 a Cabinet committee felt confident enough to issue a request to the BBC to ban 'independent comment' on foreign affairs.

An accident of personality and ambition further strengthened the government's influence over the BBC. From as long ago as 1933 Reith, now the director general, had dreamed of using his position at the BBC as the stepping stone to some even greater and more influential post. He had no desire to remain at the BBC until he retired or to find a lucrative job in the private sector. At its most extreme his ambition soared to becoming the dictator of Britain or the head of state in an imagined republic when Edward VIII's antics threatened to wreck the monarchy.

On a more realistic, but still high-flown, note, he saw himself as British ambassador to Washington or as a reforming and activist head of the War Office, preparing Britain for war. He had no taste for entering politics directly so he depended on the goodwill and the support of politicians, civil servants and other movers-and-shakers to achieve his goals. Reith became ever more contemptuous of politicians as the discussions over the renewal of the BBC charter continued and he saw the civil servants as his principal allies. He began with Sir Warren Fisher but as Wilson's star rose his allegiance transferred. Fisher and Wilson saw the value to them of having a docile director general as the real power at the BBC, and tried to choose a new chairman for the corporation on the basis that he 'wouldn't interfere'.[15]

The relationship between Wilson and Reith was the key to government influence on the BBC. One of Wilson's first tasks at 10 Downing Street had been to superintend the process leading up to the BBC's charter renewal in 1937. The abdication crisis in December 1936 cemented the BBC's subordination to the government. As he felt the ground slipping from under his feet the King tried to broadcast to Britain to explain his case over the head of the government. This would have been entirely unconstitutional on any normal topic of public affairs and the government ruled that it would also be unacceptable for the King to speak about his controversial wish to marry Mrs Simpson. Constitutional practice had evolved over centuries transforming the monarch into a mere mouthpiece for a government elected in his or her name, but it had never been faced with a conflict between monarch and government over his or her personal life. The government's ban on a direct broadcast by the King amounted to an assertion that his marriage was entirely a public matter and no different to, say, the rate of income tax. Only afterwards did Edward spot how much of a liberty Baldwin had taken on this point. Reith was entirely out of sympathy with the King and never had the slightest inclination to take up cudgels on his behalf. Reith was in close touch with Fisher and Wilson through the crisis and ensured that the King could only broadcast with the government's express approval.

The abdication crisis brought Reith's relationship with Wilson close to a simple hierarchical one between superior and subordinate. Wilson treated Reith as a junior and Reith did not demur. In May 1938 Wilson called Reith into Downing Street on a supposedly urgent matter and Reith complied. He was taken aback when Wilson asked if he had a handkerchief as he complied with the dress code of the era and kept one on display in his chest pocket. Wilson explained that he wanted Reith to 'weep with him' at the BBC having broadcast some supposed criticism of the Air Ministry, whilst the only newspaper to have mentioned it was the Labour *Daily Herald*. Wilson did not even have the excuse that the BBC risked inflaming the international situation. It was an outright question of protecting the government's reputation on a highly sensitive topic and one, moreover, where Wilson had become deeply involved himself. Two days later the government was facing the prospect of a bruising debate in the House of Commons over severe and widespread criticism – not least from Churchill – about the pace of rearming the Royal Air Force and Wilson was in the process of implementing his own solution to the problem: putting his own tame industrialist in place as the interface between the aircraft industry and the government and squeezing out the Air Secretary. Reith meekly accepted the criticism but was later moved to complain when he discovered that Wilson was wrong and even *The Times* had covered the story. Reith's surge of self-assertion was fleeting and untypical: 'I was sorry to have had this racket with Horace Wilson as he has always been so decent to me, and of course he is a great power in the land.'[16] Protecting the BBC's editorial independence took rather second place to keeping a powerful patron at the heart of government sweet. Wilson had little to complain about Reith's stewardship of the BBC. Despite some internal resistance it complied with government directions.

Churchill was anything but happy at his treatment by the BBC. He complained that his access to broadcasts when he was fighting the government over the India issue in the early 1930s had been severely restricted. When a supporter urged him to use radio to promote his political position, he replied that it was a powerful tool but was being carefully controlled. 'If we could get access to the broadcast some progress could be made. All that is very carefully sewn up over here.'[17]

The BBC stopped short of broadcasting outright government

propaganda but it willingly suppressed or removed undesirable materi-al. Matters that genuinely deserved public awareness and debate were treated as though they were irrelevant or uninteresting. To a casual listener who relied on the radio for his or her news, the international situation sounded far less threatening than it was in reality and the dic-tators were ordinary statesmen, whose behaviour both domestically and internationally did not call for comment. When a Labour MP refused to remove the statement that the dictators' policy was 'persecution, mil-itancy and inhumanity' from the script for a broadcast it was cancelled. On the night of Eden's resignation as Foreign Secretary in February 1938 the BBC was instructed that nothing at all should be broadcast about Italy or Germany as part of the government's attempts to create an innocuous narrative to explain the most severe internal challenge to appeasement that it faced. As the Czech crisis burgeoned through the summer of 1938 a series of light-hearted talks by MP and journalist Harold Nicolson under the title *The Past Week* began to stray onto the question of the Sudetenland; Wilson told the BBC to monitor closely opinions expressed in this kind of talk.[18] When Nicolson submitted a script about Czechoslovakia to the Foreign Office it was referred to the highest level in the light of Wilson's instruction and rejected. A script describing how a bishop was beaten up by Nazis at his altar was sim-ilarly rejected and the BBC proposed laughably anodyne alternatives. Eventually Nicolson broadcast about an increase in the price of milk, presumably to register his contempt for the whole process. Even then the producer was ordered to fade him out if he strayed from the topic on air. The BBC's allegiances were signalled clearly as Hitler ratcheted up his demands on Czechoslovakia to a point where he met active re-sistance from the Foreign Office. It issued a defiant communiqué which was even carried by *The Times* but the BBC refused the Foreign Office's attempts to have it broadcast in German. Reith's deputy acknowledged that there were different voices within the Whitehall establishment and that Downing Street should have the last word. Either Steward or Wilson should be able to veto Foreign Office requests. Censorship ex-tended even to children's programmes and two talks on world affairs by a distinguished journalist for the BBC's *Children's Hour* were pulled.[19]

Part and parcel of media manipulation is that the governments who practise it do not admit it and pretend, at least publicly, that their media is uncontrolled. Chamberlain was no different and Reith was perfectly happy to help connive at this. Reith cancelled a series of talks on the possible return to Germany of its African colonies that had been seized during the First World War when the government was actively contemplating such a scheme. Reith followed government direction even though Halifax told him outright that he would publicly deny having made the request.[20] Reith was complicit in covert government control of the BBC.

Reith did not stop at steering the BBC in the direction desired by the government and made sure that the Nazi regime was aware that it was not working against it. He told Joachim von Ribbentrop, the German ambassador and soon to be foreign minister, together with another senior German diplomat to inform Hitler that the BBC was 'not anti-Nazi'.[21] He invited them to send over the head of German radio – who was of course an outright Nazi propagandist – offering to 'put up the flag for him'. By conviction or calculation Reith was one of the most import allies of appeasement within the British establishment.

Reith's ambitions worked doubly to Wilson's advantage. They left him entirely dependent on his patron in the Civil Service. They guaranteed that he would serve as a tool for government control of the BBC and meant that his future could be steered to fulfil other aspects of Wilson's agenda. Reith's constant badgering to be considered for some other, grander job meant that he was practically unable to refuse when 10 Downing Street offered him a job that met the government's needs and not his. The state-controlled airline, Imperial Airways, had attracted public criticism for poor management culminating in a full-scale public inquiry that found much that needed to be done. This was all the more urgent as Imperial Airways was controlled by the Air Ministry, which was in the firing line because of rearmament. The government urgently needed to find a new high-profile chairman for the airline and its first choice for the job, the highly regarded civil servant Sir John Anderson, had spotted trouble and declined. Wilson told Reith that he had been chosen for the job with the clear implication that it was his public duty to accept. Reith obtained a brief interview with the Prime Minister as a face-saver but Chamberlain confirmed what Wilson had already told him: that he wanted Reith for the job. Imperial Airways was a miserable experience for Reith and he almost instantly regretted the move.

With Reith bound to Imperial Airways, Wilson could begin the work of finding a successor for him at the BBC who would match and surpass Reith's efforts in support of appeasement. Predictably Wilson's first candidate was a civil servant, Thomas Gardiner, the deputy director general of the Post Office. As the Post Office was the government department which oversaw the BBC, Reith had had extensive dealings with him and objected. Wilson and Fisher next put up another three civil servants as alternatives but Reith continued to object. Appointing a civil servant would rather obviously have placed the post into the gift of Wilson and his successors. Wilson cast his net wider for a 'man of experienced common sense' rather than Reith's recommendation of someone with '"a considerable cultural background", imagination, and gifts of intellectual leadership'.[22] Wilson sniffed that 'the place [the BBC] is already packed with intellect and culture'. Reith was cut out of the formal selection process and he was eventually succeeded by Frederick Ogilvie, the president and vice-chancellor of Queen's University, Belfast. He was an academic economist who had distinguished himself by identifying tourism as an important economic force. He had no experience of journalism or broadcasting. He was a poor compromise between many in the BBC who had hoped for an internal candidate and the desire of heads of the Civil Service to appoint one of their own. Reith thought Ogilvie unsuitable and the BBC's own official historian described his tenure as 'short, stormy and in some ways calamitous' but he gave Downing Street no reason for complaint.[23] Provided the BBC did not actively cause difficulties, Wilson's goal was fulfilled.

# CHAPTER NINE

# THE CENTRAL WEAKNESS

*Only too pleased if forces at our disposal enable us effectively
to threaten. There is, however, the central weakness in
the air. Cannot take the risk. (London, etc.)*

– SIR HORACE WILSON TO TRADE UNION LEADERS

O ne of the most explosive topics confronting British statesmen
between the world wars was air warfare. It inspired a terror comparable to that of thermonuclear attack during the Cold War with the
threat of mass slaughter and the collapse of civilisation. Technology had
placed in the hands of Britain's enemies a means to bring destruction
down on homes and innocent people in a previously inviolate island
nation. The air raids by Zeppelins and Gotha bombers on mainland
Britain during the First World War had exposed British people to the reality of war for the first time in hundreds of years even though the actual
damage and casualties inflicted had been trivial. The political outcry
had been so great that the Royal Air Force had been formed expressly to
meet the threat, decades before any other country created a separate and
independent air force. As European war once again became conceivable
in the late 1920s and early 1930s it was inevitable that attack from the air
should be at the forefront of people's minds. Aviation technology had
progressed so far that the next war could be even more devastating, so
the nightmare visions of H. G. Wells's *The War in the Air* appear to have
been accurately prophetic. London was held to be especially vulnerable
and tempting. It was close to potential enemy airfields, it was large and
thus an easy target, and it was home to many weapons factories and

other manufacturing industries as well as the nation's government and administration together with its ruling class.

In 1932 Stanley Baldwin, in practice the deputy Prime Minister, was preparing the ground for the reversal of the massive disarmament that had been undertaken since the end of the First World War. He chose the fear of air attack as a device to swing sentiment away from the powerful anti-war feeling created by the First World War and in favour of rearmament. Unintentionally he coined the phrase that most often tops his entry in lists of famous quotations as an emblem of the fear and defeatism of British statesmen in the 1930s:

> I think it is well also for the man in the street to realise that there is no power on earth that can protect him from being bombed. What-ever people may tell him, *the bomber will always get through* [author's emphasis]. The only defence is in offence, which means that you have to kill more women and children more quickly than the enemy if you want to save yourselves.[1]

His pessimism was taken as gospel. Less attention was paid to Baldwin's endorsement of the RAF's doctrine of deterrence so that the debate coalesced around an all-embracing and vague notion of air power. The country that was stronger in the air would dominate.

Churchill seized the issue of air defence with enthusiasm. He had been an early champion of military aviation and had even begun to learn to fly before the First World War when this was still the height of daring and originality. Air rearmament was a perfect channel for his growing fears of Britain's weakness in an ever more hostile international environment. It was an issue he could make his own to provide him with a vehicle to switch tactics in his campaign for a return to govern-ment, away from the outright opposition over the question of Indian autonomy that had proved such a failure. It had brought him no whole-hearted support from other Conservative rebels nor any meaningful public support. By contrast he could pose as a vanguard of government policy on air rearmament. He could chivvy and enthuse. He was not opposing government policy, only criticising the speed and effectiveness of its implementation. Baldwin had opened a flank to Churchill and he was not going to pass the opportunity by.

Churchill swiftly leaped on the pessimism of Baldwin's speech:

It created anxiety, and it created also perplexity. There was a sense of, what shall I say, fatalism, and even perhaps helplessness about it, and I take this opportunity of saying that, as far as this island is concerned, the responsibility of ministers to guarantee the safety of the country from day to day, and from hour to hour, is direct and inalienable. It has always been so, and I am sure they will not differ from their predecessors in accepting that responsibility.[2]

Even before Churchill had had to admit defeat over India, he was switching his campaign to defence. He proposed a motion calling for rearmament at the Conservative Party conference in 1933 which was unanimously passed. His goad was almost immediately effective in putting the government on the back foot. The new thrust of Churchill's rhetoric had the added attraction that it focused attention on Germany, at a stage when it was still possible for politicians to close their eyes to the danger that Hitler posed. The debate rapidly boiled down to the question of the relative strength of Britain and Germany in the air. When Churchill claimed that the Luftwaffe would reach twice the size of the RAF in 1937 Baldwin challenged his figures but did promise an extra 300 aircraft to maintain the RAF's lead. He also blundered into a fateful political pledge: '[A]ny Government of this country – a National Government more than any, and this Government – will see to it that in air strength and air power this country shall no longer be in a position inferior to any country within striking distance of our shores.'[3]

The shorthand for Baldwin's promise was set in stone as 'parity'. It committed the government to a dangerously simplistic imperative for the RAF to match the number of aircraft in the Luftwaffe. This left aside huge questions of availability of trained manpower, quality of aircraft, and balance of front-line and reserve strength; and, of course, it depended on unreliable intelligence as to Germany's actual strength. Baldwin doubled down on the mistake by implying a few months later that the RAF still held a considerable lead over the Luftwaffe.[4] At that point RAF intelligence was certain that Luftwaffe expansion was being kept to a slow pace because of a supposed German obsession with efficiency.[5] Baldwin's complacency was quickly shattered by Hitler himself when he claimed directly to the British Foreign Secretary, Sir John Simon, who was visiting Berlin that the Luftwaffe had already reached parity with the RAF. Hitler was lying outright but this was not clear until long afterwards.

Unintentionally Hitler had made Churchill, who had recognised his dangerous evil from the start and had become committed to opposing him, appear to be a far-sighted prophet. A network of disaffected civil servants and RAF officers steadily fed Churchill with high-level information on the problems of rearmament which he used to lambast the government. He was briefed on estimates of German strength and, crucially, the slow pace at which the RAF was being equipped with the latest designs of aircraft. With his customary emollience and shrewdness Baldwin tried to neutralise Churchill by giving him a seat on the Air Defence Research Committee, which was charged with mobilising new technology for use by the RAF. Churchill took up the offer but was too combative for this attempt to tame him to succeed. Churchill's presence on the Committee might even have worsened relations with the government. He insisted on a seat for his friend and adviser Professor Frederick Lindemann, who was arrogant and opinionated. Lindemann's vaulting political ambitions for the committee and his obsessive championship of his own pet schemes – most famously the impractical notion of aerial minefields – alienated his colleagues. As so often Churchill was right on the big picture but wrong enough on the detail to muddy the waters and leave him looking foolish and irresponsible to a conservative establishment.

The government's ability to defend itself from criticism was weakened by its choice of Lord Londonderry as Air Secretary, responsible for implementing the rebuilding of the RAF. Londonderry (coincidentally one of Churchill's many cousins) was of the old aristocracy, made immensely wealthy by the huge coal reserves on his lands. His strongest claim to political office was the obsessive snobbery that had grown in

Ramsay MacDonald, the Prime Minister, who relished his invitations to the magnificent parties at Londonderry House. He was an ineffectual minister and an unsuccessful debater even in the more forgiving forum of the House of Lords. When Baldwin replaced MacDonald as Prime Minister in 1935 he finally bit the bullet and replaced Londonderry (to his great distress).

Sir Philip Cunliffe-Lister was vastly more suitable for the job. He had moved from distinguished service in the trenches to wartime administration. He was also a close political ally of Chamberlain. He was one of the four Conservative ministers in the first National Government Cabinet of 1931 but there were limits to his ambition. Soon after he was made Secretary for Air he appears to have solicited and obtained a peerage as Viscount Swinton, a curious move on both his and Baldwin's part given the need to defend air policy in the House of Commons. He might no longer have any prospect at the top job in politics but Swinton was an energetic and competent minister, widely respected for his ability. He also brought onto his team Lord Weir, the industrial and administrative superman of the period, who was an ally of Swinton of long standing. Weir had been made a peer for his huge contribution to British munitions production in the First World War, above all in the development of the Royal Flying Corps and later Royal Air Force. Weir had no official or political status but still exercised enormous power, almost invariably to the good.

Swinton understood the complex nature of air power, above all the long time horizons demanded for the development of new aircraft and the training of aircrew. He knew from the start that one of his most important tasks was to re-equip the RAF with aircraft that embodied the latest technology. Technical development of combat aircraft was at a tipping point. The vast bulk of the RAF's aircraft were built on a pattern that had not changed since the First World War, wood and fabric biplanes with open cockpits and fixed undercarriages, armed with a couple of machine guns. The new generation of aircraft were different in almost every respect, stressed metal-skin monoplanes with retracting undercarriages and enclosed cockpits. Fighters carried eight machine guns and the bombers had two engines. This all created immense challenges for aircraft firms unfamiliar with the new technologies, still less producing such aircraft in large numbers. The process had an immediate short-term cost in the shape of a sharp drop in aircraft produced as new models were introduced. Swinton was fully prepared to accept the sacrifice, however much it hampered the goal of 'parity', which took no account of how modern planes might be.

Swinton and Weir also originated the 'shadow factory' scheme, in which established manufacturers built extra capacity alongside existing units at government expense. This was very much Swinton's own initiative and he claimed that his Cabinet colleagues were taken by surprise when he told them that the capacity was already there to meet the increase in production decided on to counter the *Anschluß*, the Nazi absorption of Austria, in March 1938.[6]

Swinton was dynamic, clear-sighted and forceful but he was also a notably abrasive personality. When he collided with the Admiralty, the most high-handed and opinionated of the service departments, over the control of naval aircraft through the Fleet Air Arm, it was inevitable that the conflict would be brutal. Both Swinton and Weir were passionately committed to the doctrine of Lord Trenchard, founding commander of the RAF, that it should have total control of all air forces. The fight was so bitter that when the government ruled in favour of the Royal Navy, Weir threated to resign and it took Sir Horace Wilson's best efforts to persuade him to remain. The struggle reached public attention and it was one of the issues that occupied Chamberlain soon after he became Prime Minister in May 1937.

The change at Downing Street if anything strengthened the government's focus on the air aspect of rearmament. It was a political Achilles heel, especially with Churchill in hot pursuit. Chamberlain disliked the concept of parity, not because it was militarily dubious but because he feared it might not be achieved. In his eyes the chief task of the British army was to provide anti-aircraft guns to defend the British mainland. Wilson had shared the common fears of air warfare when he first arrived at Downing Street in 1935.[7] He was mesmerised by the Luftwaffe's lead over the RAF and the ability of German industry to outproduce Britain's. He was dogged by the widespread fear of devastating air raids on London and even believed that such an attack had definitely been planned in November 1934.

By the autumn of 1937 the pressure was on to come up with a thorough-going and practical scheme to expand the RAF. The goal of 'exact parity' was dropped and replaced with something that would serve as an 'effective deterrent to Germany'. This brought Swinton into conflict with two ministries on quite separate issues. Naturally the Treasury opposed the Air Secretary's aim of a very large increase in the number of aircraft available by pushing for a huge increase in reserves. The other conflict set the Air Ministry and RAF against the Minister for Defence Coordination, Sir Thomas Inskip. Inskip's appointment had been widely derided given his low profile and inexperience in military matters, but he proved willing to grasp one nettle very firmly by the hand. He went beyond his formal remit to balance the demands of the individual services and challenged the RAF's operational doctrine, 'the bomber force is the basis of all air strategy'.[8] Inskip promoted the heresy that the ratio of fighters to bombers should be increased. Fighters had the merit to the bean-counters of costing less money than bombers, so cost-saving blended with strategy. With Swinton's vigorous support the Air Staff fought tooth and nail to preserve the emphasis on bombers. The Treasury won hands down on the question of total size although there was to be a significant increase in total numbers and the Air Staff had to concede a greater proportion of fighters. Swinton had done no more than argue the corner for his department and his professional advisers, but he had not been a comfortable colleague for his fellow ministers.

The drive to expand the RAF was spurred by very accurate intelligence that showed just how fast the Luftwaffe's growth had progressed.[9] The sense of the RAF's inferiority rose to new heights when a Luftwaffe delegation visited Britain in November 1937, returning a visit to Germany by the deputy chief of the Air Staff, Christopher Courtney, earlier that year at Germany's invitation. The head of the German delegation, Erhard Milch, the administrative and industrial brains behind the Luftwaffe, disclosed almost casually that the date he had given to Courtney for the expansion programme had been six months later than the reality and that the Germans would have reached a strength of 1,620 first-line aircraft by the spring of 1938. British planning had been based on the Germans not reaching this figure until early 1939. The image of the RAF that the British wanted to present to the German delegation was one of false strength and Churchill's informants gave him the material to complain to the Cabinet Secretary, Sir Maurice Hankey, 'A desperate attempt is being made to present a sham.'[10] The Germans were treated to a parade of obsolete and ill-equipped aircraft.[11]

The decisive pressure on Downing Street that action needed to be taken came from the aircraft industry and not the Air Ministry or Swinton. The flashpoint was the relationship between the ministry and the aircraft-makers. Britain's aircraft industry consisted of a slew of relatively small and often poorly capitalised companies. They had scraped by in the lean years of post-war disarmament on small orders, slowly doled out by the ministry, which – at least in their eyes – adopted a high-handed and dictatorial approach. One particular bugbear was the habit of ministry officials of turning up at production lines and demanding alterations to aircraft on the spot. The orders for the older-technology planes were not large but they were profitable; the cost of design and tooling was low. The switch to new technologies meant these orders were vanishing without being replaced by large orders for the new technologies. There was no bonanza from rearmament. The funds had been approved to expand the RAF but they were being spent only very slowly.[12]

The solution adopted by Downing Street and implemented by Wilson assumed that the balance of fault lay at the Air Ministry. In order to appease the plane-makers Wilson wanted to dilute the role of the Air Ministry and give them a direct line to the top. He knew just the man for the work. He had already pressed Charles Bruce-Gardner's services on Chamberlain a couple of years before.[13] Bruce-Gardner had no aircraft experience but he was a widely respected industrialist, firmly in the confidence of Montagu Norman, the autocratic governor of the Bank of England, a key ally of Wilson and one of the most powerful figures in British industry and finance. Bruce-Gardner ran the Securities Management Trust, the Bank of England holding company for industrial investments. Wilson had already encountered Bruce-Gardner during his time working for Jimmy Thomas, in the Labour government of 1929–31.[14] In December 1937 Bruce-Gardner was personally recruited to speed up rearmament by Chamberlain, who next persuaded the Society of British Aircraft Constructors, the plane-makers' trade association, to elect him as its executive chairman, 'to interpret the views and wishes of the industry to the Government and the views and wishes of the Government to the industry'.[15] He was knighted in the New Year's Honours list, setting the seal on his public standing. The appointment bore fruit almost immediately when Bruce-Gardner headed off his members from issuing a public protest against the Air Ministry.[16]

In practice Bruce-Gardner's authority ran far further than providing an interface between industry and government. Some of Wilson's later comments suggest that he saw Bruce-Gardner as being in charge of the air rearmament effort.[17] He certainly saw his appointment as the crucial decision in the air rearmament programme.[18] It looked like a quick fix to a problem but it came at a price. The government was placing greater confidence in a lobbyist for its commercial suppliers for rearmament than in the minister responsible. Swinton endorsed Bruce-Gardner's appointment but there is no sign that he played any part in the decision to create the job. He accepted the erosion of his responsibility.

Wilson was the key figure in shaping the political response to the challenge of RAF expansion, as well as working on the industrial and administrative levels. By some standards he crossed the line of what a civil servant could do legitimately and began to act as a politician himself. Chamberlain sought Wilson's advice instead of Swinton's, who was becoming increasingly marginalised. Wilson clearly ranked ahead of Lord Winterton, the Chancellor of the Duchy of Lancaster, whom Chamberlain brought into the Cabinet with a remit to handle air matters in the House of Commons in early 1938. As merely an Irish peer and thus entitled to be an MP, Winterton was intended to plug the gap created by Swinton's elevation to the Lords, but he had little to recommend him. He was an old-style aristocrat of the kind for whom Chamberlain had a peculiar fondness.

The Labour opposition presented Chamberlain with far less of a challenge on the issue than Churchill, but it did what it could. It was handicapped by deep internal divisions. In theory the party was solidly anti-fascist, but what counted was the approach taken to the rearmament programme and that varied according to which of the strong factions within the party was at work. One faction, represented by its former leader George Lansbury, was unconditionally pacifist and opposed to arms entirely. The extreme left, fronted by Sir Stafford Cripps, cynically saw an opportunity to cause the government embarrassment and called for workers to sabotage rearmament by strikes. The Labour Party leader, Clement Attlee, did his best to emulate Churchill's efforts and presented the government with his own catalogue of flaws in the RAF, 'not very formidable' in the views of Downing Street but it had to be answered.[19]

Chamberlain and Wilson discussed how to reply and decided that Attlee would have to be seen personally. Only afterwards was this decision passed on to Swinton as Air Secretary.[20] In a remarkable extension of his duties as a civil servant, it was actually Wilson who ended up conducting the discussion with Attlee but he failed to persuade him to abandon raising the question in the House of Commons.[21] The Labour Party plan to call for an inquiry remained on the table but handling Churchill was the real issue and here again Wilson was part of a tiny group planning the political response. Neither Swinton nor Winterton was present when Chamberlain, Wilson and the chief whip decided how to handle the next parliamentary debate on the air estimates.[22] They expected that Churchill too would call for an inquiry but Chamberlain was adamant 'an enquiry should be refused and should be refused flatly and firmly, the decision to be adhered to notwithstanding any criticism that may be raised during the debate'.[23]

The micro-politics of air rearmament were then interrupted by the *Anschluß* in the middle of March 1938. This raised the military stakes and spurred the Cabinet on to abandon the insistence that rearmament should not interfere with normal business and to authorise a dramatic acceleration of the programme of air rearmament, but they were immediately confronted by a potential obstacle to achieving anything like this pace of deliveries. Quite apart from Cripps's near-treasonous schemes, the aircraft industry faced the more mundane issue of finding additional labour, which loomed large in the concerns of the plane-makers. The Cabinet decided to discuss the question directly with the unions and Wilson was tasked with making the contact but this was a highly delicate question.[24] Handled wrongly it could appear to be an obvious attempt to split the unions from the Labour Party. It was sensitive enough for the Cabinet Secretary to leave the decision out of the formal, written record of the meeting. Wilson was well qualified for the job given his long experience of industrial labour negotiations, but it was an overwhelmingly political mission. Wilson had maintained friendly relations with Sir Walter Citrine, general secretary of the Trades Union Congress (TUC).[25] Citrine was well to the right of the movement. In a preliminary conversation between himself and Citrine, Wilson established that the key to getting the unions on side was to set out as frankly as possible the government's view of the international situation to counteract what Citrine confessed as the ignorance of some on his side.[26] Citrine very helpfully advised that the Labour Party be excluded from the conversations.

Wilson prepared a brief for Chamberlain's meeting with the TUC that amounted to a brutally frank exposé of British diplomatic and military weakness. The only way that Britain would be in a position to help sustain the ideal of collective security, to which the left was still firmly wedded, was if it rearmed.

> We can neither defend ourselves nor help others if we are not fully armed. Disarmament efforts left us weak: it inevitably takes time to recover ...
>
> Only too pleased if forces at our disposal enable us effectively to threaten. There is, however, the central weakness in the air. Cannot take the risk. (London, etc.)[27]

The stark picture was driven by the fear shared by Chamberlain and Wilson that the Luftwaffe had the power to bomb London flat with impunity. Chamberlain's talk to the unions had the desired effect. Afterwards they agreed to keep the question of supporting the rearmament programme entirely on an industrial level, 'to give a broad hint to the political Labour Party to keep off the grass'.[28]

Wilson handled both sides of the equation on the industrial relations side of the rearmament programme. Here his difficulty was the uncompromising attitude of Sir Alexander Ramsay, head of the Engineering Employers' Federation (EEF), whose members included the planemakers. Ramsay believed that the only way to release reserves of labour was 'dilution': the practice by which the work of skilled (and unionised) workers would be given to the less skilled. This had been a bogey of the unions since the First World War and they were still opposed. Wilson saw the dangers of this view and set out to mobilise his allies against the proposal.[29] They declined to intervene directly with Ramsay or the EEF, leaving Wilson to make a direct – and unsuccessful – approach to Ramsay.[30] Predictably the Amalgamated Engineering Union (AEU), which represented most skilled aircraft workers, rejected all changes in working practices. Even the information from a mole whom Sir Joseph Ball had cultivated in the AEU failed to supply a solution.[31] Fortunately for the government the heat was going out of the labour market by then. Charles Bruce-Gardner passed him the crucial information that his members were having no problems in finding the additional labour they needed to meet their expanded orders.[32]

Just before the *Anschluß* Churchill had sprung a devastatingly well-briefed memorandum on Chamberlain, setting out the deficiencies in the RAF.[33] According to Churchill's figures half of its squadrons were equipped with obsolete types. Deliveries of modern aircraft were running slowly; only a dozen or two of the latest Hurricane fighters had been delivered even though they had been ordered in 1935. Overall deliveries were running at only 200 machines per month, which Churchill put at one-third of the German pace. Training accidents were inflicting severe attrition on those aircraft that were reaching squadrons. In the crisis over Austria Churchill's memorandum had been left to one side but a month later, as another parliamentary debate on air rearmament loomed, Churchill reminded Chamberlain none too gently that Downing Street had yet to respond.[34] Wilson was prepared to be far more conciliatory than the Prime Minister had been a month earlier before the *Anschluß* and advised that Churchill should be briefed 'in the course of the next forty-eight hours' about a number of changes that were already being put in hand at the Air Ministry. Chamberlain contented himself with a perfunctory assurance that he had 'been giving the matter my very close personal attention' and alluded vaguely to '[a] number of decisions ... most, if not all of which you would, I feel sure, approve'.[35] Hidden behind Chamberlain's patronising putdown were a number of measures that Swinton had put in place. These reforms were to help break the logjam in aircraft production and contribute far more to the acceleration in output than Bruce-Gardner's appeasement of the aircraft-makers.

The Air Ministry's performance was also under challenge in the heart of Whitehall. Sir Warren Fisher sent the Prime Minister a table which showed the Luftwaffe at three times the size of the RAF and the German aircraft industry outproducing Britain's by the same factor. The value of those machines that the RAF had was undermined because a large number were obsolete, over half in the case of fighters. He put the blame squarely on the ministry: 'For some years we have had from the Air Ministry incompetence and soothing syrup in equal measure.'[36]

# CHAPTER TEN

# EVERY EFFORT TO BRING ABOUT APPEASEMENT

*The prime minister and he himself [Wilson], who was not a politician but only a civil servant, would make every effort in his limited sphere of activity to bring about appeasement. He hoped that Germany would also contribute to that end.*

– Erich Kordt's minutes of conversation with Sir Horace Wilson

Anthony Eden's resignation as Foreign Secretary in February 1938 strengthened 10 Downing Street's grip on foreign policy. The new Foreign Secretary, Lord Halifax, was far less territorial and less inclined to push back against Chamberlain's desires. The change was even more striking at the next stage down of political responsibility. Eden's junior Foreign Office minister, Lord Cranborne, had been a dedicated follower of his as well as coming from the same social and intellectual milieu. Heir to the Marquis of Salisbury, Cranborne had attended Eton and Christ Church, Oxford; he matched perfectly the Foreign Office's aristocratic style. Cranborne's replacement was notably different. Rab Butler came from a line of imperial public servants and academics and his education résumé of Marlborough and Pembroke College, Cambridge, was a distinct notch down from the Foreign Office standard. His studies and a summer spent with a German family made him nearly fluent in German and gave him a strong cultural affinity with the country. His political career was funded by marriage to Sydney Courtauld, whose father, the textile magnate, had settled on Butler £5,000 a year, about twice the salary of a top-level civil servant. It supported him in a sizeable town house in Smith Square.

Good fortune gifted Butler an early opportunity to demonstrate his competence and loyalty when the Liberal Party split and Lord Lothian, the junior India Office minister in 1931, resigned along with his Liberal Party colleagues who deserted the National Government. Butler already had extensive experience of India – his father was a provincial governor – and the government needed experts to organise the fraught passage of the India Act through Parliament. Expertise counted for more than length of service or considerations of faction and Butler was promoted to replace Lothian at the remarkably early age of twenty-eight. The India Act introduced Butler to the less attractive side of politics in the internecine conflict it unleashed in the Conservative Party. Butler was the main promoter of a fake grassroots organisation set up by Conservative Central Office to combat Churchill's vastly more successful and authentic efforts to mobilise instinctive hostility in the party's rank and file to a surrender of imperial power. In the later stages of the India Act's passage Butler took over much of the work of his senior minister, Sir Samuel Hoare, who was ill.

The India Act was an emblem of Ramsay MacDonald's National Government and of Baldwin, but its legacy extended into Chamberlain's government. It confirmed Hoare as one of the leading ministers and Butler as the one with the greatest promise. The men who fought down Churchill over the Act went on to fight him down over appeasement. Although Butler was destined for great things, neither of his next promotions brought him a ministry of his own. He moved briefly from the India Office to the Ministry of Labour when Chamberlain became Prime Minister in May 1937. That Butler should advance in the new government was no surprise, but how this came about gives a startling picture of how Chamberlain's government operated. Butler had doubts about taking another junior ministry but rather than talking over the new job with the Prime Minister or his new senior minister, Butler's reservations about the Ministry of Labour were overcome by Sir Horace Wilson.[1] Even at this early stage in Chamberlain's government Wilson was being tasked with a significant political mission. The balance of power within what was still supposedly a national government added a delicate aspect to Butler's job. Ernest Brown, the Minister of Labour, was a Liberal and from the left wing of the party at that. Wilson naturally understood the importance of keeping the ministry that was largely his own creation on a tight political leash. There is no sign that Wilson did similar work for Stanley Baldwin when he was Prime Minister and it was by any standard a remarkable extension of the normal work of a civil servant that he should serve as the government's personnel officer. Shuffling junior ministers is something of a chore for the head of government and not part of high politics but at least one of Wilson's successors has refused on principle to do this.[2] When Baldwin had first brought him to Downing Street Wilson had foreseen that he would act as a passive buffer between the Prime Minister and his ministers. Throughout Chamberlain's premiership there is no sign that Wilson felt that he should be constrained by considerations of political neutrality. The lack of a job description or terms of reference allowed Wilson to approach outright involvement in politics. By contrast he willingly claimed the civil servant's privilege of anonymity and immunity to political criticism.

Butler's move to the Foreign Office in March 1938 was vastly more important both in terms of his own career and in the priorities of the government. With the Foreign Secretary in the House of Lords it would fall to Butler to present and defend the government's foreign policy in the House of Commons. He would become the public face of Chamberlain's foreign policy at a time when it was the most important policy area for the country. In his memoirs Butler acknowledged that relations between Downing Street and the Foreign Office were at least potentially fraught, but insinuated that he himself was aligned with the professionals of the Foreign Office.[3] In reality Butler was far more deeply in sympathy with appeasement as practised by Chamberlain and Wilson.[4] A residue of suspicion at Butler's vehement support for appeasement contributed to his two failures to become leader of the Conservative Party after the war.

Within days of his appointment Butler was sending a signal to Germany that things had changed radically in the British foreign policy machine in terms of both personnel and outlook in a conversation with someone presumably senior at the German embassy in London.[5] Just as Chamberlain's African colonies plan was being prepared for launch as the spearhead of appeasing Hitler, Butler was preparing the ground with the Auswärtiges Amt with a demonstration that the government was now unanimously dedicated to making friends. He opened his pitch by setting out his personal connections with Germany and his commitment to achieving a 'close and trusting cooperation with Germany'. He went on with a critical account of how he believed that a pro-French bias had become embedded in the old guard at the Foreign Office and that this had only been challenged by Sir Nevile Henderson. He disclosed that Eden had been isolated in Cabinet, implying that it was Chamberlain's policy that enjoyed full political backing. Intentionally or otherwise the conversation also revealed just how strong Wilson's influence was as 'the prime minister's closest adviser'.

The charm offensive towards the Germans rode out the rebuff delivered to Henderson over the colonies scheme and Wilson was determined to win back any ground that might have been lost by having German grievances aired at the conversation between Hitler, Ribbentrop and Henderson. It was Wilson himself who delivered the next thrust when he spoke to Erich Kordt, counsellor at the German embassy and even more important in the limbo between Ribbentrop's dilatory and ineffective time as ambassador and the arrival of his successor.[6] Wilson began with an emollient response to the Führer's angry complaints at the British press before moving on to the true substance of appeasement. Chamberlain was determined to overcome 'leftist' opposition to pursue a policy that viewed with indifference the internal regimes of the countries at which it was aimed. England and Germany provided 'the two pillars upon which European social order could rest' and all that it required to complete the edifice was 'erecting an arch of cooperation upon these two pillars'. His policy did not involve Germany abandoning her 'national aspirations' and he even lightly qualified the mantra of non-violence: 'He hoped we would succeed *as much as possible* [author's emphasis] vis-à-vis Czechoslovakia and Austria without the use of force.' Wilson's insistence on the use of peaceful methods only held good if the 'other side' (the Czechoslovakian and Austrian governments) respected the 'prerequisite' that they 'play fair'. Wilson did not defend them when Germany complained that they were not. Kordt complained that the Austrian government had signally failed to play fair by calling a plebiscite for 9 March, the day before the conversation, aimed at resisting German encroachments on her autonomy; Wilson accepted that this move had 'created difficulties'. He concluded with a ringing affirmation that '[t]he prime minister and he himself, who was not a politician but only a civil servant, would make every effort in his limited sphere of activity to bring about appeasement. He hoped that Germany would also contribute to that end.' Wilson had not weaned himself off the notion that Hitler might be just as willing as Chamberlain to help actively in the process of appeasement.

Hitler preferred to operate in his own way and less than a week later incorporated Austria into Germany under the threat of immediate military action in mid-March 1938. The rebuff that he and Ribbentrop had delivered to the colonies plan had taken place in the quiet privacy of a diplomatic interchange, but the *Anschluß* was an inescapable and flagrant illustration that the Nazi regime recognised no limits on its action. The impact in London was rubbed in by an accident of timing. Chamberlain was told that German troops had marched whilst at a grand formal luncheon at Downing Street to bid farewell to Ribbentrop at the end of his ambassadorship. Ribbentrop had spent the morning denying knowledge that any such move was in preparation. This created an impression of bare-faced dishonesty but for once he might have been telling the truth. Hitler wanted to keep the entire credit and glory of the *Anschluß* to himself and keeping his foreign minister firmly out of the picture was part of the game plan. It is an open question whether Hitler intended to rub the noses of the British in their inability to restrain Nazi policy, but it was a painful moment for Chamberlain, all the more so as Churchill was a guest at the luncheon and the news firmly endorsed his warnings over Nazi Germany.

For the next few weeks there was no follow-up to Butler's appeasing pitch to the German embassy, as inevitably attention switched to Germany's ambitions towards Czechoslovakia which had already been amply flagged. The *Anschluß* inspired widespread suspicions that Hitler would do something similar with the Sudetenland, home of Czecho-slovakia's large German-speaking minority, which had been left under Slav rule by the Versailles Treaties. This was in part a historical accident. The main parts of Czechoslovakia were the old Hapsburg possessions of Bohemia and Moravia. These had always had a mixture of German-, Czech- and Slovak-speakers, although they had been dominated by a German-speaking aristocracy, which stood far above the middle class and peasant Slav Czech and Slovak inhabitants. There had never been a distinct German-speaking political entity so the infringement of the people's right to self-determination at Versailles had arisen because Bohemia had been given a simple democratic constitution. Inevitably this created a Czech-dominated government, given the distribution of population. Large enclaves of Hungarians and Poles further fractured Czechoslovakia's integrity.

By Balkan standards the Sudeten Germans were barely oppressed by the Czech majority but there was enough fuel for a distinctly Sudet-en political movement to develop, mainly under the leadership of the Sudetendeutsche Partei (SdP). It received large, covert subsidies from Germany with both the Auswärtiges Amt and the Nazi Party making separate payments. It became the dominant force in the Sudetenland with an overwhelming share of the vote. Its leader, Konrad Henlein, was heavily influenced by the Nazi regime but he managed to conceal this publicly. As the leader of a large ethnic minority Henlein could survive by airing grievances and demanding ever more concessions. He was under no pressure to work out a satisfactory modus vivendi with the Czech part of the country for the long term. This suited his German paymasters perfectly and they consistently held him back from negoti-ating constructively or conclusively. Henlein succeeded in persuading a range of public figures in Britain that his sole interest was merely to protect Sudeten interests and that he was neither a Nazi pawn nor working for independence or attachment to Germany. He found a ready audience amongst those who saw the injustices in the Versailles Treaties. He delivered a pitch which pretended that he was not seeking to split the Sudetenland from Czechoslovakia, which took in even Churchill.

The Prague government found itself fighting a defensive campaign against Henlein's attempts to secure greater rights for the Sudeten community but laboured under a number of handicaps. It had a poor case to present for the existing arrangements, with its inbuilt Czech domination. The Prague leadership suspected, but could not prove, the treasonous aspect of the SdP. There was no serious attempt to put the Czech case such as it was to the British, leaving Henlein's case largely unchallenged. The Czechoslovakian President, Edvard Beneš, was at persistent loggerheads with his Prime Minister, Milan Hodža. Nazi German support for the Sudeten was an ever-present force.

All that Prague could set against Nazi German influence was France's commitment to defend Czechoslovakia under a formal treaty which went back to 1924. This had originally been created as part of the French diplomatic manoeuvre known as the Little Entente, in which a group of Balkan states was sponsored to bar any resurgence of Germany or Austria, as a bulwark to protect France. By 1938 the Little Entente had singularly failed in its original goal but France had little excuse to repudiate the treaties, which would have appeared to be a craven abandonment of a long-standing ally. France was trapped in a military obligation by its treaty with Czechoslovakia that it did not feel remotely strong enough to enforce. Overt German aggression against Czechoslovakia would have triggered a war with France, which would have placed Britain in a dilemma. It had no formal agreement to support France in this case, still less any commitment to go to war alongside France, but there would have been huge pressure to do so. Britain had no strategic or economic interest in Czechoslovakia yet found itself tied to France's intentions.

Churchill was almost first out of the gate with advice on how the position of Czechoslovakia ought to be handled. He delivered this in one of his great parliamentary speeches in the debate on the *Anschluß* a few days after the event. He made no bones about Czechoslovakia being the next likely victim of German aggression. Churchill paid lip service to the League of Nations as the foundation of defence against aggression but the nub of his argument was that only a partnership of Europe's two leading democracies, Britain and France, provided a credible counter:

Not so lightly will the two great liberal democracies of the West be challenged, and not so easily, if challenged, will they be subjugated. That is the beginning of collective security. But why stop there? ... If a number of states were assembled around Great Britain and France in a solemn treaty for mutual defence against aggression; if they had their forces marshalled in what you may call a grand alliance; if they had their staff arrangements concerted ... you might even now arrest this approaching war.[7]

The 'grand alliance' echoed the coalition that Churchill's ancestor the first Duke of Marlborough had led against France's attempt under Louis XIV to dominate Europe. To Harold Nicolson it was the speech of Churchill's life and it struck a powerful chord with MPs. Even *The Times* admitted that he 'greatly impressed the House' although it avoided quoting the phrase 'grand alliance'.[8]

At the heart of Churchill's notion of a 'grand alliance' was one consideration which combined his romanticism with military reality. The French army was still Europe's largest and most effective; France's military collapse in 1940 would have as much to do with bad strategy as anything else. The French tank arm was more advanced than the Germans'. Churchill's vision of the French army was deeply coloured by his memory of the formidable force alongside which he had fought in the First World War. The spectacle of a mass review of the French army during the visit of King George VI to Paris in July 1938 nearly brought Churchill to tears.[9] Hitler recognised how powerful it might have been and devoted frantic efforts to building the *Westwall* fortifications opposite the Maginot Line in case France should have chosen to attack across the frontier whilst the Wehrmacht was engaged in the east. As it was France's military and political leadership never seriously considered this strategy, but they were in the grips of the same defeatist mentality that Churchill was trying to fight at home. Churchill lobbied hard and widely in France for full-scale military collaboration at the same time as he was arguing for a grand alliance in Britain, but he was doomed to failure as long as the political will was lacking on both sides.[10]

Chamberlain was sufficiently piqued by the attention given to Churchill's proposal that he claimed to have thought of the very same idea himself long before.[11] The Cabinet and the military chiefs had certainly examined various options over the weekend after the *Anschluß* but it was clearly Churchill's speech that forced Chamberlain and Halifax to give it some proper consideration.[12] It was rejected for two reasons: it would have involved giving the French a formal treaty commitment, long anathema to the Foreign Office let alone Chamberlain himself, and it would have triggered an all-out European war if Germany invaded Czechoslovakia. Chamberlain was handicapped by his inclination to translate any diplomatic move into a final definite, often military consequence, bypassing any judgement on how effective it might be at the level of pure diplomatic bluff. His vision of a 'grand alliance' was light years away from Churchill's: some kind of British-led *gendarmerie* that could turn back invaders at the Czechoslovakian frontier. Chamberlain was reading the mood of the country as a whole correctly. It did not want war, but it did want some show of defiance to Nazi aggression.

Churchill's speech had made him a force in government foreign policy, however briefly, and Chamberlain had to swallow his reservations and at least go through the motions of acting as though Churchill mattered as he prepared to deliver his own public response to the *Anschluß*. In the hope of softening Churchill's response to the speech, he summoned him on his own for an advance briefing at which he hinted at the considerations of Britain's military weakness which shaped his policy.[13] With his limitless capacity for finding interpretations that rebounded to his own credit, Chamberlain believed that Churchill was 'terribly pleased at thus being taken into confidence' and softened his own reply as a result. In reality Churchill was well aware that the solid government majority was never going to be swayed by anything he might say in the Commons but at that stage he did not want to burn his bridges completely.

Chamberlain was immensely pleased with the speech that he delivered on 24 March 1938: 'an éclatant success. In fact I never remember a speech by a British Minister at a critical time which has won such universal approval in Europe.'[14] It certainly hit exactly the right note with the Conservative majority in the House by explicitly ruling out any firm new commitment either to France or to Czechoslovakia yet appearing to strike a note of resolve with the claim that '[w]here peace and war are concerned, legal obligations are not alone involved, and, if war broke out, it would be unlikely to be confined to those who have assumed such obligations'.[15] He gave a high-flown but quite spurious image of a partnership between 'Great Britain and France, with long associations of friendship, with interests closely interwoven, devoted to the same ideals of democratic liberty, and determined to uphold them'. This was mere rhetoric, although sufficient listeners and readers allowed themselves to be persuaded that it meant something. It made no such impression on the Germans or professional diplomats. The German chargé d'affaires recognised immediately the emptiness of the verbiage, which he labelled as a 'vague impression'. He saw the simple point that Chamberlain had 'not undertaken any new engagements' and came to the conclusion that if things reached a crisis 'it might not in such a case come to a British intervention'.[16]

Sir Horace Wilson was not troubled by the *Anschluß* and viewed the next logical step in the creation of a Nazi-dominated *Mitteleuropa* with equanimity.[17] It did not undermine his faith in the plan that he and Chamberlain had mapped out, which he believed would soon achieve its goal, 'full of energy, self-confidence and optimism. He believed that together with Chamberlain, he was about to inscribe a new and glorious page into the book of European "appeasement".'[18] He imagined that the attachment of a series of new political and economic arrangements would dilute the monolithic strength of Nazi Germany. Britain would not be threatened but Germany's next move afterwards would be against the Soviet Union. As he hinted blatantly to the Soviet ambassador in London, Ivan Maisky, this would not be unwelcome to London.

The government was alert to any move by Churchill to involve himself deeply in Czechoslovakia. In April 1938 Churchill was due to go to Czechoslovakia on an exploratory visit with one of his old associates, Edward Spears MP, who had business interests in the country. Spears was a Francophile and broadly opposed to appeasement, but he had a surprising connection with the other camp in the person of Sir Joseph Ball. The most probable origin of the connection is through the City. Amongst Spears's interests was the Ashanti goldfields company, which later fell under the influence of Lonrho, an Africa trading company, which Ball ended up controlling. Spears tried to persuade Churchill to accept Ball as a companion on the visit to Czechoslovakia: 'he is very anxious to see the same things as you are on behalf of the Prime Minister and he is absolutely discreet'.[19] The prospect of travelling with a Downing Street spy cannot have been appealing and Churchill never visited Czechoslovakia.

Fears of armed German intervention in Czechoslovakia reached a climax at the end of May 1938. In an atmosphere of acute tension, the Czechoslovakian army mobilised amidst intelligence of an imminent attack by Germany. London and Paris protested vigorously over the weekend of 21 May. No invasion occurred but none had ever been planned. The Czechoslovakian intelligence was wrong or had been intentionally manipulated. The western powers appear never to have learned this and may have been left with an exaggerated sense of what they might be able to achieve in moderating Hitler's policy towards Czechoslovakia. They believed that they had forced Hitler into a potentially humiliating retreat. The frustration led Hitler to declare his intention to destroy Czechoslovakia.

Downing Street was unaware of the depth of the humiliation that had been inflicted on Hitler but still moved to soften the blow and flag up that it was still more than willing to accommodate German wishes in Czechoslovakia. In the wake of an off-the-record briefing to journalists, *The Times* ran a story advising the Czechoslovakian government to hold a plebiscite in the Sudetenland, which would almost certainly be a prelude to autonomy or separation. This did not seem to have registered at the higher reaches of the Foreign Office, which put out a more-or-less routine denial that a plebiscite was government policy. At the German embassy Fritz Hesse, the press adviser, knew better, having been briefed by both his usual Downing Street contact, George Steward, and by someone at the Foreign Office press section, and he set to work to persuade the Auswärtiges Amt that the article was an official feeler from Chamberlain.[20] Hesse's side-job was to act as Ribbentrop's eyes and ears at the London embassy to monitor the potentially unreliable old-style diplomats. During Ribbentrop's time as ambassador Hesse had developed a close relationship with him and was one of the few people to find him admirable. Hesse was sometimes described as the London representative of the *Dienststelle Ribbentrop*, Ribbentrop's personal apparatus within the Auswärtiges Amt, which was quite distinct from his private office staffed by regular diplomats. He later wrote memoirs, which wildly exaggerated his role in back-channel diplomacy between Germany and Britain. He had been brought up in Baghdad and, according to his daughter, had a romantic 'Arabian Nights' approach to events.[21]

It took some weeks for the message to make its way through Ribbentrop's habitually dilatory processes, but when it did Hesse was summoned to Berlin to explain the background.[22] Hesse convinced Ribbentrop, who in turn informed Hitler but failed to convince him that he could get the Sudetenland without war. Notwithstanding, Ribbentrop authorised Hesse to pass on to the English government the message that if it persuaded the Czechs to cede the Sudetenland, Hitler would acquiesce.[23] Hesse knew he was working at the limits of what the Nazi leadership would tolerate and put the suggestion to Downing Street in a much toned-down and diplomatic form.

By the time Wilson came to transmit this up the line to Chamberlain, it had been softened yet further to the assertion that the new German ambassador and his staff had been mulling over the attractions of resuming conversations for a while.[24] He used this as grounds to shift the correspondence between Downing Street and Berlin onto a friendly tone. Wilson was given an opening in the shape of some cautious wording in the Foreign Office draft of a response to a German communication, which he could challenge. He advised the Prime Minister that 'it seems [a] pity to put anything into the reply that suggests frigidity on our part'.[25] What the Foreign Office had drafted 'reminds me in tone of other remarks that have been addressed in the past five years to Germany, some of them creating the worst possible impression upon their recipients'. The alternative wording that Wilson suggested was bland in the extreme; no hint of firmness was to be allowed to intrude into what Britain said to Germany.

It seemed a propitious moment to reopen an amicable dialogue with Germany, as Wilson had just received a friendly visit from a representative of another powerful part of the Nazi bureaucracy.[26] Helmut

Wohlthat was Hermann Goering's chief economic adviser and a frequent dabbler in international affairs. Goering had no formal role in the Nazi foreign policy machine, but, in keeping with the régime's ethos of all against all, he was not content to leave his rivals unchallenged. He particularly detested Ribbentrop, so relations with Britain were a tempting area for him to interfere in. Wohlthat's personal business interests included animal fats and this had brought him to the International Whaling Conference in London in June, where he also had meetings with more than a dozen senior figures from the worlds of politics, economics, banking and the Court.* The conference was a formally established organisation that tried to regulate the hunting of whales, which was at the time a major source of fats for food and cleaning products. British firms were major players in the industry so London was a natural venue. In conversation with Wilson, Wohlthat had talked up the idea that it would be worth having discussions, implicitly with Goering's support.[27] According to Wohlthat, Wilson went even further and implied that Britain had been obliged to cooperate closely but unwillingly with France, which was swung by emotion and sensitivity. This had not stopped Britain from putting pressure on Czechoslovakia; 'Chamberlain wanted to achieve a peaceful settlement of the Sudeten German demands'. The message was repeated by Rab Butler, the Foreign Office's most committed appeaser. Over drinks at the German embassy Butler made a very sympathetic impression on Wohlthat. He too had emphasised that 'Britain is ready to treat the Sudeten German question … in accordance with German wishes'. The royal court was not shy to give its own take on appeasement. Sir Louis Greig, gentleman usher to and close friend of George VI, hinted that having Chamberlain as Prime Minister gave Germany a special opportunity to get on terms given his commitment to friendship.

Wilson had stumbled over a fault-line in Nazi foreign policy that paralleled the fracture in British foreign policy separating Downing

---

* Wohlthat's interest in natural fats had led him to help organise a German expedition to the Antarctic, then a major whaling ground. His contribution was recognised by naming a mountain range after him, the Wohlthat Massif, which keeps its name to this day. He thus has the distinction of being the only high official of the Third Reich still to be publicly commemorated.

Street from the Foreign Office. In the ferocious and chaotic war of all-against-all that raged at the top of the Nazi leadership, influence over foreign policy was just another battleground. Ribbentrop counted for nothing in other areas of policy and Goering had no compunction about trying to undermine and bypass his efforts at diplomacy. Wohlthat spoke for no one but Goering. The optimistic signals that Wohlthat and, coincidentally, Hesse were feeding to the British were just one amongst a number of facets of opinion at various points in the German government. The professional diplomats of the Auswärtiges Amt had a considerably less upbeat take on the state of affairs than the unofficial representatives. The new ambassador, Herbert von Dirksen, who had replaced Ribbentrop in May 1938, was reporting to Berlin a few days later that 'Anglo-German relations as a whole are in a state of suspense and are full of tension. They require a settlement, or at least an attempt at settlement.'[28] Dirksen was a step up from Ribbentrop in terms of competence, but he was not influential. He was an old-style professional diplomat of the kind Hitler despised, but he was not part of the clique around Ernst von Weizsäcker at the top of the Auswärtiges Amt. His mother had been an early backer of Hitler, but this now counted for little.

The flaws in British foreign policy-making created a barrier to understanding, still more to exploiting, the peculiarities of its Nazi counterpart. A dispassionate and analytical ambassador in Berlin could have explained clearly and firmly that the only thing that truly mattered was Hitler's decision. The concentration of serious decision-making into two individuals at Downing Street eliminated the chance of proper, critical analysis of policy. In practice appeasement set its own agenda. Anything that had a sniff of being a friendly overture from Germany matched the over-optimistic assumptions that lay behind Downing Street's goals and was treated accordingly.

Hard on Wohlthat's heels came another unofficial representative of the Nazi leadership, this time with a direct link to Hitler as well as being a promoter of Goering's role in diplomacy. Hitler was not above a little unofficial diplomacy of his own and staged a small exercise designed to calm British concerns whilst the true work of ratcheting up pressure on the Czechoslovakian government continued. He despatched one of his adjutants, Captain Fritz Wiedemann, to London, ostensibly to discuss the possibility that Goering might visit London and generally to spread a message of cooperation and amity. The idea of a Goering visit had been floating around for some time; its attraction lay in the unfounded belief that Goering was a pragmatist and friend of Britain, nourished by moves such as Wohlthat's recent talk with Wilson. Wiedemann was personally close to Hitler, having been his company commander during the First World War, but otherwise had no standing in the Nazi regime. The whole episode was conducted in an atmosphere of seedy operetta. The chief intermediary was one of Wiedemann's mistresses, Princess Stephanie Hohenlohe, whom he shared with the appeasing press baron Lord Rothermere. The princess was born Jewish, but happily worked for the Nazi regime. She was based in London where she conducted a long-lasting, chiefly financial but probably non-sexual relationship with Rothermere, whom she had persuaded to take up the cause of the Hungarian nation. One of her female friends knew Lady Halifax and through her arranged a meeting between Wiedemann and her husband. The conversation at the Halifax house was perfectly friendly, with Wiedemann denying that Hitler planned to use violence on Czechoslovakia. The details leaked and the story appeared in the *News Chronicle*, which opposed the government and played up the suspicions inevitably aroused by such a covert meeting.

The Goering visit to London never materialised, even supposing that it had ever been seriously considered on the German side. In the aftermath of the Wiedemann visit, Dirksen followed it up by calling on Wilson at Downing Street. He had clearly recognised that Wilson was the most useful person to talk to in London after Chamberlain. Wilson went through the motions of expressing government support for the idea, subject to vaguely expressed conditions.[29] In practice this was no more than a repetition of the standard call not to use force on Czechoslovakia as German wishes would be granted in time. More practically, Wilson wanted to alert Dirksen to the fact that Britain had a fall-back plan up its sleeve if the talks between Henlein and the Czechoslovakian government broke down without a positive result. The British foreign policy machine had seen through the false détente offered by Wiede-mann and was accurately pessimistic as to what could be achieved be-tween Henlein and Prague. Goering and Wohlthat faded away from involvement in the burgeoning Czechoslovakian crisis, but Wilson had opened an unofficial channel to Goering, which was to come into its own the following year as another crisis loomed.

*   *   *

Central Europe took centre stage from the *Anschluß* onwards but Chamberlain still wanted to appease Italy. With Eden out of the way Britain could sit down to negotiate formally with Italy in the spirit of calm amity that Chamberlain hoped would produce a long-lasting friendship between the two countries, but the change at the Foreign Office entirely failed to realign the European diplomatic balance ac-cording to Chamberlain's fantasies. The crucial proof came only weeks after Eden resigned when Germany put an end to its attempts to coerce Austria by simply absorbing it into the Reich. Austrian independence had been the one potentially difficult issue between Germany and Italy, which the British had dreamed might serve to weaken the sympathy between the fascist dictators. Mussolini understood that Italy did not have the strength, the diplomatic influence or, ultimately, the desire to fight Hitler over the *Anschluß* and accepted the move without protest. Hitler was for ever grateful to Mussolini for this show of dictatorial solidarity. There was no question of depriving Italy of the German-speaking Südtirol (Alto Adige to the Italians) region of Austria that it had been awarded at Versailles.

British foreign policy rested on the fallacy that Mussolini would willingly pay a significant price for *de jure* recognition, in particular by withdrawing Italian troops from Spain. He would not, so all that emerged from the negotiations in the short term were the 'Easter agree-ments' which were loudly cheered in Chamberlain's loyal press outlets but, in reality, amounted to little more than an amiable agreement that both sides would respect the status quo in the Mediterranean. Brit-ain was not able to reduce military spending in the region by a single penny. The question of *de jure* recognition was left open. After the middle of 1938 it barely mattered anyway. The flashpoint for instability had shifted to central Europe, where Chamberlain's willingness to sacrifice Czechoslovakian integrity mattered far more than what Britain might or might not acquiesce to in the loss of Ethiopian independence. Having swallowed the camel of the *Anschluß* there was never any prospect that Mussolini might strain at the gnat of Germany seizing the Sudetenland.

The elimination of Eden was the high-water mark of Joseph Ball's back-channel diplomacy with the Italians. It had achieved Chamberlain's overriding objective of beginning formal negotiations between Britain and Italy but it remained on tap for further contacts. Soon after the German seizure of Austria, Ball floated a feeble scheme for a summit meeting between Chamberlain and Mussolini, doubtless to put pressure on the Berlin–Rome Axis.[30] Chamberlain was to visit Switzerland for Easter and cross the border to meet *il Duce*. With the formal negotiations over *de jure* recognition still far from complete, the Italians had little compunction in letting the matter drop. No hint of this extraordinary proposal ever surfaced in Britain but the enthusiasm for a summit meeting is striking in the light of one involving Chamberlain which famously did take place a few months later. The secret channel briefly became an adjunct to formal, open diplomacy when it was used to signal that Anglo-French collaboration over Spain stopped well short of anything that would compromise Anglo-Italian negotiations.[31] Ball passed word that Chamberlain was well aware of clandestine supplies crossing to the Republicans over the Pyrenees and would take appropriate action with France.

The secret channel also served for unavowable requests from Chamberlain to Mussolini on a topic too sensitive for ordinary channels. Attacks on British shipping in Spanish waters had almost ceased after Eden's elimination, but they resumed in the early summer of 1938, providing very public proof of the aggression and bad faith of Fascist Italy. British ships were sunk and British sailors killed. On 23 June 1938 the government was savagely criticised in Parliament over an affront that only the most committed appeasers in the Conservative ranks could accept. In the words of the head of the Foreign Office, Sir Alec Cadogan, 'The House blew up about the bombing of ships.'[32] In possibly his most difficult moment in the House of Commons of the entire appeasement process, Chamberlain faced 'a pack of wild beasts when you just had to fight for your life'.[33] Unmentioned by anyone, but obvious to all, was the contrast between the government's passivity on this issue and the resolute stance that Eden had taken at the League of Nations the previous autumn, when he was still Foreign Secretary, over Italian submarine attacks on British ships under similar circumstances. Chamberlain began by attacking a British ship-owner with the conveniently Jewish-sounding name of Billmeir for supposedly profiteering and then brought out the feeble claim that his hands were tied by the non-intervention agreement, so resolute action would risk a European war.[34] The non-intervention agreement of 1936 supposedly forbad other countries to become involved in the Spanish Civil War; Britain respected it to the letter, France mostly, but Germany and Italy ignored it. Publicly and officially Chamberlain had to maintain the pretence that this was purely a question for the Spanish Nationalists; the aircraft now carrying out the attacks carried Nationalist markings, but they were supplied by Mussolini with Italian crews based on Mallorca. Britain's well-connected and effective consul in Mallorca, Alan Hillgarth, was well aware of the true position.[35] Churchill had a field day, lambasting the government for the 'debasement of a currency ... [T]he British flag is not giving protection to persons proceeding about their lawful vocations.' He skewered Chamberlain with the suggestion that the 'Prime Minister should use his personal influence with Signor Mussolini', which he had devoted 'so much exertion' to cultivating. Chamberlain ruefully admitted that 'Winston was far more subtle and kept quiet except his banditti were sniping when they could'.[36]

Churchill had thrown down a challenge to Chamberlain and, hidden from sight, Chamberlain tried to use the secret channel to take it up and defeat it. Pleading intense political pressure on Chamberlain, Ball begged for Mussolini to make a public statement that could be set against suspicions in Parliament that these attacks were pre-planned and conducted by Italian forces.[37] By then the balance of power had shifted far in Italy's favour. Chamberlain did not get his declaration, but he did receive a comforting telephone call from the Italian foreign minister, Galeazzo Ciano.[38] Dino Grandi, the ambassador to London more attuned to the need to rescue Chamberlain, urged Rome to discourage Franco from making attacks on shipping 'for the next days'. The secret channel had failed to deliver and the pressure of criticism forced the government to concede with an open complaint in Rome that was then disclosed to the press.[39]

Churchill rapidly frittered away any benefits from his tactical victory over Chamberlain by blundering into a parliamentary quagmire, once again involving the Committee of Privileges, in an unhappy echo of his tactical blunder in the campaign against the India Bill. Churchill's son-in-law Duncan Sandys was a Territorial Army officer as well as an MP and through one of his fellow officers acquired some useful information of the weakness of anti-aircraft defences. He used this to try to pressurise Leslie Hore-Belisha, the War Secretary. Here the authorities over-reacted and Sandys found himself threatened with prosecution for revealing military secrets. Presented with a perfect opportunity to hammer home the government's desire to hide the inadequacy of anti-aircraft defences behind excessive secrecy, Sandys with Churchill's support over-played his hand by bringing the matter before the Committee of Privileges as an infringement of the constitutional rights of an MP. This was a grave tactical error. An easy presentational win was transformed into a procedural slogging contest that dragged on in futility over weeks, incomprehensible to the public and which played to the government's built-in strengths. Chamberlain found it as tedious as anyone even though Churchill's misjudgement was working to his advantage: '[T]he House is beginning to be aware that [they] have been humbugged by Winston & Sandys and they don't want to hear much more about it.'[40]

The affair brought out one of the deficiencies of the Official Secrets Act: the ferociously prescriptive Section 6, which imposed a duty on anyone to denounce any breaches of secrecy. Wilson was put in charge of a committee of civil servants, who were given the job of burying an attempt to reform the Act.[41]

# CHAPTER ELEVEN

# A NICE FRAUDULENT
# BALANCE SHEET

*[A] lot of the old ... death-traps ... could have been turned out in any
quantity and would have produced a nice fraudulent balance sheet.
All this influenced critics to think it all ought to be much easier.
Chamberlain made up his mind he must sacrifice me
in order to get an easier time in Parliament.*
– LORD SWINTON

The *Anschluß* brought only a brief distraction from the difficulties
in air rearmament and, anyway, made it even more urgent. The
government was still under severe pressure. The changes at the Air Ministry that Chamberlain had mentioned to keep Churchill quiet proved
to be highly effective at increasing aircraft output over the next year. At
the level of the crude political imperatives that were being played for,
though, they hardly set the pulses racing. They occurred at the initiative
of the Air Secretary, Lord Swinton, but he was not to be allowed to
reap his reward. Swinton instituted a small committee, the Air Council
Committee on Supply, which grouped representatives of the Air Ministry, Sir Charles Bruce-Gardner for the industry and its most significant
member, Edward Bridges, soon to become Cabinet Secretary. Bridges represented the Treasury and his presence was the keystone of the
committee's unprecedented power to authorise spending. The logjam
of time-consuming paper shuffling between the Air Ministry as the
spending body and its paymaster, the Treasury, was broken. One of the

Royal Air Force's forgotten heroes, Air Marshal Sir Wilfrid Freeman, was promoted, combining responsibility for aircraft design and aircraft production. This dual function allowed Freeman to drive through the introduction and full-scale manufacture of the RAF's most famous and effective aircraft types of the Second World War.

Bruce-Gardner's membership of the Air Council Committee on Supply was a bright spot in a generally tense relationship between him and Swinton. The direct dealings between the two men were overshadowed by a triangular dialogue with Horace Wilson as the third participant. Swinton and Bruce-Gardner competed for Downing Street's support via Wilson. Both Wilson and Bruce-Gardner briefed each other on their contacts with Swinton but the full extent of their relationship remained hidden from the Air Secretary. Wilson was far more closely aligned with Bruce-Gardner. At one point he expressed 'the hope that the line which you and I discussed the other day will prove acceptable to him'.[1] A civil servant and the head of a trade body were combining to set government policy behind the back of the minister responsible. They enjoyed a huge tactical advantage in the battle for the Prime Minister's approval in that they both aimed for the same thing: a crude target of increasing the number of aircraft produced, with quality taking only second place. Bruce-Gardner followed up the advantage with an alarmist picture of the gap between British and German output, 'very disturbing figures and, for that reason any decision arrived at "by the few" should be made with the best information available and this, so far as I am concerned, I have endeavoured to provide'.[2] Bruce-Gardner had anointed himself as provider of strategic intelligence to Downing Street as well as its adviser on the duties of national defence. Swinton challenged Bruce-Gardner on his true goal, 'the desirability of placing orders in the largest possible quantity and covering longer periods', and told him firmly that this was a question for the Air Ministry. Wilson was happy to relay Bruce-Gardner's complaints to Chamberlain but insisted that he hold back from the economic heresies of 'imposing war conditions' or going far 'in the direction of interference and control'.[3]

The underlying dispute between Swinton and Bruce-Gardner concerned the level of orders, but the inevitable explosion was triggered by the news that the Air Ministry was sending a mission to the United States to examine the possibility of buying aeroplanes from American makers. This provoked the Society of British Aircraft Constructors (SBAC) to rage. Bruce-Gardner succeeded in preventing its members from making a public protest by reading out the letter he was going to send Swinton, 'complaining in the strongest terms with regard to the proposal to buy American war planes'.[4] As well as hurting their export business it would signal that the British industry was fully loaded, which they believed was not true. The mission provided ammunition for an MP who also owned an aircraft company to complain of 'the inefficiency of the Air Ministry' at a time when 'many companies in the aircraft industry were dismissing their workpeople through lack of orders'.[5]

Bruce-Gardner brought out the big stick and waved his privileged position with the Prime Minister at Swinton to force a decision in his favour. He wanted to come to the Air Ministry with a small delegation of his members to settle a lengthy list of grievances. Bruce-Gardner's decisive weapon was a long paper he had composed on the basis of information from SBAC members. It argued that the Air Ministry's wilful refusal to grant orders meant that aircraft output was only half the level that the industry could attain. The catch was that the missing aircraft were of types that SBAC members were willing to produce and not necessarily the ones that Swinton, the Air Ministry or the RAF wanted. Prominent in Bruce-Gardner's list of planes that could be produced quickly in large numbers were the near-obsolete Gladiator biplane fighter and the Hampden bomber and its derivatives, which might charitably have been described as a stop-gap design. At the other extreme, Bruce-Gardner promoted orders for types which did not even exist as prototypes, notably a twin-engine version of the calamitous Fairey Battle light bomber, which was never to see the light of day. Bruce-Gardner's paper was not just aimed at the civil servants and the air marshals of the Air Ministry. It featured basic descriptions of the types of aircraft that he favoured, which the professional readers would already have known by heart. The real target readers sat in Downing Street and Bruce-Gardner knew how to play on the panic factor at the highest level of government. He painted a vivid picture of the lack of progress in production fully six weeks after the *Anschluß*, which he had described to Wilson as a 'gypsy's warning'.

Swinton fought back at a meeting in the Air Ministry on 25 April 1938 where Bruce-Gardner had to face the massed ranks of politicians and civil servants alone.[6] The Air Secretary delivered a blunt message to the industry to warn it away from the vision of easy and lucrative orders for obsolescent aircraft types:

> [H]e wished to secure the co-operation of Sir Charles Bruce-Gardner in making it clear to contractors that they would not be doing their duty merely by accelerating output of existing types. It was of the utmost necessity that the new types should be brought in at the earliest possible date and he would be very disappointed if, as the outcome of the discussions, acceleration of new types was not achieved.

Swinton dominated the meeting, but the ground was being cut from under his feet at Downing Street. Wilson forwarded Swinton's paper and covering letter to Chamberlain, noting that it 'suggests that the industry is not being fully utilised'.[7] He presented Bruce-Gardner's paper as an answer to the burning question for Chamberlain, 'what is the maximum the industry could produce in the next two years'. Parity might have been abandoned as a formal target but its spirit lingered on. Wilson fed in a panic factor of his own: '[U]neasiness is widespread and may come to a head quite soon.'[8] He reported conversations with other industrialists and concluded that 'a wave of dissatisfaction with the Air Ministry is developing fast'. For good measure he forwarded to the Prime Minister samples of open complaint at the pace of air rearmament together with Churchill's reminder that his memorandum of March had yet to answered, to ram home the political stakes involved.

Swinton was losing ground in his insistence on quality over quantity. Chamberlain explained to a Cabinet meeting on 27 April 1938 that Bruce-Gardner had promised that his members in the aircraft industry would be in a position to deliver 4,000 aircraft by the end of March 1939 and a further 8,000 the following year.[9] Chamberlain's goal was 'maxiumum output' through the 'acceleration of suitable types now in production and of bringing into production as early as possible the latest improved types'. He said nothing of matching the Luftwaffe, but focused on dealing with political criticism, 'especially from Mr. Winston Churchill'. The Cabinet 'authorise[d] the Air Ministry to accept as many aeroplanes as they could obtain up to the maximum of 12,000 machines in the next two years'. There was no mention of quality in the Cabinet resolution.

Swinton's fate was sealed by the House of Commons debate on air on 13 May. As a member of the House of Lords he was unable to take part in the debate and Lord Winterton failed lamentably. Winterton wildly misread the mood of the House and put up a miserable performance of defending the government's record against well-briefed attacks from Churchill and the Liberal leader, Sir Archibald Sinclair. Winterton's dismissal afterwards was a foregone conclusion – although he kept his seat in Cabinet – but Chamberlain caused raised eyebrows by sacking Swinton as well. Lord Weir resigned as adviser to the Air Ministry in disgust almost immediately. Swinton's abrasiveness had not made for a quiet life and he had become a lightning rod for the discontent of the aircraft industry. Wilson had backed the industry fronted by his man Bruce-Gardner against the ministry. Together Wilson and Bruce-Gardner were happy to play a political numbers game. Downing Street had chosen how it wanted to overcome the obstacles on the way to rebuilding the RAF and Swinton was not part of the plan.

In his memoirs Swinton bemoaned the forces that had led to his removal:

There were not wanting manufacturers who would like to have built a lot of the old Hinds and Harts, death-traps which could have been turned out in any quantity and would have produced a nice fraudulent balance sheet. All this influenced critics to think it all ought to be much easier. Chamberlain made up his mind he must sacrifice me in order to get an easier time in Parliament. This was not unnatural for a Prime Minister who was not much interested, at the time, in rearmament and was convinced that war could be avoided.[10]

He was exaggerating by suggesting that Bruce-Gardner and Wilson wanted to produce such true antiques, but was accurate in recognising that the political imperative of quantity had trumped the need for quality.

Sir Kingsley Wood, who replaced Swinton as Air Secretary, was far more of a professional politician. He had a gift for promoting schemes which attracted favourable publicity. As Postmaster General he had been credited with a successful drive to market telephones to the public. He had moved on to the Ministry of Health where he had pursued slum clearance, a topic close to Chamberlain's heart from his own time at the ministry. Superficially the change was an improvement: 'Kingsley has lots of energy and business sense and creates public confidence without antagonising people as Philip [Swinton] does.'[11]

Almost Wood's first move in office was designed to kill three birds with one stone. Above all it would provide spectacular evidence that the government was addressing the question of aircraft manufacture, on which it had taken such a severe beating in Parliament at the hands of Churchill. It would also elegantly bury two embarrassing parts of his legacy from Swinton in the same grave. Soon after Swinton had been appointed his abrasive personality had contributed to an embarrassing and venomous public squabble with Lord Nuffield, Britain's leading car manufacturer, over a small aircraft engine company that he owned personally.[12] Wood saw scope for major dividends from conciliating Nuffield, whose industrial empire might be used to good advantage in the rearmament effort. In particular, it could be used to make good the problem of producing Spitfires. Swinton was the political father of the Spitfire and earned enormous credit in driving its adoption by the RAF, but actually manufacturing it had become a nightmare. Supermarine, the company who designed the Spitfire, had only one small factory in Southampton, vulnerable to German air attack. The Spitfire was the key aircraft in modernising the RAF's fighter force and it would have to be produced in volume. Wood and Nuffield agreed that Nuffield would build and operate a massive factory at Castle Bromwich near Birmingham, which would build 1,000 Spitfires.[13] Publicly this was touted as the largest aircraft order ever placed, although the agreement fell well short of a legal contract. The Treasury was appropriately sniffy about the whole procedure, especially as it had not been consulted. The factory cost the then gigantic sum of £3½ million and was equipped with the most modern machines available. Wood ensured that every ounce of possible favourable publicity was wrung from the scheme.

The combination of Wood as minister and Bruce-Gardner as Downing Street's link-man to the plane-makers appears to have satisfied Downing Street that all was back on track. There is no sign that any attempt was made from the top to chase progress on making good the lag in production. Relations between government and plane-makers calmed down. Wood could work undisturbed and he, in turn, made no changes to the new men and structures that he had inherited from Swinton. In Wilfrid Freeman's words, 'We spent the money and Kingsley Wood left us alone.'[14]

With perfect political cynicism, the government could ignore the SBAC's self-serving complaint at the possibility of buying in the United States once it had served its purpose in undermining Swinton. The mission led to orders for two aircraft types that played an important part in the RAF's arsenal in the Second World War: the Harvard advanced trainer and the Hudson light bomber and maritime patrol aircraft. These were the first of many US aircraft without which Britain would have been severely handicapped. Swinton and Weir had recognised that the British domestic aircraft industry did not have sufficient capacity to meet the needs of a full-scale air war.

The change in minister did not lead to any let-up in the government's fight with Churchill over air rearmament; if anything it intensified. Churchill wrote to Wood with a barely veiled threat to intensify his criticism of the government's air rearmament and to ally himself with the opposition parties. He bemoaned the slow progress that the Air Defence Research Committee (ADRC) was making and openly regretted that he had ever accepted Stanley Baldwin's invitation to join it as, 'with the support we had from the Liberal and Labour Parties in the house, we could have enforced more attention to this subject, than by being members of these committees'.[15] Baldwin had used this as a device to muzzle Churchill and Churchill knew that it had succeeded.

The threat added fuel to the fire of the conflict between Churchill and another top-level member of British bureaucracy. Since he had severely attacked the visit by Erhard Milch in November 1937, Churchill had been increasingly at loggerheads with Sir Maurice Hankey, the Cabinet Secretary. Hankey had been particularly annoyed at the level of confidential information that was reaching Churchill through his network of disaffected RAF officers.[16] Even though Hankey had operated in almost the same way together with David Lloyd George during the First World War to circumvent entrenched complacency in the armed services, he had now aligned himself squarely with the government against Churchill. Hankey prepared an unconvincing rebuttal of Churchill's complaints about the ADRC and forwarded it to Chamberlain as ammunition against Churchill with a covering letter that reads more like the work of a dedicated politician than a civil servant. It recommended the material for its value in 'counter attacking him' and relished the prospect of it being used in a 'withering counter-blast' when the time was right.[17] The key weapon would be a public announcement of the 'epoch making inventions that have been adopted', radar clearly to the fore. Chamberlain enthusiastically supported the idea to 'keep the cards up our sleeve till we are ready to play them with effect'.[18]

Churchill kept up the pressure on Wood although he switched his attention to technical matters. He challenged Wood on the question of intercepting bombers.[19] Churchill had grasped the crucial fact that was to become all too obvious in the course of the Second World War, that a heavily laden, long-range bomber was at a permanent disadvantage to defending fighters in terms of speed and armament. This simple fact proved that the fear that 'the bomber will always get through' and the terror that the Luftwaffe inspired in the hearts of the appeasers was quite false. As so often happened, Churchill was right on the big picture but wrong on the detail. He was less perspicacious in the way he advised that this imbalance should be exploited and argued in favour of turret-armed fighters to attack bombers on the beam and against fighters with conventional fixed, forward-firing weapons such as the Spitfire. Here Churchill found himself unwittingly in the same camp as Bruce-Gardner. One of the aircraft types that featured in

Bruce-Gardner's list of favoured machines of which output could easily be stepped up if only the Air Ministry would issue firm orders was the turret-armed Boulton-Paul Defiant. The Defiant proved an utter failure in combat and was pulled out of action within weeks.

The battle between the government and Churchill using Britain's defence secrets and technological choices as ammunition was never fought. Churchill was in fact well briefed on radar. His correspondence with Wood dwindled into a more-or-less courteous lobbying effort for aerial mines. Hankey's hopes of being asked to continue in office were dashed and he went into retirement following a power struggle with Wilson and Sir Warren Fisher which is discussed elsewhere. The burgeoning crisis over Czechoslovakia squeezed out other questions through the summer of 1938.

# CHAPTER TWELVE

# A WISE BRITISH SUBJECT

*[I]n case conversations broke down he [Chamberlain] proposed to have*
*a wise British subject available to slip off quickly to Central Europe*
*to try and get the parties together again.*
— CABINET MINUTES

Britain's next move in the Czech crisis had been prepared well before Fritz Wiedemann's visit as a contingency plan should negotiations between the Czechoslovakian government and the Sudetens reach an impasse. After minimal consultation with anyone involved, it was announced that a British mediator would come to Czechoslovakia to help negotiate a deal between the two sides.

The way in which the decision was taken marked another step in the transformation of British foreign policy from a collegiate process exposed to criticism to one decided solely by Chamberlain and Wilson. The colonies scheme had gone through the process of discussion at the Cabinet Foreign Policy Committee (FPC) and had been executed by a collective decision. The mediation mission to Czechoslovakia was simply announced on 22 June 1938 – albeit as a 'proposal' to the full Cabinet and the FPC in advance; 'in case conversations broke down he [Chamberlain] proposed to have a wise British subject available to slip off quickly to Central Europe to try and get the parties together again'.[1] No attempt was made to explain it, still less to invite discussion in either the full Cabinet or the FPC, and there is no indication that Chamberlain talked to the Foreign Office about it beforehand. The lack of visible political or even diplomatic discussion before the mission is puzzling given its importance. A former senior diplomat understood immediately that 'it committed HMG up to the hilt'.[2] Britain had taken the responsibility of solving an internal Czechoslovakian problem, even though it had no formal or direct interest in the question. Not only had there been no domestic British consultation but there had been none with France, which was directly interested through its treaty obligation to protect Czechoslovakia from a German attack. For a choice of such importance, there has been remarkably little analysis of it, although Chamberlain's parliamentary private secretary, Lord Dunglass, later thought it 'a mistake. It drew us in too much.'[3]

A curious feature of the 'wise British subject' mission was the laughably transparent pretence that it was not an official move by the British government. Chamberlain told Parliament that it had been launched at the request of the Prague government. This fiction had the double attraction of implying that Prague would have to accept any recommendation that the mission might make and helping Downing Street's case in the turf war within the British foreign policy machine. An official mission would have fallen squarely under the remit and control of the Foreign Office, whilst an 'unofficial' one would not be subject to the same constraints of practice and demarcation and could be shaped more to the taste of Downing Street. Wilson was deeply involved from a very early stage. He drew up an eclectic list of 'wise British subjects' as possible candidates for the job which he sent to Lord Halifax.[4] It was a truly British exercise in nominating 'the great and the good'; there was one representative each from retired politicians, the judiciary, academia, industry and the bar. Wilson tucked into his list an oblique hint that this was essentially a Downing Street show and not a Foreign Office one. He grudgingly admitted that the Foreign Secretary might have wanted to consider former ambassadors for the task, but hinted that they were unsuitable as a tribe by mentioning that Lord Lothian, the ambassador to Washington, albeit not a professional diplomat, featured amongst his 'many rejects'. He claimed that the list was drawn up in random order but the first two names – Lord Runciman, the Liberal shipping magnate whom Chamberlain had sacked from his Cabinet job as President of the Board of Trade on becoming Prime Minister, and the Scottish judge Lord Macmillan – were manifestly the most likely candidates. Chamberlain preferred Macmillan but eventually the choice fell on Runciman, who resisted at first but was eventually persuaded to accept the mission by Alec Cadogan of the Foreign Office.[5]

Wilson had appreciated from the start that choosing Runciman would not be enough in itself to keep Downing Street in control of the mission: 'Someone would have to accompany him and to do most of the work.'[6] Whoever was chosen for this task would be able to influence the mission enormously. The man selected was Frank Ashton-Gwatkin, the head of the Foreign Office's recently created economics section, and he was a perfect candidate from Downing Street's point of view. Wilson would have known him as a member of the British delegation to the Imperial Conference of 1932 in Ottawa, which had very much been his personal creation. He supported ardently the vision of central Europe dominated economically by Germany. Runciman asked for Ashton-Gwatkin personally on the basis of having worked with him as President of the Board of Trade, but he had been prompted to do so. The eternal Foreign Office intriguer Willie Tyrrell, who actively supported appeasement, claimed that he had advised Runciman to ask for him. Ashton-Gwatkin was anything but an obvious companion for a firmly grounded businessman and politician like Runciman. He was a moderately successful author of sexually ambiguous novels and flippant in his approach to his work. He enlivened the stresses and tedium of the mission by composing light-hearted doggerel, which featured a dim view of the Czechs as a people. Ashton-Gwatkin's presence on the mission was important enough for the Downing Street press manipulation machine to put a heavily positive, but not wholly accurate, spin on the choice. He was presented as an expert on the region 'well-versed in Danubian affairs' (true perhaps in regards to its economy) although his true diplomatic expertise was on Japan.[7] The choice of Ashton-Gwatkin was important enough to be referred to the Cabinet. Cadogan found the request to have him on the mission 'rather objectionable', but Halifax supported it and obtained the support of Chamberlain and the rest of the Cabinet.[8]

One of the Foreign Office's most aggressive opponents of appeasement, Wilson's *bête noire* Rex Leeper, had tried very hard but inevitably in vain to promote a rival candidate for Ashton-Gwatkin's slot.[9] Robert Bruce Lockhart was not merely an outsider, a secret intermediary with the Russian Bolsheviks during the Revolution, now turned journalist. He was a frequent visitor to Czechoslovakia and a friend of both President Beneš and the ambassador to London, Jan Masaryk, son of the first President of the country. '[I]t would be too dangerous, as I knew too much! In other words, Germans would object to me as biased in favour of Czechs!'[10]

The prospects that Britain would support Czechoslovakia were not especially strong – the main objective of Chamberlain's policy was to keep Germany happy – but the Czech leaders unknowingly did their own standing at Downing Street immense damage. Beneš and Masaryk both had a low opinion of Chamberlain and expressed this without restraint or decency in phone conversations between Prague and London:

> Masaryk: The wicked old [obscenity] is longing to lick Adolf's backside. His tongue is hanging out.
>
> Beneš: Stuff it back in again! Bring him to his senses.
>
> Masaryk: The old beast hasn't any senses left, except to smell out the Nazi ashheap [probably a euphemism] and hang around it.
>
> Beneš: Then have a talk with Horace Wilson. Ask him to warn the Prime Minister that England is in danger too if we do not stand firm. Can't he be made to understand this?
>
> Masaryk: How can you talk to Wilson? He is nothing but a jackal.[11]

The telephone line passed through German territory and the conversations were intercepted by Goering's *Forschungsamt* (research office), the bugging operation which was one of the keys to his power. Theodor Kordt, who had joined the German embassy in London a few months before, when his brother returned to Berlin, was tasked with passing on the transcripts to Wilson, who was annoyed that the British bugging operation had apparently failed to tap these conversations itself. It turned out that British intelligence had in fact been doing just that, but had been restrained by tact and awareness of Chamberlain's extremely thin skin from passing them on to Downing Street.

Chamberlain had never held a high opinion of the Czech people: 'not out of the top drawer – or even the middle'.[12] The vulgar abuse by the Czech leaders added a personal edge to this dislike. He barely recognised them as individuals. Revealingly, he mentioned Beneš only once in his letters to his sisters and Masaryk not at all. Throughout the entire crisis Chamberlain was at the forefront of the British approach of settling the Czechs' fate directly with the Germans and with minimal reference to their leaders. Wilson was even more brutal: 'From the start we were up against the fundamental difficulty that Czechoslovakia had no business to exist as it was.'[13]

The Runciman mission laboured through the sweltering heat of a central European August. For weekend relaxation the party would usually stay at the country home of a great Bohemian noble. As they were German-speakers the impression inevitably grew that Runciman had a bias against the Czech population, as expressed in a popular ditty: '*Wir brauchen keinen Weihnachtsmann,* | *Wir haben unseren Runciman.*'[14] ('We don't need Father Christmas, we've got our Runciman.')

Little emerged of substance from the negotiations, which involved a constant shuttle between the two sides. Whilst this was going on, most of London including most of the senior members of the Foreign Office had departed on holiday. Chamberlain was dogged by ill health and rotated between Downing Street, Chequers and Scotland. Only Wilson appeared an immovable feature at Downing Street. To a greater extent than ever he was the link between the Prime Minister and the rest of government.

Wilson pursued his private channels to assure the Germans that he shared their view that the position of Czechoslovakia was 'unnatural and absurd'.[15] In a confidential meeting at the home of his 'sleuth' on Germany, Philip Conwell-Evans, that was not reported to the Foreign Office, he spoke to Theo Kordt at the German embassy, who had provided his starting point for attempts to restart dialogue with the Germans after Hitler's rebuff of Chamberlain's colonial scheme in March 1938. The British government was prepared for serious negotiations over Czechoslovakia. All Germany had to do was to abstain from violence. He repeated the vision of Britain and Germany as the 'twin pillars' of

European culture that he had made in March. They provided the best defence against Bolshevism, anarchy and barbarism.

Wilson had monitored Runciman's work apprehensively but a visit to London by Ashton-Gwatkin near the end of August brought a surge of relief.[16] Ashton-Gwatkin went first to the Foreign Office where he met Wilson amongst others to brief them. Afterwards, tellingly, he had lunch with Wilson on his own.[17] The picture that Wilson absorbed showed the Czech side in a far more helpful mood than they had been before, agreeing to a new basis for negotiation. Three autonomous districts might be created in which Sudetens would be predominant. The mood was light enough for Wilson and Ashton-Gwatkin to begin building castles in the air. Runciman would soon be in a position to deliver some hopeful public pronouncement before Hitler's much-anticipated speech at Nuremberg. To prepare the way for Hitler to support the new proposals Konrad Henlein, the Sudeten German leader, was to go to Nuremberg and tell the Führer that he was 'impressed by the fair-mindedness of the English'. Even better, Henlein 'proposes to add that in his view acceptance [of the new proposals] could be regarded as the first step in improved Anglo-German relations'. The crisis would not merely be defused but the way in which it was solved would make a positive contribution to appeasement. Henlein's visit might even be followed up with a visit to Hitler by Runciman himself to firm up the Führer's commitment to the plan. Intentionally or otherwise Henlein had struck on exactly how to keep up morale at Downing Street via Ashton-Gwatkin, who was acting more or less as his mouthpiece. This 'fairly encouraging news' was swiftly passed on to Chamberlain on his country holiday.[18]

The moment of optimism was brief. When the Czech side embodied these new bases into a formal 'Third Plan', the Sudetens rejected it out of hand. They complained to Runciman that it was so hedged about with conditions as to be worthless and, amazingly, he agreed with them. Warnings of imminent military action began to come through, notably those personally delivered by a retired senior German officer, Ewald von Kleist-Schmenzin, in the course of a clandestine visit to the UK. Kleist-Schmenzin visited Churchill, who passed his warnings on to the government. The crisis was back on at full tilt. British attention focused on the speech Hitler was scheduled to deliver to the Nuremberg party rally on 13 September, which was widely expected to announce that the Czech problem would be solved by force. A meeting of ministers was summoned at short notice for 30 August in conditions of great and utterly ineffective secrecy, and Sir Nevile Henderson was recalled from Berlin 'for consultations' with instructions to make this widely known. Chamberlain was prepared to send a gentle message to the Germans that he was unhappy with events but not too vigorous a one. With the sole exception of Duff Cooper, the ministers did not dissent from Chamberlain's opinion and no one ventured any positive solution. The conclusion was to wait and see, labelled as a strategy of 'keeping the Germans guessing'. For once the hackneyed diplomatic phrase 'recalled for consultations' was strictly true. Wilson briefed Henderson on an emergency fall-back plan that he and Chamberlain had devised if the crisis should reach a hopeless point.[19] It was vital that they had someone at the Berlin end who was fully briefed.

The day after the Cabinet meeting the Soviet ambassador, Ivan Maisky, found Wilson in a quite different mood to the one that had followed the *Anschluß*. He 'looked somewhat gloomy, anxious and fad-ed'.[20] Their conversation 'assumed a despondent almost panicky tone'. Wilson was caught between fixation on Hitler and his capacity for harm and the weakness of Britain and France. He rejected Maisky's advice to deliver a firm statement of solidarity with France. Wilson accepted that it might prevent war, but he was horrified at the idea of challenging Germany, which he described as no more than 'a hypothetical danger that will not become pressing for a few more years'.

Chamberlain had departed for Balmoral for the quasi-obligatory few days with the sovereign, leaving Wilson in London to handle develop-ments. Given the inefficient (and insecure) telephone system of the era, much of the dialogue between the two was conducted by letter, which provides an unusually comprehensive picture of the relationship in action at a crucial moment in the Czech crisis. Wilson had no positive ideas for how to progress, but he could work to eliminate any thought of potential solutions which went against his or Chamberlain's instincts.

His first task was to fend off unsolicited advice by Churchill, who had managed to speak to Halifax and followed up with a letter. Whilst Halifax was usually reliable, there was a greater danger that he might not treat Churchill's heresies with the full contempt that they deserved. It was easy to deal with Churchill's suggestion that President Roosevelt might be called into the crisis.[21] Roosevelt's intervention was no more desirable over Czechoslovakia than it had been in January when he had unwittingly set the ball rolling towards Anthony Eden's resignation. The most that Wilson would accept was that the US President might be informed of what was going on but was definitely not to be asked for an opinion or 'still less for any action'. As Halifax merely wanted to keep in reserve the possibility of bringing in Roosevelt, this would be enough, but the Foreign Office showed an unacceptable inclination to wobble in a potentially far more dangerous direction. Churchill had managed to speak to Halifax and had proposed a variant of his Grand Alliance scheme, which he had been arguing for vainly since the *Anschluß*. In this, once Runciman had finalised a set of proposals, Britain, France and the Soviet Union should urge Germany to accept them. Halifax mentioned this idea to Wilson, who predictably found it anathema, a 'mixture of diplomacy and threat', and he delivered a barrage of counter-arguments, which Chamberlain could deploy if Halifax showed any inclination to take the idea further, notably military weakness and German hostility to the Soviet Union.[22]

This was all small beer compared to a move that Halifax and the Foreign Office were contemplating on their own. Halifax was considering making a speech to the press at Geneva, where he was going to address the League of Nations.[23] A few days earlier the Chancellor of the Exchequer, Sir John Simon, had made a speech at Lanark in which he had set out the long-established formula that Britain would support France. Even though it contained nothing new, Simon's speech had attracted considerable attention in British newspapers and some criticism in Germany, but Halifax did not think it had done enough to remind the Germans. A speech by the Foreign Secretary 'might reach quarters in Germany which would not have paid much attention to what John Simon had to say'.[24] Wilson disliked the idea of a speech at all, but if he could not prevent it entirely he was determined that in both timing and content it should have the least prospect of registering on the Germans.[25]

The draft of Halifax's speech was discussed at a meeting with Wilson, Sir Robert Vansittart, the anti-German chief diplomatic adviser, two other Foreign Office officials and, as a late entrant, Malcolm MacDonald, the Colonies Secretary, son of Ramsay MacDonald. None of them showed any inclination to back Wilson's line and he had to appeal directly to the Prime Minister to impose his views on Halifax. The only part of the draft that he supported was admonishment to the Czechoslovakian government to be more helpful, which Halifax thought had been lacking in Simon's speech at Lanark. Some of those at the meeting felt that the draft was so severe on this point that it would encourage Germany to hold out for the stiffest terms and asked Wilson to say so to Chamberlain. Wilson complied but made no attempt to follow up this aspect; the Germans could screw up their demands on the Czechs as high as they wanted as far as Wilson was concerned. He concentrated his fire on the passages in the draft that he construed to be a threat to Germany and explicitly attacked the Foreign Office's supposed enthusiasm for a firm line towards Hitler:

'They [the British people] might be swept to stern action...'
   'We are strengthening our defences...'
   'We could give a pretty good account of ourselves...'
   'We need not fear war...'
   'I have spoken frankly...'
   It seems to me that any intelligent journalist, reading these paragraphs in this sequence, could draw one deduction, namely that we were threatening Germany. It amounts, it seems to me, to precisely what the Foreign Office have been pressing for all along, namely March 24th and May 21st, 'but more explicit'.[*][26]

In the event, Wilson did not need to bring the Prime Minister in action

---

[*] See pp. 135, 137.

against the Foreign Secretary and Halifax softened the draft later that day, perhaps after another conversation with Wilson. That evening Wilson could telephone a message to Chamberlain at Balmoral in considerable relief that Halifax had agreed to drop most of the contentious paragraphs in the draft.[27] The speech was never delivered; Halifax cancelled his journey to Geneva because the crisis had become so intense, but the haggling provides a clear indication of how much Halifax had travelled away from pure appeasement and how hard Wilson fought to soften the effect.

Wilson was so obsessed with avoiding any risk that he was opposed to giving Hitler even a private but explicit warning that Britain would support France if it were attacked by Germany, when the discussion turned to what should be done if the chance arose for a private conversation between Henderson and the Führer at the Nuremberg Rally, or *Parteitag*.[28] By then Wilson felt that Halifax had gone native and absorbed the dangerous values of the Foreign Office, lumping them together as 'Halifax and his people' when he argued against the suggestion of a warning. As well as his general aversion to risk, Wilson manufactured a theoretical scenario to sustain his case: Hitler 'might resent it as a threat ... [He] might even use it as an excuse for doing what he would otherwise hesitate to do...' Once again Halifax backed down although he attempted to keep alive the possibility that Henderson might make such a statement if negotiations hit a difficult patch.[29]

Even a direct and confidential appeal from a German contact of long standing, who was risking his life, failed to move Wilson. Theo Kordt came secretly to Downing Street in the first of a number of visits in which he also met Halifax and Cadogan. Inevitably the accounts of the meetings are somewhat sketchy. To protect Kordt, no records were kept of any of them and, even in his private diaries, Cadogan referred to Kordt only as X. Kordt warned, wrongly as it turned out, that military action was being launched on 19 or 20 September and that a conspiracy was afoot amongst bureaucrats and generals to remove Hitler if Britain gave a clear sign of resolution. Wilson practically ignored what Kordt was saying. He did not broaden his contingency planning to cover an unannounced invasion of Czechoslovakia and no attempt was made to give a warning to Germany. The best explanation that Wilson could produce afterwards was to the effect that 'we could not see what could be done to bring it [the plot] to a head' as though Kordt had not pleaded for a firm declaration by the British government to precisely this end.[30] To Wilson, Kordt was merely a convenient conduit into the German foreign policy machine for the appeasement message; his advice on how to handle Germany mattered as little as the advice emanating from the British Foreign Office. The possibility, however uncertain, of removing Hitler was to be ignored, if there was any risk that it might compromise appeasement to help it on its way.

# CHAPTER THIRTEEN

# THE BEST THE ENGLISH CAN DO

*So that is the best the English can do. In any case it has gradually become clear to them that they will achieve absolutely nothing with us by bluff.*
– ADOLF HITLER, OF SIR HORACE WILSON

Neville Chamberlain's flight to Germany to prevent war by talking directly to Hitler remains one of the defining episodes in the entire Czechoslovakia crisis. It set in motion the series of meetings that are simply known as 'Munich' in which war was prevented by sacrificing Czechoslovakia's interest. The flight was entirely the work of Chamberlain and Wilson, who had developed it in the course of a late-night conversation upstairs at Downing Street. In its first version it featured two variants. 'Plan X' was downright outlandish: Chamberlain, referred to as 'Mr X', would get on a plane to Germany and arrive in Berlin unannounced and then seek a conversation with Hitler. In 'Plan Z' Hitler would be asked beforehand to accept Chamberlain's mission. It shows the pressure under which Chamberlain and Wilson were working as well the perils of concentrating decision-making so narrowly that Plan X was even considered.

Control of the plan was kept firmly in the hands of the two men in Downing Street. The first person to be told about it was Nevile Henderson, the British ambassador, who had to be briefed to put the plan into operation from the Berlin end. It was only on 8 September, a week and a half after the plan's inception, that there was any discussion of the idea that Chamberlain would go to Germany amongst an informal ad hoc group of politicians and civil servants. The two options were first put to Chamberlain's close Cabinet allies, Sir John Simon and Halifax, as well as to Alec Cadogan. Halifax insisted that Robert Vansittart also attend and he was the only one to argue against Chamberlain going at all, likening the proposal to the Holy Roman Emperor Henry IV's humiliating journey to Pope Gregory VII at Canossa.[1] Chamberlain was tempted by a Micawberish inclination to wait until after the Nuremberg Rally was over and leaned towards Plan X. Cadogan and Vansittart disagreed and spoke in favour of doing something before Hitler's speech and in favour of preparing a brief beforehand. In the event a cautious public statement was issued which fell far short of a clear warning to Hitler.

From Nuremberg, Henderson was advising vehemently against a warning of any kind. His messages were sent via the Foreign Office but were addressed directly to Wilson, rather than to Halifax, his direct political boss, Cadogan, his direct professional boss, or even the Prime Minister. The situation was too critical to indulge in the usual formalities. Henderson knew who could truly make the decisions.

With Plan Z held as a contingency plan, Wilson fought for a hard line towards the Czechs and a soft line towards Germany. He vigorously supported the idea of a plebiscite in the Sudetenland when it resurfaced. British endorsement of a plebiscite would have been tantamount to saying that Czechoslovakia should cede the Sudetenland to Germany, and the Foreign Office was hostile to such a complete prostration. Wilson was whole-heartedly in favour, precisely because a plebiscite would lead to the break-up of Czechoslovakia and, in his eyes, a permanent solution of the problem.[2] The Czechs had objected to the loss of the Sudeten territories on military and strategical grounds but Wilson countered this argument with the assertion that the *Anschluß* had fatally undermined this objection. He wanted Britain to be ready with a firm scheme available to force on the Czechs.

The informal group that had met to discuss Plan Z had now become a formal sub-committee of the Cabinet with proper minutes being taken. Chamberlain's other closest ally, Sir Samuel Hoare, had joined the group, which informally came to be known as the 'Inner Cabinet'. Membership was fluid but unless Chamberlain or Wilson were in Germany, they were present. It continued to meet until the crisis had finally been resolved, including three times on the day after Hitler's long-awaited speech on 12 September. Hitler gave little clue as to his intentions beyond violent personal abuse of President Beneš but pressure was growing. Konrad Henlein, the Sudeten leader, rejected another set of proposals from the Prague government out of hand and widespread disorder was developing in the Sudetenland, possibly fomented intentionally. British secret intelligence sources sent repeated warnings that Germany was about to launch a military attack on Czechoslovakia. The moment for desperate measures had arrived.

Chamberlain and Wilson were suddenly confronted by a proposal that would have cut the ground from beneath Plan Z. The French started talking about a three-power conference to address the Czech question, which threatened to pre-empt Chamberlain's private mission.[3] Their Prime Minister, Édouard Daladier, was chivvying Chamberlain for a conversation by telephone, but Chamberlain refused. Chamberlain decided to launch Plan Z – presumably in consultation with Wilson – and this was rubber-stamped at the Inner Cabinet's last meeting at 10 p.m.[4] Discussion was minimal and only Chamberlain, Halifax, Wilson and Cadogan were present. The Cabinet as a whole was only told once Britain had been committed to the mission. There is no sign that there was any open debate as to who should accompany Chamberlain on the mission. Chamberlain wanted Wilson and that was that. To begin with Wilson expected that only Foreign Office officials would accompany Chamberlain but the Prime Minister – with the support of Sir John Simon – insisted that he come.[5]

All Chamberlain wanted from the Berghof meeting on 15 September was to establish a relationship with Hitler and to get an agreement to settle the Sudeten problem by negotiation. It was practically impossible for Hitler to refuse the second part and, thanks to Wilson's credulity, Chamberlain could travel back to London in the deluded belief that he had more than succeeded in the first goal.

The next step for the British was to soften the French commitment to

Czechoslovakia. This was not a hard task. Georges Bonnet, their foreign minister, was a defeatist and appeaser firmly in the league of Chamberlain and Wilson. Together with Daladier, Bonnet visited London on 18 September, two days after Chamberlain returned from the Berghof. The French worked out a settlement with the British, under which Czechoslovakia was to cede districts with a majority Sudeten population to Germany and the frontiers of the remainder of Czechoslovakia would be guaranteed by Britain and France. The closing communiqué of the talks stated bluntly that transfer of these districts to Germany was vital. Chamberlain outflanked those in the Cabinet who objected by asserting that no pressure would be exerted on the Czechs to accept this. In reality Britain and France began to force Prague into line almost immediately. Theodor Kordt of the German embassy gave an edge to Chamberlain's enthusiasm for bullying the Czechs into submission with another crop of phone intercepts featuring Beneš and his London ambassador Masaryk exchanging vulgar abuse of Chamberlain.[6] At 2 a.m. on 21 September the British and French ambassadors told Beneš that unless he accepted, France would feel itself freed of its obligations to defend Czechoslovakia. Beneš bowed to the pressure.

It now remained to persuade Hitler to take what the appeasers had negotiated for him and Chamberlain set off on his second flight to Germany to meet Hitler at Bad Godesberg on the Rhine. The venue had been chosen by the Germans as a favour to Chamberlain because it involved a shorter flight from London, although there was a limit to German tenderness and the British delegates had to spend forty minutes driving from their hotel on one bank of the Rhine to Hitler's on the other for the meetings. It was equally inevitable that it was Wilson who accompanied Chamberlain to Bad Godesberg for the substantive talks on the future of Czechoslovakia. Here Chamberlain and Wilson were confronted with the reality of actually negotiating with Hitler rather than dealing in generalities. Moreover, they had already flagged to him that they were negotiating from weakness. The phone taps were telling Hitler that he now had Prague on the back foot and he wanted to destroy any hope Beneš might have entertained of British support by confronting them with categorical demands.[7] The Führer now wanted the Czechs to cede the Sudetenland almost immediately to Germany, without even the formality of a plebiscite. The German army was to march in within days to set the seal. This was presented as a non-negotiable ultimatum to the British delegation, with the implication that Britain should make the Czechs agree unless they wanted war. All that Chamberlain was able to wring from Hitler in a late-night discussion was to change the word 'demand' into 'proposal' and to put back the date for German occupation of the Sudetenland by three days to 1 October. Hitler had got the measure of his man and sweetened the pill with the ludicrously flattering assertion that Chamberlain was the first man for many years who had ever won any concessions from him.[8] Just as he had swallowed the drivel that the German side – abetted by Wilson – had fed him on his first visit to Hitler, Chamberlain saw this as proof that 'he had established some degree of influence over Herr Hitler'.[9] Hitler rounded off the work of gulling the British Prime Minister with the outright, comforting and justly famous lie that he had 'no more territorial ambitions in Europe'.[10]

As Chamberlain and Wilson were paying the price for beginning negotiations at a disadvantage at Bad Godesberg, Downing Street was confirming to the Germans just how weak they were by revealing the pressures that they were facing at home. The press officer, George Steward, told his embassy contact, Fritz Hesse, that the events at Bad Godesberg were bolstering Chamberlain's domestic enemies. If he failed to ride out the pressure he might be overthrown and replaced by a 'Cabinet under Eden and Churchill, which could only be described as a War Cabinet'.[11] To protect Chamberlain the Germans should cease giving the impression that they were issuing ultimata. The Germans would get their deal from Chamberlain, but no one else.

Chamberlain reacted to Hitler's twist of the screw at Bad Godesberg with a mixture of fear and delusion. As he flew back to Britain through clear skies, looking out over the vast expanse of London's houses, he put himself in the place of German airmen approaching the capital on a bombing mission. Acutely conscious that the building blocks for a proper expansion of the Royal Air Force had only just been put in place, he saw the capital as a practically undefended target. It was a chilling vision he shared with Wilson on the plane and, later that day, with the Cabinet. Britain was just not ready for war and it should not be risked. Cadogan of the Foreign Office was appalled that Chamberlain seemed to be telling the Inner Cabinet that 'total surrender' was the only option. In his analysis, the Prime Minister had been 'hypnotised' by Hitler.[12] Chamberlain's rationale was practically to parrot out what Hitler had put to him at Bad Godesberg. Even as Chamberlain tried to stave off war by bowing abjectly to Hitler's demands, the mirage of full appeasement was drawing him forward. He rationalised that Hitler's memorandum was not much harsher than terms which had already been agreed to. He contrived to find positive benefits in surrendering to Hitler's terms. This would clear the air for a broader settlement. In Chamberlain's eyes, 'if we got this question out of the way without conflict it would be the turning point in Anglo-German relations. To the prime minister that was the big thing of the present issue.'[13]

When the press had been briefed about Bad Godesberg, Chamberlain had declared, 'It is now up to the Czechs.'[14] It was a vain hope that they would swallow Hitler's ultimatum and they ordered a partial mobilisation of their army, which made it clear that acceptance was highly unlikely. This was put beyond doubt when Jan Masaryk, the ambassador to London, brought the formal Czech response the following afternoon. Predictably enough, the government formally rejected it in high-flown terms, calling on British and French help to support them: 'The nation of St Wenceslas, John Hus and Thomas Masaryk will not be a nation of slaves ... we rely on two great democracies to stand by us.'[15] The ball was firmly back in the British and French court.

On the day of his return from Bad Godesberg Chamberlain had faced no immediate opposition in either the full or the Inner Cabinet and it looked as though there would be a straight run to give British endorsement to Hitler's demands. But the following day he encountered two quite unexpected obstacles. Cadogan had worked on Halifax's conscience on the Saturday evening and the Foreign Secretary swung around completely from his endorsement of Chamberlain's position at a full Cabinet meeting on the morning of Sunday 25 September. Chamberlain was 'horrified', but could at least reserve his position until the French position was known. The French ministers, Daladier and Bonnet, were on their way to London for discussions. Chamberlain was counting on them continuing their practice of falling in line with any British move that looked as though it could save them from having to respect their obligations towards Czechoslovakia, but he was in for an unpleasant surprise. Daladier 'raised the strongest objections to the Hitler plan' and repeatedly insisted that France was ready to do its duty.[16] Hitler's Bad Godesberg demands had been pitched so high that they finally reached a level unacceptable to all but the most committed appeasers. Even a brutal cross-examination of the French by Sir John Simon in his most remorseless courtroom style failed to bludgeon them into following the British. Chamberlain could not hide the reversal in the French position completely from the Cabinet, when it met for the third time that day near midnight, but he was less than frank. He described their answers to Simon as 'evasive' and implied that, because they had not pressed the British for a commitment to join them in war against Germany, they were bluffing.[17]

Chamberlain appeared to be caught in a corner, but he then sprang on the Cabinet a proposal which must have been worked with Wilson in one of the breaks between its meetings. Britain should try to avert war by proposing a tripartite commission comprising Germany, Britain and Czechoslovakia to solve the Sudetenland issue. The proposal was to be sent to Hitler in a personal letter, delivered in person by Wilson. If the letter failed to draw a response, Britain would finally issue a direct warning that it would go to war along with France if the appeal were rejected. The Cabinet's most anti-appeasement member, Duff Cooper, tried to persuade Chamberlain to include this warning in the letter itself, but the most the Prime Minister would accept was that Wilson would deliver the message orally. He gave himself – and Wilson – a further escape clause by insisting that the terms of any oral message delivered would depend on further information of French intentions. The Cabinet agreed with Chamberlain and Daladier endorsed the plan the following morning in an unminuted meeting with Chamberlain and General Gamelin, the French army chief of staff. They also decided the precise wording for the oral message for Wilson. William Strang of the Foreign Office, who had been observing these goings-on, acidly observed, 'As so often in the way of diplomacy, a decision was reached behind the scenes which seemed to bear little relation to what had been said around the conference table.'[18]

Chamberlain had ensured that the execution of his desperate appeal to Hitler to ward off conflict was in the hands of Wilson, whom he trusted completely and on whom he could rely to take no chances of provoking Hitler by the kind of blunt warning that others had argued for. The tripartite plan was little more than a pretext for Wilson's mission. To make certain that Hitler understood that only Chamberlain's words were of any significance, confidential and unrecorded instructions were passed to Henderson in Berlin to inform the German side that they should ignore any reports on the negotiations with the French and the Czechs that did not come from him. 'Any press or other messages which might appear should be disregarded as pure guesswork.'[19] Wilson was, of course, exempt from this. Chamberlain wrote a brief letter to Hitler saying that he had full confidence in Wilson and that Hitler could 'take anything he says as coming from me'.[20] The significance of the move was immediately clear to Hitler, who discounted any bellicose noises from London.[21]

These were wise precautions. Whilst Wilson was in Berlin on the afternoon of 26 September, the Foreign Office put out a communiqué which stated bluntly that if Germany attacked Czechoslovakia, France and Russia would go to war and Britain would 'certainly stand by France'.[22] It was drafted and issued by Wilson's *bête noire*, Rex Leeper of the Foreign Office News Department. This was precisely the kind of direct warning that Wilson had been struggling constantly to prevent. Leeper had shown it to Halifax for approval beforehand and he did not demur, but Wilson was later to blame Leeper entirely for the move and he seethed against it as evidence of Leeper's 'disloyalty'.[23]

Wilson's first meeting in Berlin took place on 26 September in Hitler's vast office in the Reichskanzlei with everyone seated on low chairs or sofas. Both Ribbentrop and Henderson were there, in a rerun of the discussion of the doomed colonies scheme six months before. It was an even more miserable experience and this time it did not need Ribbentrop's efforts to undermine the proceedings with his hostility. Even by his own demanding standards, Hitler's behaviour was wild. Paul Schmidt, his Auswärtiges Amt interpreter, wrote that this was the only time that he saw Hitler entirely losing control of himself.[24] He was due to deliver a speech about the Czechoslovakia crisis to the massed ranks of the party faithful at the Sportpalast only a couple of hours later and had already worked himself up into a mood of aggression and hostility.

Wilson first passed over Chamberlain's letter of authority and then handed Schmidt Chamberlain's longer letter for him to translate to Hitler. This began with the Czechoslovakian government's formal rejection of the Bad Godesberg memorandum. It proposed that Czechoslovakia hold talks with Germany with the British providing benign assistance; the tripartite scheme that Chamberlain had put to the Cabinet had become severely diluted. At this Hitler exploded and began to rant, screaming, 'There's no point to negotiate anything at all any more.' He got to his feet, followed by the other members of the German party, and headed for the door. Wilson kept his nerve and remained in his seat, as did the rest of the British group, which seems to have persuaded Hitler that it would be unacceptable to abandon the discussion and leave his visitors to find their own way out of his office. Wilson was moved, partly by calculation and partly by annoyance at the 'boorish rudeness to one who, in addition to being an Englishman, was a visitor'.[25] Afterwards he complained that Hitler had treated him as a 'lackey' and he became distinctly hostile to him personally, but this did not undermine his commitment to appeasing him.[26]

The conversation resumed in shambolic form with Schmidt trying to complete the translation of Chamberlain's letter, whilst everyone else, except for Ivone Kirkpatrick from the British embassy, talked across each other. Kirkpatrick, who had been brought along as a note-taker, was unable to take his eyes off Hitler in full spate and, to Wilson's horror, froze with his pencil poised above the paper.[27] At one point Hitler got to his feet again and made as if to leave, which Wilson again ignored. Towards the end of the meeting a modicum of calm was re-stored and Hitler invited Wilson to attend the Sportpalast meeting, to the Englishman's embarrassment. Hitler thought it would let him find out what the German people truly thought about the Czechs. Wilson's response, that he would simply listen to it on the radio, gave Hitler the opening to tell him that he would miss the full atmosphere if he did. Having failed to intimidate Wilson in a diplomatic meeting, Hitler was dropping the unsubtle hint that a Nazi Party rally in thrall to the Führer would be an even more frightening experience. In view of the furious atmosphere Wilson decided not to try to deliver his oral message to Hitler, fearing that he might treat it as an ultimatum and announce military action in his speech. All that was decided was that the talks should resume the following day.[28] The meeting had, though, achieved something for Wilson. Somewhere in the rambling discussion Hitler had been told that Leeper's communiqué was merely 'authorised' and not 'official'.[29] Once again the Foreign Office's desire to send a clear warning to Hitler had been sabotaged.

Wilson did not relish the prospect of delivering the oral warning to Hitler and was looking for a way to make it unnecessary or at least to give him something with which to console him. After a restless night, Wilson cabled London advising that maximum pressure should be put on the Czechs to concede.[30] The Czechs could save their pride by simply withdrawing troops from the area to be occupied and letting the Germans march in unopposed. He did not trust the London ambassador to tell Prague accurately that Chamberlain believed that nothing could stop a full invasion of Czechoslovakia. It was even worse now. The British military attaché in Berlin had just toured Czechoslovakia and found 'morale is poor and resistance will prove to be feeble'. In fact, this was counter to what the British military attaché in Prague was reporting.

Unbeknownst to the British party, Hitler had decided before the meeting with Wilson that he would keep the door open for further discussions even though he was unwilling to soften his terms. He appeared to be better briefed about the internal challenges that Chamberlain was facing in London, which Steward had set out to the German embassy, and saw the attraction of strengthening him.[31] He would 'build golden bridges to London and Paris'. As well as the by-now ritual abuse of Beneš, the Sportpalast speech included favourable references to Chamberlain and his work to promote peace and agreement. This was duly noted by Kirkpatrick, who was transcribing the speech at the British embassy over a tray of food, whilst Wilson and Henderson dined properly. It also registered in London, where Chamberlain put out a statement thanking the Führer for his kind words and practically endorsing his refusal to trust the Czech government.[32] He took personal moral responsibility for the Czechs' meeting their promises and committed the British government to obliging the Czechs to carry them out promptly. Instructions were sent to Wilson in Berlin to make sure that this had registered on Hitler.[33]

Until his second conversation with Wilson the following day, Hitler had been unsure whether the British were bluffing or whether they meant to be serious.[34] His first meeting with Wilson had given him a pretty good idea that they had no serious intention of going to war and the second meeting was decisive and put this beyond doubt.[35] Afterwards he knew that the British would not fight for Czechoslovakia. It was one of the moments in the crisis that he happily retold once it was over. Supposedly it was the moment when Britain was going to give Hitler a final warning, but Wilson ensured that the warning lost any force it might have had. Wilson began with craven flattery of Hitler's oratorical performance at the Sportpalast the previous evening. When Hitler told him that he had no message to give to London beyond his thanks for their efforts and that the only option for the Czechs was to accept the Bad Godesberg terms, Wilson finally delivered the verbatim text of Chamberlain's oral message in what he described as his best attempts at the tone that Chamberlain himself would have used:

> If the Czechs reject the German memorandum and Germany attacks Czechoslovakia, we ha[ve] been informed by the French Government that they [will] fulfil their obligations to Czechoslovakia, and that, should the forces of France in consequence become actively engaged in hostilities against Germany, the British government would feel obliged to support them...[36]

Wilson sandwiched the prepared declaration between comments designed to soften its impact. Once again he trotted out Hitler's supposed

vision of Britain and Germany as the 'twin pillars' of European civilisation and lauded the potential benefits of harmony between the two
countries.[37] Ernst von Weizsäcker was struck by the frequency with
which Wilson 'referred to the possibility of an Anglo-German understanding on a number of questions'.[38] Far more importantly, he added
the gloss to the declaration that the French had chosen their words carefully and that they did not specify that France would attack Germany.
As Sir John Simon had mercilessly established in his cross-examination
of Daladier and Bonnet, the French could decide that simply manning
the Maginot Line defences against Germany would be sufficient to
meet their commitments. Wilson had opened himself up to a question
from Hitler that finally settled his doubt as to whether Britain would
act. What if the French did, after all, attack Germany? Would the British join in? Were they prepared to trigger a world war? Wilson had no
answer to give and that settled any doubts Hitler might still have had:
it meant that Wilson was backing down.[39]

At the end of the meeting as the others of the British party had left
the room, Wilson drove the final nail into the coffin of hopes that
Britain might stand up for Czechoslovakia. He gave Hitler a personal commitment to attempt to coerce the Czechs to fall in line with
German wishes: 'I will still try to make those Czechos sensible.'[40] Hitler
knew that the game was his: 'So that is the best the English can do. In
any case it has gradually become clear to them that they will achieve
absolutely nothing with us by bluff.'[41]

He naturally told Wilson that he would welcome his efforts in this
direction and wound up the meeting by saying, 'England could wish
for no better friend than the Führer'.[42]

# CHAPTER FOURTEEN

# THEIR JUST DEMANDS HAD BEEN FAIRLY MET

*[The German people could] feel that their just demands had been fairly met and [were] ready to take their place at the Council table of the Nations.*

– SIR HORACE WILSON ON THE OUTCOME OF MUNICH

Hitler knew that he had the British exactly where he wanted them. The Sudetenland was his; the only decision was whether to seize it by force or to have it handed to him. The door had been held open a crack, but war looked imminent. To keep his options open, he could extend another 'golden bridge' towards London and he accepted Ernst von Weizsäcker's advice to write to Chamberlain, ostensibly replying to the letter that Wilson had brought him.[1] The letter was composed as Wilson was on his way back to London. In London war seemed imminent. The Royal Navy was mobilised as a precautionary measure, although it was soon believed that this was a major factor in what happened next.

When Wilson reported on his conversations in Berlin to the Inner Cabinet, he gave no room for hope that Hitler was anything but determined to have his way. His account of what Hitler had told him did not dissent from the Führer's views and, short of saying outright that he agreed with him completely, he made it plain that the Führer's views were the ones to which Britain would have to respond.[2] He was almost acting as Hitler's spokesman to the British Cabinet. When he quoted Hitler as claiming that the British 'were being made dupes by the Czechoslovak government' and accusing the Czech government of being responsible for an imminent world war because it was being 'dilatory', it was plain in which direction his sympathies lay. The only way he saw to avert war was that Britain should telegraph Prague immediately 'suggesting' that the government 'tacitly accept occupation by German troops of the areas up to the red line'. Chamberlain was scheduled to broadcast to the nation at 8 p.m. and at this point the Inner Cabinet were turfed out of the Cabinet Room by a squad of BBC sound engineers. They adjourned to Wilson's office next door, where Halifax and Cadogan tried to argue against sending the telegram. Chamberlain backed down far enough to accept that the proposal be put to the full Cabinet.

There was no guarantee that the Cabinet would not revolt against Wilson's last-ditch plan of pressurising Prague, and Chamberlain made his broadcast in a doom-laden tone. 'How horrible, fantastic, incredible it is that we should be digging trenches and trying on gas-masks here because of a quarrel in a far away country between people of whom we know nothing.'³

In this distinctly non-inspirational fashion, the Prime Minister warned the people of Britain that they might soon be at war. By the time the full Cabinet meeting began, Wilson had drafted his cable to Prague and Chamberlain opened with a barrage of arguments in favour of urging capitulation on the Czechs. Nevile Henderson had just telegraphed a warning that Germany would invade Czechoslovakia in its entirety unless Prague complied. Chamberlain quoted the opinion of the military attaché in Berlin that the Czechs were already defeatist. The dominion Prime Ministers were also advising pressure on Prague. Chamberlain then opened the floor to Wilson, who was constrained from giving the kind of direct advice that he had given the Inner Cabinet but he did deliver a strengthened version of his presentation.⁴ Hitler was convinced that Beneš was a 'twister' and explained that it was via phone taps that the Germans knew that the Czechs believed 'they had got France and Great Britain exactly where they wanted them'. Duff Cooper was first out of the gate opposing the telegram, but it was Halifax's opposition which swung the meeting to reject the Prime Minister's proposal.

Only after this setback was Chamberlain told that another glimmer of hope had come into view with the arrival of Hitler's letter ostensibly replying to the one that Wilson had brought him.[5] Hitler did not soften his demands but he did suggest that Germany might formally guarantee the frontiers of the rump of Czechoslovakia in proof that the Sudetenland was, indeed, his last territorial demand. He did not repeat his deadline but left it to Chamberlain whether he would continue his efforts to 'bring the Government in Prague to reason at the very last hour'. It was enough for Chamberlain to hope for 'some ground on which a further proposal for a peaceful settlement could be based', but he found himself fighting one final rearguard action of the meeting. He admitted to the Cabinet that he would have to be more specific to the House of Commons, when he spoke the following day, than he had been in his BBC broadcast. He suggested that he should describe how Wilson had delivered the 'special message' to Hitler – even after Hitler had heard it, Chamberlain was loath to call it a warning – but stopped short of saying he would make a commitment to any immediate declaration of war if Germany invaded Czechoslovakia. This was too cautious for the balance of opinion amongst the ministers, who insisted that he should nail Britain's colours to the mast and say that Britain would fight alongside France if the French 'engaged in active hostilities' to meet their obligations.

Whilst all this was going on another German feeler was reaching towards London, which might have been one of Hitler's 'golden bridges' and which Wilson took up avidly. Fritz Hesse, the German embassy press man, had been passed a scheme from Berlin for a phased transfer of the Sudeten districts to Germany over fourteen days, which supposedly met objections to the Bad Godesberg scheme.[6] Supposedly this had originated with Hitler and then been passed by his press secretary to Hesse's boss. On the evening of 27 September Hesse broached this with Kordt at his flat, where Philip Conwell-Evans, Wilson's tame Germany expert, was also present. Conwell-Evans offered to arrange for Hesse to pitch the plan to Wilson. At that stage Wilson did not know Hesse personally, but George Steward at Downing Street was already well aware of his unusual level of access in the German foreign policy machine. Steward must have passed this on to Wilson, so he was willing to take up an approach from an otherwise insignificant figure. Then or later, Wilson also acquired a wildly exaggerated notion of Hesse's closeness to Hitler. Only something that looked like a genuine prospect for avoiding war could have deserved an hour of Wilson's time on such a critical day.

Wilson and Hesse met under suitably furtive and melodramatic conditions at 8.30 a.m. the day after Wilson's return from Berlin. Wilson and Conwell-Evans collected Hesse from a street corner in a taxi and they proceeded to cruise randomly around London as the discussion continued.[7] The driver became increasingly annoyed at his passengers' inexplicable, furious desire for locomotion and thought they were drunks. After an initial squabble over which country was responsible for the impasse, Wilson told Hesse that Britain could accept any German demand, except for the Wehrmacht moving into the Sudetenland; German police would be acceptable.[8] Form was what mattered and not substance. The current shape of the Bad Godesberg plan was an insurmountable obstacle to the British recommending acceptance to the Czechs. Nothing would be more welcome to Britain than a Czech capitulation, but Wilson saw no way to bring it about, except – by implication – if the Germans softened the appearance of the Bad Godesberg scheme. He tipped Hesse off that Chamberlain's speech that afternoon would leave the door open and not commit Britain to be drawn into war if Germany saw its plan through. Wilson concluded with his one note of firmness in the whole conversation: if Germany marched into Czechoslovakia, Britain would declare war. In the privacy of a London black cab, this lacked the force of a statement by the Prime Minister in the House of Commons. The taxi-driver's annoyance almost boiled over when Wilson told him to stop at the back door of Downing Street, which was forbidden to non-government vehicles.

The decision as to whether Europe went to war lay in the hands of Germany. Britain had sent ample signals that it would acquiesce to almost anything. The French would follow and the Czechs were powerless. It was one of the rare occasions when Nazi Germany resorted to something approaching collegial decision-making. Hitler was momentarily undecided and the Nazi leadership was split.[9] Ribbentrop was violently opposed to any concession to the British, but Goering and Goebbels would accept. The former foreign minister Konstantin von Neurath had been admitted to the group and also supported concessions. The fact that he was there at all probably tells us more about Hitler's low opinion of Ribbentrop's advice than the value of Neurath's. Goering indulged in a savage attack on Ribbentrop. Germany had secured what it wanted as far as avowable objectives went. The only way that Hitler would be able to achieve his heartfelt desire to destroy Czechoslovakia entirely was if war broke out. The Bad Godesberg memorandum limited what could be obtained by negotiation. The gap between German demands and what the democracies would tolerate was only a question of process, as Wilson had recognised in his conversation with Hesse that morning. When the idea of using Mussolini as a mediator was floated it was accepted. The British and French had already solicited his help.

Chamberlain was actually making his speech to the House of Commons when a note was passed to him saying that Hitler had accepted a last round of negotiation. As Europe pulled back from the brink of war the House erupted in hope. The four-power conference at Munich was set for the following day and, once again, Chamberlain and Wilson headed off to Germany. The three other heads of government – Hitler, Mussolini and Daladier – were accompanied by their foreign ministers, but Halifax was left in London with Wilson at his accustomed place alongside the Prime Minister.

The outcome of the Munich conference was a foregone conclusion, with Germany making only minor concessions. Wilson's taxi-borne insistence that the Wehrmacht should not execute the occupation was quietly forgotten. At Chamberlain's request two Czechs had been summoned to Munich, but purely as observers. They stayed at the same hotel as the British delegation, the Regina Palast, but were left to their own devices until Frank Ashton-Gwatkin of the Foreign Office, whose duty on the Runciman mission was now done, appeared at 7 p.m. He resolutely refused to engage in any substantial discussion, which made it abundantly clear to the Czechs what their status was.[10] Three hours later the Czechs were favoured with a few minutes of Wilson's time and he set out the new plan with a map, showing the Sudeten areas which were to be occupied immediately. Wilson twice answered the Czechs' questions on the plan with a formal statement that he had nothing to add and paid no attention to what they said about the districts involved. Only once the conference had concluded and the British delegation had returned from the Nazi headquarters where it had taken place were the Czechs favoured with any substantial account of their fate. At 1.30 a.m. they were summoned to Chamberlain's suite in an atmosphere of defendants receiving the verdict and their sentence in court. Chamberlain explained the new terms and after perfunctory answers had been given to questions from the Czechs, Wilson 'gave a pretty broad hint ... the best course for his [the Czech] government was to accept what was clearly a considerable improvement upon the German [Bad Godesberg] memorandum'.[11]

The final act of the Munich conference, the Anglo-German 'peace for our time' declaration, was entirely Chamberlain's work, but the seed might have been sown weeks before when the crisis was approaching its height. The industrialist Lord Weir still maintained a good relationship with Wilson, even after resigning in disgust from the air rearmament programme when Lord Swinton was sacked. At the very beginning of September he called to see Wilson for a chat at Downing Street and to mull over ideas. One of these struck a chord with Wilson and he set out to sell it to Chamberlain, deploying his keen knowledge of the vanity that drove his master. Wilson told Chamberlain that Weir had identified three 'big people' in the world – Hitler and Roosevelt were the others – who had to cope with the misbehaviour of the 'little people' like Beneš and Henlein.[12] The world expected two or all three of them to 'propose to do something jointly beginning with a declaration that there must be no war' and this 'on direct personal grounds'. Undisclosed to Weir, the basis for the personal agreement between two of the 'big people' was already in place in the shape of Plan Z. What was to become the Anglo-German Declaration sounds uncannily like Weir's proposal for a joint declaration.

It is unlikely that Chamberlain even discussed the specifics of the declaration with Wilson beforehand. It was drafted by William Strang of the Foreign Office for Chamberlain to take with him, when he visited Hitler the morning after the conference. Having overcome the obstacle of the Sudetenland, Chamberlain saw the time as ripe to actively pursue friendship with Germany. Chamberlain could delude himself that Hitler's signature meant that he believed this too. Predictably, Wilson's account of Munich written in 1941 puts a favourable spin on events where possible and where the events are incriminating, they are either treated cursorily or ignored entirely, but with the skill learned from composing hundreds of parliamentary answers for ministers, Wilson avoided demonstrable, blatant falsehood. It was only in his story of how the declaration came about that he succumbed and resorted to near-outright dishonesty. The declaration was the keystone of Chamberlain's delusion that he had brought lasting peace to Europe. By then Wilson knew the declaration was an error, but still tried to protect the memory of his, by then dead, friend. He too shared the delusion. He implied – entirely falsely – that the initiative for the final conversation came from Hitler: 'Next morning the Prime Minister went alone to Hitler's flat – in accordance with an invitation given and accepted during one of the waiting periods over the night.'[13] He did not mention that Alec Dunglass accompanied Chamberlain; perhaps he felt Dunglass was so insignificant that his presence simply did not count. Slightly less blatantly, Wilson obfuscated the authorship of the declaration itself: 'Hitler had agreed to the modifications arranged at the Munich Conference, followed the next day by the joint declaration.'

Wilson stopped short of subscribing to the self-serving version of the declaration that Dunglass peddled afterwards when his own reputation as a politician might suffer from association with such an embarrassment. In this version, the declaration was an astute diplomatic trap designed to make Hitler's responsibility plain to the international community, notably the USA, if he triggered a war, and was to be publicised accordingly.[14] Nothing else suggests that Chamberlain had any such motives; everything else shows that he believed in the literal effect of the declaration, including Dunglass's own statement a year and a half later that 'he [Chamberlain] and Horace believed that by the sacrifice of Czechoslovakia they could achieve permanent peace and that Hitler would be satisfied'.[15] The fiction is repeated to this day.

For all the adulation poured on Chamberlain in praise of his having averted war, Wilson knew that the agreement would face criticism. On the flight back from the Munich conference he set Strang to work to compile a list of the points in which the agreement presented an improvement on the Bad Godesberg memorandum.[16] Strang was struck by the superficially impressive list that resulted, but later accepted that apart from a few days' delay in transferring part of the territory, they were 'worthless'.

The most potent line of attack that Wilson visualised was the accusation that there would have been a better result if Britain had 'made it clear earlier that we should be at war with Germany, if she invaded Czechoslovakia'.[17] This was the kind of move against which Wilson had struggled throughout the crisis. He had had his way but now had to explain why he had been right. He sat down to compose a rebuttal for Chamberlain to deliver in the House of Commons. He began with a few feints including the laughable claim that German public opinion had contributed to Hitler shying away from war. The cheers Chamberlain had received from the people of Munich were heartfelt and fuel for his vanity, but they did not mean that the fear of a war from which they had been freed had influenced Hitler at all. The true substance of Wilson's analysis was that Britain had been right to sacrifice the Czech state.

Suppose that the move had been successful in its immediate object [making Hitler back down], what would then have been the prospects of lasting peace? The German people would have felt that this country had twice within a short time prevented them from rectifying an injustice … I believe that we should have failed to solve the problem: and that, on the contrary, we should have 'brought war nearer'.

The principle of self-determination was firmly on Wilson's side but he had swallowed the lie of Hitler's 'last territorial demand' hook, line and sinker. Removing the Czech obstacle meant that the German people could 'feel that their just demands had been fairly met and [were] ready to take their place at the Council table of the Nations'. Munich was merely the prelude to a golden age of appeasement.

When Chamberlain waved the declaration in the air on his return to Heston and announced that he was bringing 'peace for our time' he meant every word. A few days later Lord Swinton sounded out his private views before pledging the Prime Minister his support.[18] He offered to back him but only on condition that Chamberlain was 'sure in your mind that you have been buying time for our rearmament'. Chamberlain was offended and drew out the declaration (which he seems to have been carrying around as a talisman) and waved it at his former minister. 'But don't you understand? I have brought back peace.'

# CHAPTER FIFTEEN

# CLEARLY MARKED OUT
# FOR THE POST

*There can I think be no doubt as to my successor.*
*H.J. [Wilson] is clearly marked out for the post.*
– Sir Warren Fisher to Sir P. J. Grigg

The combination of Wilson's strong relationship with Chamberlain and the Prime Minister's style of government meant that for all practical purposes, Wilson was by some measure the most powerful figure in the British Civil Service, but his formal status in the hierarchy was still ambiguous and other men held titles and job descriptions that might have made them seem to be his rivals. Wilson was perfectly aware that he needed to consolidate his position as reflected in *The British Imperial Calendar and Civil Service List.*

Wilson's first major step to shape the Whitehall machine to his own tastes was a joint effort with his old patron, Sir Warren Fisher. For Fisher it was a piece of long-unfinished business that he had hoped to settle for good many years before. David Lloyd George had promoted two men from relative obscurity to high positions in Whitehall that had practically been tailor-made for them. They had coexisted in uneasy harmony for almost two decades but it was inevitable that the tension between the two would break out sooner or later. One was Fisher, who had stamped the force of his personality on what had begun as a weak claim to the head of the Civil Service and transformed it into one of the dominant features of the inter-war administration. He ruled almost all government departments with a rod of iron but his empire had never quite swallowed the Cabinet Secretariat, Lloyd George's other administrative innovation, which operated as the personal fiefdom of Sir Maurice Hankey, Lloyd George's other favourite. Hankey used an ingenious sleight of hand to ward off Fisher's attentions. Hankey was also the secretary to the Committee of Imperial Defence (CID), Britain's highest forum for setting military strategy, which he staffed with service officers and operated as a military body. He used his Royal Marine rank of colonel, even though he had long ceased to have any day-to-day connection. He resisted vigorously any suggestions that he was a civil servant. He jumbled the two bodies and palmed his organisation off as one that was more military than civilian.

Hankey's glory days had come when Lloyd George was Prime Minister and he was the privileged adviser and confidant on almost the whole spectrum of government issues. When Lloyd George fell from power Fisher and Hankey fought a ferocious battle over the status of the Cabinet Secretariat. It seemed Fisher's moment to subordinate the Secretariat to the regular Civil Service, but Hankey survived, somewhat diminished but with his state-within-a-state intact. Fisher was forced to accept Hankey's status but only on the understanding that this was a personal status attached to Hankey's unique personality. It remained a thorn in Fisher's flesh. As permanent secretary to the Treasury he saw himself as the chief adviser to the First Lord of the Treasury – the Prime Minister – by right. With the Cabinet Secretary standing outside his empire there was always the risk that his rightful position might be usurped as Hankey had done under Lloyd George. In Fisher's vision the pyramids of political and Civil Service power touched at their summits and only he and his successors had any right to stand at the latter summit.

Hankey reached the normal retirement age of sixty in April 1937 but continued to serve. He had informal agreements with Fisher to work until 1940 and with Chamberlain to continue 'as long as possible'.[1] He was, though, acutely aware that his pension entitlement was small and cast around for lucrative employment in retirement.[2] The decisive moment came in May 1938 when he was called in by Fisher, who together with Wilson pressed on him the merits of their own candidate as his successor, the then comparatively junior Treasury civil servant Edward Bridges. Hankey would have preferred some way in which he could preserve his legacy intact with a free-standing operation straddling politics (through the Cabinet Secretariat) and the military (through the CID). It was a scheme that neither Fisher nor Wilson found palatable and Hankey was handicapped by the lack of anyone willing to try to take over all his responsibilities.

Hankey's strategic and diplomatic ideas were closer to Wilson's than Fisher's. Hankey was acutely aware that the British Empire was at the last gasp of strategic over-reach. It had been built in the days when France was its only challenger but now Germany, Japan and the United States had the resources to put its standing to the severest of tests. Hankey was desperate to avoid policies or commitments that might expose the empire to this kind of challenge, which he knew in his heart it would be hard pushed to resist. Wilson's vision of Britain as powerless against Germany was less complex but it led to the same conclusion. However, Wilson did not need allies in Whitehall to promote his vision. The Prime Minister already shared it. What mattered to Wilson was to bring the Whitehall machine firmly under the control of Downing Street.

Hankey lobbied hard but there was a different king on the throne and one far less sure of his position. Hankey tried frantically to persuade people from his organisation to rise to the challenge and offer to replace him completely, but they foresaw the pitfalls. It was Wilson who delivered the death blow to Hankey's foredoomed struggle. Hankey had been looking forward to occupying his retirement with one of the juiciest and most lucrative quasi-sinecures that the British government could offer, a directorship of the Paris-based Suez Canal Company, which formed a key part in Britain's global infrastructure as well as being an enormously profitable business in its own right. Wilson hinted darkly that Hankey might not receive this reward if he continued to make trouble. Hankey fumed that this was a piece of 'effrontery' and a 'bluff and blackmail', but quietly withdrew.[3] That left just two big beasts in the Whitehall jungle.

Hankey was succeeded as Cabinet Secretary by Fisher and Wilson's man, Edward Bridges. Bridges did not even hold a knighthood at that stage and manifestly ranked far below Wilson or Fisher. The Cabinet Secretariat had been tamed and Bridges operated as a dutiful subordinate to Wilson for the remainder of Wilson's time in the Civil Service. When Churchill became Prime Minister in 1940 he viewed Bridges with considerable reserve and suspicion as a holdover from the old regime that had treated him so badly, but Bridges was a civil servant of the utmost integrity and dedication who served Churchill just as loyally and efficiently as he had served Chamberlain. Bridges went on to become one of the towering figures of the twentieth-century British Civil Service. He was acutely conscious that between them Fisher and Wilson had left a legacy that inspired fears of partisanship and megalomania. Arguably Bridges's greatest gift to the Civil Service was the steps he took to untie this poisoned history.

Barely six months later Fisher fell into the same trap as Hankey, when he too made preparations for his own sixtieth birthday and retirement in September 1939. He went even further than Hankey, going so far as to tell the man he planned to take over from him as permanent secretary to the Treasury, Sir James Grigg, that the appointment was his. The true choice, of course, lay with the Prime Minister. Whatever chance Fisher might have had to impose his will evaporated during the Munich crisis. He violently opposed the desertion of the Czechs and labelled British support for German behaviour as being an accessory to a crime.[4] His mauling of the government's record on air rearmament might have been private but it had also placed him in the same dangerous camp as Churchill.

As Grigg prepared to return from India, where he had been working as the head of finance for the Indian government, Fisher found himself compelled to disappoint his would-be successor. He shamefacedly told Grigg that Wilson was 'clearly marked out for the post'.[5] Grigg swallowed the setback and went on to head the War Office before switching to politics, at least of the wartime technocratic style. It was duly announced that Wilson would become permanent secretary to the Treasury on Fisher's retirement. Fisher awarded himself three months pre-retirement leave, so Wilson took over all his functions in May 1939.

Fisher's dream had finally been realised. The permanent secretary to the Treasury was the uncontested principal adviser to the Prime Minister. The only catch was that the permanent secretary concerned was not Fisher. Wilson held the position, because the Prime Minister of the day trusted him entirely, not because of any of Fisher's daft constitutional theorising. Wilson finally had the grand title and status that embodied the solid power that he had only been able to exercise from a distinctly indeterminate position in the Civil Service hierarchy.

Wilson did not turn his back on the day-to-day source of his power, the constant proximity to the Prime Minister and the rest of the Cabinet. He began his day in the strategic master room at Downing Street, and only in the 'latter half of the day' did he move to the grand room in Treasury Chambers, from which he exercised the more mundane functions of the head of the Civil Service.[6] The day-to-day tasks of the head of the Civil Service took a distant second place to Wilson's role as Chamberlain's adviser.

# CHAPTER SIXTEEN

# THE APPALLING SUMS IT IS PROPOSED TO SPEND

*In view of the appalling sums which anyway it is proposed to spend*
*on bombers none of the alternatives seems to be 'cheap'.*
– Sir Horace Wilson to Neville Chamberlain

The Munich crisis exposed brutally the extent of the Royal Air Force's unpreparedness for war. The sense of its inferiority to the Luftwaffe played a major part in Chamberlain's unwillingness to risk war. To repair the RAF's deficiencies the Air Minister, Sir Kingsley Wood, had extended the alphabet of expansion plans with Scheme M, which would boost fighter numbers by one third. The surge in activity renewed Downing Street's baleful interest in air force matters as suspicion grew that Wood had succumbed to the old bureaucratic trap of going native and adopting the values of the tribe he was supposed to keep in order. Wilson could tolerate the substance of the plan, but was appalled at the thinking behind it and the proposal to broadcast this thinking publicly. He leaped into action to call the wayward minister to order. Wood's most heinous crime had been to suggest that parity with the Luftwaffe once again be the 'overriding consideration'.[1] This was doubly objectionable to Wilson. It threatened to skewer Chamberlain with the same futile and dangerous commitment that had opened Baldwin to Churchill's criticism, when air rearmament first became a hot political topic in 1932, 'parity ... in at least as dangerous form as it has ever been stated'. It was one thing to push quantity ahead of quality when it was a question of undermining an objectionable minister but quite another to risk a public commitment. Even worse, a surge in rearmament could compromise what Wilson considered to be Chamberlain's great achievement at Munich. Not only would the Germans just match the increase in output of warplanes but they 'would … take it as a signal that we have decided at once to sabotage the Munich Declaration'. Rearmament was not to be allowed to compromise peace for our time.

Wood had come perilously under the spell of the air marshals and he then sprang one of their cherished projects on Chamberlain in a way that suggested that he had not learned the lessons from being slapped down by Wilson on the question of 'parity'. The way to address the Luftwaffe's superiority in bombers was to build larger ones, and the Air Staff formulated its goal of an 'ideal bomber' that would do the job. Thus, without increasing the headline number of bombers the military strength of the RAF might be increased. It had been relatively simple to design modern fighters using the new technology, but a far more complex one to use it to the full in bombers. The medium bombers of both the RAF and the Luftwaffe were compromise solutions. The Luftwaffe did not plan to do much more than serve as an adjunct to the army, but the leaders of the RAF were determined to apply the principle of strategic bombing and wanted aircraft capable of that job. This was to lead to the Short Stirling, Handley-Page Halifax and, ultimately, Avro Lancaster four-engine machines with which Bomber Command conducted its devastating offensive against Germany. Wood heartily recommended the plan to the Prime Minister as it 'would offer substantial advantages in all respects'.[2]

Wilson lined Chamberlain up to challenge Wood on the bomber plan. His main concern was money and not military strategy: 'In view of the appalling sums which anyway it is proposed to spend on bombers none of the alternatives seems to be "cheap"!'[3] Wilson was suspicious of the pseudo-management jargon rolled out by the Air Staff such as 'total bomber lift', but he rejected the thought of finding some tame expert outsiders to torpedo the plan. Both Chamberlain and Wilson were deep in a fog of ignorance as to how air forces and the minds of air marshals worked. They were dubious of the big bomber not on military (still less on ethical) grounds, but because they saw it as a device to manipulate and circumvent budgetary constraints in the traditional struggle between a spending department and the Treasury. Wilson came up with a wildly false analogy with the Royal Navy's first Dreadnought battleships, and warned that 'we shall presently be told that in order to safeguard the very large bomber it will be necessary to accompany it by the appropriate number of very fast fighters so as to protect so large and costly a machine from enemy attack'. He was entirely wrong; the air marshals worked under the firm delusion that bombers could defend themselves, until the Luftwaffe demonstrated their mistake in the early days of the Second World War. Wilson secured the Prime Minister's authority to set the Chancellor of the Exchequer and, if necessary, the Prime Minister himself loose on Wood to explain the error of his ways, but Wood spotted that Downing Street was bringing the heavy artillery up to use on him. All Wilson needed to do was hint at the threats and the errant minister returned to the path of righteousness. Wood accepted that orders for bombers would be held at a level to keep the factories ticking over and no more.[4]

The debate over whether 'strategic' bombing is a viable strategy or not rages on, but it did not concern Chamberlain and Wilson. They understood the vital importance of rearming the RAF, but they had no interest whatever in the technical aspects of how it should be done. In part the explanation lies in the fact that Chamberlain and Wilson hoped fervently – and indeed, rather believed in the aftermath of Munich – that none of this would be put to the test of battle. To play and win the numbers game of 'parity', what mattered was the unit cost of each of the counters, nothing else. Chamberlain and Wilson were content to play the crude numbers game, because that was what counted in the House of Commons, and Charles Bruce-Gardner, Wilson's man in the aircraft industry, offered them an easy win. Chamberlain wanted to rearm in the air because he was terrified that the Luftwaffe would bomb London flat. Perversely, even though this fear was so strong as to shape his whole diplomacy, he paid minimal interest to the details of how the threat was to be countered.

The only air force topic that exercised Chamberlain at all seriously was the dispute over the Fleet Air Arm. Otherwise it was handled as a strictly political or budgetary question. This stands in glaring contrast to the extensive and detailed information that Churchill gathered on the RAF and the Luftwaffe and used to lambast the government. Even when high-grade information and advice was offered to him on a plate, Chamberlain was not interested. Roy Fedden of the Bristol Aeroplane Company was a key figure straddling British aircraft engineering and intelligence on German output. In November 1938 he returned from a tour of Germany full of information and Tom Jones, David Lloyd George's crony and friend of Wilson's, pleaded unavailingly with Chamberlain to see him.[5] 'I got no further than "Send him to see Kingsley Wood". L.G. would have pressed a button and had Fedden to breakfast tomorrow morning if not tea that afternoon … Neville, said L.G. once, has a retail mind in a wholesale business.'

Chamberlain was content to work on the simplistic picture that Bruce-Gardner fed him via Wilson. Bruce-Gardner remained very much in favour with Wilson, feeding him a detailed account of developments at the Air Ministry, together with a French journalist's estimate of French and German aircraft output, as though normal Civil Service channels and the British intelligence machine were somehow unreliable.[6] Bruce-Gardner also supplied Wilson with ammunition to use against Churchill's demand that a Ministry of Supply should be established. He spun his evidence to suggest that the creation of a Ministry of Supply would lead the air marshals to practise the heresy that he had detected in Lord Swinton, of putting the production of modern planes ahead of the output of large numbers of older types. Bruce-Gardner recognised the overwhelming force of crude numbers even if they had been dumped as a formal commitment, saying, 'I do not believe Parliament will allow Baldwin's parity formula to go away.'[7]

The raw numbers finally delivered the result that Wilson had striven for on Chamberlain's behalf. In early April 1939 Bruce-Gardner reported that monthly output had nearly quadrupled from the levels of early 1938 and was set to rise further.[8] Delightedly Wilson passed this on to Chamberlain with the rider, 'If you want to stand up to Hitler now, you can do so.'[9] This casts an important light on Chamberlain's policy in other areas afterwards. It is debatable whether he would have taken steps such as the introduction of conscription if the air picture had not given him confidence. By the summer of 1939 Bruce-Gardner was cheerfully telling his patron Montagu Norman, governor of the Bank of England, that he was now 'well satisfied' with aircraft production.[10] Both Wilson and Bruce-Gardner were correct as far as crude total numbers went, but there were still ample grounds for concern when the detail was examined. Much of the increase in production came from aircraft types of dubious military value such as the Fairey Battle and Handley-Page Hampden. When the RAF tried to stem the Wehrmacht's advance through France in May 1940, Battles were massacred for little military gain.

Wilson and Bruce-Gardner appear to have ignored what actually came of Wood's award of the Castle Bromwich project to Lord Nuffield soon after he had replaced Swinton in May 1938. Whilst this step had made favourable headlines, it did not make Spitfires. Behind the scenes the project failed almost totally. Nuffield was well past his prime and his autocratic and eccentric methods compromised the plan from the beginning. He insisted that Castle Bromwich was not to be classed as a 'shadow factory' (and associated with the hated Swinton) and it operated entirely under his control, outside the national network of fighter-building factories that the Air Ministry established. Nuffield did not understand that the technology of manufacturing aircraft in smallish batches was utterly different to the completely standardised assembly of thousands of cars. He could do nothing about the deplorable labour relations at Castle Bromwich, which mirrored those of the Nuffield car factories in Birmingham. Nor were Spitfires high on Bruce-Gardner's priority list. It was not one of the aircraft types where he had identified scope to increase output, because orders had already been placed for as many as could – theoretically – be produced. Even at the height of the Battle of Britain, Castle Bromwich was only producing a dribble of Spitfires. Swinton estimated that under competent management Castle Bromwich could have produced 1,000 Spitfires that were sorely needed.[11] Swinton cursed Wood's decision as one taken on purely political grounds.

Wilson's confident remark also shows how he and Chamberlain had become focused on one single measure of military strength. Even if apologists for Chamberlain are correct in asserting that Munich gave Britain a year's breathing space to rearm, German rearmament also continued after Munich. Chamberlain fixated on the financial strain this produced, but not on the boost to German military potential. Downing Street paid no attention to British intelligence that the Germany army was increasing in strength.[12] They ignored the huge addition to German industrial strength from the factories seized in the rump of Czechoslovakia. A British intelligence appreciation of July accepted that industrial capacity was no longer a brake on German army expansion. Sixteen to seventeen new divisions could be equipped annually and it would be possible to put two-thirds (or eighty) of its divisions into line 'fully armed and equipped in the most modern fashion'.[13] Amongst the booty from Czechoslovakia was the excellent T38 tank and the plant to produce it. The T38 was superior to the Panzer Mk II, the mainstay of the German tank force at the time, and gave good service well into the Russian campaign. The Kriegsmarine was also expanding, with the widely publicised launches of its first battleships, *Bismarck* in February 1939 and *Tirpitz* in April. Less publicly but perhaps more menacing, the number of U-boats delivered in 1939 amounted to 40 per cent of the total figure delivered between 1935 and 1938.[14]

After the Czech crisis Churchill moved into open opposition to Chamberlain and his campaign of criticism on the narrow issue of air rearmament dwindled in importance. The topic, though, remained a live one for him and he followed progress with anything but the complacency of Chamberlain and Wilson. Unfairly he neglected what had been achieved by Swinton's final reforms at the Air Ministry, but he was acutely aware that much could still be improved. One of his early acts as Prime Minister in May 1940 was to appoint his long-standing crony Lord Beaverbrook as Minister of Aircraft Production with a remit to make good the failings of the Chamberlain government. One of the most acute questions that Beaverbrook faced was Castle Bromwich and it was only solved when in his early days as Minister of Aircraft Production he transferred control to the Vickers arms company, which had taken Supermarine over.[15] Only then did the factory begin to contribute usefully to production, eventually building more than half of the Spitfires that flew.

# CHAPTER SEVENTEEN

# WELL ANCHORED

*[I]t is important that the subject should be well anchored for it is one that needs to be handled with care. Much harm may be done and much money wasted unless the peace-time activity is kept within strict limits.*
– Sir Horace Wilson memorandum

The years between the world wars were the first golden age of media. Technology and industry had transformed the world of communications radically. Radio and talking movies had become fully established, reaching the vast bulk of populations in the developed world. The print media had developed huge infrastructures and massive economies of scale so that posters, newspapers and magazines could be reproduced in colossal numbers and high quality, then distributed around a country rapidly and cheaply. The transformation of print spawned a generation of artists and designers who learned how to produce striking and effective images that could translate this media reach into powerful commercial and cultural messages. The spread of literacy meant that the written word had an almost universal impact. By the 1930s the entire population of a country could be presented with the same pictures, words and sounds within a few hours. Governments and political parties were not slow to spot the opportunity and propaganda was soon a major branch of political activity. Steering public opinion had become a key objective even when the rise of dictatorships devalued the public vote. Communist and fascist regimes espoused this new world whole-heartedly; the democracies were rather more tentative.

The new world did not appeal to Sir Horace Wilson. He despised propaganda and did not think that it deserved consideration by serious statesmen. It might be part of the armoury of foreign dictators but he saw no need for Britain to respond. Even when the Second World War had actually broken out, he seriously contemplated dispensing entirely with a propaganda ministry. He admitted that this was part of an old-fashioned outlook on the world, but to him propaganda was the antithesis of what a government should be doing, not an aspect of it, as he informed Chamberlain in one of his rare discursions on the theory of government: 'Having been old-fashioned for many years, I find myself unable to show enthusiasm for propaganda by this country & I still cannot bring myself to believe that [it] is a good substitute for calmly getting on with the business of govt. including a rational foreign policy.'[1]

This outburst was triggered by one of the unintended outgrowths of kicking Sir Robert Vansittart sideways at the turn of 1938. In one of his last acts as Foreign Secretary, Anthony Eden had appointed Vansittart to head a committee tasked with studying Britain's projection of itself abroad. The move was aimed to keep Vansittart occupied and out of mischief after his demotion, as well as addressing the question of how Britain should counter the aggressive propaganda of the fascist states. Wilson's idea of a 'rational foreign policy', of course, meant appeasing the dictators. If Britain indulged in the same style of open self-assertion created by the simplicities of propaganda messages, the dictators would be upset and the policy compromised. The removal of Eden had allowed another drive to make friends with Mussolini and this might be put at risk. Vansittart's efforts should not 'ginger up every agency to fulminate against Italy here and now'.[2]

The formation of Vansittart's committee was announced publicly and this instantly attracted the displeasure of the dictator states. It was bad enough that Britain's uncontrolled press should abuse the dictators and their policies, but it was doubly unacceptable that the British government should in any way contemplate adding its voice to the chorus. When the British ambassador called with the doomed proposal to appease Germany with African colonies, the Führer personally lambasted him for 'inflammatory reports' by various organisations, including

Vansittart's committee. The ambassador, the devotedly pro-appeasement Sir Nevile Henderson, was at pains to insist that the Vansittart committee was not involved in anti-German propaganda. As it had not even started work at this stage, this was an assurance that he could give with complete safety. The message from Germany was clear: propaganda by Britain was unacceptable. There is no sign that Henderson took the opportunity to point out to the Führer that he had at his disposal the huge Ministry for Propaganda and Popular Enlightenment under the control of Joseph Goebbels and that other countries might fairly consider what they might do to match this formidable tool for influencing domestic and foreign opinion. Hitler was notoriously susceptible to hostile comment about him and his regime abroad.

Much though he might sympathise with Hitler's fury on these points, Wilson's hands were rather tied. His influence over the British press was strictly limited and he would only be able to mitigate the effects of the Vansittart committee once the time came to implement any recommendations it might make through the British bureaucratic apparatus. The picture was not all black in Downing Street; Vansittart's efforts were not the only moves that Britain was making in the direction of propaganda and here Wilson was in a far stronger position to ensure that appeasement was not going to be hampered. In 1938 the bureaucratic swansong was heard of the Cabinet Secretary, Sir Maurice Hankey, one of Wilson's most powerful rivals for power in Whitehall.

Before Wilson had fully established himself as a power in the land from his base at 10 Downing Street, Hankey had made gentle moves in a direction that was fraught with risks in Wilson's eyes. Hankey had included the creation of a Ministry of Information (MoI), on the lines of the original British propaganda machine of the First World War, in his long-range contingency planning for potential and hypothetical wartime arrangements when the Abyssinian crisis of 1935 flared up. Hankey was not an instinctive supporter of propaganda and certainly not an advocate of provoking the dictators, but his thorough and tidy military instincts impelled him to put the bare bones in place so that should the evil day come, it would not be necessary to do everything from scratch. The MoI would also handle more mundane questions, such as censorship, which were far closer to Hankey's heart. In Hankey's plans the MoI had taken on a menacingly concrete shape. A government minister, Colonel John Colville,* was designated to serve as Minister of Information and a full-time director general was taken on and set to work on drafting more detailed plans for the ministry if it was to be called into being. On the positive side of the ledger this was all still treated as highly confidential and its affairs could be dealt with firmly out of the glare of public attention. The contingency plans had been developed and were administered by the Committee of Imperial Defence and its myriad sub-committees, the cornerstone of Hankey's apparatus for driving policy that he had built up and nurtured as practically his private domain for more than twenty years. But now Hankey was on his way out and it would be an easy task to unpick any aspect of his legacy that was not to the taste of the government.

Wilson's first opportunity to keep the MoI as theoretical and unmenacing to the dictators as possible came at almost the moment that Hankey departed into retirement. In July 1938 Colville decided that he wanted to be relieved of the responsibility of being minister designate. By that stage, Wilson was well enough entrenched for the decision as to a successor to arrive on his desk. And it stayed on his desk. Chamberlain seems to have been content for the matter to be settled amongst civil servants with Wilson to the fore; in all the internal debates over propaganda policy Chamberlain emerges as a passive spectator, signing off measures that Wilson proposed. Wilson used his power to ensure that no one was given the task who might have threatened appeasement. His choice lighted on Lord Stanhope, the President of the Board of Education, whose activities 'would not be of the first importance in war'.[3] Stanhope was a throwback to an earlier era, when a hereditary peer with a modicum of political ambition would have a reasonable chance of a seat in Cabinet. He had neither a significant political following nor administrative competence. Low profile counted more with Wilson than other considerations and he brushed aside the concerns of Edward Bridges, whom Wilson had chosen to take over

---

* No relation to Chamberlain's private secretary, the diarist 'Jock' Colville.

from Hankey as Cabinet Secretary. Bridges had spotted that they were dealing with 'a very ticklish matter' and that the new minister designate should be one who 'inspires the fullest confidence'.[4] Stanhope's shadowy appointment lasted only two months until he was promoted to be First Lord of the Admiralty to replace Duff Cooper, who had resigned in protest at Munich. Wilson adopted an even more radical solution to the question of finding a minister sufficiently insignificant to ward off any risk that the MoI might amount to anything. He simply did nothing for a further two months and only after some prodding did he come up with a candidate to become 'Minister', the quotation marks showing how little he thought of the task. His candidate was even less impressive than Stanhope: Lord Rushcliffe, who had moved from active politics to chair the Unemployment Assistance Board as long before as 1934. Wilson added a double layer of insurance against the risk that the minister designate might succumb to the temptations of empire-building and excessive enthusiasm for propaganda in peacetime: he was only to hold the post until the outbreak of war, when the actual ministry would pass to someone who had yet to be chosen. It is not clear whether Rushcliffe was even approached about the idea; certainly nothing came of it. Rushcliffe did call on Wilson around this time, but, if the topic of the Ministry of Information arose at all, it was not something Wilson mentioned to Chamberlain afterwards.[5] Wilson was keeping the dangerous plaything of propaganda policy firmly out of the hands of the politicians.

Wilson was well ahead of the game in taking control of the MoI's political leadership – or the lack of it. The position on the ministry's administrative leadership was a far less satisfactory one from his perspective. The director general designate was everything that Wilson did not want for the job. Worse, he was the only individual working practically full time on the mission. Sir Stephen Tallents was one of the emblematic figures of the inter-war publicity world. He had been the secretary and the driving force of the Empire Marketing Board, whose goal was to promote trade, mainly by creating a strong image for imperial food products. In 1932 Tallents had written the highly influential pamphlet *The Projection of Britain*, which argued that the use of modern publicity techniques should be extended to other aspects of British culture and values abroad, as an adjunct to traditional diplomacy. He moved on to the General Post Office where he inspired the ground-breaking Film Unit, which had done so much to create a clear image of the work and ethos of the organisation. From the moment of his appointment to the MoI in 1936 Tallents had driven its planning forward with the same enthusiasm and vigour. This was bad enough in itself, but far, far worse in the eyes of the appeasers was that he saw that the propaganda part of the MoI's work would be directed against Germany and applied the same energy to this part of his work.

The MoI was briefly activated during the Munich crisis, which set the scene for a ferocious, albeit uneven, contest between Tallents's vision for the ministry and Wilson's. Mobilisation subjected the MoI and Tallents's leadership to the acid test of operating within the Whitehall environment, where the MoI demonstrated a significant capacity for nuisance, if not actual mischief. On what appears to have been its own authority, and in a completely extempore fashion, it mounted preparations for a huge air-dropped leaflet campaign on Germany immediately on the outbreak of war.[6] On the ultimately faulty premise that Germany would confiscate private radio sets and perhaps switch to mass broadcasts through wired sets in public places, Tallents believed that such a drop would be the only method available to broadcast propaganda to the German people. Unsurprisingly the attempt to prepare the operation at such short notice did not go smoothly, entailing a number of fraught meetings between MoI, Foreign Office and Air Ministry officials. It was not a good advert for an active Ministry of Information or Tallents's administrative skills. Curiously, the plan for a leaflet drop endured until war came, with a number of senior backers in government, but Chamberlain and Wilson were definitely not amongst them. The plan became the focus of various manoeuvres in the succeeding months, even after Tallents had left the scene.

The fumbles over the leaflet scheme were bad enough, but Munich also encouraged Tallents to promote a dangerously ambitious vision for his ministry. To him the crisis was a wake-up call that showed how important it was to step up the work on the MoI. He recommended that some of its components should actually begin to operate. An 'Enemy Publicity Department' was to start work, targeted specifically against Germany. The MoI was also to provide publicity and press relations for government departments which did not have sufficient capacity of their own.[7] It should begin to operate openly, as a corollary of its move to active operations, for news of the plans for the MoI had appeared in the press immediately after the crisis – they were anyway an open secret on Fleet Street. All of this was highly controversial. Wilson had drawn precisely the opposite conclusion from Munich: 'it became unnecessary to take anything other than very preliminary action'.[8] Peace for our time applied to propaganda as well. Tallents's proposal would also cost money as well as providing unarguable evidence that Britain felt war was more likely rather than less. His wild plans for Enemy Publicity were especially deplorable; they involved the preparation of measures hostile to Germany and thus provocative to Hitler.

Tallents was a dynamic and effective publicist, but he was an innocent in the ways of bureaucracy. He nailed his colours to the mast by launching his proposals as formal recommendations with no preliminary softening up of anyone else involved. Whitehall, of course, swarmed with people who thought they had a stake in the question, many, if not most, of whom had far greater bureaucratic firepower at their command. The plans for Enemy Publicity stamped firmly on the toes of the Foreign Office, which jealously guarded its peacetime monopoly of publicity overseas.[9] The Foreign Office was not the favourite Whitehall department of Chamberlain or Wilson, but they were not about to cut it down to size by encouraging a maverick whose ideas about propaganda against the dictators were far more radical than anything they could contemplate. Tallents had made an implacable and powerful opponent of a potential key ally. Wilson knew that the time had come to turn his big guns on Tallents. He took personal charge of an all-out Whitehall counter-offensive: '[I]t is important that the subject should be well anchored for it is one that needs to be handled with care. Much harm may be done and much money wasted unless the peace-time activity is kept within strict limits.'[10]

Downing Street set out to bring the plans for the MoI and propaganda firmly under its control. The ground was well prepared for a meeting of the Committee of Imperial Defence sub-committee that oversaw Tallents's work some weeks after Munich. With Hankey in retirement, it was child's play to shape the sub-committee according to Wilson's wishes. Wilson circulated a note setting out what it was 'advisable to steer the Committee towards deciding', Whitehall-speak for what it would decide, in particular that 'the minimum of activity about propaganda in enemy countries should be displayed now'.*[11] He followed this up with a small meeting of top-level colleagues which rehearsed the meeting and made 'tentative arrangements' for Tallents's future.[12] The committee meeting was chaired by Sir Warren Fisher, who was 'contemptuously rude throughout' towards Tallents and did not even seem to have read the papers Tallents had submitted.[13] Wilson attended the meeting to enjoy the fun. Tallents's proposals were flatly rejected after a brutal discussion. Even after this rebuff, Tallents persisted in advocating action. He ignored the advice of a friendly senior civil servant 'not to commit hari-kari' and refused to withdraw the letter.[14] He was duly sacked in January 1939.

Wilson was not too squeamish to refuse the services of an unnatural ally in the manoeuvres to neutralise Tallents. Sir Campbell Stuart had been one of the leading lights of the British propaganda operation against Germany during the First World War and had published a self-glorifying memoir under the title *The Secrets of Crewe House*. He had been given retrospective credibility by the Germans themselves through their campaign to pin their defeat on anything but incompetence and defective military strategy. They wildly exaggerated the pernicious effects on civilian morale of British propaganda as part of the 'stab in the back' legend, according to which craven civilian politicians betrayed the German army. Stuart was desperate to relive these glories, but his attempts to create a role for himself at the MoI had been rebuffed by Tallents and Stanhope in one of his few detectable contributions.[15]

Stuart turned to Wilson and Fisher, who were far more accommodating because they understood that in any bureaucratic fight over a

---

* Wilson unguardedly accepted that the dictatorships were hostile.

technical question, you need a tame technical expert to put up against anything the other side might have. Stuart fitted the bill very nicely, and he had an additional and priceless advantage. He argued that propaganda was an extension of Secret Service work and should thus be treated as completely confidential. Anything Stuart might do under cover would not provoke the Germans. He was given vague authority to develop a covert propaganda operation, but once the skids had been placed under Tallents his usefulness was at an end and he was stood down, saying, '[T]he Prime Minister felt that in the Munich meeting he had achieved world peace and I was instructed to suspend my operations' – further evidence that Downing Street believed that the declaration did mean peace for our time.[16] Stuart had to pull in his horns, but he had achieved a precious strategic advantage. He had been acknowledged as the British propaganda maestro, a position he asserted vigorously until well into the Second World War. It was the beginning of a long chapter of divided responsibilities and conflicting spheres of influence that hamstrung British propaganda policy for a long time to come.

Stuart was not just Wilson's (semi-)tame propaganda expert who could be used to shut up anyone else with a dangerous pretension to know anything about the topic; he had a further claim to Downing Street's goodwill on questions of propaganda and, this time, it went directly to Chamberlain himself. Stuart's main job was chairman of Cable & Wireless Ltd, a supposedly private company but in reality controlled by the government. It operated the global telegraph system, which served as a key part of the British imperial command and control apparatus, and it was also the parent company of Wireless Publicity Ltd, the British arm of Radio Luxembourg, which broadcast commercially to Britain in direct competition with the BBC, to the fury of Sir John Reith. At the height of the Munich crisis the services of Wireless Publicity Ltd and Radio Luxembourg were offered to the British government for propaganda into Germany via Sir Joseph Ball. Radio Luxembourg also broadcast to Germany.[17] The offer was taken up with enthusiasm and Ball proposed using translations of Chamberlain's speeches for the broadcasts. He had already built up great kudos with Chamberlain by featuring him extensively in publicity films for the Conservative Party and further playing on his vanity by claiming that his performances had been extremely well received. Radio Luxembourg was soon broadcasting recordings of Chamberlain's speeches and other material into Germany. The operation was strongly backed by Chamberlain himself and continued until the eve of the Second World War despite protest from Germany. This was one of the rare instances in which Wilson's ultra-conservative instincts did not carry the day in shaping British propaganda operations. Ball was willing to award Chamberlain (or at least his words) a direct role and the risk of upsetting the Germans was put to one side.

# CHAPTER EIGHTEEN

# ABANDONMENT AND RUIN

*They [the American people] realise perhaps more clearly than the French and British publics have yet done, the far-reaching consequences of the abandonment and ruin of the Czechoslovak Republic.*

– WINSTON CHURCHILL, BROADCAST TO THE UNITED STATES

During the Czechoslovakia crisis Churchill had taken care not to break with the government outright, even though his views did diverge from the appeasers'. The consideration was reciprocated. He rated highly enough in the political firmament to receive a number of high-level briefings, mainly from Lord Halifax, even during the most intense phases of the action. As had happened over the *Anschluß* debate, Downing Street was manifestly anxious to head Churchill off from open dissent with government policy. Predictably Churchill championed the kind of clear warning to Hitler that Wilson was vehemently opposed to.[1] When he was advised that the French were looking for a way out of their commitment and were not keen to fight, he flew to Paris for talks with two of Édouard Daladier's more resolute ministers. On his return he issued a public statement warning of both the military and the symbolic damage that would be done if Czechoslovakia were deserted.[2] Activity amongst British politicians outside government was just as frantic as the diplomatic activity. Churchill held or attended a series of meetings with a range of dissidents and semi-dissidents from both the left and the right of the Conservative Party but stopped short of any moves directly against the government. He was desperately afraid that Chamberlain would cave in to Hitler but, when the severity of the Bad Godesberg terms became manifest, he thought that Chamberlain would, at last, resist, although this did not lift him very high in Churchill's estimation. When it briefly appeared possible that Chamberlain might actually trigger war whilst still at Bad Godesberg, Churchill questioned whether the Germans would be so stupid as to prevent 'our beloved Prime Minister' from returning to Britain.[3]

Partly because he was being briefed by Halifax, Churchill greatly over-estimated Chamberlain's willingness to stand firm against Hitler's extreme demands. The gap between what Churchill expected that the government would do and what actually was to happen widened to an abyss as the Bad Godesberg memorandum was discussed. Churchill saw both Chamberlain and Halifax at Downing Street before Rex Leeper's communiqué was despatched and believed that it fully expressed what the government believed.[4] It was only when the terms of the Munich agreement reached Churchill at a meeting of the Other Club at the Savoy that he realised the extent of the government's cave-in.[5]

The abandonment of the Czechs under the Munich agreement was enough to tip Churchill into serious revolt. He advised the Czechs in London privately against abandoning their fortifications immediately.[6] Far more important, he spoke against the government in the four-day debate on the Munich agreement in the House of Commons and was amongst the twenty or so Conservative MPs who rebelled and abstained from the vote on the government's policy. By some accounts, he was amongst those who remained ostentatiously seated whilst the MPs went through the division lobbies, in a very public display of his rebellion.

Churchill complained not just about the agreement, but about the way in which the policy that brought it about had been shaped. He had correctly identified the concentration of decision-making in the hands of a small number of ministers, the 'Big Four', the Inner Cabinet of the crisis days. Churchill called for Parliament to be recalled into session so as to create some kind of counter-balance.[7] This produced one of the most bad-tempered Commons clashes of the crisis, when Chamberlain refused to consider an extension of the sitting. Chamberlain and Churchill each called the other unworthy. To Chamberlain's relish the mood of the House was against Churchill and he was poorly received but the acrimony lingered.[8]

The abstention of Churchill and the other Conservatives was a strictly symbolic gesture in the light of the massive government majority and the weakness of the official opposition parties. The comparatively small size of the revolt shows how weak Churchill's support was. The other abstainers included Churchill's son-in-law Duncan Sandys and two of his long-term loyalists, Bob Boothby and Brendan Bracken. Duff Cooper, who was the only member of the Cabinet to resign over Munich, also abstained, perhaps inevitably. It was immensely courageous and risky in view of the immense public support shown for the Munich agreement and marked Churchill and the others as unreconciled enemies of appeasement. Had Chamberlain and Wilson been right about Hitler's preparedness to keep his word, the rebels could have been left on the political scrapheap, but history proved that it was Churchill who understood Hitler better. The rebellion reshaped Conservative politics for a quarter of a century; the next three Conservative Prime Ministers – Churchill, Eden and Harold Macmillan – were amongst the abstainers. A generation had to pass before an appeaser, and a junior one at that, Chamberlain's parliamentary private secretary, Lord Dunglass, entered 10 Downing Street.

The publicity given to Wilson, who had been practically unknown to the general public before the crisis, because of his flights to Germany, inevitably inspired some hostile comment. The truth was filtering out that Chamberlain preferred the advice of someone with almost no grounding in foreign affairs to that of the Foreign Office. The anti-appeasement National Labour MP Harold Nicolson wrote a speech in which he accused Chamberlain of shunning the advice of foreign policy experts in favour of Wilson's, 'which was never inconvenient'.[9] He thought better of such a directly personal attack when he came to deliver the speech and left the passage out of what he said but by then the party office had issued copies of the first text. Nicolson was widely criticised for the phrase but the accusation lingered. A few weeks afterwards another anti-appeasement Liberal MP, Geoffrey Mander, asked a Parliamentary question as to Wilson's role. Chamberlain immediately went onto the counter-offensive with a bland statement that Wilson had been seconded to the Treasury for service to the Prime Minister in 1935, which anyone could have found in the Civil Service List, before launching a ferocious assertion that Wilson should benefit from the traditional anonymity granted to civil servants to ensure the impartiality of their advice. Mander then unintentionally gave Chamberlain an opening for a crushing double blow when he asked a supplementary question which incorrectly implied that Chamberlain had not been accompanied by any Foreign Office official on his visits to Germany. Chamberlain told the House of Commons flatly that Mander's question was factually wrong; the legitimate question as to why his most senior Civil Service adviser by far on foreign policy was not in the Foreign Office was left unasked.

The upper ranks of the government were solidly in favour of the Munich agreement, but some voices saw the Czech crisis as a political turning point and advised Chamberlain to reshape the government, notably Halifax, who thus completed his betrayal of Chamberlain's approach at the Cabinet meeting after the Bad Godesberg negotiations. He and other advocates of a genuine national government were defeated by Chamberlain's instincts and Wilson's opposition. As they returned from Heston aerodrome for Chamberlain's triumphal welcome, Halifax advised Chamberlain to bring in the Labour and the Liberal leaders. According to Halifax, Chamberlain said, "'I'm not sure about that. You had better speak to Horace about it." And Horace did not approve.'[10] Halifax kept up the pressure and even wanted Chamberlain to bring Eden back into the government.[11] Even as loyal a follower of Chamberlain as Sir Samuel Hoare supported the idea of bringing Eden back, although he explicitly ruled out any approach to Churchill even before his revolt in the Munich debate.[12] Others were giving the same advice, some even going so far as to suggest bringing Churchill in. It was only in the aftermath of the Munich debate that Chamberlain was able to lay the idea to rest completely.[13]

It was a sign of how weak Chamberlain's Cabinet team was reckoned to be that he had been forced to consider the idea at all. He did accept that the government needed to be strengthened and made some changes, but his choices were unadventurous if not downright minimal. Lord Runciman came into the Cabinet as Lord President of the Council after his efforts in Czechoslovakia. The choice of a peer, Lord Stanhope, to replace Duff Cooper at the Admiralty could only be explained by Chamberlain's affection for a generous house-party host. Stanhope came from an old aristocratic family and had been decorated for bravery in the First World War but was hopelessly out of his depth. The most high-profile new House of Commons appointment did not even add political vigour but did give a clear idea of Chamberlain's policy priorities. Sir John Anderson, who had transferred from the Civil Service to the government benches via a by-election a few months before, came into the Cabinet with responsibility for air raid precautions. Britain's weakness in air power was a question of defending the country from the Luftwaffe, and nothing must be said that could be construed as a potentially offensive measure against Germany. Chamberlain was infuriated when he had to cancel an interview with a journalist from the normally loyal *Sunday Times* and found that the newspaper had written up progress in the air in terms of boosting RAF bombing power.

Churchill took another long step towards outright opposition to Chamberlain when he broadcast to the United States on 16 October 1938. It was one of his most eloquent and sweeping attacks on the dictators and British policy. He reminded his audience of his futile call for a Grand Alliance and repeatedly hammered home the fate of Czechoslovakia, 'abandonment and ruin', 'sacrifice' and 'destruction'.[14] The broadcast drew a back-handed compliment from Chamberlain, who felt it 'was much more damaging to our cause' than a recent speech by David Lloyd George.[15] He credited Churchill with not denigrating Britain, but persuaded himself that the speech would somehow alienate US sentiment by seeming to lecture the Americans on the need to help Britain.

The Conservative Party machine was unleashed against Churchill and the other rebels. The challenge to Churchill in his Epping constituency was led by Colin Thornton-Kemsley, who had previously been an enthusiastic supporter of his, but now seemed to be working for Conservative Central Office to weaken Churchill. Thornton-Kemsley led the attack on Churchill at a special meeting of the West Essex Unionist Association held in the City of London on 4 November.[16] His speech read like a prospectus for appeasement in its purest form. Armed opposition to Germany had failed and there was no real conflict of interest between Germany and Britain. A 'policy of friendship' amongst the Munich powers would prevent war in Europe. The chairman, Sir James Hawkey, steadfastly supported Churchill against this assault and an artfully worded resolution urging Churchill 'to continue his work for national unity and national defence' was carried by a healthy majority. Churchill had survived, but Thornton-Kemsley continued his campaign, trying to force Churchill to stand as an independent. 'We wanted to support the Conservative administration, not to discredit them.'[17] Churchill was still fighting off attempts to undermine him in his constituency the following March, just as Hitler was to reveal himself in his true colours by seizing the remainder of Czechoslovakia.[18]

One of the Munich rebels, the Duchess of Atholl, went to the extreme of resigning her seat as an MP and fighting the resulting by-election as an independent against the official Conservative Party candidate. Churchill came very close to an open breach with the party when he wrote the duchess a letter of support, in which he implied that she was closer to the 'finest principles' of the party and 'your defeat would be relished by the enemies of Britain and of Freedom'.[19] Atholl was defeated, in part because of her unpopular vocal support for the Republican side in the Spanish Civil War, and Churchill was faced by the exultation of government supporters. At a house party at Blenheim Palace, James Stuart, the deputy chief whip, told Churchill that he should leave the Conservatives in terms that even he admitted were harsh and left a 'wound that took a long time to heal'.[20]

# CHAPTER NINETEEN

# RIDING THE TIGER

*Supposing however that the P.M. was forced into having a General Election, what would happen then? It is extremely probable that, if the S. of S [Halifax] resigned on a 'Defence of the West' policy, or something like it, coupled with a real rearmament effort, whereas the P.M. stood self-declared for 'Riding the Tiger' i.e. concessions without a quid pro quo, a substantial number of Ministers would resign with him.*

— SIR ALEXANDER CADOGAN, MEMORANDUM

The end of Munich left Chamberlain exhausted but exalted. By his sole, personal efforts he had saved Europe from war. The frantic cheers of the crowds were the proof that his mastery of statesmanship was recognised. His achievement was not purely the negative one of preventing war; he had opened the way to a new era of peace and harmony founded on friendship between Europe's two dominant powers. In Chamberlain's eyes, this was the true success of the Munich declaration. Now that Hitler had committed himself to the project, the last potential diplomatic stumbling block had been removed.

If Chamberlain's euphoric state was his moment of hubris, nemesis came only progressively. He had to face the test of the House of Commons debate, which he admitted that he found 'draining' even though there was never any risk of serious challenge.[1] Churchill's rebellion was essentially symbolic but it still raised Chamberlain's ire. He had been alerted to Churchill's contacts with the Czech embassy by phone taps and relished the fact that Churchill was unaware of this hidden power. He put the whole episode down to a 'regular conspiracy' between

Churchill and the Czechs and complacently took Churchill's assessment of his vulnerability as 'demonstrat[ing] how completely Winston can deceive himself when he wants to'. Even though the House was against Churchill on the point, Chamberlain was stung by the accusation of 'unworthiness'.

Chamberlain's access to bugged conversations involving Churchill raises the question of whether there was systematic covert surveillance of his opponents. The evidence is mixed. Foreign embassies were routinely bugged by MI6's Section X, which would have disclosed Churchill's conversations with Masaryk.[2] MI6's involvement suggests that the embassies were treated as foreign territory seemingly exempt from the system of Home Office Warrants that regulated domestic wiretaps and was strictly enough adhered to to require the Home Secretary's approval for wiretaps on the King at the height of the abdication crisis.[3] As Home Secretary, Sir John Simon strongly supported appeasement, but nothing has emerged publicly to indicate that he was called upon to authorise an extensive operation. After war broke out draconian rules were used to justify a wiretap on an opposition Liberal politician.[4] During the war Joseph Ball bragged to a former dissident Conservative MP who suspected that his line had been tapped under Chamberlain that he himself was responsible for this.[5] Given Ball's habitual mendacity and fondness for flaunting secret service contacts, there is reason to be suspicious.

It was a more taxing business for Chamberlain to deal with doubts in the ranks of his supporters. He was confronted by the 'defection of weaker brethren'. One Cabinet minister, Duff Cooper, had actually resigned and two others threatened to do so, Oliver Stanley and Harry Crookshank. They were persuaded to stay in the fold, but not before rumours of fresh resignations had become widespread. Crookshank put up an especially demanding and egocentric performance, which was particularly stressful for Chamberlain to deal with.

The strains of the crisis, the ensuing House of Commons debate and the ministerial defections – successful and attempted – proved too much even for Chamberlain's resilient health and strength of personality. He had already come 'nearer to a nervous breakdown than I have ever been in my life' when he came back from Munich.[6] Lord Home, the father of Chamberlain's parliamentary private secretary, Lord Dunglass, invited Chamberlain and his wife to The Hirsel, his estate on the Scottish borders with its reposeful salmon fishing. He spent ten days on the Tweed largely sheltered from the stress of his work.

Whilst Chamberlain was recuperating in Scotland, Downing Street was setting down the ground rules for the next phase in Anglo-German diplomacy. Chamberlain would have to live with Halifax and the Foreign Office but could at least take steps to prevent a recurrence of Rex Leeper's communiqué of 26 September or any similar interference in foreign policy by such unhelpful individuals. At the height of the crisis Sir Nevile Henderson had informed the Germans that they were to pay no attention to anything unless it came from Downing Street. They were now to be told that this held good for the future and, if anything, even tougher rules applied. This time, though, Downing Street cut out all official channels to send its message. Around 10 October, the Downing Street press man, George Steward, gave a lengthy briefing to Fritz Hesse, his contact at the German embassy who doubled as Ribbentrop's informer in London. By way of explanation, Steward treated Hesse to an indiscreet account of how the splits inside the Cabinet had played out during the crisis, with the result that British policy-making had passed into the sole hands of Chamberlain and Wilson. Halifax, the Foreign Secretary, was no longer part of the picture and the Foreign Office had actively tried to sabotage Chamberlain's policy and 'had sworn to be "revenged" on Germany'.[7] The Germans should bypass the Foreign Office entirely and 'all future ... major questions should be dealt with direct'. Only Downing Street counted and the Foreign Office should be ignored. Even Henderson, the ambassador in Berlin, was to be cut out of the loop because he had displayed a lack of discretion in passing information to the Foreign Office in London and might do so again, which could 'caus[e] all kinds of obstruction and undesirable publicity'. It was implicit that these instructions came from the highest level at Downing Street. Steward distanced Chamberlain from any enthusiasm for rearmament. The primary purpose of the rearmament programme was to strengthen Chamberlain domestically and smooth the way for him to win a general election; Hitler could sleep safely. Chamberlain was Germany's friend; if he was not supported, he might be replaced by politicians who were downright hostile.

Hitler gave the first indication that Chamberlain was wrong to think that Britain and Germany had become close friends at Saarbrücken on 9 October 1938, in his first major speech after the crisis.[8] Noting the House of Commons debate on Munich, he laid into British criticisms which were compromising ties between the countries:

Only one thing, however, which applies to our relations with England. It would be well if people in England gave up certain airs and graces of the Versailles epoch. We will not tolerate admonitions to Germany as by a governess [*gouvernantenhafte Bevormundung*]. Investigations by British statesmen or members of Parliament into the fate of Germans within Germany are out of place.[9]

The appeasers had, of course, rigorously avoided this kind of provocation, but Wilson knew how bad an impression Hitler's words would make on the Prime Minister and warned him, 'Master, I'm afraid you are not going to like this.'[10] All was not lost, though, and Chamberlain could still take comfort from his achievement, and there was Churchill to blame as well. He lashed out against Churchill's hunger for publicity and rested his confidence in Hitler: 'Hitler has promised me, and I believe him. We have made Europe safe.' But for all his outward confidence, Chamberlain had seen 'the red light'.[11]

Even worse was to follow. MI5 and the Foreign Office played the same trick on Chamberlain that the Germans had played on Edvard Beneš and Jan Masaryk. Intercepted telegrams revealed that Hitler was describing Chamberlain as an 'arsehole' and MI5 used these to catch the Prime Minister's eye.[12] Halifax underlined the obscenity three times in red on his copy of the report.[13] Chamberlain's self-esteem was challenged and the reports made a very distinct impression on him.[14] They were another instance of 'the red light' and began to feed a reaction against Hitler.[15]

As well as a less rosy picture on the German side than he had brought back from Munich, Chamberlain faced internal obstacles to completing his work. Anthony Eden, the determined enemy of deals with the dictators, had been removed from the Foreign Office and Robert Vansittart had been side-lined but their replacements had shown themselves to be broken reeds during the crisis. Alec Cadogan had egged Halifax on to revolt against accepting the Bad Godesberg terms in open Cabinet, but Chamberlain had little alternative but to keep Halifax in place. It would have been suicidal to push out a second Foreign Secretary in so short a space of time. Chamberlain's colonies scheme had failed abjectly to interest the Nazi regime but he was still determined to find a peg on which to hang a broad agreement.

When Chamberlain returned to London from The Hirsel, he could not begin the work of follow-up appeasement immediately. His first job was to reshape the Cabinet, from which he had lost a second minister, Edward Stanley, the Dominions Secretary, through the accident of death. Chamberlain had barely settled the new appointments when the Nazis launched the *Kristallnacht* pogrom. The public euphoria generated by avoiding war had already started to ebb; it was clear that the government was confronted by serious fights in by-elections at Oxford and Bridgwater where the opposition had united behind a single anti-appeasement candidate. Public revulsion at the treatment of the Jews was a powerful factor in opinion of the government's foreign policy. The semi-defection of Halifax had been rather predictable, but from his lair in Downing Street, Wilson had started to sniff treason even amongst men who had previously been unswervingly loyal. He was revolted by the behaviour of Sir John Simon and Sir Samuel Hoare, who, 'with ambitions to succeed him, hovered round him like vultures, anxious to be in at the kill ... They impeded his recovery.'[16] Wilson expected the same level of personal loyalty from Chamberlain's political colleagues as he himself lavished as a civil servant. A renewed appeasement drive to translate 'peace for our time' into something more solid would have to be handled very carefully and, to begin with at least, very discreetly.

Further attention was absorbed by a glaring piece of Chamberlainite vanity and duplicity. Chamberlain had dreamed up a visit to Paris together with Halifax and their wives, with the primary intent 'to give the French people an opportunity of pouring out their pent-up feelings of gratitude and affection'.[17] Paris's population duly stepped up to the plate by lining the route with cheering crowds.[18] Flagging solidarity with France publicly also cleared the way for a far more meaningful diplomatic project: a visit to Mussolini that Chamberlain was planning for January. Had Chamberlain gone to Rome before Paris, it would have been all too obvious that France meant little to Chamberlain but Italy meant a great deal. There were practically no serious diplomatic discussions, apart from over terms of a guarantee to the rump of Czechoslovakia, which could safely have been handled at ambassador level. Halifax's presence served to demonstrate the inconsequentiality of the operation. Under adult supervision, the Foreign Secretary could be let out to help in a task of secondary importance. Almost the only sacrifice that the trip demanded of Chamberlain was to feed the vanity of the Duke and Duchess of Windsor with the first call on them by a top-level politician since the duke's abdication as King two years before.

When, on 15 November 1938, the Cabinet Foreign Policy Committee finally met to discuss how to execute Chamberlain's desire to 'follow up' Munich the foreign policy professionals had little to offer by way of concrete ideas.[19] The best that Cadogan had come up with for Halifax was his 'King Charles's head', trying to push the Germans into a clear statement of their wishes. This was, of course, quite contrary to Hitler's way of working and, as the destruction of Czechoslovakia stood at the top of the Nazis' list of desiderata, would not have yielded anything like an honest answer. Worse, Halifax and Cadogan produced ample evidence that Hitler and other Nazi leaders had seen Munich as a humiliation and now ranked Britain as the chief enemy of the German people. Chamberlain inevitably dissented on the Foreign Office analysis of German intentions and believed Britain should 'do all in its powers to encourage the moderates'.[20] Chamberlain had at least partially shaken off the ill-effects of learning how Hitler referred to him privately and pooh-poohed intelligence reports of his hostility, showing his usual ability to see a thimbleful of wine at the bottom of a glass as a glass half full: 'There was no suggestion that Herr Hitler contemplated any immediate aggressive action.'[21]

LEFT Sir Horace Wilson, GCB, GCMG, CBE. 'Age 55 – height 5' 9" – medium build; dark hair – fresh complexion – clean shaven – large straight nose – blue eyes (squint in right eye) – dark rings under eyes', according to an MI5 surveillance operative, unaware that he or she was describing the country's most powerful civil servant. © Elliot & Fry/Hulton Archive/Getty Images

RIGHT Sir Horace and his master walk across Horse Guards Parade, umbrellas furled despite the rain. The civil servant keeps a deferential half pace behind the Prime Minister. This might not have reflected the true balance of power between them. © Davies/Topical Press Agency/Getty Images

LEFT Winston Churchill as an infantry officer in the First World War. He had a great fondness for the distinctive French *Adrian* helmet (his is displayed at his home, Chartwell) and had an emotional attachment to the French army. He understood that it offered the most powerful military force to counter Nazi Germany, but he underestimated the weakness of France's politicians and generals. © The Print Collector/Alamy Stock Photo

RIGHT Bricklaying provided a new consolation for Churchill as he drifted towards the political wilderness, but joining the builders' trade union as a publicity stunt backfired embarrassingly despite the fact that he had sought the advice of Wilson as an expert on the unions. © Keystone Press/Alamy Stock Photo

ABOVE Sir Joseph Ball operated behind a smokescreen, making great play of his contacts in the intelligence world. Through an acquaintance from Gray's Inn he established a secret channel to Fascist Italy and controlled the magazine *Truth* as a covert propaganda tool. © Picture Post/Hulton Archive/ Getty Images

ABOVE Ball shared a passion for fly-fishing with Chamberlain and invited him to his house at Kimbridge on the river Test, which cemented their friendship. Photo courtesy of Peter Hayes of the Flyfishers' Club

ABOVE LEFT Field Marshal Goering explains the finer points of bison rearing to Foreign Secretary Lord Halifax on his sprawling estate, Carinhall. Halifax was impressed by Goering's expansive style, finding him a 'composite personality, film star, great landowner interested in his estate, prime minister, party-manager, head gamekeeper at Chatsworth'. Goering claimed that Germany's African ambitions reached no further than the Cameroons and Togoland, which inspired Chamberlain to propose to Hitler a deal over the colonies. © Bundesarchiv, Bild 102-17989/Georg Pahl

ABOVE RIGHT Lord Halifax (*right*) avoided the kind of bitter confrontation with Chamberlain over foreign policy that had doomed Eden. Sir Alec Cadogan (*left*), Permanent Under-Secretary of the Foreign Office, was a pragmatist, in contrast to his ferociously anti-German predecessor, Sir Robert Vansittart, and he worked hard to cooperate with Wilson. Halifax did push for a stronger line against the dictators, and won most of his open disputes with Chamberlain, but neither he nor Cadogan seems to have recognised how much Downing Street bypassed them through back channels. Author's collection

The catastrophic Fairey Battle, a 'fast' bomber, which was 100mph slower than German fighters.

The obsolescent Gloster Gladiator; its enclosed cockpit was its chief concession to modern design.

The inadequate Handley-Page Hampden, known as the 'Flying Suitcase'.

The Boulton Paul Defiant, misconceived and dangerously useless in combat.

Wilson's chosen troubleshooter for the aircraft industry, Sir Charles Bruce-Gardner, wanted as many of these produced as possible. Chamberlain, too, put quantity before quality. This served to deflect Churchill's criticisms but saddled the RAF with too many aircraft of minimal value.

Plan Z goes into operation. The Foreign Secretary and the head of the Foreign Office were allowed to see Chamberlain off to Germany, but only Wilson and a comparatively junior Foreign Office official, William Strang, accompanied him on the mission. © Herald Archive/SSPL/Getty Images

ABOVE Joachim von Ribbentrop's dismal failure as ambassador in London had made him violently anti-British, but he was still on hand to accompany Hitler's visitors. © Sueddeutsche Zeitung Photo/Alamy Stock Photo

RIGHT The German foreign ministry's Paul Schmidt interprets between Hitler and Chamberlain. Only when the Germans refused to give the British Schmidt's transcript of the first conversation between the two leaders did the British feel the need to include a fluent German speaker in their team and even then only as a note-taker. © Bundesarchiv, Bild 146-1977-159-11/Hoffmann

ABOVE The leaders pose to mark the signature of the Munich agreement. The French Prime Minister, Daladier (*second left*), looks decidedly unimpressive; Mussolini and his foreign minister, Ciano (*first right*), look decidedly thuggish. Wilson lurks in the background. © Bundesarchiv, Bild 183-R69173/o.Ang.

MIDDLE The British team in the Munich negotiations was tiny and depended on the Germans for transport. Wilson later joked that the outcome might have been different had the British fielded a more impressive delegation and that he could have been rewarded with an earldom. © Bundesarchiv, Bild 183-H12987/o.Ang.

BELOW The *Kristallnacht* pogrom was severely criticised by the world's media, but Reuters news agency, run by Wilson's ally Sir Roderick Jones, gave the Nazi regime a platform to provide its version of events. © Historic Collection/ Alamy Stock Photo

Fritz Hesse was the personal agent of foreign minister Joachim von Ribbentrop at the London embassy; he was a borderline fantasist who had long been of interest to MI5, from whose file on him this picture is taken. Wilson wrongly ascribed to Hesse close ties to Hitler comparable to Hewel's; he may simply have muddled the two men.
© The National Archives

Helmut Wohlthat was firmly in Hermann Goering's camp; his official function as economics adviser provided Wilson with handy cover when their discussions were leaked publicly.
© Historic Collection/Alamy Stock Photo

Germany's traditional diplomats, and above all ambassador Herbert von Dirksen, took over the undisclosed talks with Wilson from Wohlthat after the leak.
© Historic Collection/Alamy Stock Photo

Walther Hewel (*left*) was a long-standing friend of Hitler, with whom he had been in prison after the Beer Hall Putsch. He fed the British with misinformation, including the fateful fiction that Hitler was prepared to be patient over Danzig.
© Bundesarchiv, Bild 146-2005-0012/o.Ang.

Montagu Norman (*right*), the autocratic, anti-Semitic and individualistic Governor of the Bank of England, was tasked with the economic appeasement of Germany, but he had to face the opposition of the Foreign Office and the dismissal of his German contact, Hjalmar Schacht (*left*), the last voice of reason in the German leadership. He lobbied almost successfully to have Sir John Simon removed as Chancellor of the Exchequer. © AP/Shutterstock

Wilson believed that it was a legitimate part of his job to advise the Prime Minister on political matters, including the choice of ministers. In their different ways, six Cabinet ministers (*from left to right*) – Anthony Eden, Sir John Simon, Sir Thomas Inskip, William 'Shakes' Morrison, Leslie Hore-Belisha and Lord Swinton – did not measure up to what Wilson wanted. Only Simon survived, and then only because Wilson's candidate to replace him declined the job. © Tophams/Topham Picturepoint/Press Association Images © PA/PA Archive/PA Images © Len Putnam/AP/Shutterstock

The University of London Senate House became the wartime home of the Ministry of Information. Wilson's guiding principle in peacetime preparations for its establishment was not to offend Germany. The result was a fiasco. © Adrian Phillips

Chamberlain had dreaded the prospect of having Churchill as a Cabinet colleague again, and the first weeks of the War Cabinet proved him right. © Granger Historical Picture Archive/Alamy Stock Photo

Germany was experiencing its own internal institutional turf-fight over who should influence foreign policy, which found its way into the use of back-channel intermediaries. Joachim von Ribbentrop had to bear the brunt of Hitler's frustration that he had been deprived of a war to annihilate Czechoslovakia, and complained that he had been left to take on the British alone.[22] He was anxious to protect the Auswärtiges Amt's – that is, his own – remaining influence over foreign policy. Ribbentrop explained the dilemma to his man in London, Fritz Hesse, when the latter came to Berlin. Back in London Hesse set to work to create some proof that the Auswärtiges Amt was capable of bringing something useful to the table. He now had a direct line to Wilson, established at the fateful moment of the Sudeten crisis when Europe hovered on the brink of war, and contacted him. Wilson was in a receptive mood and ready with a concrete suggestion for him to try on Berlin: he asked Hesse to sound out German feeling as to a possible agreement designed to humanise war by forbidding poison gas and the bombing of civilians. The agreement would naturally have to be reached directly between Chamberlain and Hitler, outside normal diplomatic channels, but for the actual signature Ribbentrop, or even Hermann Goering, could come to London. Ribbentrop had just visited Paris to sign a comic imitation of the 'peace for our time' declaration so that the French would not feel too left out of things. Pointless though this exercise had been, it did make it painfully obvious that no senior German statesman had deigned to visit Britain. Once Germany had repaid numerous British visits, Chamberlain might again travel to Germany to discuss with the Führer but not before. Despite Wilson's petulant insistence of some token of active German interest, Hesse read Wilson's pitch as proof that 'Britain is ready, during the next year, to accept practically everything from us and to fulfil our every wish'.[23] Hesse had been especially taken by the care with which Wilson explained the measures the British government 'had spontaneously taken to bring to an end the bad feeling resulting from anti-Semitism in order to remove this particular cause for friction in our relations'. *Kristallnacht* was not to stand in the way of appeasement.

Hesse's initiative led nowhere, but it did alert the Foreign Office to the existence of Downing Street's parallel diplomacy. An MI5 agent at the German embassy obtained a copy of the first draft and the final draft of the letter Hesse sent to Ribbentrop reporting the conversation, which soon arrived on the desk of Cadogan.[24] Cadogan agonised over whether to disclose what he had discovered to Halifax or to suppress it. He set down in writing the pros and cons of each course of action.[25] Above all he feared dire internal consequences from involving himself in a fight between two ministers, including dragging the Foreign Office into politics, but was desperate to frustrate the policy of appeasement, 'Riding the Tiger' as he put it, 'i.e. concessions without a quid pro quo'. Perhaps the decisive consideration, though, was the power of honesty. Cadogan was alert to the danger that the secret negotiations might leak out and put the Foreign Office in the invidious position of having been aware of them yet failing to warn the Foreign Secretary. In the end Cadogan did tell Halifax but he does not appear to have pursued the matter thoroughly. MI5 had wrongly identified Hesse's contact as George Steward; had it been known that it was Wilson, the question would have been considerably more serious.[26] The sole outcome was that 'a member of the Prime Minister's staff was eventually warned by Sir Horace Wilson against indiscreet talk'.[27] Cadogan optimistically noted that 'this will put a brake on them all', but in fact the upshot was far closer to the fear that Cadogan had listed as an argument against disclosure to Halifax, that Chamberlain would 'make a scapegoat of somebody' and 'carry on with his clandestine negotiations'.

# CHAPTER TWENTY

# THE RIGHT LINE
# ABOUT THINGS

*Sir Roderick [Jones, chairman of Reuters] was anxious that Reuters
should always take the right line about things.*
– SENIOR REUTERS JOURNALIST TO SIR NEVILE HENDERSON

K eeping Churchill out of government became as much a goal of
the Nazi regime as it was of Chamberlain's political strategy. Nazi
abuse and Downing Street suspicions created a self-feeding circle in
which the more Joseph Goebbels and his cohorts attacked Churchill,
the more provocative it would have seemed to bring him into government. There was never any doubt that Churchill was an obstacle
to friendly relations between the Nazi regime and Britain, and in the
wake of Munich the German leadership launched a virulent campaign
against him and, to a lesser extent, the other senior Tory dissidents,
Anthony Eden and Duff Cooper. Goebbels issued instructions to the
German press to miss no opportunity to attack them.[1]

The verbal assault on Churchill was closely intertwined with the acceleration of the Nazi persecution of the Jews in the autumn of 1938.
Hitler had been deprived of his war of annihilation against Czechoslovakia by the peaceful settlement of the Sudeten crisis, but there were
other outlets for his craving for violence. The Nazis' first move was
to expel from Germany the 20,000-plus Jews who were Polish citi-
zens. The Polish government did everything short of formally blocking
their return to Poland, so they were caught in a miserable dilemma,

trapped on the frontier. The child of one of these families, a young man called Herschel Grynszpan, was in Paris where he took drastic and fateful action, shooting and fatally wounding a German diplomat. This provided a trigger and pretext for the massive, nationwide Nazi pogrom against Jews in Germany organised a week later on 9 November. *Kristallnacht* marked the next step in Nazi racial policy towards one of outright violence, intended to force the Jews out of the country.

Hitler opened the assault on Churchill, even before Grynszpan's attack, with a speech chiefly devoted to complaints at criticism from abroad. He laid into Churchill's call for a change in regime in Germany with the advice to 'traffic ... less with traitors and more with Germans'.[2] He permitted himself a dig at 'umbrella-carrying' bourgeois politicians, but reserved his fire for 'war agitators' like Churchill. After Munich, Hitler had conceived a particular dislike of the neatly furled umbrellas invariably carried by the likes of Chamberlain and Wilson, and it became his shorthand for the feeble but irksome British statesmen who had tried to defy his will during the crisis. After the Paris shooting, the Nazi Party newspaper *Der Angriff* stepped up the attack, practically accusing 'the Churchill clique' of having ordered Grynszpan to undertake the assassination. Hitler retreated a little from his contempt for Chamberlain, contrasting him favourably with the 'war agitators', and sent him a pointed message to keep Churchill out of government: 'In France and Britain men who want peace are in the Government. But to-morrow those who want war may be in the Government. Mr Churchill may be Prime Minister to-morrow.'[3]

He contrasted his democratic credentials with those of Churchill, but could not resist another dig at Chamberlain or anyone else who fancied they could interfere with Germany from outside. 'If ever a man represented a people, my dear British members of Parliament, I am that man. Mr Churchill may have an electorate of 15,000 or 20,000. I have one of 40,000,000. Once and for all, we request to be spared governessy tutelage.' Hitler was repeating the phrase '*gouvernanten-hafte Bevormundung*' that he had used in his first major speech after Munich, which gave an early warning to Britain that the new era of

Anglo-German friendship that Chamberlain imagined he had initiated was a long way from being a reality.

The German state had already launched an all-out propaganda offensive against anti-appeasers. The press was instructed to miss no opportunity to criticise the 'eternal trouble-makers against Germany', Eden, Churchill and Cooper.[4] German embassies were instructed to do likewise, which prompted Ernst von Weizsäcker to complain.[5]

The reaction to *Kristallnacht* was predictably muted in Downing Street. Chamberlain expressed personal revulsion at what was going on, but this was tinged by frustration that horror at Nazi anti-Semitism was holding up his drive for appeasement: 'I am horrified by the German behaviour to the Jews. There does seem to be some fatality about Anglo-German relations which blocks every effort to improve them.'[6] He gloomily foresaw the need to say something in Parliament that steered between condoning the atrocity and criticism. Chamberlain was now entirely convinced that criticism of Hitler would inevitably provoke him to even greater excesses and lead to worse persecution.

The same thought pattern drove Wilson's approach to handling a resurgence of fears amongst British settlers in Africa that Munich heralded a sell-out of their interests there to Germany. These had to be calmed without shutting the door totally on colonial appeasement.[7] Above all the government statement had to be couched so as to avoid offending Hitler, notably through any inference that 'perhaps recent happenings' in Germany might be influencing British policy against concessions. Wilson could just bring himself to this squeamish and prissy euphemism for Nazi persecution of the Jews in a confidential letter, but otherwise 'these ought not to be mentioned'. There is no sign whatever that Wilson had any personal sympathy for Hitler's victims and long afterwards asked a historian, 'Did you ever meet a Jew you really liked?'[8] Chamberlain was no more sympathetic: 'No doubt Jews aren't a loveable people; I don't care about them myself.'[9] He complained that his hopes of détente were uncertain 'as long as the Jews obstinately refuse to shoot Hitler!'[10]

Amidst the welter of international press condemnation of *Kristallnacht*, the Nazi regime could draw comfort from one facet of Wilson's sedulous campaign to coordinate British media in support of appeasement. Much of this had taken the form of suppressing material and opinion that Downing Street judged to be dangerous to the policy, but now one of Wilson's stable of tame outlets provided a platform for outright Nazi propaganda.

Nothing illustrates better the strength of Wilson's position at the centre of the web of the British state apparatus than his relationship with the Reuters news agency. When the Führer delivered his tirade against the British press to Sir Nevile Henderson, the British ambassador, when he was peddling the doomed colonial scheme in March 1938, he had also taken a swipe at Reuters. Goebbels had taken violent but fleeting exception to a story from the Reuters Vienna bureau about defecting Luftwaffe officers.[11] Reuters was often bracketed with the BBC and *The Times* as a voice of the British government. In fact, the Reuters news agency had minimal formal ties to the British state, but it was the only significant British international news agency and had a correspondingly high profile. The news agencies of the dictator states, above all Germany's Deutsches Nachrichtenbüro, were outright propaganda organs, so it was inevitable, however falsely, that Reuters should be viewed in rather the same light. The British government had no formal tools to hand to oblige Hitler by transforming Reuters's coverage to something more to his taste, but the accidents of personality and business management were soon to give Wilson a powerful means of influencing Reuters. Under the autocratic leadership of Sir Roderick Jones, Reuters had been losing ground to its US commercial competitors globally and was further hampered because its European and Japanese competitors were heavily subsidised by their governments. Jones had also used a rejig of Reuters's share ownership to make himself a very wealthy man, rather than bringing fresh capital into the agency. Reuters's outside shareholders were rapidly losing confidence in Jones and lobbying for a dilution of his power.

Jones turned to the government for financial help and in the spring of 1938 found himself negotiating with Wilson on the terms of an agreement between the government and the agency. Jones made great play of Reuters's ability to counteract unwelcome or distorted reports carried by its foreign competitors as a bargaining counter. By July 1938 they had reached a draft agreement which gave the government a powerful and formally recognised voice in the affairs of Reuters even if it stopped short of outright control. The government would

> make a payment to Reuters for the purpose of assisting them to extend and improve their foreign news service, i.e. not only the collection of news but in particular its distribution overseas, with the object of providing Governments and the public overseas with an accurate and impartial service of news, especially on topics in which British interests are concerned ... Reuters will at all times maintain the closest cooperation and liaison with the Foreign Office and other Government departments at home ... While maintaining complete independence of direction or control by HM Government they will at all times bear in mind any suggestions made to them on behalf of the Government as to their news service or as to the topics or events which from time to time may require particular attention.[12]

The subsidy was to amount to £39,500 annually. In exchange Jones would gradually withdraw from undiluted control over Reuters. A chief general manager, 'acceptable to HM Government', was to be appointed who would step up to a higher position in five years' time. In his conversations with Wilson, Jones went even further in committing himself to bow to Wilson's wishes. Wilson did not 'of course' include in the letter 'the personal assurances which you have given me throughout as to your desire to co-operate as we would wish'. By an astute combination of a relatively small amount of government money and a willingness to leave Jones in a powerful position at Reuters for some years, Wilson was set to transform the relationship between Reuters and the government into an even closer one than with the BBC.

Even before the agreement had been drafted, Jones was showing how Reuters could redeem any earlier hostility to Nazi Germany and contribute to the project of appeasement. He offered Reuters's services to send 'one of my most trusted representatives' to interview Hitler and give him an opportunity to present his own views on Czechoslovakia, where the crisis was building, to the entire world.[13] Jones would give the project his 'personal attention and direction from start to finish'. Nothing came of the idea but as the Czech crisis lurched towards war in September 1938, he sent his associate editor in London, Gordon Young, out to Germany to cover Chamberlain's mediation efforts under his personal direction. When Young interviewed Sir Nevile Henderson, he could assure him that 'Sir Roderick was anxious that Reuters should always' meet his wishes that the press would 'take the right line about things'.[14] Henderson was notoriously hostile to any British journalists who dared to criticise the Nazi regime in their reports. Young had privileged access to the British team in the negotiations including (at Jones's behest) Wilson himself. At the Berghof, where Chamberlain had gone for his first conversation with Hitler, Young appeared to be operating as Wilson's PR man rather than an independent journalist. Even at this early stage of the talks, Wilson was fearful that the truth of his desire to sacrifice Czechoslovakia would become obvious and that there would be 'an outcry at home that there was a plan to "sell out the Czechs"'. Wilson did not want to prejudice opinion on the discussion between Hitler and Chamberlain until the Cabinet had met, so he and Young 'outlined together' the despatch that Young was to send to London.

Reuters could set itself apart from less appeasing sections of the world's media when the Nazi regime unleashed its worst atrocity yet. The *Kristallnacht* pogrom was deservedly excoriated in newspapers across the globe but Reuters was willing to provide Germany with a platform to put its own side of the story. Young flew out to Berlin to interview Goebbels, chief architect of the pogrom, who was acutely conscious of this unfavourable coverage. He began by making a good impression with sympathy for Goebbels's complaints against the attitude of the British press.[15] Goebbels hoped Young would write this all up and when Reuters published the interview, he was not disappointed. He was happy with the prominence that it was given and was happy to release it for publication in the German press, which gave it extensive coverage.[16] Of course Goebbels could very easily have placed a similar interview in German media outlets, but the fact that it was carried by a powerful and reputable outlet from a major democracy lent it a unique force and credibility.

# CHAPTER TWENTY-ONE

# ADVICE FROM THE DEVIL

*I have pleaded when it was already late; and perhaps my Right Hon.*
*Friend may remember I have even adjured him not to be deterred from*
*doing right because it was impressed on him by the devil.*
– WINSTON CHURCHILL IN THE HOUSE OF COMMONS

Chamberlain was unmoved when a long-standing shibboleth of committed rearmers was given another outing in the wake of Munich and *Kristallnacht*. The painful demonstration of British military weakness which had shaped Chamberlain's policy encouraged the War Secretary, Leslie Hore-Belisha, to agitate for the establishment of a Ministry of Supply.[1] This was the First World War's Ministry of Munitions by another name. Its creation under David Lloyd George had been emblematic of the shift to total-war conditions, bringing huge swathes of industry under direct state control to increase arms output. To resurrect it after Munich would have been a clear public statement that the government was committed whole-heartedly to rearmament. Behind the scenes an influential Civil Service group, the 'Principal Supply Officers Committee with its Supply Board and rabbit-warren of sub-committees', had been working for years to plan a switch from civilian to military production.[2] Progress had been made, but now its bureaucratic leading light judged that it needed to move from a purely advisory role to one where it had executive powers, but the political decision was adamantly against. Once again, the nub of the question was that Chamberlain imagined that he had obtained lasting peace, and that it was foolish to see Munich as a lesson that Britain needed to rearm more vigorously. He said, 'A lot of people seem to me to be losing their heads and talking as though Munich had made war more instead of less imminent.'³ He feared unspecified 'friction' that a Ministry of Supply would create and, with blind optimism, foresaw that the need for one might actually diminish.

One of the key features of Chamberlain's credo of appeasement was that traditional, conservative economic management was a vital part of the country's military resources. To him a sound economy was the fourth arm of defence. He was on less sure ground in the belief that Britain's ability to deter the dictators depended on maintaining this policy. Like so much else that he held dear, Hitler and Mussolini simply paid no attention to it whatever. Chamberlain shied away from the realities of a full-scale war against a major industrial power, but he was far from ignorant of them. His miserable experience as Director of Manpower during the First World War had introduced him brutally to the demands of a command economy and the unpleasant compromises that were required to retain some shreds of democratic control when one was needed. Britain's economy was stretched to the limit by the First World War, and lurking behind Chamberlain's fear of war lay the foreboding that it would be broken by a Second.

Churchill strongly supported the creation of a Ministry of Supply. He himself had been one of the ministers of munitions in the First World War. It marked one of the high points of his first wartime career and of his partnership with Lloyd George, who had braved the hostility of the established Conservative Party to bring Churchill back into government in this job after a year and a half on the back benches and in the trenches following the Gallipoli fiasco. Becoming Minister for Munitions would have provided Churchill with a platform to drive his campaign for serious rearmament, just as he had vainly hoped that Stanley Baldwin would make him Minister for Defence Coordination in 1935. As early as 1936, Churchill had campaigned repeatedly to create a Ministry of Supply to drive forward rearmament in the face of what he saw as lethargy and complacency. When the opposition Liberals tabled a motion proposing one in November 1938 it was almost sure of some support from Churchill. The question was: how far would he go? When he had last spoken in favour of a Ministry of Supply in May 1938, he had displayed his inclination to invent or misremember historical parallels to support his case. He claimed that the hermit St Anthony had been castigated by the early fathers of the Church for refusing to do something that was right when the devil told him to do it.[4] Six months later he returned to the theme: 'I have pleaded when it was already late; and perhaps my Right Hon. Friend may remember I have even adjured him not to be deterred from doing right because it was impressed on him by the devil.'

But Churchill knew what his reputation was in the government and that there was little hope that Chamberlain would listen to him. Sir Thomas Inskip, Minister of Defence Coordination, argued against the imposition of controls and the resulting loss of liberty, and Chamberlain blandly asserted that there were no problems to solve anyway.[5]

The unstated, but more potent, reason for opposing a Ministry of Supply was that it might compromise appeasement. The Air Secretary, Sir Kingsley Wood, admitted privately, 'We can do little without a Ministry of Supply, but to appoint such a Minister would arouse the anger of Germany.'[6] The cause was a lost one but for the first time since the India Act debates, Churchill actually voted against the government. The only two Tory rebels who joined him were Harold Macmillan, the most awkward of the awkward squad, and Brendan Bracken, one of Churchill's most faithful disciples. Two years before, Churchill had restrained himself to display sufficient loyalty to the government so as not to spoil his chances of being asked back into government, but after Munich he was condemned to open opposition.

The question of a Ministry of Supply had been the subject of intense debate within the government. Two successive Cabinet meetings in October 1938 looked at the question: first in its pure form with powers of compulsion, and then in a severely diluted form with merely voluntary powers. None of the ministers gave serious support to either variant and Chamberlain could consign the question to oblivion and move on to other matters.

The combination of the crushing vote against a Ministry of Supply and Chamberlain's emphatic rejection of the idea in the House of Commons on 17 November might have seemed to have hammered the final nail into its coffin, but the idea did not go away for long. By the beginning of 1939 it once again returned to the agenda. The prime mover here was Inskip, who performed a dramatic volte-face from his previous position. At the meeting to discuss a Ministry of Supply with compulsory powers, he had spoken firmly against the proposal. In a paper dated 18 January 1939 he had changed his tune almost entirely, arguing that everything, bar the formal creation of a Ministry of Supply, should be undertaken immediately. Worse, he gave a clear signal that he expected war to come before too long: 'Public opinion will compel us to set up a Ministry of Supply in the full sense in emergency. We must, therefore, make all preparations for it in peacetime which the time now at our disposal permits.'[7]

This was not just a reversal of what he had advised recently, it was a denial of practically his entire *raison d'être* as Minister of Defence Coordination. Inskip had been given the job in 1936 by Baldwin as almost explicitly an anti-Churchill with the modest task of ruling on priorities amongst the service ministers and not acting as the advocate of measures to push the preparations for war on any faster. He was now as good as reciting a shibboleth of Churchill's that was anathema to Chamberlain and the Cabinet as a body. There is no evidence as to why Inskip should have changed his view so radically. For some weeks rumours had swirled that he could usefully be replaced as Minister of Defence Coordination, rumours which accurately named the man who was supposed to take over.[8] He had also been one of the targets of a revolt by junior ministers led by Robert Hudson, supposedly frustrated at the anaemic policy of the government. Inskip may just have decided to go down fighting.

Even before Inskip's fateful paper was fully completed Chamberlain had wind of its contents. Chamberlain called him in and invited him to resign on the vague grounds that '[y]our position in the H. of C. + in the country + in the press had gone back lately'.[9] Chamberlain practically admitted that the Hudson revolt had played a part because he tried to console Inskip with the claim that his departure would not provoke the same exultation as sacking Hore-Belisha would have inspired, the War Secretary being the prime target of Hudson's manoeuvre.

Inskip remained in office for another fortnight because Admiral Lord Chatfield, who was to take over from him, was still in India. He used the time to good effect. At a meeting of the Committee of Imperial Defence to discuss his paper on 26 January he doubled up on his heresy by claiming that things had got worse since October. This was tantamount to the ultimate sin of questioning the permanency of Chamberlain's achievement at Munich.

> There was ... present, I think, the feeling that the situation has so far changed for the worse since October that the decision then made [not to contemplate a Ministry of Supply] does not hold good now. There was also the feeling that, if we are anyhow to envisage a Ministry of Supply in war, its establishment in war conditions would be so difficult an operation as to make it most advisable that the outbreak of war should find it already established and running as a unit of administration.[10]

With one minister prepared to rebel against Chamberlain others crept out of the woodwork. Both Lord Halifax and Hore-Belisha backed Inskip and the committee instructed him to set out their feelings in writing to the Cabinet.[11]

The rebellion was nipped in the bud. Two days after the Committee of Imperial Defence meeting, *The Times* was running a story that Inskip was to be moved from his position. His actual dismissal came the same day. Afterwards he was guarded as to why he had been sacked, but did write that Sir Horace Wilson, David Margesson, the chief whip, and Hudson 'all had a part in it'.[12]

# CHAPTER TWENTY-TWO

# THE MOUNTEBANK

*We heard tonight that that mountebank Montague [sic] Norman is off to Berlin … he mentioned it to the PM and Nevile Henderson, both of whom thought it a good thing. Such a visit can only do harm – by encouraging the pro-German proclivities of the City, by making American and foreign opinion think we are doing another deal with Germany behind their backs – and another example of the PM's pro-Nazi tendencies – and finally in Germany itself where it will be regarded as proof of our anxiety to run after Hitler.*
– OLIVER HARVEY DIARIES

With the Paris jaunt behind them Chamberlain and Wilson could turn to the serious question of resuming friendly dialogue with Germany. The first seed of a new potential approach had been sown before the crisis had even reached its height. As well as unconsciously mapping out the 'peace for our time' declaration when he called at Downing Street, Lord Weir had looked forward to the sunlit uplands beyond and Wilson was equally keen to convince Chamberlain that Weir was onto something worthwhile. The flattery with which Wilson had watered Chamberlain's penchant for personal diplomacy served just as well to bed in the new line of approach.

Assuming that the present difficult corner is turned, we ought to take advantage of the changing mood in Germany and of the indications of questioning the regime by jumping in and proposing a new line, namely economic development through the use in Germany and the neighbouring countries of spending power which otherwise is being directed to the increase of armaments.[1]

The difficult corner had been turned and the spontaneous cheers of the German crowds in Munich provided a reason to believe that the mood had indeed changed – at least to those who were already inclined to believe this.

The key figure in the next phase of attempted appeasement was a long-standing ally of Wilson, Montagu Norman, governor of the Bank of England and one of the dominant figures of inter-war Britain. Rather like Sir Warren Fisher at the top of the Civil Service, and Sir Maurice Hankey at the Cabinet Secretariat, Norman had reached his position in the years immediately around the First World War – 1920 in his case – and retained it for twenty years and more. Wilson and Norman had worked closely together on industrial affairs ever since Wilson's time working for Jimmy Thomas, in the Labour government of 1929–31.[2] Norman was an arch-conservative in economic matters and resolutely approached any Keynesian notion of reflating the economy to counter the Great Slump exactly in line with Chamberlain's views. He was unusually active in influencing industrial restructuring, which brought him into long-standing and fruitful contact with Wilson in his days as chief industrial adviser and beyond; Charles Bruce-Gardner, whom Wilson parachuted into the aircraft industry as Downing Street's troubleshooter, came from Norman's stable of trusted men. In 1934 Norman had praised Hitler as a bulwark of civilisation in Germany and had a distinct prejudice against Jews.[3] He cultivated an eccentric style, sporting a trimmed goatee beard and a long black cloak and travelling under aliases.

Norman had strong links to Germany through Hjalmar Horace Greely Schacht, president of the German central bank, the Reichsbank. Schacht and Norman were friends and collaborators of long standing. Schacht had already tried his hand at broader questions of diplomacy between Britain and Germany with his scheme for a colonial settlement in early 1937. Norman and Schacht were the driving forces behind the creation of the Bank for International Settlements (BIS), the bank for central banks, and met regularly at its board meetings in Basel. Schacht had risen to the presidency of the Reichsbank at a quite young age in the aftermath of the First World War, but in 1934 he had become minister of economics in the Nazi government, even though he was not a Nazi Party member. He was, though, an economic nationalist. He was not an outright financial conservative like Norman but progressively fell out with the Nazi economic policy of autarky as expressed in Goering's armaments-focused Four Year Plan. Goering was the true force in German economic policy and Schacht resigned as minister in early 1937 to be replaced by Walter Funk, up until then the chief press spokesman and an utter cypher. In 1938 Schacht was still at the Reichsbank, the last senior person in the German leadership who had any claim to moderation or balance.

By the end of November the time was ripe, and Norman came to see Wilson at Downing Street to discuss arrangements for Schacht to open talks with Chamberlain.[4] The plan was treated with great caution and Norman ensured that a letter he sent to Chamberlain via Wilson about the idea was returned to him. For all this caution the story did leak that Schacht was on his way to London and Chamberlain gave a briefing to the full Cabinet.[5] Chamberlain's ostensible explanation for Schacht's visit to London was that he was coming to discuss schemes to finance the emigration of Jews from Germany and the expatriation of their property in the face of new Nazi anti-Semitic legislation.[6] It is an open question as to whether any of the ministers were taken in by the suggestion that some new-found concern for the welfare of Jewish refugees on Chamberlain's part inspired the slew of high-level meetings announced for Schacht in London. Chamberlain's insistence on secrecy was another warning sign that he had other fish to fry with the German central banker. He did cover himself to undertake the true business of Schacht's visit with a vague reference to the possibility of 'obtain[ing] some useful information as to Germany's economic position which was giving her cause for great anxiety' and the desirability of 'do[ing] all we could to encourage the Moderates'. The Foreign Office was fed a story that Schacht was bringing proposals from the German side.[7]

Schacht travelled to London together with Norman direct from a BIS meeting and stayed together with him for the entire visit. They went to Downing Street three times, once to see Wilson on his own and the other times to see Chamberlain.[8] The conversations with Chamberlain did not produce any result immediately in terms of a wider agreement on economics or anything else and Alec Cadogan was left with the impression that Schacht had poured cold water on the scheme, and 'told him [Chamberlain] straight there was no "appeasement" with Hitler'.[9] All that has survived of Chamberlain's record of the conversation is the conclusion that '[t]his [?] would maintain information of both sides and keep open personal contracts which might be useful'.[10] Schacht knew the dynamics of Nazi politics perfectly well and did not share the Auswärtiges Amt's preoccupation with keeping British hopes warm, so he could be considerably more frank. He was also aware how shaky his own position was in the German hierarchy. Schacht fed a useful titbit to one of his other contacts by disclosing how vain Funk was and how easy it would be to play on this by inviting him to London. When Frank Ashton-Gwatkin, the head of the Foreign Office's economics section and an enthusiastic appeaser, raised the idea of following on from the Munich agreement, Schacht treated him to a scathing and direct answer that it was a delusion to imagine any such thing was a possibility given Hitler's contempt for the old notion of international agreements.[11] Moreover he pooh-poohed British notions of supposed extremists advising Hitler against collaboration with Britain; all that mattered was Hitler himself. 'There are four great men in Germany today. They are Hitler and Hitler and Hitler and Hitler. No-one has any influence on him.' The door was left open a crack with the ambiguous claim that 'there can always be cooperation between us'.

Cadogan was wrong to think that the conversation between Chamberlain and Schacht had drawn a line under the initiative. Without consulting anyone at the Foreign Office, Norman prepared to repay Schacht's visit to London with one of his own to Berlin on a mission for Chamberlain and Wilson. The christening of Schacht's grandson, to whom Norman was godfather, in the first week of January provided a suitable pretext. The story leaked in the British press and few took seriously the claim – 'stoutly maintained' as even *The Times* wrote, dripping with sarcasm – that this was an entirely private affair. The following day

*The Times* reported, with all the hallmarks of an off-the-record briefing by George Steward at Downing Street, that there was 'good reason to believe that he may take the opportunity to discuss whilst in Germany matters of economic and political importance concerning German relations with Europe' and spoke of a proposed delegation of British industrialists to Germany. The Foreign Office had already been tipped off in Germany and reacted furiously:

> We heard tonight that that mountebank Montague [*sic*] Norman is off to Berlin ... he mentioned it to the PM and Nevile Henderson, both of whom thought it a good thing. Such a visit can only do harm – by encouraging the pro-German proclivities of the City, by making American and foreign opinion think we are doing another deal with Germany behind their backs – and another example of the PM's pro-Nazi tendencies – and finally in Germany itself where it will be regarded as proof of our anxiety to run after Hitler.[12]

Cadogan took action to hobble the attempt at backstairs appeasement and got Lord Halifax to authorise a letter to Norman, pointing out that Norman had not even mentioned the visit to Halifax and 'warning him to engage in no serious negotiations!'[13]

Norman was so infuriated in his turn by the letter that he stormed over to the Foreign Office to confront Cadogan. He argued that his visit had been agreed long before with the Prime Minister, the Chancellor of the Exchequer, Henderson and Wilson.[14] Cadogan was convinced that Norman's journey to Berlin was 'a stunt of No. 10' and stood his ground, pointing out that the press reports in themselves were grounds for concern. Norman calmed down but they parted on an acrimonious note:

> Cadogan: Well, I hope you will let us know of any results.
> Norman: There won't be any results!
> Cadogan: *Tant mieux.*[*15]

---

\* French, 'So much the better'.

Halifax followed up the interdict on Norman with another smaller move to clip the wings of the economic appeasers. Ashton-Gwatkin, the champion of *Mitteleuropa*, economically dominated by Germany, and Lord Runciman's pro-Sudeten official, was due to visit Germany in his regular capacity as head of the Foreign Office Economics Department. At the last moment Halifax ruled against this, albeit not permanently.[16] Norman was frustrated that even this relic of his scheme for economic appeasement was being blocked. He recognised that there were dissensions within the Foreign Office and he blamed the influence of Sir Robert Vansittart for frustrating it.

The whole episode was another waymark in the degeneration of relations between Downing Street and the Foreign Office into near-total dysfunction. It shows how Henderson was now serving two competing masters and reserving his full loyalty for only one. Norman had claimed that he had arranged to see no one but Schacht and, if this were true, the meeting was doomed before it began. Schacht was finally dismissed from the Reichsbank two and a half weeks later, ostensibly for opposing the latest splurge of borrowings. Two of his senior officials were purged at the same time. Schacht was again replaced by Walter Funk, who combined the presidency of the Reichsbank with his job as economics minister, as Schacht had done himself in his glory days. The moderates whom Chamberlain had fondly imagined he could cultivate had been practically eliminated.

Even after Schacht's removal Downing Street kept up its hopes for economic appeasement. Chamberlain happily believed an informal comment from Herbert von Dirksen, the German ambassador, that Hitler was worried by Germany's economic position and keen to improve exports.[17] In a mirror image of the dread with which Hitler's speech to the Nuremberg *Parteitag* had been awaited for what it would say about Germany's possibly violent intentions towards Czechoslovakia, Hitler's speech to the Reichstag, marking the sixth anniversary of his rise to power on 30 January 1933, was awaited hopefully for any positive signs. Cadogan spotted the phenomenon and recognised its dangers:

> Much too much attention paid to these periodical performances and we are too much 'agog' ... went over to the PM at 10. I *hope* he isn't

too relieved at the speech and won't think now that everything is the best in the best of all possible worlds. I don't *think* so.[18]

Cadogan was again quite wrong; Chamberlain took Hitler's speech as evidence that 'at last we are getting on top of the dictators'.[19] One of the keys was that 'the economic situation in Germany is bad and everyone knows it so Hitler has had to acknowledge it publicly'. To take advantage of this it had been 'quietly arranged' for Oliver Stanley, the President of the Board of Trade and thus Funk's ministerial opposite number, to visit Berlin.[20] The decision to send Stanley to Germany had been inspired by Chamberlain's discussion with Schacht in December. Schacht's hint to Ashton-Gwatkin showed that Funk's vanity made him a soft target. Even after Cadogan had headed him off from political talks in Berlin, Norman had been working with Wilson to prepare the mission.[21] Chamberlain fancied that Hitler and Ribbentrop were so worried about the economic position that they would welcome British assistance to improve it. Chamberlain's optimism soared to white heat after Hitler supposedly tweaked a speech by the Duke of Coburg to the Deutsche-Englische Gesellschaft (the German equivalent of the Anglo-German Fellowship) to make it more friendly.

To prepare for the Stanley mission the interdict that Halifax had imposed on Ashton-Gwatkin travelling to Germany in the wake of Norman's abortive political talks was lifted. As Ashton-Gwatkin was head of the Foreign Office economics section and a frequent visitor to Germany, with a broad range of contacts in banking and industry as well as the German government, this was an unexceptional and quite natural task. He was certainly a welcome visitor and he was granted appointments with both Ribbentrop and Goering, which might have rung alarm bells with anyone at the Foreign Office concerned that he might have a broader political agenda than serving as a sherpa for Stanley's visit. They would have been prescient if they had. After some initial fencing Ashton-Gwatkin admitted to Ribbentrop that he 'had concrete ideas but that these extended beyond the limits of economy into the sphere of politics'.[22] An agreement on trade would be a powerful register of confidence between the two countries that might influence considerations of rearmament. It was only at the end of the conversation that Ashton-Gwatkin proposed one very concrete step that Ribbentrop might take, which puts it beyond doubt that he was travelling as Wilson's emissary with a far wider political remit than had been disclosed to his masters at the Foreign Office: Ribbentrop should invite Wilson to Berlin. Once again Wilson could act as Chamberlain's personal emissary to the Führer. Unsurprisingly, Ashton-Gwatkin did not mention this idea in his report to the Foreign Office on his visit.[23] Ribbentrop declined, pleading the need for clearer relations between Britain and Germany. By the time Wilson would have had the opportunity to digest this latest rebuff of a hand of friendship from Downing Street, the government had been confronted with rather more dramatic evidence of true German intentions.

# CHAPTER TWENTY-THREE

# COMBATING HOARE'S
# HERESIES

*I greatly hope that I can rely on your (or H.J.'s) help
in combating S.H.'s heresies if necessary.*
– Sir Percival Waterfield to Sir Warren Fisher

The world of propaganda was too tempting a playground, rich in career opportunity and political profile, for it to remain the exclusive preserve of Wilson's appeasement-minded caution for ever. The void that Wilson had created by eliminating all but the most low-key players was bound to suck in other, new pretenders to the propaganda crown. Sir Stephen Tallents had been easy meat for Wilson and his Civil Service cohorts, but the next figure to emerge as an enthusiast for serious propaganda activities presented a far stiffer set of challenges.

Sir Samuel Hoare, then the Home Secretary, was one of Chamberlain's closest political allies and a member of the unofficial Inner Cabinet that made up the heart of his government. As a British operative in Rome during the First World War, he had been involved in unavowable clandestine propaganda operations, bribing Mussolini to swing his newspapers in favour of Italian participation in the war on the side of the Allies. At the end of February 1939 Hoare launched his campaign to take control of British propaganda policy, offering his 'services' and demanding that it be taken out of Civil Service control and handed to the politicians.[1] Behind the scenes he and his close ally the press baron Lord Beaverbrook discreetly sounded out Sir John Reith with the unspoken, but implicit, offer of a major part in a reordered propaganda world under their control.[2]

Hoare was a loyal supporter of appeasement and there was no immediate risk that he would use propaganda policy in ways that would provoke the dictators, but propaganda had become an area that Wilson had ear-marked for his own attention and control. It was a given in Whitehall that 'he is already de facto a member of any body dealing with propaganda'.[3] He was not going to give up this power willingly. And certainly not to Hoare, one of the senior ministers whose behaviour in the aftermath of Munich had revolted him, with an opportunist ambition to succeed Chamberlain. Hoare's links to Beaverbrook were widely known and Beaverbrook was widely distrusted throughout Whitehall. He had vigorously supported appeasement through his calls for British isolationism, but it took more than this to get into the good books of Chamberlain and Wilson. Beaverbrook's greatest sin was that he was also a close ally of Churchill, and their scandalous partnership in support of Edward VIII during the abdication crisis had been viewed as tantamount to treason.

Wilson sat down with Chamberlain to work out how to stymie Hoare's drive into the world of propaganda. Their immediate conclusion was that Hoare should be subjected to an even stricter restriction on his propaganda mandate than his political and bureaucratic predecessors. He should only 'act as Minister designate, for the time being' with the appointment of someone else as minister designate proper as a next step.[4] This point was hammered home a couple of days later when Hoare met a group of top-level civil servants, which naturally included Wilson and Sir Warren Fisher, to begin to get to grips with the Ministry of Information (MoI). Their starting point for the meeting was that the 'prime minister does not propose at the moment to designate a prospective Minister of Information, but he has asked the Home Secretary to act as though he were Minister Designate and take responsibility for the peacetime preparations for a Ministry of Information'.[5] Hoare was a make-believe minister, who could serve as a fall guy if anything went too wrong publicly. The meeting proceeded in a blizzard of patronisation and irrelevance of the kind that allows the Civil Service to neuter even the most senior minister. Hoare was invited to familiarise himself with the excellent and extensive work that had already been done to prepare for the MoI. One of the civil servants came up with the marvellously baffling suggestion that the Ministry of Health should be given responsibility for some parts of information policy.

Under other circumstances this might have marked the end of Hoare's grab for propaganda power, but the occupation of the remainder of Czechoslovakia barely a week after his unpromising start with the top tier of the Civil Service undermined the argument that everything necessary was being done on the topic already. Hoare returned to the charge and showed that Wilson was not the only one who knew how to work the Whitehall machine. He was attending another, rather more senior, sub-committee of the Committee of Imperial Defence, the Strategic Appreciation Sub-committee, of which Wilson was not a member, and railroaded it into giving him a blank cheque in the form of the authority to establish a committee of ministers, in which he would be the senior minister, to examine propaganda in enemy countries.[6] Even more startlingly, the meeting formally concluded 'that it was of the highest importance to take immediate propaganda action against Germany'. This was, of course, a major revolt against the policy of low-key passivity championed by Wilson. Hoare had the bit between his teeth and his tame committee quickly held two meetings close together, in one of which it committed the ultimate heresy of declaring itself to be 'the controlling body for all propaganda questions' in a direct challenge to Wilson's *de facto* domination.[7] Hoare's committee even revived Tallents's plan for a massive leaflet drop on Germany the moment war began. This, though, represented the high-water mark of Hoare's propaganda coup attempt. He faced a tough and determined opponent and began to make mistakes himself.

Hoare's scheme to seize control of propaganda began to run into the sand when he took on Downing Street in the kind of attritional battle that played to the strengths in Wilson's position. His mistake was to try to impose his own ideas of who should and should not be part of the future MoI. He succeeded in cancelling the appointment to the ministry of Lord Macmillan, a Scottish judge with small experience of propaganda but great ambitions, who stood high in the favour of Chamberlain and Wilson. Macmillan had been Wilson's preferred candidate to lead the British mission to Czechoslovakia in the summer of 1938. Hoare then badly over-reached himself by attempting to block Sir Joseph Ball from the ministry.[8] Here he was tartly overruled; whatever justification Hoare had dreamed up to object to Ball's appointment, most likely the fact that he was a Conservative Party propagandist, would count for little in wartime when his 'suitability' for the job would count for more.[9] Probably Hoare's worst blunder was attempting to have Sir Christopher Bullock appointed as deputy director general designate. Bullock had been forced to resign as a civil servant by Fisher in an ethics scandal three years before. Even though Fisher was fading from the scene by then, he enthusiastically backed Wilson's refusal to accept someone who had signally failed to behave like 'an officer and a gentleman'.[10] To round off the damage, Hoare brought a cuckoo into his nest by insisting on the services for the MoI of Sir Percival Waterfield, who promptly volunteered his services to Fisher to fight any inclination on Hoare's part to succumb to the influence of Lord Beaverbrook on such a sensitive topic as propaganda: 'I am very apprehensive of the new Minister's ideas, which seem to me largely misconceived. (I gather he has been talking to Beaverbrook) ... I greatly hope that I can rely on your (or H.J.'s) help in combating S.H.'s heresies if necessary.'[11]

The post-Prague mood of seriousness exposed one part of Wilson's scheme to keep the MoI at barely tick-over level as wildly anomalous. Wilson had chosen an individual to replace Tallents as director general designate who showed the lengths to which Wilson would go to avoid any risk of activity or provocation. The candidate had to pass the Whitehall test for being a 'safe pair of hands', a conservative and cautious person who would not rock the boat in any way, above all who would not show any inclination to repeat Tallents's excessively proactive approach to the task. Sir Ernest Fass was a trained lawyer and his main job was suitably prudent and low-key. He was the Public Trustee, the government official who dealt with cases where the state took control of the affairs of people or organisations under strictly regulated conditions, such as certified lunatics or the estates of people who had died without leaving a will. To make doubly certain that the appointment was essentially token, Fass was subjected to the same rule devised for the minister designate: that the role would be limited to peacetime. Fass was utterly ignorant of propaganda, information policy or the background to the MoI. The sum total of his work on the ministry was some tentative and unavailing attempts to find out what Sir Campbell Stuart was up to, and a trivial and pointless dispute over demarcation with the Secret Service. Now it was Wilson who had over-reached himself, by coming up with such a ludicrously unsuitable individual. When the government got wind that his appointment was about to appear in the press, Fass was dismissed the day before the stories appeared.[12] There were limits to the public embarrassment that could be accepted in the name of appeasement. Fass's successor was only a small improvement. Lord Perth, formerly Sir Eric Drummond, had been a notable supporter of appeasement as ambassador to Rome. He had actively opposed any propaganda against Mussolini. His chief interest in the job was its pay and obtaining an exception to government rules to allow him to serve as a director of the family bank. He celebrated his appointment by taking a month's leave.

As Hoare floundered around on questions of personnel and Prague faded from attention, the time fell ripe for Wilson to stage a counter-attack. Hoare's private committee had opened a vulnerable flank by actually proposing a concrete measure. The Civil Service is always adept at identifying the weak spot in a scheme that allows it to be torn apart. The plan to drop leaflets on Germany had never appealed to Wilson – in fact it entirely failed to live up to the hopes of its promoters when it was implemented in the early weeks of the Second World War – and he set to work. He began by looking at the financial cost of printing leaflets in peacetime before they were needed as a potential objection, but spotted quickly that the sums involved were far too trivial to carry weight. He struck a far better source of ammunition on a key question of principle. Hoare's committee was welcome to play around with leaflets as a contingency scheme, but when it came to whether to put the scheme into effect, the decision would have to be taken at the top level. The mere existence of a scheme 'does not prejudge the question whether at the time there should in fact be this distribution. That decision can and ought to be taken by the Government of the day only in the light of the then circumstances.'[13] Wilson was not quite satisfied with the implication that this could all be so far in the future that the government might have changed and added another layer of hypothesis to ram home that this was all very theoretical and divorced from day-to-day reality. The matter would only become a live topic 'if and when hostilities break out, let us say, with Germany'.[14] Less than three months before war broke, Downing Street's faith in 'peace for our time' was still strong enough to relegate Germany to one of a number of hypothetical opponents.

When Britain declared war, it was possible to consign Hoare's efforts to the dustbin of history. There was never any question of bending Downing Street's strict peacetime-only restriction on appointments in Hoare's favour. The true balance of power between the minister and the civil servant was obvious in the MoI's personnel. The first actual minister appointed to lead the MoI was none other than Lord Macmillan, in what would have been taken as a slap in the face for Hoare, who had excluded Macmillan from a more minor job in his brief moment of influence. Wilson had firmly opposed the appointment of 'some great panjandrum' at the MoI.[15] Wilson personally informed Macmillan of his promotion.[16] Lacking political, administrative or excessive propaganda experience, he was never going to jump the MoI off the comfortable rails laid down by Wilson over the preceding year. Ball was put in charge of the ministry's film division, echoing his work for the Conservative Party and doubtless serving as Downing Street's eyes and ears inside the organisation.

The MoI as it came into being in the first days of the war was Wilson's creation. It had been shaped to meet a series of essentially negative targets. The constant changes of leadership, the arbitrary restrictions on the men in place and their unfamiliarity with the topic meant that Wilson had achieved his goal of doing as little as humanly possible about propaganda. Nothing had been done to provoke the dictators. Stuart's 'private command' in foreign propaganda lurked in the undergrowth. Vast practical questions of organisation and wartime news management had been left unresolved, but these had never figured in Wilson's priorities.

# CHAPTER TWENTY-FOUR

# THE END OF THE RAINBOW

*All the Press carries a ridiculous 'Rainbow story' ... Much too optimistic. Traced it to interview by PM yesterday evening to Lobby correspondents. He really shouldn't do this – or at least he should consult H. before.*

– Sir Alexander Cadogan diaries

In the first months of 1939 Chamberlain was living in a bubble of optimism filled by his belief that economic difficulties were forcing Hitler into a compliant mood. He was entirely correct in seeing that breakneck rearmament was straining the German economy badly, but entirely incorrect in believing that this would make Hitler more co-operative. He could also feed off the reputation he had acquired after Munich and dream of using it in troubled regions elsewhere. When a representative of the local Arabs in Palestine offered him some craven flattery, 'Your excellence has everywhere acquired the title The Father of Peace & we look to you to give us peace', Chamberlain took this as grounds for optimism that his personal status might help redeem the catastrophe of British policy there.[1] Chamberlain was confident that he was on entirely the right track and that his critics were in the wrong. It was they who threatened peace and not the Fascist dictators. He indirectly accused Churchill of warmongering and pointedly claimed that he was 'Bogy No. 1 in some parts of Europe'.[2]

Wilson was less exultant than his master, but he too believed that everything was well on course for appeasement to succeed. Chamberlain's obstinacy was a positive virtue and a cult of the personality around him was positively beneficial. Resisting alternatives to their policy was the key, at a time when we [are] steadily enhancing our position – at home & abroad by quietly getting on with the job and by refusing to be driven off course by puffs whether from within or from without. My impression is that the consistency & persistency of the PM's policy are telling more & more. By rigidly refusing to indulge in verbal fireworks he is impressing the people that really matter…

I expect you will agree that the more we build up Chamberlain the greater is the contribution we can make to the sense of firmness which must develop a bit if we are to see it grow into a sense of security in Europe.[3]

Chamberlain's optimism boiled over as the prospects for broader harmony in Europe were given another boost when the Spanish Civil War drew to a close. Following the speedy collapse of Republican resistance in Catalonia at the end of February, Britain and France had recognised Franco's regime officially and it was only a matter of a few weeks before the remainder of the Republic crumbled too. The issue which had bedevilled British and French relations with Italy for three years was about to vanish. This was enough for Chamberlain to see marvellous visions of an appeased and peaceful Europe, which he shared with one of his favourite audiences, the docile lobby correspondents of the British newspapers, who could be relied upon to relay faithfully and uncritically the Prime Minister's insights.[4] Chamberlain spelled out in detail his glorious vision on 9 March. By an amazing leap of imagination and faith he prophesied that the removal of the Spanish complication would help rapidly disperse Italy's newly invented claims against France around the Mediterranean and on the Red Sea. He hinted at the imminent success that awaited the policy of economic appeasement. The poor state of Germany's economy made the regime there crave the kind of industrial cooperation that Oliver Stanley was going to discuss in Berlin. Hostile articles in the German press, inspired by Goebbels, could safely be ignored as they did not represent the true state of affairs. With tension dissipating throughout Europe, talks on disarmament were just around the corner. This was not just a triumphal declaration to the British people that appeasement had almost succeeded, it flagged to Berlin and Rome that the leaders there had a friend in London who trusted them to deliver their part of his vision.

None of this had been discussed with the Foreign Office beforehand. If anything, it had been withheld. Alec Cadogan had been at Downing Street talking to Wilson whilst the briefing was actually taking place but had not even been told that it was happening, still less what it contained.[5] Downing Street had achieved the appeasement of Europe on its own despite the hindrance of the Foreign Office and it was right that credit should be given accordingly. The first that Halifax or Cadogan heard of what the Prime Minister had been telling the lobby was when the newspapers ran this 'rainbow story' in similar terms the following morning. Its origin was unmistakable, and the shock was enough to send Halifax round to Downing Street to protest personally to Chamberlain, but the Prime Minister had already left for Chequers.[6] Halifax sat down to write possibly the most hostile letter to the Prime Minister in his time as Foreign Secretary. Beginning with a sarcastic congratulation on Chamberlain's wisdom in having gone to the country already, he explained the disastrous consequences that his briefing was likely to have: the Germans would think that Britain needed to slow rearmament more than they did and the French would think that Britain was about to stab them in the back over the Italian claims.

Chamberlain delivered a gushing but brief apology to Halifax with an insincere promise to harmonise statements on foreign affairs in future but in reality, he was utterly unrepentant. He made no attempt to withdraw or mitigate his comments.[7] His only serious regret was that the journalists had not hidden their source better. It was his usual reaction to blame someone else for the problem. The press had been 'pretty clumsy' in repeating what he said verbatim.[8] But for this the briefing would have been treated simply as background. Chamberlain entirely ignored Halifax's practical complaints about the briefing and reaffirmed his faith in why he had delivered it in the first place: '[N]o harm has been done & indeed it is a good thing that dictators should be made to feel our confidence.'[9]

The 'rainbow' briefing marked the nadir of Chamberlain's journey into a world of illusion. At some point it was inevitable that he would have to deal with the world as it existed and not as he dreamed it. Far worse punishment lay in store for Chamberlain for this moment of hubris than an ineffectual telling off from his placid Foreign Secretary, and it was to be meted out by the man whom he saw as his principal partner in achieving appeasement. Hitler had never for one moment abandoned his dream of destroying the Czechoslovakian state. The secret of his intentions was not especially well guarded in Berlin and a steady flow of warnings had been reaching London since the start of the year through secret and other channels that Hitler had more up his sleeve.[10] One very precise and well-sourced warning came from someone whom Downing Street would usually have trusted. Frank Ashton-Gwatkin returned from Berlin at the end of February with one very valuable piece of intelligence. He, like many others, had picked up gossip that Germany was planning another move in eastern Europe and had asked a German friend, who enjoyed access to Hitler, what might lie behind these rumours. The friend had recently spoken to Hitler and was certain that what was left of Czechoslovakia was the target for near-full integration into the German sphere of influence.[11] Ashton-Gwatkin duly reported this to London but there is no sign that this registered with anyone, still less that it affected what Downing Street expected Hitler to do. The perception in Downing Street of Hitler's intentions was set by its man in Berlin, who was quite immune to fears that Hitler was about to do anything unwise. Sir Nevile Henderson advised London against paying attention to 'wild stories of attacks in various directions'.[12] By the day after the 'rainbow' story appeared in the newspapers the flow of warnings had become a torrent with both MI5 and the Secret Intelligence Service coming up with their own versions.[13]

The immediate trigger for German action in Czechoslovakia had been provided by a movement amongst the Slovak minority to gain autonomy and free itself from the rule of the ethnic Czechs in Prague. It reached a crisis the very day the 'rainbow' story was published, when Czechoslovakia's new and inexperienced President dismissed the Slovak leaders and imposed martial law in the province. Just as Chancellor Kurt Schuschnigg's unexpectedly resolute move in calling a plebiscite in Austria had triggered the *Anschluß*, so Emil Hácha's move sparked the occupation of the ethnic Czech areas of the old Hapsburg provinces of Bohemia and Moravia by Germany under threat of devastating military action on 12 March. For the first time, the Third Reich swallowed an area with a non-German population and Hitler's claim that the Sudetenland had been his last territorial demand was exposed for the lie it always had been. In contrast to the Sudeten crisis, which had developed over months, the Slovak crisis put an end to Czechoslovakia in a matter of days. Britain was spared the long agony of deciding how to respond. As the Wehrmacht marched into the Czech capital, 'Prague' became a shorthand for this decisive piece of Nazi aggression, just as 'Munich' had become a shorthand for the process that had ended the Sudeten crisis the previous September.

Chamberlain was entirely unprepared; he received the news whilst he was away fishing with Ball.[14] The move came as a complete shock and total humiliation to him, a painful demonstration that the confidence he had had in Hitler's honesty had always been utterly misplaced. The shock was so bitter, even months afterwards, that he had difficulty facing up to the truth of his credulity in the face of Hitler's lies. Wilson did not want him reminded of it and tried to suppress an otherwise friendly journalist from referring to Chamberlain's having been 'duped' and made to look a fool.[15] Chamberlain had been deeply hurt but, to begin with at least, was unable to face the reality that his policy had been disastrously misconceived. By chance, there was a regular Cabinet meeting that day, which was naturally dominated by a discussion of what steps to take. Chamberlain began with a casuistical statement of what was to be the public stance of the British government. He asserted that the guarantee of Czechoslovakian independence, promised after the Munich agreement, had not become operative and that it could now be ignored, as the state it was supposed to protect had just ceased to exist. He trivialised the military occupation of Bohemia as 'symbolic', and proposed to make a brief and anodyne statement in a debate in the House of Commons merely 'regretting' the military occupation and cancelling Stanley's visit to Berlin.[16]

The meeting rejected the idea of recalling the British ambassador from Berlin, the traditional diplomatic way of signalling serious annoyance, but Halifax wanted a far more resolute public statement than Chamberlain proposed, something that 'would imply that Germany was now being led onto a dangerous path'. But Chamberlain fought off any attempt of the Cabinet to impose on him what he should say.[17] The exact wording was thrashed out in a discussion after the Cabinet meeting with Wilson and Cadogan. Inevitably Wilson's instincts prevailed. To Cadogan's disgust, Chamberlain chose to expand the draft he had read to the Cabinet and to say outright that his policy was not going to change because of Prague: 'He would go with his "policy" (? "appeasement"). Fatal!'[18] Chamberlain told the House that he would not be deflected from 'our' course.

It soon became clear that this extreme business-as-usual approach was no longer acceptable to Chamberlain's colleagues or to the public. Privately and predictably, Chamberlain blamed the opposition for his foray into the depths of denying reality because they called a debate 'before we knew all that had happened'.[19] He now knew that he would have to modify appeasement. The first move was to recall the British ambassador, albeit only briefly. The next step was to try to repair the damage done by his initial promise in the House of Commons. It had long been planned that he would speak to the Birmingham Conservatives on the Friday and he used the speech to distance himself from the statement he had made in the Commons on 15 March, with the feeble claim that he had not been in full possession of the facts. The rest of the speech was unfavourable to Hitler but hardly a ringing denunciation. The closest he came to direct criticism was to remind the audience of Hitler's promise that Sudeten had been his last territorial demand. Chamberlain even brought himself to mention how the Jews had been treated, breaking the taboo that Wilson had enunciated in the aftermath of *Kristallnacht*. Chamberlain did not tie himself to a major change in British diplomacy, but he conceded a hint of something afoot in a non-committal double negative that 'other [countries], too, knowing that we are not disinterested in what goes on in south-eastern Europe, will wish to have our counsel and advice'. It is a register of just how whole-heartedly Chamberlain had striven for conciliation with Hitler up until then, that even this passed muster as a reversal of policy. The speech was also the first step in restoring Chamberlain's self-esteem, as it provided him with the usual material for self-congratulation. 'The speech seems to have come through splendidly & I have had countless messages of approval.'[20]

This small change in the direction of British diplomacy did not involve any change in the way Chamberlain conducted it and the Foreign Office remained out in the cold. 'The FO were as usual pretty barren of suggestions but I have worked out a plan which a few Ministers have accepted today & which I shall put to the Cabinet tomorrow. It is pretty bold and startling...'[21] Prague had not dented Chamberlain's capacity for smugness and self-dramatisation. This plan for a declaration by four powers – Britain, France, Russia and Poland – that they would consult in the face of any further aggression showed all the weakness of something cooked up on the spur of moment without adequate discussion and intended chiefly for public consumption. It was announced before there was any serious discussion with the other countries supposedly involved. The scheme had never amounted to more than – in the words of a Foreign Office official – 'amateur collective security'.[22] It was finally torpedoed by – justifiable and justified – Polish suspicions of Russia. Chamberlain and Wilson were deprived of a public coup which would have helped restore Chamberlain's reputation. Wilson complained long after, 'It seemed quite unjust that having decided to revolutionize his attitude, he should be prevented from demonstrating its drive and its object.'[23]

The weeks after Prague saw a period of frantic diplomacy with alarms and excursions of all kinds. Germany seized Memel [now Klaipėda] from Lithuania and rumours abounded about further landgrabs in prospect. Most famous of these was a quite unfounded tale that Germany was just about to attack Romania; there were persistent stories of an imminent invasion of Poland. The final outcome was an unconditional British and French guarantee to Poland against German aggression, which was announced a fortnight after Prague. This was precisely the kind of binding commitment to Continental intervention that Chamberlain and Wilson had battled to escape the previous year. It was a necessary corrective to the extremes of appeasement, but to become fully effective as a deterrent Hitler would have to be convinced.

The guarantee to Poland remains one of the most vigorously debated parts of Chamberlain's diplomacy; it was the step that forced directly Britain's declaration of war on Germany.[24] When historian Martin Gilbert questioned Wilson on the move long afterwards, his explanation provided a vital but simple reason: 'It was then impossible, politically, not to give the guarantee.'[25] The statement also gives the key to understanding most of Chamberlain's post-Prague moves. He often appears as an entirely pragmatic figure, concerned solely to find and drive the right policy. In reality he could not count on unqualified support from his MPs, however large their majority in the House and however ruthlessly they were whipped. The raucous debate on bombing British ships in Spanish waters the previous summer had shown that there were limits to the tolerance of Conservative MPs. Like the Birmingham speech and other moves yet to come, the guarantee was imposed on a reluctant Prime Minister by ordinary political considerations.

Mistrust of Chamberlain was still – deservedly – widespread. When *The Times* ran a leader the day after the Polish guarantee that pointed out that it did not cover Poland's existing frontiers – 'The new obligation which this country yesterday assumed does not bind Great Britain to defend every inch of the present frontiers of Poland. The key word in the declaration is not integrity but "independence"' – many thought that it had been inspired by Downing Street so as to undermine the effect of the guarantee.[26] The wording had certainly been thrashed out in great detail between Geoffrey Dawson, the newspaper's editor, and the leader-writer concerned, who admitted in his journal, 'Possibly G.D. and I between us put too much stress on the limitations to the guarantee, & not enough on its implications.'[27] The words 'integrity' and 'independence' had certainly been proposed by the government. Chamberlain whole-heartedly endorsed *The Times'* qualifications and added one of his own which left the right to decide whether the guarantee became operative in his own hands: '[W]hat we are concerned with is not the boundaries of states but attacks on their independence. And it is we who will judge whether their independence is threatened or not.'[28]

Churchill instantly recognised the significance of the *Times* leader.

He was delighted by the guarantee as proof of firmness in the government, but appalled at any move to dilute it. In the House of Commons he pointed up the frightening similarity between this leader and the one which had foreshadowed the dismemberment of Czechoslovakia the previous September: 'There was a sinister passage in the *Times*' leading article on Saturday, similar to that which foreshadowed the ruin of Czechoslovakia, which sought to explain that there was no guarantee for the integrity of Poland, but only for its independence.'[29]

If Chamberlain had imagined that the new direction in British foreign policy would work to restrain the dictators, he was soon to be disabused by Mussolini. Frustrated that Hitler had launched Prague without consulting him, Mussolini repaid the compliment with a futile and unannounced invasion of Albania over the Easter weekend on 7 April. This was not quite as public a humiliation for Chamberlain as Prague, but once again British diplomacy was on the spot. Astoundingly, Chamberlain's immediate reaction was as submissive as his first reaction to Prague. He classed the move as a 'lapse' by Mussolini and did not want it to disturb relations with Italy. Obligingly, Churchill provided Chamberlain with further evidence that he was right to be passive. By then, all it took was for Churchill to push for something, and it was *ipso facto* dangerous. Chamberlain complained of the pressure for a recall of Parliament from 'Winston, who is the worst of the lot, telephoning almost every hour of the day ... I know there are a lot of reckless people who would plunge us into war at once but one must resist them...'[30] In the wake of Prague, Chamberlain had called on Mussolini to mediate and manifestly still hoped for something from this direction. Even Wilson was sufficiently shaken by this cavalier approach to point out to Chamberlain that the invasion of Albania had provoked public outrage, which made at least a token gesture necessary.[31] Wilson's advice was not strong enough and Chamberlain still resisted pressure from Halifax to issue guarantees against further Italian aggressions. This time Halifax was able to override the Prime Minister and Britain committed itself to protecting Greece and Romania on 13 April 1939.[32]

The combined humiliations of Prague and Albania were enough to dent even Chamberlain's self-confidence and for the first time he wavered. His annoyance and frustration were magnified by the domestic political pressure on him. The House of Commons debate on Albania inspired the petulant outbursts that it 'does not show that I have been wrong as my partisan critics declare' and 'it does enable my enemies to mock me publicly and weaken my authority in the country'.[33] He verged on self-pity: 'I confess to feeling very dispirited & very lonely.' He even called in the chief whip to discover whether his position in the party had been weakened. Chamberlain's spirits had fallen low enough for him to give some serious consideration to the idea of bringing Churchill into the government, even though Churchill had made a speech in the debate whose supportive words were, to Chamberlain's ear, offset by an 'acid undertone which brought many cheers from the Labour benches'.[34]

At this moment of the deepest doubt, he turned to Wilson for advice and summoned him to Chequers on Sunday 16 April. They walked through the Buckinghamshire woods, which were showing the first signs of spring, discussing ways in which the Prime Minister could show his new resolve to take on the dictators in a way that would convince the public without compromising his core strategy. The conversation ranged over Churchill, the possibility of introducing conscription and a notion that had occurred to Chamberlain as a way of satisfying enthusiasts for all-out economic control without establishing a full-scale Ministry of Supply: a halfway Ministry of Supply purely for the Army could be set up. They did not reach a conclusion and Wilson's advice can only be inferred from later events. After they had returned to the house to continue talking, Wilson was interrupted by a phone call informing him of an abortive initiative by President Roosevelt, which was to lead nowhere but briefly put everything else on hold. Within one week, the attenuated Ministry of Supply came about, as did conscription. Churchill, however, remained firmly outside the government. Chamberlain knew that Hitler and Mussolini would see it as a challenge if Churchill were brought in and this was a risk that Chamberlain did not want to run: '[T]he nearer we get to war the more his [Churchill's] chances improve and vice versa.'[35]

Wilson's visit to Chequers marked the low point for Chamberlain and, from then on, his spirits began to turn upwards. A full week went by without another diplomatic crisis. Best of all, unofficial contacts in Berlin fed stories to Chamberlain that offered the hope that Hitler might be starting to see the error of his ways, and might even be seeking a way to resume friendly contact. Whenever Chamberlain saw dregs in a glass, it was half full of the finest vintage to him. The hopeful stories came from two well-connected and pro-Nazi British aristocrats, who had gone to Berlin to join the celebrations of Hitler's fiftieth birthday. Lord Brocket was both highly placed in the Anglo-German Fellowship and a confidant of Chamberlain.[36] He bombarded Halifax with a stream of advice and comment on relations with Germany. The Duke of Buccleuch was personally close to Rudolf Hess and had been appointed as Lord Steward by George VI.[37] This was one of the most senior jobs in the royal household, carrying the task of liaison between the sovereign and the House of Lords. It had traditionally been held by a significant politician. After arriving in Berlin, Brocket and Buccleuch rather belatedly sought guidance from the British embassy on what to do should they be invited to Hitler's birthday party itself. Buccleuch was advised that attending the party would be taken as a sign that the Court was not harmonised with government policy, although the final decision was left to Buckingham Palace. The Palace clearly agreed with the embassy and Buccleuch departed for London, but not before he had accompanied Brocket on a number of his calls to German officials. The embassy left Brocket as a private citizen to decide for himself and he spent the best part of a week seeing everyone from the Führer downwards.[38] Everywhere he was told how positive it had been that the recall of the British ambassador had only been a brief one. Brocket insisted that he was there purely in a private capacity, but he did appear to be delivering messages on Chamberlain's behalf. He pestered most people he spoke to with the request that Hitler make some favourable reference to Chamberlain in his speech, which has the feel of a plea from Chamberlain himself. He told Hitler he hoped that he and Chamberlain might meet again. When Ernst von Weizsäcker, the head of the Auswärtiges Amt, asked Brocket whether it was too late for a rapprochement between Britain and Germany, Brocket said that

Chamberlain wanted friendship, but Prague and British public opinion made it difficult.

Chamberlain had learned at least something from his previous errors and was not entirely taken in, but his compulsive optimism had not died and he was ready to believe that '[p]erhaps Hitler has realised that he has now touched the limit and has decided to put the best face on it'.[39] Hitler saw the same in mirror image. In his eyes, the aristocrats had been sent to Berlin as the personal emissaries of Chamberlain, whatever the truth might have been. To him it meant that appeasement was back on. 'England would again like to find a bridge to us. Chamberlain has already put out his feelers.'[40]

Brocket brought back a concrete idea for how one such bridge might be built. He had seen Walther Hewel, the liaison between Hitler and Ribbentrop, who was known to be very close to Hitler. Hewel claimed that he wanted to counteract supposed British misunderstandings about Hitler and floated the idea to Brocket that 'a really influential Englishman who could speak German fluently could come and have a long talk to Hitler about Anglo-German relations'.[41] As well as the language barrier Hitler had not been impressed by the calibre of the British individuals whom he had met. Over the next few weeks this proposal acquired a life of its own and was taken up by Sir Joseph Ball, Herbert von Dirksen, the German ambassador in London, and Leo Geyr von Schweppenburg, a former German military attaché, now on Ribbentrop's staff, as well as by Wilson.[42] The main difficulty it faced was that neither side could come up with a compellingly good candidate; too few British spoke German. It became part of the litany of suggestions from the German side of ways to defuse the burgeoning crisis that was trotted out with ever-decreasing sincerity as war approached.

\*   \*   \*

January 1939 had brought another increase in Wilson's already heavy workload. After years of inactivity the Irish Republican Army (IRA) published a 'declaration of war' against Britain and launched a bombing campaign in mainland Britain under the grand title of the 'S Plan'.

The campaign lasted until March 1940, killed ten people and injured ninety-six or so in about 300 separate explosions. Five of the terrorists were convicted in December 1939, of whom two were hanged.

Wilson coordinated the British response to the attacks.[43] Little else is known even though there must have been a substantial effort by the security forces; the episode does not feature at all in the official history of MI5. Wilson had some oversight of MI5 and in June 1940 personally sacked Sir Vernon Kell, its first director general.[44]

# CHAPTER TWENTY-FIVE

# PAY WHATEVER PRICE
# MAY BE NECESSARY

*He [Dingli] was most emphatic in stressing the importance, in his view, of*
*paying without delay whatever price may be necessary to satisfy Italy.*
— SIR JOSEPH BALL TO SIR HORACE WILSON

Mussolini received his reward for intervening in the Czechoslovakia crisis a few weeks after the Munich conference. The question
of *de jure* recognition of the Italian conquest of Ethiopia had been put
on hold at the Easter agreements of 1938, but this was still very much a
goal for Mussolini. The final step of the process was an unseemly haggle
in which Britain finally recognised Vittorio Emanuele III as the world's
second King-Emperor alongside George VI in exchange for the with-
drawal of a large, but still token, number of Italian troops from Spain.

This left the way clear for the next – rather deferred – stage of Chamberlain's drive to make a friend of Fascist Italy. This was to be achieved
by a personal visit by Chamberlain to *il Duce* in Rome which had been
planned since the autumn of 1938. The visit was set for January 1939 and
the timing suited Mussolini and his foreign minister, Galeazzo Ciano,
perfectly. Hardly had Chamberlain and Halifax left Paris on their visit
of the previous November than the Italians launched a noisy campaign
to press a series of purely opportunistic claims against France: Djibouti,
seats on the board of the Suez Canal Company, Tunisia and even Cor-
sica. Having paid France the token courtesy of visiting Paris before he
visited Rome, Chamberlain saw no need to change his plans. British

solidarity with France counted for less than a vague and ineffectual challenge to the strength of the Axis. It is hard to identify any more concrete goal that Chamberlain had for the excursion. The visit had become a touchstone of continued appeasement. When one of his correspondents advised Chamberlain to cancel it and 'to make a grand Alliance against Germany', this would have been to 'abandon my policy and adopt Winston's!'[1] Obstinacy had become a virtue.

As with the Paris jaunt Chamberlain indulged Halifax by taking him along with him. Neither the Prime Minister nor the Foreign Secretary made themselves disagreeable to their hosts by raising the question of Italian claims against France. Chamberlain was mightily relieved that Mussolini did not do so either.[2] Appeasing Italy ranked well above helping France. He and Halifax cold-shouldered the French ambassador, prompting the bitter reflection in his memoirs 'that they did not trouble themselves to show me publicly and visibly, however, signs of sympathy that would have been very opportune; as they would, however, have meant that the entente between Great Britain and France remained a constant and could not be shaken'.[3]

Chamberlain judged the visit 'truly wonderful', relishing the enthusiastic welcome by the Italian crowds, just as he had relished the reception in Paris.[4] Feeding the Prime Minister's vanity seemed to have become a major object of British diplomacy. Chamberlain was also charmed by what he mistook for a genuinely good impression he had made on Mussolini. In fact, *il Duce* was anything but impressed by his visitors: 'These men are not made of the same stuff as the Francis Drakes and the other magnificent adventurers who created the Empire. These, after all, are the tired sons of a long line of rich men, and they will lose their empire.'[5] Predictably, nothing practical whatever was achieved.

The secret channel rather went to sleep as Chamberlain launched these unproductive excursions into conventional diplomacy, but shortly after the Rome jaunt it reappeared in a second and rather different incarnation. It was revived from the Italian end, initially as a conduit to convey misinformation to Downing Street. The trigger was Prague, which gave Italy an opening to try to pass itself off as the moderate face of the Axis. Adrian Dingli, the legal adviser to the Italian embassy in

London and Joseph Ball's point of contact from the start, passed on the claim (quite possibly true) that Germany had given no warning to Italy of its plans and quoted Dino Grandi, the ambassador, describing Hitler as a 'mad dog'. The Italians' underlying goal was to drive a wedge between London and Paris. Britain's influence was called upon to help Italy in its negotiations with France over its new shopping list of demands.[6] After the Anglo-French guarantee to Poland, Ball and Dingli returned to the charge with the assertion that the guarantee made it all the more important to pay Mussolini's price before it increased any further. Intriguingly, Ball espoused the Italian claims whole-heartedly and echoed Dingli's assessment that Britain should 'pay ... without delay whatever price may be necessary to satisfy Italy'.[7]

Alas for Ball's efforts, Mussolini picked the very day of his second letter to emulate his fellow dictator and to invade Albania in an act of outright gangsterdom, which tested the tolerance even of Chamberlain: 'I am afraid such faith as I ever had in the assurances of dictators is rapidly being whittled away.'[8] It was not enough to daunt Ball, who appeared to be working by this point as Italy's conduit to Downing Street. He conjured up another clandestine, personal channel between Rome and Downing Street, together with an imaginary reworking of Italian politics and diplomacy to accommodate the messages that it would feed to Downing Street. The cast had been extended to include a former US diplomat, now naturalised as a British citizen, and George Glasgow, the diplomatic correspondent of *The Observer*, presumably from Ball's stable of tame journalists. The Italian end of the connection appeared decidedly unqualified for the task; Mario Manenti was a sculptor who had been living in London for thirty-seven years.[9] He supposedly had a family link to Arturo Bocchini, Mussolini's police chief. This, together with Ball's endorsement, was enough to persuade Wilson to become directly involved in back-channel contacts with Italy and he invited Manenti in for a conversation.[10] Manenti began with the doubly false claim that Mussolini was using him as a channel because the regular diplomatic avenues had been hijacked by pro-Germans. In Manenti's version of the world, the foreign minister, Ciano, was now entirely under German influence, but Mussolini himself was not committed to the Axis. The invasion of Albania had been a move against Germany, rather than anything else. Manenti then reverted to the shopping list of points which Britain was to use its influence on France to grant to Italy.

Chamberlain's confidence in Mussolini was still weak enough for him to dismiss Manenti's proposals as 'vague or impractical', but he did latch on to the idea of appeasing Italy at France's expense even if this involved formal diplomacy by Britain.[11] In contrast to the first incarnation of the secret channel, which had been kept rigorously secret, Wilson disclosed the Manenti contacts to the Foreign Office. He rounded off his minute of the meeting to Alec Cadogan by quoting Manenti's regretful claim that 'the French were making things much more difficult for Mussolini', implying that this was also the Cabinet's view of matters.[12] Cadogan seems to have ignored Wilson's pointed suggestion that 'perhaps something could now be done'. He was a great respecter of proper procedure and he took his orders from his proper political boss, Halifax. He was equally unresponsive to Wilson's suggestion that he meet Manenti.

Despite Chamberlain's scepticism about Manenti's concrete proposals and Cadogan's unhelpfulness, Ball's new channel had got off to a promising start. Wilson was happy to see George Glasgow when he asked for a meeting. Glasgow reiterated Manenti's accusation that Ciano had fallen – probably corruptly – under German influence. Growing anti-German sentiment in Italy would supposedly underwrite a three-way pact between Britain, France and Italy. This was further fuel for Wilson's drive to mobilise the Foreign Office to pressurise France into a more accommodating stance towards Italy. By then Chamberlain had calmed down enough from Albania to see 'Mussolini as the best agent for commencing discussions with Germany as and when the opportunity occurred'.[13] Wilson had another go at Cadogan to follow up the Prime Minister's hankering for France to move towards Italy, speaking of 'the need … to urge the French to do everything they could to arrange for a settlement with Italy'.[14] Cadogan politely but firmly poured cold water over the idea and this scheme for indirect appeasement went on hold for a few weeks.

With Albania fading into the background, secret contacts could be passed back to their more accustomed and conventional intermediaries. Ball was soon transmitting rank flattery from Grandi via Dingli of Chamberlain's 'great wisdom with regard to Albania', which Chamberlain was reminded was aimed against Germany.[15] Predictably a Franco-Italian settlement remained at the foreground; 'it was vitally important that agreement [between France and Italy] should be reached with the least possible delay'. This would strengthen Italy within the Axis and enable it to hold at bay German attempts to force it into a military alliance. For once, Dingli actually provided useful information by warning that Ribbentrop was going to visit Rome in search of just such an alliance. The outcome was the 'Pact of Steel', signed on 22 May, which explicitly tied the two dictators far more closely than their informal ties.

The pact created some difficulties for the secret channel in its first two incarnations but they were far from fatal. In Rome Grandi passed as excessively pro-British and anti-German and he found himself fighting to hold on to his position. He made a fulsome speech in favour of the pact to Italian and German diplomats, which he tried to justify to Downing Street fittingly enough via Dingli. Ball was willing to accept that internal considerations forced Grandi to do something that seemed to belie the amicable face that he was showing to Downing Street. Ball's standing in Downing Street, too, had been diminished by the Pact of Steel and he was reduced to having to ask Wilson for a few minutes of face-to-face conversation with the Prime Minister.[16] Even before Albania Wilson had been moving to take personal charge of the secret channel and filter the communications it was feeding from Rome before they reached Chamberlain.[17]

Cadogan had forced Wilson to pause, but not abandon, the strategy that Ball had promoted of appeasing Italy at France's expense. Here Wilson had a far better-placed partner than Ball in the shape of the pro-appeasement British ambassador to Paris, Sir Eric Phipps. Phipps in turn had a good line to Georges Bonnet, the ultra-appeasing French foreign minister. The stage was set for a drive to shift French policy in the direction that Mussolini wanted, behind the back of the French Prime Minister and largely bypassing the British Foreign Secretary. Wilson began by producing his own alternative to a draft letter to Daladier that

the Foreign Office had produced for Chamberlain. Chamberlain's draft
was an outright plea for Daladier to ignore French public opinion and
to make concessions to Italy with no *quid pro quo*.[18] Wilson's covering
letter to Chamberlain gives an intriguing sense of his deployment of
flattery as a tool in managing politicians. The draft referred improbably
to Daladier's 'unrivalled authority', which Wilson implied was due to
Chamberlain: 'Daladier owes his position to you & to what you have
done for him.'[19] Phipps advised against sending the letter immediately
out of tactical considerations, but continued to intrigue with Bonnet
to bounce Daladier into making concessions to Italy, using Britain
as a lever. The letter that Chamberlain eventually sent was rather less
abject than Wilson's first draft and did not directly urge Daladier to
accept Italian demands but it repeated the dubiously flattering sketch
of Daladier's political strength.[20] Daladier turned down the proposal in
a blizzard of ornate French phraseology.[21]

By the early summer of 1939 Ball's status as the gatekeeper to the
secret channel was under threat as Wilson displaced him as the advocate of appeasing Italy at France's expense. Worse, Grandi's position
in London was looking shaky as Mussolini drifted into Hitler's arms.
There was a hint of desperation in the idea that Ball passed on of a
rerun of the Munich conference as a way to settle the burgeoning crisis
over Danzig.[22] This time, though, the country that was to be carved
up, Poland, was to be allowed a voice in the proceedings. The Pope
would also lend a hand. None of this helped Poland, Grandi's career or
anything else. Grandi was replaced as ambassador and recalled to Rome
to serve as minister of justice.

# CHAPTER TWENTY-SIX

# CATCHING THE MUGWUMPS

*It is a most ingenious idea for it is calculated to catch all the mugwumps and at the same time by tying the thing to Art XVI we give it a temporary character. I have no doubt that one of these days Art XVI will be amended or repealed and that should give us the opportunity of revising our relations with the Soviet* [sic] *if we want to.*
– NEVILLE CHAMBERLAIN TO HIS SISTER

Prague forced Chamberlain to retreat on a number of fronts, as his policy of extreme appeasement was ever less viable and the clamour for a more resolute stance towards Hitler grew. He had held back from practical steps to prepare Britain for the possibility of war because of the double fear that they might be regarded as provocations by Hitler and that they might damage Britain's economy. Britain still lagged far behind the transformation of Germany into an armed camp, supported by an autarkic economic system.

The political pressure that had forced Chamberlain to make the Birmingham speech did not go away. In the wake of Prague he was compelled to take a series of steps to prepare Britain for war. They were taken more or less reluctantly. No distinct faction within the Cabinet or the Conservative Party called for these moves specifically, but Chamberlain's overriding consideration was presentation and political impact. Military calculation lagged far behind. When Chamberlain spoke to a large meeting of the 1922 Committee, he was braced for trouble because he expected both Eden's and Churchill's supporters to be there.[1]

The first of the moves was to double the Territorial (volunteer reserve) Army in size. This came about almost by accident, prompted by
Wilson in search of an announcement that would show the government
taking military preparation seriously. Chamberlain had picked up that
he would face questions about how actively the Territorials were being
used and Wilson wrote to Halifax, suggesting that Territorial training
schemes be stepped up.[2] Halifax wanted to go far further, and proposed
that conscription be introduced. The idea had been in the air for some
time, but it would have been a radical move. Wilson objected on the
grounds that he judged that the trade unions would be opposed. The
unspoken but more powerful objections were that Chamberlain had
promised there would be no conscription and that Hitler would be
upset. The question was referred to the Prime Minister, who predictably sided with Wilson. Spontaneously and extempore, Halifax suggested doubling the Territorial Army and Chamberlain jumped at the
idea. Wilson took charge and marshalled Halifax as Foreign Secretary
and Sir John Simon as Chancellor of the Exchequer behind the scheme
in the space of a day.[3] The Treasury noted that it was 'not based on
a strategic plan', but Simon overrode his officials, having seen which
way the political wind blew.[4] The purpose was 'the necessity for impressing Europe as to our military determination'. Chamberlain's only
significant contribution to the process was to decide that he himself
should make the announcement to the House of Commons, not the
War Secretary, Leslie Hore-Belisha. It was not even discussed with the
Army Council. The scheme confronted the Army with vast problems,
in the form of finding training resources, equipment and facilities,
which had not even been considered in advance, still less set in hand.[5]
As the principal role of the Territorial Army had been transformed into
air defence, Germany could not complain that this was an aggressive
measure. It also depended on men actually volunteering to serve if it
was to acquire any substance.

Doubling the Territorial Army did, though, demand some bureaucratic adjustment to allow it to happen and the first fruit of Chamberlain's walk in the woods with Wilson was the announcement of an attenuated Ministry of Supply (MoS), dedicated solely to the needs of the

Army, on 20 April. At the political level the choice of minister deprived the announcement of any force as a register of new-found resolution. Symbolism was just as important as practical effect. Leslie Burgin, the National Liberal Minister of Transport, was as near a total nonentity as it is possible for a Cabinet minister to be. Few doubted his competence but his appointment to the position proclaimed an 'anyone but Churchill' doctrine very loudly indeed. Chamberlain cheerily reflected, 'The new Ministry of Supply was certainly not the post for Winston.' It glaringly advertised Chamberlain's confidence that Churchill's services were not required. The anti-appeasement MP Harold Nicolson was unsure whether the House of Commons reacted to Burgin's name with 'a gasp of horror' or 'a deep groan of pain'.[6] Whichever might have been the case, he saw it as clear proof that 'Chamberlain's obstinate refusal to include any but the yes-men in his Cabinet caused real dismay'.[7] In the words of an Edenite diplomat, Burgin was a 'ghastly selection'.[8]

A few days later Chamberlain followed up the attenuated MoS with the even more dramatic announcement that for the first time ever Britain was to have military conscription in peacetime. It was a measure that France had long been pushing for.[9] As with the MoS, it failed to make the political impact it should have had. A flavour of grudging concession hung heavy round both measures. The call-up was limited to men between the ages of twenty and twenty-one so a total of only 200,000, according to public statements, or only 180,000 when Chamberlain was talking to the trade unions. All that was involved was six months of compulsory training with the option of voluntarily joining the Territorial Army at the end. A supposedly defensive dimension was injected by emphasising that some of the men involved would be trained in searchlights and anti-aircraft guns. The only part of the Army's mission that interested Chamberlain was defence against the Luftwaffe.[10] Another leader might have taken the opportunity to advertise national service as a patriotic move to rally the country behind diplomacy, but Chamberlain's approach was decidedly apologetic. There had been no discussions beforehand with the Labour Party, who could assail him in the House of Commons for breaking Baldwin's pledge of April 1936 not to introduce conscription. Wilson had reverted to his old metier of negotiating with the trade unions to prepare the way, but even in his true field of expertise he had not achieved much.[11] Chamberlain's private discussions with the Trades Union Congress leaders went no better, but their reservations were quite different to the ones Wilson had feared they would raise. They were taken aback that such efforts were being made for so few men.[12] A broader measure, promoted more energetically, would have been hard to resist and would have improved Chamberlain's threadbare credentials as a national leader. Chamberlain and Wilson seemed to have ignored the obvious economic fact that removing men from the labour market improves the bargaining power of those left active. Sadly, it is difficult to form a more complete judgement as the relevant file from Downing Street has long vanished.[13]

Chamberlain rejoiced that conscription had succeeded as a minimalist and token measure with his habitual orgy of self-congratulation:

> More & more I am convinced that much of the art of statesmanship lies in accurate timing, as the fisherman knows when he is trying to get a long cast out. In the present case I believe we hit the right moment when public opinion was ripe for the move and when the foreigners would not have been satisfied to wait much longer.[14]

Chamberlain was determined to keep any offence to Germany to a minimum. Nevile Henderson had been sent back to Berlin as an explicit 'counter-weight' to the decision after his brief post-Prague recall.[15] Henderson called on the Auswärtiges Amt with a formal statement of the defensive aspect of British conscription and repeated assurances of the government's peaceful desires and intentions.[16] Harold Nicolson was delighted by the fact of conscription, but Chamberlain's performance in explaining the measure to the House of Commons inspired another bilious outburst: '[I]t is the combination of real religious fanaticism with spiritual trickiness which makes one dislike Mr Chamberlain so much. He has all the harshness of a self-righteous man, with none of the generosity of those who are guided by durable moral standards.'[17]

Concern at Chamberlain's performance over Prague was strong enough to drive together the disparate groups inside the Conservative

Party opposed to him into joint action, for the first time since the Munich debate. Churchill, Duff Cooper and Leo Amery signed a Commons motion tabled by Eden calling for a truly national government. The whips stamped on the motion brutally using the commanding resources at their disposal, amending it into one of slavish praise for the Prime Minister. This was no more than a demonstration of how a large majority of docile MPs can be mobilised, but Chamberlain persuaded himself that 'the motion put Anthony back a mile both for its disloyalty and its futility'.[18]

Churchill understood that the moment had come to make a serious diplomatic attempt to bring in the Soviet Union as a counter-weight to Nazi Germany. But he also saw clearly the difficulties this kind of move would bring with the other eastern European nations. He launched his drive at the close of day's work at the House of Commons near 11 p.m., in a direct appeal to Ivan Maisky, the Soviet ambassador, who was at the House that day:

> Now look here, Mr Ambassador, if we are to make a success of this new policy, we require the help of Russia. Now I don't care for your system and I never have, but the Poles and Rumanians like it even less. Although they might be prepared at a pinch to let you in, they would certainly want some assurances that you would eventually get out. Can you give us such assurances?[19]

The instinctive reaction of most Conservatives at such an idea was unrestrained horror. Rab Butler's ultra-appeasing parliamentary private secretary, Chips Channon, observed the conversation: 'I saw him with Lloyd George, Boothby and Randolph, in a triumphant huddle surrounding Maisky. Maisky, the Ambassador of torture, murder and every crime in the calendar.'[20]

Prague had opened the Pandora's box of Soviet involvement in British diplomacy. Chamberlain's extempore four-power declaration led nowhere, but as the spring of 1939 wore on, relations with the Soviet Union became the elephant in the room of British diplomacy and politics.

Moscow had been kept at arm's length, if not further, during the Sudeten crisis. It was never remotely contemplated to ask the Soviet Union to the Munich conference. It is a measure of just how severe the domestic pressure on Chamberlain was after Prague that he included the Soviet Union in his spur-of-the-moment four-power declaration scheme. Treating the Soviet Union as a respectable diplomatic player had long been a left-wing shibboleth. Before the First World War successive governments had insisted that the realities of diplomacy meant that liberal opinion would have to accept the unpleasant fact of collaborating with the absolutist Tsarist regime. Labour could now assert that this same diplomatic pragmatism demanded collaboration with an avowedly socialist regime. The logjam was finally broken and the Soviet Union brought into the mainstream of European diplomatic calculations. Thus began four tortuous and ultimately futile months of discussion and negotiation in which the British and the Soviets repeatedly tried to find an effective modus vivendi which might serve as a brake on Hitler.

Creating an effective alliance with the Soviet Union was a daunting task, facing two very distinct problems: mutual suspicion and geography. Neither side trusted the other. Stalin was suspicious of Chamberlain's thoroughly capitalist approach to life. Chamberlain was eternally suspicious of the Soviets and had suspected serious conspiracies on their part since the early phase of the Sudetenland crisis, 'the Russians stealthily and cunningly pulling all the strings behind the scenes to get us involved in a war with Germany'.[21] Chamberlain's opinion of the Soviet Union was not helped by the fact that Lloyd George, whom he loathed even more than he loathed Churchill, was the most vocal advocate of a Soviet alliance: '[H]ysterical passion of the Opposition egged on by L.l.G. who have [*sic*] a pathetic belief that Russia is the key to our salvation.'[22] Chamberlain's letters to his sisters regularly contained more of the same.

Chamberlain's views, however, were positively objective and balanced compared with some members of his government. Maisky was a particular hate object for Chips Channon, who described him as 'the smirking cat ... so sinister and smug (are we to place our honour, our safety in those blood-stained hands?)'.[23] Channon was representative of widespread attitudes at the centre and right of politics. Nor were the unqualified friends of the Soviet Union in Britain an impressive group, topped by the purblind naivety of Sidney and Beatrice Webb and the near-treasonous willingness to subordinate British interests to the Soviet Union's displayed by those on the extreme left such as Stafford Cripps. It is easy to forget that Stalin had far more blood on his hands at this stage than Hitler. He had murdered several hundred thousand people in the Great Purge alone, which had only just drawn to an end. The elimination of the large majority of the senior officers in the Red Army had seriously degraded its ability to fight. It is nonetheless worth noting that Chamberlain appeared to be even less well informed of the internal structure of the Soviet regime than of Germany's. He barely mentioned Stalin by name and at no point showed any awareness that his was the only opinion that mattered. Few would argue with his distrust of the Soviet Union, but it was part of a remarkably unbalanced view of diplomacy when contrasted with his never-failing willingness to trust Hitler and Mussolini.

The raw fact of geography was a further obstacle. The Soviet Union had no borders with Germany and to apply military power it would have required the support of smaller countries which did. These were quite rightly just as suspicious of Soviet as of German motives, and Chamberlain knew this fully: 'Moreover she is both hated and suspected by many of the smaller states notably by Poland Rumania and Finland so that close association with her might easily cost us the sympathy of those who would much more effectively help us if we can get them on our side.'[24]

Predictably enough the Germans complained vociferously at any rapprochement with the Soviet Union, as they did at any diplomatic overture to countries to their east. They applied the hostile term 'encirclement' (*Einkreisung*) to this and Chamberlain was sensitive to their fears. He swallowed the pitch by the Polish foreign minister, Colonel Józef Beck, that agreement with the Soviet Union might actually spur Germany into an otherwise avoidable attack.[25]

It is hardly surprising that Chamberlain opted to give priority to keeping Germany's smaller neighbour on side. After the Poles had blocked his four-power declaration scheme he pursued the logic to the end: 'If bringing Russia in meant their [Poland's and Romania's] running out I should think the change was a very disastrous one.'[26] Wilson was deeply unhappy about the British guarantee to Poland in itself, but he approved thoroughly of Chamberlain's priorities, saying, 'Stick to the Poles – you can't trust the Russians.'[27] At this stage there seemed to be a binary choice between Poland and the Soviet Union as allies. The previous year it had been axiomatic that Czechoslovakia would be incapable of military resistance to Germany, but in 1939 there was little inclination to assess Polish military strength seriously.

Churchill was inevitably associated with forces pushing the government towards an alliance with the Soviet Union. In the course of a House of Commons debate, Channon scored, or thought he scored (his is the only account), a tactical victory over Churchill.[28] The President of Poland had written privately to Churchill saying he had no objection to a British alliance with the Soviet Union. The anti-appeasers hoped to inveigle Chamberlain into saying that Poland opposed an alliance, giving Churchill the opportunity to prove him wrong. According to Channon, an indiscreet anti-appeasement MP unwisely bragged about Churchill's letter to him, and he was able to warn Chamberlain of the trap.

The Soviets resolutely refused any notion of a halfway house and insisted on a full-scale mutual defence pact. When the Soviet Union made the offer/demand of a formal three-power alliance at the end of May, Chamberlain was put firmly on the spot. The Poles had finally relented and raised no objection. Worse, the Cabinet was firmly in favour of an alliance. All his instincts screamed at him to resist in the face of overwhelming support for the idea. Not only would it call for him to surmount his hatred of the Soviet Union but, worse, it would finally spell the death of appeasement. Aligning with anyone against Germany was the antithesis of the policy that Chamberlain had pursued throughout his premiership.

There was no sign of opposition to the alliance in the press and it was obvious that refusal would create immense difficulty in the House even if I could persuade my Cabinet.

On the other hand I had and have deep suspicions of Soviet aims and profound doubts as to her military capacity even if she honestly desired & intended to help. But worse than that was my feeling that the Alliance would definitely be a lining up of opposing blocs and association which would make any negotiation or discussion with the totalitarians difficult if not impossible.[29]

The only one of his ministers who supported Chamberlain's analysis was Butler, 'and he was not a very influential ally'.[30] Just as he had done in the aftermath of Prague when he came under pressure to bring Churchill into government, Chamberlain sent for Wilson to try to find a way out of the dilemma.

Together the two men cooked up a way of sabotaging the alliance. It had superficial elegance, invoked another shibboleth of liberal opinion and was thoroughly dishonest. The alliance was to be linked somehow to Article XVI of the Covenant of the League of Nations, which sanctioned the use of force to enforce League rulings. The article had never been applied in any serious case – the moment to attempt this had been missed when Mussolini invaded Ethiopia in 1935 – and it was practically a dead letter. Chamberlain had never been a great believer in the League and the principle behind Article XVI, however ineffective it might have proved, remained a bugbear for him.

It is a most ingenious idea for it is calculated to catch all the mugwumps and at the same time by tying the thing to Art XVI we give it a temporary character. I have no doubt that one of these days Art XVI will be amended or repealed and that should give us the opportunity of revising our relations with the Soviet [*sic*] if we want to.

The entirely hypocritical injection of the League of Nations into the proceedings by Chamberlain and Wilson was emblematic of the British contribution of bad faith and half-heartedness to the formal proposals for an alliance delivered to the Soviet government. The Soviets detected this instantly and replied that 'the League of Nations was included in the British proposals simply for the purpose of creating impediments to a fast reaction to an attack by an aggressor'.[31] This set the tone for the formal and ultimately futile talks over an alliance that dragged on for the next three months. Chamberlain continually tried to apply the brakes on the British side.[32]

> I put as little value on Russia's military capacity as I believe the Germans do. I believe they would fail us in an extremity & even to talk to them has already got us into trouble with our friends. I would like to have taken a much stronger line with them all through, but I could not have taken my colleagues with me.[33]

It is hard to believe that the talks with the Soviet Union would have ended in quite such a total failure had Chamberlain dedicated to them a fraction of the enthusiasm and tolerance with which he pursued friendship with Hitler and Mussolini. Moreover, hidden from all but Chamberlain and Wilson, Downing Street was conducting foreign policy far more to its taste. Chamberlain viewed the prospect of failure in the Soviet talks with complete equanimity and even saw it as inevitable.[34]

Churchill was clear-sighted enough to know that a Soviet alliance was hard to achieve. In private conversation with a senior British general he set out a remarkably accurate list of predictions for how war might evolve,[35] beginning with the 'crippling or annihilation of Poland'. As it turned out, it was the Germans and the Soviets themselves who removed the obstacle of Polish doubts by partitioning the country in September 1939. Only at the end of the list came 'an alliance with Russia, when the latter sees how the land lies'.

# CHAPTER TWENTY-SEVEN

# TALKING APPEASEMENT AGAIN

*Went to see H.J.W. about a telephone intercept, which looks as if No. 10 were talking appeasement again. He put up all sort of denials to which I don't pay much attention. But it's a good thing to show we have our eye on them.*
– SIR ALEXANDER CADOGAN DIARIES

As the half-heartedness of Chamberlain's concessions to the anti-appeasers over conscription and the Ministry of Supply became all too apparent, informed circles also started catching signs that the supposed switch in Britain's diplomatic stance towards Germany was superficial rather than profound. Harold Nicolson reported, 'There is a very widespread belief that he [Chamberlain] is running a dual policy – one, the overt policy of arming, and the other the *secret de l'Empereur*, namely appeasement plus Horace Wilson.'[1] The appeasers' house journal, *The Times*, was read closely as a register of the true thinking at Downing Street and it duly provided evidence that the old policy of appeasing remained in force. It published a leader in late April that was judged to be at best flabby on protecting Poland and, more important, on 3 May a letter from Lord Rushcliffe, an insignificant former Conservative minister, which presented Hitler as a potential force for peace, reaffirmed the spirit of Munich and, sinisterly, asserted that the British guarantee to Poland entitled London to oversight of Warsaw's foreign policy.[2] Fairly or otherwise, it was widely assumed that Rushcliffe's letter had been written at Wilson's behest.[3]

Inside the Foreign Office doubts over the true stance of Downing Street went beyond mere suspicion. As they had done in the wake of

Munich, the intelligence services alerted the professional diplomats to what Downing Street was doing behind their backs. By then Alec Cadogan recognised that this was not mischief perpetrated by a junior employee and that Wilson was deeply implicated in what was going on. The split of the British foreign policy machine into two opposing camps was practically complete. 'Went to see H.J.W. about a telephone intercept, which looks as if No. 10 were talking appeasement again. He put up all sort of denials to which I don't pay much attention. But it's a good thing to show we have our eye on them.'[4]

Yet again Cadogan was being too optimistic. The fact that the Foreign Office knew what was afoot did not in any way deter Downing Street from going ahead with its overtures to Germany. It only became more circumspect.

The channel from Downing Street via Fritz Hesse to Ribbentrop which had been blown the previous autumn does not seem to have been used. Downing Street's other line to Ribbentrop, through Philip Conwell-Evans of the Anglo-German Fellowship, had vanished as Conwell-Evans defected to the anti-appeasement camp in the wake of Munich and devoted his efforts to Sir Robert Vansittart. Instead a new intermediary came on the scene, this time a British one. Henry Drummond Wolff was the grandson of a late Victorian diplomat and minor politician. He had briefly been a Conservative MP, affiliated to the very far right wing of the party in contact with Sir Oswald Mosley's Fascists.[5] He was an obsessive bore of the first magnitude, unstable and with a wildly exaggerated notion of his own abilities. His entry on the scene also complicated Wilson's back-channel diplomacy by involving Sir Joseph Ball in the German side of this; hitherto Ball had only dealt with Italy. After his brief spell in Parliament, Drummond Wolff had tried to interest Ball in a plan to finance the Conservative Party through a subscription scheme and stayed in touch with him afterwards. His mind buzzed with grandiose schemes to reorganise trade throughout the Empire. He was obsessively anti-Semitic, endorsing Nazi fears of 'efforts at world economic domination effectively fostered by the Jews' which he saw as aimed against the interests of the British Empire.[6] He was also obsessively hostile to the Anglo-American trade agreement of 1938, which gave the United States Most Favoured Nation status. Drummond Wolff saw this as a hostile act aimed against Germany, tantamount to a declaration of war inspired by the Jews (and the Catholics, who had sneaked into the plot somehow).[7] Drummond Wolff had anointed himself as an expert on economic relations between Britain and Germany and in early 1938 he had gone to Berlin to see Hjalmar Horace Greely Schacht at the Reichsbank, who proved unreceptive to his advice.[8] The pace of his activities picked up in early 1939 when he went to Berlin twice. These visits were ostensibly private, but he was enjoying a far higher level of access than an insignificant former MP might normally have expected. Drummond Wolff discussed his journeys in advance with Ball and he later implied that he had travelled at Ball's suggestion.[9] He met – under pledges of mutual secrecy – Hermann Goering and his economic diplomacy side-kick, Helmut Wohlthat, who had struck up a relationship with Wilson the previous summer. Goering claimed vociferously that Germany wanted friendly relations with Britain, with an economic deal as a prelude to a wider political settlement. He was vague as to content and methods in either case, but repeated the stock German plea for the British press to abandon criticism of Germany.[10] He had kindly words for both Chamberlain – 'warmest appreciation' – and for Wilson – 'respect and admiration'. Wohlthat's reports of his contact with Wilson the previous summer had clearly made a favourable impression. On his second visit, Drummond Wolff was fed a similar suggestion to the one that Lord Brocket had brought back from Berlin: that a 'special envoy' should travel privately to smooth the way for formal negotiations.[11]

In the aftermath of Prague, Drummond Wolff's Berlin contacts in Goering's camp latched on to him as a suitable conduit for stories that it was Ribbentrop who was attempting to poison Hitler's mind against Britain, with the implication that the route to a settlement between Britain and Germany lay through avoiding the foreign minister and relying on contacts with them.[12] Drummond Wolff was easy prey for this pitch. He had persuaded himself by then that his and Ball's 'joint efforts … had brought us substantially nearer to a settlement with Germany'.[13] In a series of letters and face-to-face meetings, Drummond

Wolff badgered Ball to take all possible steps to calm German fears of 'encirclement' and to attend to Germany's economic wants. Perhaps unconsciously, he was setting the scene for the final acts in the campaign of economic appeasement of Germany.

Ball had little interest in Drummond Wolff's fantasmagoric schemes for imperial development, but recognised that he could act as a channel to signal that the time had come to reopen confidential contacts with Germany. In early May he authorised Drummond Wolff to tell the Germans that he was travelling to Berlin with the 'knowledge of the Prime Minister's closest economic advisers'.[14] According to Drummond Wolff, Ball added another layer of governmental sanction by promising to inform 'the appropriate intelligence authorities that my mission had been approved'.[15] Drummond Wolff further talked up his pretensions to be the mouthpiece of the British government by telling his contact at the German embassy 'in confidence' that he had spoken more than once to Wilson, most recently at some length. On the strength of these credentials Drummond Wolff broadened his range of access in Berlin and his contacts spanned every camp in the various forces struggling to influence German foreign policy: the established forces of the Auswärtiges Amt and its increasingly irrelevant attachment to the practices of formal diplomacy; Ribbentrop's personal operation represented by the former military attaché in London, Leo Geyr von Schweppenburg, now serving on his staff; the Führer's own circle in the shape of Walther Hewel, Hitler's friend and liaison to Ribbentrop; and finally his old stamping ground of Goering's empire with Wohlthat to the fore again.[16] The crowning achievement of the visit was a three-and-a-half-hour conversation with Goering himself, following which Drummond Wolff declared himself to be 'on terms of friendship and trust' with the field marshal.[17] This time the conversation with Goering went beyond generalities and the field marshal 'undertook to send a special representative to London to obtain confirmation of my proposed agreement and to make specific arrangements for official negotiations'.[18] Drummond Wolff put himself under an oath of secrecy to tell only Chamberlain, Wilson or Ball about what had been discussed. It is unlikely that Goering was any more interested in Drummond Wolff's broader schemes than Ball, but indirect contact had been established between the top levels. He was told to wait for a telegram which would launch the next step in the negotiations. Ball and Wilson were enthusiastic about the progress that Drummond Wolff had made in preparing the ground, and he was instructed to act immediately the moment he received the signal.[19]

Goering's special representative was none other than Helmut Wohlthat, and he arrived in London a couple of weeks later. The high point of Drummond Wolff's time as the secret sherpa for top-level meetings between Britain and Germany came when he hosted a dinner for Wohlthat on one side and Wilson and Ball on the other. The venue was the London town house of the Duke of Westminster. The Duke of Westminster and Drummond Wolff knew each other from financing Ball's right-wing Conservative propaganda operation.[20] The duke was an enthusiastic appeaser and a virulent anti-Semite. He was a member of the Link, a generally pro-Nazi stablemate of the Anglo-German Fellowship, aimed at a wider public than the Fellowship's avowedly elitist target. Despite his aristocratic rank and immense wealth he had conspicuously failed to be invited to perform any major public service. By contrast, his brother-in-law Lord Beauchamp had been a minister, a knight of the Garter, a lord lieutenant and chancellor of London University amongst many distinctions. An even more bitter cause of resentment was that Beauchamp had also fathered three sons despite his flamboyant homosexuality whilst none of Westminster's marriages produced an adult heir.[21] Westminster's divorces had been punished with the customary social ostracism of the era but the double standards and hypocrisy of the time meant that Beauchamp's standing was not hurt as long as the fiction was maintained that his sexual orientation was secret. When the opportunity arose, the duke applied himself with relish to providing King George V with hard evidence of Beauchamp's homosexuality, forcing him to flee the country in disgrace.

The dinner was extremely confidential and only Drummond Wolff's later account of it has survived. Wilson told Wohlthat that the British government would be prepared to negotiate on the whole range of issues. On his side, Wohlthat said that he wanted Britain to send someone suitable to Berlin to continue the negotiations and Drummond Wolff fondly imagined that he himself was the ideal candidate. Ball immediately disabused him and proceeded to give sad proof of his ineptitude as a negotiator (and perhaps an overly enthusiastic partaker of the ducal wine cellar). He spontaneously told Wohlthat that there would be no difficulty in handing back the pre-war Imperial German colonies in Africa, 'so as to put the Union of South Africa in its place'.[22] Wohlthat had not been expecting negotiations to open immediately, and certainly not in this fashion. The dinner ended inconclusively.

Drummond Wolff was riding the crest of a wave of illusion that took him to the heights of secret British diplomacy despite the damper Ball administered at dinner. In reality he had outlived his usefulness. His attempts to follow up from the Wohlthat dinner were ignored until he treated Ball to a peremptory note demanding that he and Ball 'should be empowered to carry through the work already successfully started' and select a British emissary to Hitler as had been agreed at the dinner.[23] This gave Ball the opportunity to close the door very firmly (and presumably with a combination of relief and relish) on the enthusiastic and persistent amateur. Drummond Wolff had unwittingly supplied Ball with further ammunition by demanding that the activities of a clutch of rival private intermediaries, most notably the aristocratic visitors to Hitler's birthday celebrations, be closed down to leave the field clear for himself. Ball waved the big stick of Wilson's authority to make absolutely sure that Drummond Wolff backed off, telling him:

> [Wilson] and I cannot help thinking, however, that private and unofficial conversations of the kind which have recently been carried on by Buccleuch, Brocket and others are potentially very dangerous, in that they may encourage that section of opinion in Germany which has always held that Britain will never fight ...
>
> [T]his policy does not, of course, rule out a settlement of outstanding questions by negotiation ... We are however, both satisfied, after full consideration of all the facts that it would be dangerous for such negotiations to be undertaken otherwise than through normal official channels.[24]

Wilson and Ball clearly had a very elastic definition of 'normal official channels', as this was far from the end of the conversations with Wohlthat. Ball's supposed anxiety not to feed German perceptions that Britain was defeatist was chiefly a convenient pretext for shutting down Drummond Wolff, but it was unconsciously accurate as an analysis of the actual achievements of Downing Street's back-channel diplomacy.

*   *   *

With the Soviet Union talks stalled and the back channel to Berlin opening again, the British government decided to send the Germans an explicit statement of its foreign policy. In part, this reaffirmed the new firmness that lay behind various measures of preparation for war, which had been forced on Chamberlain in the wake of Prague, but it also made plain that the way to dialogue was still open. In practice this formalised a shift in avowed British policy from a quest for agreement with Germany to a blend of resolution and rapprochement, but this was masked by the pretence that this had been British policy all along. The message was delivered by Halifax in a long-planned and high-profile speech at the appropriate venue of Chatham House, the home of Britain's pre-eminent foreign policy think tank, the Royal Institute of International Affairs. It was also broadcast live to Britain and the United States. Its importance was clear from the start and much effort went into composing the speech; Cadogan noted that it had been 'the bane of our lives for weeks'.[25] The haggling over Halifax's planned speech to the League of Nations in the midst of the Sudetenland crisis in August 1938 gives a flavour of what must have been involved.

In the event Halifax stiffened his text at the last moment, prompted by rumours of a coup in Danzig and reports that Ribbentrop was telling Hitler that Britain would not fight.[26] He was vigorously cheered for assertions such as 'We know that if international law and order is to be preserved, we must be prepared to fight in its defence' or 'Great Britain is not prepared to yield either to calumnies or force'.[27] This kind of declaration occupied most of the time. This shows how far the balance of power had shifted in the Foreign Office's favour at the expense of Downing Street since the episode of the Geneva speech, but the appeasers did not go away empty-handed. The door was left open to negotiation provided that Germany mended its ways. 'British policy rests on twin foundations of purpose. One is determination to resist force. The other is our recognition of the world's desire to get on with the constructive work of building peace.' The report in *The Times* gives a better sense of what Downing Street thought were the speech's priorities. Its second sub-heading announced 'THE DUAL POLICY'. Most listeners rejoiced at Halifax's firm tone, but the appeasers still had something more emollient with which to work.

Halifax's own approach to his speech shows perfectly his ambivalence towards appeasement. The delivery and the bulk of the text was aimed at those who wanted a firm policy to Germany, but the 'dual policy' aspect was a vital part of the message. It was Halifax himself who briefed the editor of *The Times* before delivering the speech.[28] To his credit he did not retreat from the stance even after the policy had failed. When he quoted the speech in his memoirs, the opening sentence was, 'British policy rests on twin foundations of purpose.'[29]

In Germany Goebbels caught the two distinct notes in Halifax's speech. He heard a 'mixture of threat and religiosity [*Devotion*]'.[30] It did not change his analysis of what the British would do, but he paid it far more attention than a speech by Chamberlain a few weeks later which he simply dismissed as 'the old rubbish'.[31]

# CHAPTER TWENTY-EIGHT

# MORE WAYS OF
# KILLING A CAT

*There are more ways of killing a cat than strangling it and if I refuse to take Winston into the Cabinet to please those who say it would frighten Hitler it doesn't follow that the idea of frightening Hitler or rather convincing him that it would not pay him to use force, need be abandoned.*

— NEVILLE CHAMBERLAIN TO HIS SISTER

Before the British could roll out the 'dual policy' fully, Downing Street had to deal with Churchill. Joseph Ball completed the work of persuading Henry Drummond Wolff to back down with another argument, this time rooted in domestic politics, that 'the PM's hands were tied owing to Winston's action'.[1] In early July 1939 Churchill's allies had launched a full-scale press campaign demanding that he be included in the government. Lord Camrose's *Daily Telegraph* broke completely with the government party line and lent its force. All of Churchill's private attempts to persuade the government to take him back in had been rebuffed and this was practically the last roll of the dice that was available to him. Ball was more honest on this point. The press campaign was a strong reason for caution in secret diplomacy, but it certainly did not force Downing Street to abandon the overtures to Germany.

Chamberlain had no intention whatever of taking Churchill into government. By then, he was convinced that doing so would be tantamount to a declaration of war on Germany and was delighted when

Australia's pro-appeasement high commissioner to Britain, Stanley Bruce, called to back him up, leading Chamberlain to remark, '[T]hey [Australia and South Africa] think as I do, if Winston got into Government it would not be long before we were at war.' The ineffectuality of the pro-Churchill campaign merely served to nurture Chamberlain's sense that he held the whip hand. The only wrinkle was that Camrose, a normally reliable supporter of the government amongst the press barons, should have joined in.[2] Camrose was called in to Downing Street for the error of his ways to be explained.

In a mirror image of the anti-appeasers' tendency to blame things on Wilson, Chamberlain saw the hand of the Soviets and dismissed the drive as 'a regular conspiracy in which Mr Maisky [the Soviet ambassador] has been involved'.[3] Maisky would naturally have been pleased if Churchill had entered the Cabinet, but was in reality sceptical about the drive, of which he observed wearily, 'How many have there been now?'[4] Chamberlain was so confident of his position that he did not make even the slightest gesture of conciliation towards Churchill. Keeping Churchill out of government had become almost an end in itself and a challenge to Chamberlain's most mulishly obstinate instincts, topped up by his total blindness to the workings of Hitler's mind.

> There are more ways of killing a cat than strangling it and if I refuse to take Winston into the Cabinet to please those who say it would frighten Hitler it doesn't follow that the idea of frightening Hitler or rather convincing him that it would not pay him to use force, need be abandoned.[5]

It is improbable that Chamberlain would ever have frightened Hitler. It is even less likely that he could have driven the Führer to make the kind of bloodless calculation of respective military strengths that permanently held the appeasers back from action. The press campaign achieved nothing and ran out of steam. Chamberlain gloated at Churchill's – quite possibly imagined – depression.[6] Once again Harold Nicolson read what was going on at Downing Street more accurately: 'Chamberlain's obstinate exclusion of Churchill from the Cabinet is taken as a sign that he has not abandoned appeasement and that all gestures of resistance [to Hitler] are mere bluff.'[7] He also detected how Chamberlain had been reinvigorated by the resumption of his cherished policy: 'The Prime Minister at question time was so buoyant and perky that it looks as though appeasement was going well.'[8]

Chamberlain's allies were in a position to dish out more substantial reprisals for Churchill's effrontery. In 1936 Ball had secretly taken control of *Truth*, a small-circulation political weekly, using funds provided by Lord Luke of Pavenham, the Bovril magnate.[9] *Truth* had been the powerful mouthpiece of Radicalism in the Victorian era, but had since faded away.[10] It is doubtful whether *Truth* was remotely as influential as it had been in its heyday, but it still served as a vehicle to deal out savage criticism of Chamberlain's opponents. Under Ball's reign a virulently anti-Semitic angle crept into its content. Days after the pro-Churchill articles appeared in the *Daily Telegraph* and elsewhere, *Truth* devoted its entire first page to a sneer at what it labelled as an 'intrigue'.[11] Chamberlain relished what he read as Churchill's 'distress' at the 'witty' articles 'making fun of the suggestion that he could help matters in the Cabinet'.[12]

The press campaign in favour of Churchill having faded away, the field was clear for appeasement to be resumed. Downing Street might now be promoting the idea of a dual policy of firmness towards aggression and willingness to talk, but it was the second part that still appealed more to Chamberlain. As ever his approach was suffused with wild optimism and an abject misreading of Hitler. The greatest obstacles that he could identify were the misconceptions and sensitivities of those who did not recognise that appeasement was right and that the assumptions on which it was based were correct:

> It is very difficult to see the way out of Danzig but I don't believe it
> is impossible to find, provided that we are given a little time and also
> provided that Hitler doesn't really want a war. I can't help thinking
> that he is not such a fool as some hysterical people make out and that
> he would not be sorry to compromise if he could do so without what
> he would feel would be a humiliation. I have got one or two ideas

which I am exploring though once again it is difficult to proceed when there are so many ready to cry '*Nous sommes trahis*'* at any suggestion of a peaceful solution.[13]

It was the Germans themselves who presented Chamberlain with one of these ideas. They were sounding out indirect lines of approach to Downing Street and came upon the hugely successful popular historian Arthur Bryant. Bryant was one of the most prominent and least appealing of the 'fellow travellers of the right', open Nazi sympathisers in Britain, an extreme apologist for Nazi Germany and an anti-Semite.[14] Bryant was closely connected to the top level of the Conservative Party, he edited the *Ashridge Journal*, the quarterly associated with the party's think tank of that name, and he had just published a gushing celebration of its previous leader, *Stanley Baldwin: A Tribute*. He edited a collection of Chamberlain's speeches up to the end of the Munich crisis under the title *The Search for Peace* for which he had obtained an impressive publisher's advance.[15] Bryant's introductions to the speeches praised the Prime Minister lavishly: 'Mr. Chamberlain, however, disregarding criticism and abuse alike, went quietly forward with the long-neglected task of European appeasement...'[16] They read like a manifesto for 'the twin pillars of the Prime Minister's policy, which he describes as the freeing of Europe from past quarrels maintained by the dead hand of the past, and the simultaneous repair of those breaches in our defence caused by the policy of unilateral disarmament'.[17] Bryant blamed disarmament exclusively on the 'Socialist Party', as he invariably referred to Labour.[18] He contrasted Chamberlain favourably with the opposition and 'their programme of military alliances and provocatively self-righteous declarations [which] would almost certainly lead to war'.[19] Bryant made a point of reminding readers that Churchill had promised to support Chamberlain as leader of the Conservatives when he became Prime Minister in May 1937, implying that any doubts Churchill might express about appeasement were those of a disloyal

---

* French, 'We have been betrayed'.

renegade.[20] It is little surprise that Bryant was very much *persona grata* with Chamberlain.

Bryant responded avidly when he received an overture from a former Hitler Youth leader now on the staff of Walther Hewel, Hitler's friend, old comrade in arms and link-man to Ribbentrop. Bryant asked Chamberlain whether he should follow up the approach and go to Germany. Chamberlain declined to get involved directly, but welcomed the idea that Bryant should go to Germany himself provided that there was no suggestion that he was going as anything other than a private individual.[21]

Bryant flew to Berlin but was summoned far south to Salzburg, to speak to Hewel, who was staying there in attendance on Hitler at the Berghof. Bryant faithfully trotted out the dual policy towards Germany. The key thing was not to use violence; if Germany attacked Poland, Britain would go to war, but, 'speaking purely as a private individual British opinion was not so much concerned in keeping Danzig out of the Reich'. Germany should also have its place in the Balkans ('a strong German Reich with her own proper economic sphere in eastern and south-eastern Europe') and its place in the sun ('British opinion would have been ready to follow a British statesman who was prepared to negotiate a settlement of the colonial problem').[22] Hewel dutifully stuck to the fiction that Bryant was an intermediary with Chamberlain. His most important message for the British was that Hitler had not fixed a definite date for the solution of the Danzig question: 'The day of its return might be neither this year nor next.' This was amongst the statements that Chamberlain marked when he read Bryant's report.

Four weeks after the dinner at the Duke of Westminster's, Helmut Wohlthat had another, and this time publicly admissible, reason to visit London: the 1939 meeting of the International Whaling Conference. After attending in 1938 – and opening his relationship with Wilson – it was natural he should be a delegate. At the German embassy in London Wohlthat made no pretence that his mission was anything other than to prepare for conversations with the British government. He also made clear that it was the British who had taken the initiative for the conversation.

Hewel's contact with Bryant fed directly to the Führer himself; it did not affect what Goering was up to and the channel through Goering's man, Wohlthat, remained open. Wohlthat's second contact with Wilson in 1939 went in considerably more business-like fashion than the semi-chaotic dinner at the Duke of Westminster's house. Cutting Henry Drummond Wolff and the oafish presence of Sir Joseph Ball out of the picture made life much simpler. Wilson saw Wohlthat on his own at his office. In Wohlthat's version, Wilson opened the conversation 'in a very sympathetic way that "he wanted to speak to me as one who was a colleague and a friend" with a joint interest "in maintaining orderly forms of government and in not exposing present-day civilisation to a crisis of the greatest magnitude in the shape of such a clash"'.[23] This was mildly qualified by a ritual assertion that Britain was ready for war. Wilson then attempted the standard negotiator's gambit of trying to draw Wohlthat into stating what Hitler wanted to discuss, but Wohlthat stonewalled, which forced Wilson to move on to the next part of his programme: a typed list that had already been prepared of all the good things that could come from a negotiation. Each item was prefaced 'in the assumption of', presumably German good behaviour. The main features were pacts of non-aggression and non-interference in the other country's spheres of interest, in Germany's case eastern and south-eastern Europe. Wilson played down the British guarantee to Poland as once the pacts had been agreed, it would be 'superfluous' and 'Danzig would play a minor part for Britain'. A declaration on arms limitation would follow and a new era of peaceful cooperation between the countries would be the next stage. It was the old, optimistic vision of an appeased Europe, now looking decidedly threadbare with over-use. The Führer could be 'a statesman for peace'. For the moment the talks would have to be held secretly, with both France and Italy kept out of the picture. Wilson hammered home the need to keep things quiet: 'You have Mr Chamberlain's political future in your hands. If this leaks out, there will be a great scandal and Mr Chamberlain will be forced to resign.'[24]

Wohlthat also saw Ball, but the only thing he took away from the conversation worth reporting was the remarkably indiscreet information of the intended November date for the next general election. This was a clumsy attempt to suggest to Wohlthat that there was only limited time for Hitler to respond to the overtures, together with an indirect reminder that Chamberlain was Germany's friend and needed all the support he could get against opponents of appeasement. Wohlthat was probably unaware of how privileged he was to be told this; there is no sign that anyone but the narrowest circle around Chamberlain had the date.

These well-hidden moves to revive appeasement were transformed into a public sensation by the actions of a minor British politician, who muscled in on the act. Robert Hudson was a junior trade minister who had been due to accompany Oliver Stanley on the mission to Berlin, aborted by Prague. Even by the standards of rising politicians, he was burningly ambitious and widely disliked. In the aftermath of Munich, he had led an abortive revolt of junior ministers, ostensibly in protest at the lethargy of government policy, but in reality aimed at undermining their more senior and deadbeat colleagues. Through the services of a Norwegian delegate to the whaling conference, Hudson arranged to talk to Wohlthat. They discussed broad trade matters, a possible colonial settlement and the possibility of Britain lending money to the Reichsbank to finance disarmament. Except for the firm idea of a loan to Germany, this was practically the same pitch as the programme for economic appeasement which had been put on ice after Prague.

Had things gone to plan, Wohlthat would have returned to Berlin with the message that there was still scope for both political and economic appeasement if Germany behaved itself, but, even whilst Wohlthat was still in London, the story broke in the anti-appeasement *News Chronicle*, just as Wilson had feared it might. The source was Hudson himself and Wilson thought that Hudson intentionally leaked the story to sabotage the talks, because he was opposed to appeasement.[25] Hudson certainly compounded the damage by giving an off-the-record interview to the *Daily Express*, which splashed the supposed size of the disarmament loan at the then astronomic figure of £1 billion. The leak might, though, have been accidental, although the accounts that point in this direction are more colourful than probable and thus have the smell of an attempt to put out a smokescreen. Fritz Hesse, the German embassy press man, was told that Hudson had drunkenly dialled the wrong phone number and spoken to a newspaper editor rather than Chamberlain. Wohlthat was told that Hudson had simply been over-heard talking too loudly to the Spanish ambassador, the Duke of Alba.[26]

Chamberlain was predictably furious that the story had leaked, but the reaction suggests that Hudson's conversation with Wohlthat had not been wholly a private venture by a junior minister. As usual, Chamberlain blamed someone else. He fumed that Hudson 'had a very bad reputation as a disloyal colleague ... it is a favourite device of his to take ideas on which other people have been working for years and put them forward as his own'.[27] The loan, though, Chamberlain labelled as not part of the package and he felt on firm enough ground to deny to the House of Commons that there was any plan for a loan. He could pass off the talks between Wohlthat and Hudson as more-or-less routine, although he had to admit that the Cabinet had not known in advance. As for how Wilson had come to be talking to Wohlthat, his long-ob-solete title as chief industrial adviser came in handy as a pretext that Chamberlain could use to explain it away.

Wilson was caught unawares by the leak and had to track down Wohlthat the night before the story appeared to agree what line to take with the press.[28] He knew that trouble was in store. Not only had the Cabinet not been informed, neither had the Foreign Office. The only British record of the talks was Wilson's memorandum of his conversation, which was, perhaps predictably, far less substantial than Wohlthat's and reads quite differently.[29] It did not mention the list of points at all and the only reference to further talks was 'the now very familiar [idea] that someone should visit Hitler prepared to talk to him about political, military and economic questions'. Wilson's account reads like a general chat about the state of relations between Britain and Germany, which leaves the reader wondering quite why it should have taken place. Wilson said very little to Wohlthat except for repeating a claim that Britain's actions had been forced on it by Germany's 'trouble-some' behaviour, emphasising the scale of British military preparations and insisting that any initiative must come from the German side.[30]

Wilson claimed that he said a number of times that British policy was fully explained in Halifax's Chatham House speech and gave Wohlthat a copy of *The Times* with a report of the speech when Wohlthat confessed that he had not read it.

Wilson's memorandum was dated 19 July, the day after the conversation with Wohlthat, but it was not passed on to Halifax until 24 July, two days after the story was leaked in the papers, and then only when the Foreign Secretary asked for it.[31] Even if the conversation had been as superficial as Wilson's account suggests, it is still remarkable that the Foreign Office had not been informed beforehand. It is hard to avoid the suspicion that the memorandum was composed and ante-dated to cover Wilson and the Prime Minister from the disclosure of their secret diplomacy. Long afterwards Wilson admitted that his reports on back-channel conversations were 'perhaps somewhat inadequate'.[32]

# CHAPTER TWENTY-NINE

# MR BOOTHBY EXPECTS
# A RAKE-OFF

*The attached letter implies that claimants will suffer if they do come under Mr Boothby's wing (which is untrue); Nathan states that Mr Boothby has had long and arduous negotiations with the Treasury (which is untrue); and Weininger may be held to imply that Mr Boothby expects a rake-off.*
– SIGISMUND WALEY TO SIR HORACE WILSON

During his wilderness years Churchill was both a substantial figure in politics and a political pariah. He cut a lonely figure in the House of Commons. There was no large group of dissident MPs around him. He made no effort to build one and few would have been tempted to join, given the ferocity of the whips and his dwindling prospects of ever returning to power. Of the twenty or so MPs who abstained in the Munich debate only three were linked to him, his son-in-law Duncan Sandys, Bob Boothby and Brendan Bracken. The two latter had been his followers for a long time. Boothby had been Churchill's parliamentary private secretary whilst he was Chancellor of the Exchequer from 1924 to 1929, and Bracken had helped him in election campaigns in 1923 and 1924. Supporting Churchill was bad enough in the eyes of Conservative mainstream opinion, but Boothby and Bracken had lurid reputations in their own right. Boothby was a heavy and unsuccessful speculator on the Stock Exchange, involved in second-rank financial businesses, and was conducting a long-term and flagrant affair with the wife of a fellow MP, Harold Macmillan. Bracken played up his obscure origins to the point of apparently encouraging utterly un-founded rumours that he was Churchill's illegitimate son. Bracken was the driving force behind the creation of a group of financial newspapers and magazines. He was highly paid and flaunted his affluence with a chauffeur-driven Hispano-Suiza and a house in Lord North Street. In traditional Conservative circles he was viewed as practically a criminal. Boothby and Bracken both offered tempting targets for indirect attacks against Churchill and opposition to appeasement.

Bracken and Boothby had both put themselves very firmly in the firing line over the Czech gold scandal of May 1939. After Prague the Germans had naturally wanted to get their hands on Czechoslovakia's gold reserves, but they were physically held outside the country. Luckily for them, the Bank for International Settlements (BIS) docilely began to hand the reserves over under the influence of Montagu Norman, gover-nor of the Bank of England and partner in Wilson's attempts to appease Germany economically in January 1939.[1] This was done in secret but, in one of the greatest feats of investigative journalism ever, Paul Einzig, who wrote for Bracken's *Financial News*, broke the story that £6 million worth of gold had been handed over to the Nazis. When the scandal was debated in the House of Commons, Sir John Simon, the minister responsible, put up a dishonest and contemptible performance even by his own high standards. He was severely harried by Bracken, Boothby and Churchill, who was able to indulge in pointed wit at Simon's dis-comfiture when he wound up the debate:

> Here we are going about urging our people to enlist, urging them to accept new forms of military compulsion; here we are paying taxes on a gigantic scale in order to protect ourselves. If at the same time our mechanism of government is so butter-fingered that this £6,000,000 of gold can be transferred to the Nazi Government of Germany, which only wishes to use it, and is only using it, as it does all its foreign exchange, for the purpose of increasing its armaments ... it stultifies altogether the efforts our people are making in every class and in every party to secure National Defence and rally the whole forces of the country.[2]

A couple of months later in July 1939, Boothby presented Wilson with a near-perfect opportunity to even the score, when he opened himself to an attack on a question of financial ethics, involving another set of Czech assets. One of Boothby's business partners, who had become a close personal friend, was a Czech-Jewish businessman called Richard Weininger, who had been an officer in the Hapsburg army during the First World War. Weininger had moved to Britain in 1938, but he and his family had left considerable assets in Czechoslovakia, which they hoped to get out of the country. After Prague this became immensely more difficult. Boothby and another MP, Colonel Harry Nathan, formed a committee to try to help Czech refugees claim compensation for assets frozen in the now Nazi-controlled territory. These naturally included Weininger's family. Boothby began to lobby on behalf of holders of Czech assets who signed up to the committee. This was all in the public eye and perfectly above board. Boothby was not paid for his work on the committee.

Boothby's committee worked in parallel with a far more prestigious one. A well-established City of London organisation – the Council of Foreign Bondholders, which had represented British investors in securities issued by defaulting entities abroad since the late nineteenth century – had established a committee to advise the Treasury on Czech assets. It featured luminaries such as Sir Edward Reid, a partner in Baring Brothers, the prestigious merchant bank, and Sir Otto Niemeyer, who had moved from the Treasury to the Bank of England. They viewed Boothby's upstart operation with 'some misgivings'.[3]

What was not disclosed was a private arrangement under which Weininger agreed to pay Boothby 10 per cent of anything recovered for him. Weininger put the family assets involved at £242,000 (worth perhaps £25 million today) so Boothby's share would have been £24,200. This would have been enough to pay off some very pressing debts with which he was faced, including £6,000 to another former MP, the sinister figure of Alfred Butt, who doubled as a theatrical impresario and money-lender. Even more dubiously, Boothby had helped transfer the legal ownership of the Weininger assets to a British company, Zota Limited, and ante-dated this transaction to a week before Prague. At a point when it was unclear whether British holders of Czech assets would be treated more favourably than Czech émigrés, this looked like an attempt to paint a Union Jack on the Weininger claim using forged documents.

All this was to remain hidden for over a year, but where Boothby came unstuck in the summer of 1939 was by trying to recruit some more wealthy Czechs to his committee. The Petschek family of bankers and industrialists might have claimed to be the Rothschilds of Czechoslovakia and, being Jewish, had fled their homeland. The cousins Paul and Walter Petschek had even greater assets frozen in Czechoslovakia than Weininger, approximately £900,000. They had heard of Boothby's committee, but had no interest in it and preferred to deal directly with the Bank of England. Boothby began to pester them to associate themselves with his committee. Had he left it at that, it is unlikely anything would have happened, but he then over-reached himself badly. Walter Petschek told Colonel Nathan that his family refused to join the committee. Nathan replied, implying quite falsely that the Boothby committee was the authorised channel for compensation claims and that the Petscheks' claim would suffer if they persisted in staying outside. Even Boothby accepted that Nathan's letter was blackmail.[4]

Boothby also tried to apply pressure on Petschek from another direction, which was even more risky. Louis Infield, the brother of one of Boothby's lawyers, was a very junior civil servant at the Ministry of Health. Boothby persuaded him to assist in the scheme. Infield duly telephoned Paul Petschek, asking him to come to his office at the Ministry of Health without explaining why he wanted to speak to him. Conscious of his vulnerability as a refugee in a foreign country and with the Continental's deference to the caprices of bureaucracy, Petschek agreed and went to see Infield. He was taken aback when it turned out that Infield wanted to persuade him to join Boothby's committee, suggesting that it would be 'advisable' for him to do so.[5] At this Petschek brought the interview to as rapid a close as he could.

Petschek was prompted to protest at all this and sent a copy of Nathan's blackmailing letter to Sir Edward Reid, who in turn passed it on to a senior civil servant at the Treasury, Sigismund Waley. Petschek might only have been a refugee, but he could operate in far more rarefied spheres of power and influence than Boothby. The correspondence worked its way up the system and landed on Wilson's desk together with a covering letter from Waley giving the background to the two committees. Waley suspected predatory intentions on Boothby's part: 'Mr Boothby expects a rake-off.' He also made the welcome suggestion that Boothby's pretensions might be disposed of by way of a parliamentary question, for which he had attached a draft. This gave Wilson the opportunity to bring the political heavy artillery to bear on Boothby. He forwarded the papers to Sir John Simon, together with the recommendation that the parliamentary question route be used. The very next day, Simon told the House of Commons that Boothby's committee had no official standing and that all holders of Czech assets who filed their claims with the Bank of England would be treated equally. Boothby's claim to being able to do anything useful on behalf of Weininger, the Petscheks or anyone else had been very publicly flattened.

Merely squashing Boothby's scheme was not enough for Wilson. He had struck a rich vein of material deeply discreditable to Churchill's parliamentary acolyte, and he set out to mine it to the full with minimum delay. Wilson called Paul Petschek in for a conversation that same Friday. He opened by telling Petschek that Infield's suggestion that the Petscheks would be at a disadvantage if they did not place their claim via Boothby was 'one which we in this country could not tolerate'. Wilson did not say so outright but he clearly implied that Infield had behaved quite wrongly and asked Petschek to 'help him get a full and clear picture of the whole incident'.[6] He was beginning to prepare the indictment of Boothby. Petschek was desperate to avoid getting involved in any controversial issues given his and his family's status, but bowed to the inevitable and reluctantly agreed to send Wilson copies of all the correspondence involved. Wilson promised that he would be discreet about their involvement.

The following Tuesday Wilson moved on to the next potential source of dirt on Boothby. Infield was a far softer target than Petschek. He was petrified at being called in by the head of the Civil Service at very short notice. He did not admit to having intentionally pressurised Petschek, but otherwise sang like a canary. He described in detail how Boothby had recruited him and provided crucial testimony to the damning fact that Boothby had personally asked him to call Petschek in. Wilson accepted Infield's claim that he had been naive and that he had not been given any financial incentive to do what he had done.[7] Infield agreed happily to provide a full written account of what had gone on. Wilson had no reason to punish Infield; he was far more useful as a junior civil servant terrified for his job and correspondingly willing to cooperate. The chief civil servant of the Ministry of Health agreed with Wilson that Infield had been 'indiscreet & foolish' but no more and that a severe reprimand would 'meet the case'.[8] Given the gravity of what Infield had done, he had got off lightly, but he was more valuable on tap on the government payroll for future operations against Boothby.

Boothby himself had to be left to the politicians and Simon called him in for the final scene in the first act of the drama. Simon warned Boothby that the ground was about to be cut from under the feet of his committee by the parliamentary question. In what was to prove a near-suicidal move, Boothby repeatedly assured Simon on his honour that he had no financial stake in the affair. This was true in the narrow sense that he was not being paid anything but expenses by his committee and that he had no direct financial motive to persuade the Petscheks to join; he made no mention of the 'rake-off' from Weininger's claim that had already been agreed. Boothby's economy with the truth at this point would come back to haunt him the following year, but for the time being Wilson and his allies could be content with having hobbled Boothby's committee.

# CHAPTER THIRTY

# TOO MANY PEOPLE AT THE JOB

*This seems to be a reason for hesitation about Mr Tennant*
*(it won't do to have too many people at the job, even if*
*they begin by going to different quarters there).*
– SIR HORACE WILSON TO ARTHUR RUCKER

Chamberlain moaned that 'Hudson's gaffe' had done harm, but there is no sign that he believed that it was lasting. He certainly did not share the view of Cadogan's private secretary, Gladwyn Jebb, one of the opponents of appeasement inside the Foreign Office, that '[t]he immediate effect of this piece of super-appeasement has been to arouse all the suspicions of the Bolsheviks, dishearten the Poles ... and encourage the Germans into thinking that we are prepared to buy peace'.[1] Chamberlain was confident that 'there are other and discreeter channels by which contact can be maintained for it is important that those in Germany who would like to see us come to an understanding should not be discouraged'.[2] When Chamberlain claimed at the start of July that he had 'one or two' ideas for keeping up contacts with Germany to offer Hitler a face-saving exit from the Danzig crisis, it was something of an understatement. The chain that led from Helmut Wohlthat to Herbert von Dirksen was far from the only avenue that Downing Street was exploring. Throughout July and August 1939, two more high-profile British visitors came to Germany, carrying messages from Downing Street, albeit usually in the guise of purely private contributions to good relations between Britain and Germany. Wilson was the ring-master of this particular circus, just as he had handled

Wohlthat. He made sure that his various intermediaries stuck to the 'dual policy' line, but it was the 'willing to talk' part of the policy that mattered most.

Chamberlain did not think that much needed to be done to convince Hitler of how firm a line he would take after all the various posturings in the aftermath of Prague. In fact, the risk that Chamberlain saw was that Hitler would launch a pre-emptive strike before Britain became too strong:

> In fact I have little doubt that Hitler knows quite well that we mean business. The only question to which he is not sure of the answer is whether we meant to attack him as soon as we are strong enough. If he thought we did he would naturally argue that he had better have the war when it suits him than wait till it suits us. But in various ways I am trying to get the truth conveyed to the only quarter where it matters.[3]

Chamberlain's conviction that he had persuaded Hitler of Britain's resolution was the last in the series of convenient delusions about him that had fed appeasement throughout. It had begun with the belief that Hitler was actively competing with Mussolini for Britain's affections. When Hitler failed to follow up the Munich declaration, Chamberlain convinced himself that he was being forced back to talks by Germany's economic problems.

Downing Street's choice of intermediaries and the simple fact that they were coming sent the signal that Britain wanted to talk. Downing Street discounted the risk that this would undercut the firmness aspect of the dual policy. The Germans were only too happy to oblige with a suitably impressive level of reception for the visitors. Anything that stayed the British hand was welcome. The professionals of the Auswärtiges Amt genuinely wanted to avoid war, but Hitler and Hewel just wanted to string the British along, in a rerun of the 'golden bridges' of the Sudeten crisis. Ribbentrop was temperamentally hostile to Britain but told Hitler whatever he thought he wanted to hear. Ribbentrop's man Hesse gave him a precious direct line to Wilson. Goering was not going to be left out of the competition to control German relations with Britain and made sure that he had dogs in the fight. Thus every single element of the chaotic world of Nazi foreign policy became involved in Wilson's efforts at back-channel diplomacy.

Hardly had Arthur Bryant set off on his mission to Germany than another significant figure volunteered his services as an intermediary. Ernest Tennant was a City of London financier, descended from the Scottish chemist and industrialist Charles Tennant, who had made a huge fortune from industrial bleaching techniques and established one of Britain's wealthiest dynasties. He was also a constituent of Rab Butler, with whom he was on good terms. Tennant had come to know Ribbentrop just as he was setting out on his campaign to make friends for Germany amongst the British elite in 1934. He had become probably Ribbentrop's oldest and closest British friend, and at his suggestion had been one of the founders of the Anglo-German Fellowship, in which he played a major role. It was precisely this access to Ribbentrop that Tennant offered to put at Chamberlain's service in a letter written on 4 July.[4] He dangled the dream of winning Ribbentrop away from his present hostility to Britain and back to the frame of mind in which he had come to Britain seeking friendship five years before. To begin with Wilson was sceptical, aware of the risk of flooding the market for back-channel links between London and Berlin: 'This [Bryant's mission] seems to be a reason for hesitation about Mr Tennant (it won't do to have too many people at the job, even if they begin by going to different quarters there).'[5]

There were also grounds for reservations about approaching the German leadership through Ribbentrop, who was the most glaring and notorious representative of 'that section of opinion in Germany which has always held that Britain will never fight'. When Ball and Wilson had been trying to head Henry Drummond Wolff off from his own efforts at mediation, they had been aware (or at least claimed to be aware) of the danger of encouraging these forces in Germany.

Wilson's reservations did not weigh as heavily on Chamberlain, and he instructed Wilson to see Tennant on his behalf, on one of the rare occasions on which Chamberlain can be seen to have overruled him.[6]

Wilson did not try to dissuade Tennant from going. Tennant certainly made the right noises to Wilson, assuring him that he supported the government's 'dual policy' and saying that he would tell Ribbentrop that Britain was ready to fulfil its obligations to Poland. Even if it was already a done deal with Chamberlain that Tennant should go, Wilson still subjected him to a full catechism, which balanced the stick with the carrot:

> [I]t was important that he should confine his conversation to the lines that he had just expressed to me, namely, his interpretation of the whole-hearted way in which the British public is behind the Government in its policy, first, of determination to assist any state whose independence is threatened, but, secondly, of willingness to reason with reasonable people.

Even before the leak of the Wohlthat talks, secrecy and deniability were major preoccupations for Wilson. On no account was Tennant to tell anyone that he had seen Wilson, or in any way been in touch with the Prime Minister. It was all right for Berlin to be subjected to a parade of prominent British people arguing for good relations, but they should at least seem to be travelling of their own volition.

Downing Street's willingness for Tennant to undertake his mission survived the public furore over Wohlthat, even though the publicity did give Tennant pause for thought. Ultimately, he decided that his personal links with Ribbentrop were already so well established that he was in a strong position to put over the line that he had agreed with Wilson. He had also devised his own, personal take on Hudson's scheme to offer Germany financial incentives to behave itself.[7] Germany was to be credited with an imaginary sum of £100 million, notionally invested in the major world equity indices. Tennant fully expected that an Anglo-German settlement 'would bring about a very large rise in the value of securities'.[8] Once Hitler had signed the agreement, the resulting profit of £50 million, or £100 million if he were really lucky, would be credited to Germany, probably under the condition of being spent 'entirely within the British Empire'. Wilson produced a tactfully watered-down version of this intriguing proposal for the files, which was promptly sabotaged when Chamberlain's private secretary, Arthur Rucker, passed on to Chamberlain Tennant's original letter. Wilson was terrified that there might be a repetition of the Wohlthat fiasco and topped up his initial briefing to Tennant with a copy of Lord Halifax's Chatham House speech and a very firm instruction 'not to give the slightest indication that there were any "proposals" in our mind'.[9]

Tennant made only a half-hearted pretence that he wanted to see Ribbentrop as part of a routine business trip to Germany.[10] Under the feeble pretext that he found Ribbentrop's magnificent office at the Auswärtiges Amt daunting as a private individual, he proposed a quiet dinner and 'real talk as we used to do in the old days'. He was duly asked to come to Ribbentrop's Austrian country *Schloß* at Fuschl, followed by an invitation to join Ribbentrop on the eleven-hour train ride back to Berlin the following day. On the train he had a long conversation with Walther Hewel, who was travelling as part of Ribbentrop's retinue for the trip.

Tennant's mission to reopen the dialogue was doomed from the beginning. Ribbentrop was too far gone in his hostility to Britain to behave like a rational shaper of foreign policy. Tennant was treated to some hours' worth of monologue by the foreign minister at his most verbose and a slightly more restrained performance by Hewel. Ribbentrop's rant ranged from the debilitating effect on Britain of dominance by the Oxbridge caste to Hitler's status as a figure of millennial importance, on a par with Muhammad. Whatever hopes Wilson might have entertained that Tennant would either convince Ribbentrop that Britain would fight or prepare the way for a conversation between 'reasonable people', they were to be disappointed. When Tennant reported to Wilson on his return to London, he apologised for the 'absence of argument' by saying that he thought it was 'better to encourage Ribbentrop to talk than to divert him into an argumentative channel'.[11] Tacitly, Tennant was accepting that Britain would have to live with Ribbentrop as an implacable enemy. If Wilson had seriously hoped that Tennant would deliver a ringing statement of Britain's commitment to defending smaller states, he was in for a disappointment. Hewel peremptorily rejected Tennant's tentative suggestion that Hitler might be interested in a temporary agreement to hold further expansion, leaving Tennant with no proposals to take back to London except for the demand that Poland should stop 'insulting' Germany, that the British press should be muzzled and that the Poles should be convinced of the futility of military resistance to Germany, with the clear implication that Britain should stop encouraging them in this folly.

Ribbentrop treated Tennant to barely disguised warnings that Germany was mobilising technology to prepare for war. A huge plant was being constructed to convert coal into oil, making good Germany's poor access to mineral oil. Other projects aimed at generating power by splitting the atom, solving the problem of perpetual motion and making wool from potato peelings. This early warning of German nuclear ambitions did not get quite the attention it deserved, perhaps because it was mixed in with projects respectively fantastical and bathetic.

Tennant was given ample reason to understand just how perilous the situation was: 'R. gave me the impression that war has almost been decided upon.' Hewel topped this up by telling Tennant that Hitler was bent on avenging Polish 'insults' and was convinced that Britain was so dominated by Jewish influence that 'there is nothing to be done but fight'. Tennant returned to London sure of the seriousness of the position, but once he was exposed to the calming influence of Wilson's company, he began to see things in a more optimistic light; 'he formed the impression from something that Hewel said at the close of their discussion that he, Hewel, for all the threatenings, felt sure that there would not be any serious trouble'. Tennant recorded Hewel saying that Hitler was prepared to wait a year, but this hardly seems to justify this late surge of delusional optimism.

The mixed messages from Tennant were not the only reason why Downing Street failed to take fully on board the warning signs that he brought back from Germany. On the same day that Tennant had dined with Ribbentrop, another unofficial envoy had spoken to the Führer himself and had come away with a far more comforting story. Lord Kemsley, chairman of the Allied Newspaper group, unlike his brother Lord Camrose, had remained a faithful supporter of the policy of appeasement. Kemsley controlled the *Daily Sketch* and the *Sunday Times*, Chamberlain's most slavishly obedient press outlet, in his own right. How he came on the scene featured yet another example of the persistent inability of some senior people in Britain to recognise Nazi propaganda stunts and their inclination to treat them as serious attempts to build good relations between the countries.

In May 1939 Kemsley's attention had been caught by an article in the Nazi Party newspaper *Der Völkischer Beobachter* by Otto Dietrich, Hitler's press secretary.[12] Dietrich claimed that he had proposed a deal to the head of 'one of the most important newspaper groups in the United States' under which he would put the entire German press at the disposal of this group's best writer provided that a reciprocal article putting the German case was published by this group. According to Dietrich his offer was rejected. The American group was not named and the whole story may have been an invention. Nonetheless the idea caught Kemsley's fancy and he contacted Dietrich with the offer to implement the same deal between his newspapers and the German press. Having promoted the whole notion in the first place, Dietrich would have been ill placed to slam the door on Kemsley and preparations went ahead on the British side.

Downing Street had evidently been satisfied with Arthur Bryant's performance as a spokesman for the British cause as he was commissioned to produce the British contribution for the Dietrich–Kemsley article swap, instead of another writer whom Kemsley had first nominated. Bryant put aside other pressing commitments and began the work. Downing Street took the scheme very seriously indeed and Wilson personally took charge. Bryant went through his draft together with Wilson and obediently amended it on a number of points, which Wilson wanted, most notably to remove the statement that Hitler had duped Chamberlain through Prague.[13] For all the effort that Wilson and Bryant put into the task, it was to come to nothing and Bryant's efforts remained hidden in government files for thirty years.

Kemsley began his mission with something of a lag in the back-channel appeasement stakes. He was invited to Germany by Dietrich, ostensibly at least to discuss the newspaper articles exchange scheme, but the possibility of an audience with Hitler hovered in the background from the beginning. Kemsley's mission began with the customary passage through Wilson's office and the ritual catechism. There was no pretence that he was anything but Downing Street's messenger. 'Kemsley has gone away with what is, I hope, a right impression of what he should say – if received – and he has promised to stick closely to the line.'[14]

Quite what Wilson told Kemsley to say can only be inferred from his note of the conversation, but there is no indication that it was any different to his briefing to Tennant. It seems that he was excused from reading Halifax's Chatham House speech. The one notable difference is that the total secrecy with which Tennant's mission was shrouded was somewhat lifted for Kemsley's. Wilson was not worried that news might get back to the Foreign Office and he asked Sir Nevile Henderson to look after the press lord, who was duly invited to the embassy.

Kemsley got off to a promising start in Berlin. He had begun proceedings by a preliminary meeting with Alfred Rosenberg, the Nazi's chief ideologist and another old friend of Hitler, who rather nonplussed his visitors by referring to Chamberlain as Britain's Führer. Rosenberg clearly reported favourably and Kemsley was told that Dietrich would see him not in Berlin, but in Bayreuth. It was a high honour and a strong hint that Kemsley would be received by Hitler himself. The annual festival of Wagner operas at Bayreuth was the high point of the Nazi cultural calendar and a fixed date in the programme of anyone who was anyone in Nazi Germany. Hitler's passion for the composer put Wagner squarely at the top of the German pantheon of creative geniuses. Hitler attended every festival from 1930 until his decision to invade the Soviet Union in 1941 curtailed his social programme. It was at Hitler's urging that the festival became an annual event. Kemsley's chances of seeing Hitler were thus riding high. The festival had been directed from 1930 by Winifred Wagner, the English-born but mainly German-raised widow of the composer's son Siegfried. Winifred was utterly devoted to Hitler personally but she never joined or publicly supported the Nazi Party.

The conversation between Hitler and Kemsley had almost been pre-scripted as an Anglo-German lovefest. The British party were struck by Hitler's friendliness throughout. The Führer kicked off with the claim that 'he personally had never been anything but friendly towards Britain'. Kemsley played his part to perfection, adopting the guise of the bluff, apolitical businessman. The arms race between Britain and Germany was just as futile as a price war that he and a rival publisher had fought, until the intervention of a mutual friend had brought the folly to an end. He faithfully trotted out the dual policy of firmness and openness to dialogue that Wilson had laid out. Officially Downing Street's policy balanced firmness and friendliness, but the dreams of the pure spirit of appeasement were still the dominant feature; Kemsley endorsed Chamberlain's optimistic view of the Munich declaration as 'the forerunner of a different relationship with Germany in the future'. The pitch he delivered for Britain's new firmness was decidedly flabby. He did not tell Hitler explicitly that Chamberlain would stand by the guarantee to Poland if Germany attacked; instead he used a distinctly abstract formula which also left Chamberlain with a broad escape route. 'If the Prime Minister considered that Germany had done something so serious as to affect the security of the world, and announced in Parliament that he had decided to declare war on Germany, the whole House would rise in support.'[15]

Hitler was direct as well as friendly. He sniffily distanced himself from the Hudson–Wohlthat talks: 'Germany was not after money.' He wound up with a proposal that was music to the ears of Chamberlain and Wilson, spontaneously suggesting that each country put in writing what it wanted. This was precisely the kind of structured approach to negotiation that the British had dreamed of from the start. The Germans made every effort to impress on Kemsley's party just how well things had gone. The interpreter Paul Schmidt told them how favoured Kemsley had been to receive a full hour of the Führer's time instead of the ritual twenty minutes. Hitler himself conspicuously received the British party in the first interval of the performance of *Parsifal* later that day. Hitler's crazed British aristocratic groupie, Unity Mitford, sought out Kemsley and informed him that Hitler himself had told her of the discussion.

The British motives in the Kemsley talks were idealistic; Hitler's were far more cynical. It was of course in his interests to keep them guessing as to his true intentions, especially with the German negotiations with the Soviet Union at an early stage. Hitler was using the same tactics that he had used ahead of the Sudeten crisis, although for the one and only time he involved himself directly in the business of stringing the British along. The first hint of this had come a fortnight before the Kemsley visit, when Hitler and Goebbels discussed how Goebbels would respond publicly to Halifax's Chatham House speech.[16] He expected the British and French to climb down if – as had happened before Munich – Germany built a 'golden bridge' for them, as it was indeed soon about to do. Hitler might have been in diplomatic, rather than natural, mode when he spoke to Kemsley. Dietrich, who had originated the conversation and knew Hitler far, far better than the British visitors, was much less convinced that he was truly being friendly. He 'was struck by Hitler's marked reserve throughout the talk'.[17] All the evidence of German enthusiasm may simply have been staged. The Germans were not remotely deceived by Wilson's efforts to conceal Downing Street's involvement and to depict all this as the private efforts of individuals. Wilson's hopes that this would put over both halves of the dual policy equally effectively were similarly illusory. Goebbels knew that Kemsley had 'come obviously [*selbstverständlich*] as Chamberlain's emissary' and that his message was that 'Britain did not want war'.[18]

All this was hidden from Downing Street, and hopes soared when Kemsley briefed Chamberlain and Wilson about his conversation with Hitler.[19] Kemsley urged them to follow up his discussion. Wilson imposed the most stringent secrecy on Kemsley, who proudly told him that he had already fobbed off attempts by his fellow press baron Lord Beaverbrook to worm the true story out of him by sticking to the article exchange cover story.[20] The vision of a deal with Hitler shone brightly enough for Downing Street to bring the official side of British foreign policy into the equation, although this was to be limited to Halifax and Sir Alec Cadogan. Cadogan was by then too hard-bitten to do more than wish Downing Street joy of this latest exercise, but Halifax loyally did his duty. Between them, Chamberlain and the Foreign Office chose to take the most proactive route available to pursue the opening:

Kemsley should get in touch with Dietrich as soon as possible to explore how Britain and Germany might put their demands in writing. There was no question that this was to be handled other than at the highest level, and Wilson drafted a letter for Kemsley to sign. It was acceptable for a professional diplomat and the Foreign Office to know what was going on, but the actual mechanics of the contact remained firmly in Downing Street's hands.

Whilst Kemsley was treated to a charade of Hitler's interest in appeasement future, the ghost of appeasement past was roaming the streets of Bayreuth.[21] Unofficial contacts with Germany had overtaken traditional diplomacy as Downing Street's chosen way of approaching Hitler. Not only had Nevile Henderson failed to build a worthwhile dialogue, but the throat cancer that was to kill him was already draining his strength. It seemed that he was only kept in position as a symbol of the government's commitment to appeasement.[22] Henderson knew of Kemsley's visit and was almost certainly aware that a conversation with Hitler was in prospect. Scenting the chance of getting to speak to the Führer himself, he decided to get in on the act. That, after all, is what ambassadors are supposed to do and he had a flimsy pretext. By chance, when he was studying German as a young man, he had shared lodgings with another Old Etonian, who was otherwise as different from him as possible. The future Lord Berners was a high aesthete and eccentric who had schooled Henderson in the musical detail of Wagner's Ring cycle, which the diplomat had never forgotten.[23] Claiming affection for Wagner's music ('[t]hough absolutely unmusical'), Henderson set off for Bayreuth but was delayed by a car breakdown so he arrived only after Hitler had departed for a tour of inspection of the *Westwall* fortifications. Winifred Wagner, whom Henderson knew, tried to help him, but all she could do was to keep him amused until Hitler returned with occupations closer to Henderson's heart such as a trout-fishing excursion in nearby Berneck.[24] It was all to no avail. When Hitler returned, no invitation arrived and all Henderson got was a glimpse at the performance of *Die Walküre*.

\*   \*   \*

In contrast to Downing Street's enthusiasm for covert contacts with Germany that it inspired directly, there was little interest in an unsolicited approach from dissidents. General Ludwig Beck was closely aligned with anti-Hitler elements and had resigned as the Wehrmacht chief of staff in August 1938 in protest at the proposed invasion of Czechoslovakia. In July 1944 he was to pay with his life for his part in the bomb plot against Hitler. In July 1939 he sent a staff officer, Colonel von Schwerin, to warn the British of German plans to invade Poland and to suggest means by which Hitler could be deterred. Unlike Theodor Kordt, who had at least got a hearing from Wilson, Halifax and Cadogan the previous year when he tried to get British help for the dissidents' conspiracy, Schwerin was given only a low-key reception: James Stuart, the deputy chief whip, and a former military attaché in Berlin.[25] Schwerin doomed the initiative from the start by arguing for bringing Churchill into power as 'the only Englishman Hitler is afraid of' and claiming that Hitler 'was convinced that British foreign policy was thoroughly flabby'.[26] Stuart was a Chamberlain loyalist and closed the conversation with the blank statement that Schwerin's ideas were politically impossible.

# CHAPTER THIRTY-ONE

# ENTITLED TO DEMAND CONCESSIONS

*The British Government would use its influence in Warsaw to induce the
Polish Government to cede to the German demands ... because Britain
was giving Poland so much political backing she [Britain] was entitled
to demand from the Polish concessions in order to avoid
an entanglement with Germany.*
– Sir Horace Wilson to Herbert von Dirksen

The summer of 1939 in Britain was not swallowed by the same atmosphere of looming crisis as the summer of 1938, when Czechoslovakia had dominated everything. Britain had set down two public
markers with the Polish guarantee and Halifax's Chatham House
speech. There was nothing comparable to the Runciman mission,
which had sucked Britain into the agonised detail of German claims in
the Sudeten dispute. Berlin, Warsaw, the Germans of Danzig and, in a
last faint evidence of its existence, the League of Nations could be left
to sort things out amongst themselves.

But there was still a crisis, and no one was more aware of this than
Churchill. He was determined that the British Parliament should have a
voice in whatever Britain might do. In a normal year it would have been
unexceptional for Parliament to go on holiday for the months of August
and September, but not in 1939. Churchill saw the danger that a normal
parliamentary recess would appear to be a retreat that allowed the forces of
appeasement to hold sway. He wrote to the press baron Lord Rothermere:

Evidently a great 'crunch' is coming and all preparations in Germany are moving forward ceaselessly to some date in August. Whether H. will call it off or not is a psychological problem which you can judge as well as any living man. I fear he despises Chamberlain and is convinced that the reason he does not broaden his Government is because he means to give in once Parliament has risen.[1]

Churchill feared that 'the Government would run out over Poland as it had over Czechoslovakia'.[2] With Churchill's support, the Labour Party formally proposed that the holiday be limited to a couple of weeks. Chamberlain was enraged and put the move down to a manoeuvre by Churchill against him personally: '[T]he real protagonists of a change are Winston (backed by L.G. [Lloyd George]!) and Archie [Archibald Sinclair, Liberal leader] and their real object is of course to attack and weaken the PM.'[3] Fuelled by the twaddle that Walther Hewel had fed to him via Arthur Bryant, Chamberlain was smugly complacent that Hitler was backing down. Churchill was not to be allowed to challenge this view or the plans for an extension of appeasement that Chamberlain and Wilson had been brewing.

Whether I shall be able to carry out my plans remains to be seen. All my information indicates that Hitler now realises that he can't grab anything else without a major war and has decided to put Danzig into cold storage. On the other hand he would feel that with all these demonstrations here, mobilisation of the fleet, territorials & militiamen training, bombers flying up and down France, he must do something to show that he is not frightened. I should not be at all surprised therefore to hear of … large bodies of troops near the Polish frontier, great flights of bombers, and a crop of stories of ominous preparations … That is part of the war of nerves and no doubt will send Winston into hysterics. But to summon Parliament to ask questions & demand counter measures is to play straight into Hitler's hands and give the world the impression that we are in a panic.[4]

Just to ram home his belief that genuine foreign policy considerations had far less to do with the motion than partisan self-interest, Chamberlain told the House that the vote was one of confidence in the government even though the whips had not issued a formal three-line whip. Even allowing for the risk of some Tory defections, this upped the ante greatly, as there was no serious risk that the government would be defeated. Chamberlain had goaded Churchill in a brief conversation before the debate, which fed a bitter exchange during the debate itself.[5]

The government inevitably won with a healthy majority, leaving Chamberlain to relish Churchill's annoyance. He could depart for his summer holiday fishing with the Duke of Westminster at his luxurious house at Lochmore in the Scottish Highlands.

*　　*　　*

Churchill had been entirely prescient in his instinct to keep Parliament involved in British foreign policy. Just as the recess began, Wilson undertook one last and quite outrageous attempt to appease Germany.

Senior Nazi leaders attended Bayreuth regularly, whatever their tastes in music or lack of them. Joseph Goebbels was the most assiduous attender. It provided an opportunity to meet the Führer in a relatively relaxed atmosphere, as he indulged in his musical passion. His other greatest place of relaxation, the Berghof, remained a very private space to which invitations were strictly rationed. Sometimes this access came at a cost, such as the occasion when Hitler tried to use the swan motif from *Lohengrin* as a device to wean Goering away from his passion for blood sports. The Nazi leaders might not have enjoyed the music but the event provided a forum for their usual occupations of backstabbing, intrigue and point-scoring as they manoeuvred to win the Führer's favour and poison his mind against their rivals. The atmosphere was an even more claustrophobic and oppressive extension of the Führer's court in Berlin, with its power plays conducted in the confined area of a small provincial town. The 1939 edition did not prove to be an exception to this rule. Hitler attended and appropriately the first performance he saw there was *Götterdämmerung*, 'Twilight of the Gods'.

In August 1939 Hermann Goering was gifted the opportunity to lob

– intentionally or otherwise – a couple of sizeable stones into Joachim von Ribbentrop's pond. The public disclosure of the Wohlthat talks had stymied Goering's foray into back-channel diplomacy with Britain, but he could always use the affair to score off his rival. Ribbentrop was attending Bayreuth and appears to have been focused on the socio-cultural goings-on there, where the festival had been running for more than a week, rather than on what Germany's various representatives, official and unofficial, were up to in London. One of the reasons why he had been a failure as ambassador to Britain was that it was more important to him to stay close to the regime's internal political ma-noeuvres in the Führer's vicinity, and he spent far less time in London than any normal ambassador would have done. As foreign minister his priorities were unaltered and he approached the conduct of diplomacy in a decidedly hands-off fashion. Even though Herbert von Dirksen, his ambassador in London, had reported promptly and fully what he knew of Helmut Wohlthat's dealings in London to the Wilhelmstrasse, this had not registered with Ribbentrop. He was thus in for some nasty shocks when Goering, who had been paying close attention to what his man, Wohlthat, had reported to him face to face on his return from London, sprang his surprise in the shape of his own account of the mission. Goering took the opportunity to rub the foreign minister's nose in the fact that Britain's leaders had started to conduct high-level political talks with someone out of his own stable. Potentially even worse, Wohlthat had held his talks with the knowledge and acquies-cence of Ribbentrop's own man, the ambassador to London.

Confronted by his own sloppy inattention, and perhaps suspicious that Dirksen was shifting his allegiance towards his great rival for in-fluence over German foreign policy, Ribbentrop was incensed. He tele-phoned the Auswärtiges Amt in Berlin and dictated a curt telegram to Dirksen demanding an immediate report explaining Wohlthat's 'politi-cal' conversations and how they came to be held with the ambassador's knowledge. He wanted to know how Goering's man had been allowed to trespass so far onto Ribbentrop's own turf. Ribbentrop also demand-ed an explanation as to why he had not been informed of Wohlthat's actions, but the foreign ministry 'provisionally' deleted this sentence in the light of a report from a week before in which Dirksen had given a full account.[6] There was no need to make Ribbentrop look more rude, negligent and foolish than he was.

The diplomats at the Wilhelmstrasse and the London embassy saw a silver lining in their political master's furious attempt to repair the damage done by being outmanoeuvred by Goering. Wohlthat's initiative had looked dead in the water after the newspaper leak, but now that Ribbentrop insisted on finding out what lay behind it, they could sound the British out on whether they had actually been interested. If they had been, discussions could resume, this time conducted by professionals. Goering's amateur operation could be cut out of the process. Ernst von Weizsäcker, Germany's chief diplomat, followed up Ribbentrop's telegram to Dirksen with one of his own a few hours later.[7] It echoed Ribbentrop's instructions, adding two implicit questions. Was the Wilson feeler an official move by the British? What were the British up to with the Soviets, or, in German parlance, the 'encirclement negotiations'? The second item had the additional benefit that it allowed Weizsäcker to wag his finger at the amateurish efforts of Goering and Wohlthat, by pointing out that this 'obvious' question had not been raised with Wilson. This was enough ammunition to resume the conversation, albeit gently.

Word was passed to the British that the Germans wanted to find out whether there was anything of substance in the Wohlthat conversations by Weizsäcker's man in London, Theodor Kordt, who called on Rab Butler at his grand house on Smith Square. Kordt had been called back to Germany and wanted to talk to some 'very authoritative person' before he left.[8] In practice this meant Wilson himself. Kordt mis-stated and exaggerated the impact of Wohlthat's talks on the Nazi leadership by claiming that Goering 'had influenced Ribbentrop to the good' by briefing him. Moreover, according to Kordt, '[t]he Führer had shown interest'. Butler told Chamberlain about the conversation and the Prime Minister sent instructions that Wilson was to see Kordt or Dirksen. The discussions begun with Wohlthat were back on. Helpfully, Butler told Wilson that he would inform Lord Halifax of what was going on, covering Wilson's back against future claims that he was bypassing the Foreign Office.

The proceedings were markedly more furtive than Wilson's July contact with Wohlthat. After the Wohlthat debacle, Wilson was secretive in the invitation he sent to the German embassy. Their representative – Wilson was not even sure who was coming – was to come to his private address and was to park his car at a distant corner before continuing on foot. In the event it was Dirksen who came to Wilson's flat in Kensington the following day. Dirksen does not appear to have known that the British would have been happy to talk to Kordt instead, or that the meeting was more of a German initiative, albeit following on from the Wohlthat talks, than a British one. Kordt had talked up the extent to which the Wohlthat talks had interested Berlin and also appears to have been economical with the truth in the interest of getting his ambassador involved in the discussions.

The conversation was a long one, taking around two hours, which gave ample time to cover a lot of ground and different topics. Both participants wrote accounts of it, but, as happened with the British and German accounts of the Wilson–Wohlthat conversation, they have so little in common that they might as well be of different discussions. The discrepancies began with why the conversation was taking place at all. Wilson's version had Dirksen engaging in little more than a sounding-out exercise, obeying Ribbentrop's instructions to explore the subject of the Wohlthat talks further and '[c]lear his own mind as to the line which Kordt could take (and perhaps he himself later) as to the future'.[9] Strikingly, Wilson at no point claimed that it had been necessary to put the German straight as to what he might or might not have said to Wohlthat when they met. If the newspaper leaks had been incorrect, this surely would have been the moment to make this clear to Dirksen. The most likely explanation is that Wilson's memorandum (the only account he ever gave of the conversation) was intended to get something on file that touched on a sufficiently large number of topics in an innocuous way to give him a 'correct' version of events to set against anything that might leak out later. If Dirksen's take on the conversation was remotely accurate, Wilson had good cause to want material to hand with which to support an alternative version of the conversation.

Wilson was much more frank with Dirksen than he had been with Wohlthat as to the British side's enthusiasm for getting out of the guarantee to the Poles and leaving them to their fates. Dirksen was interrogated at length by the Americans in 1945 after the German surrender and what he told them had to come from memory. His strongest recollection of the talk was a 'startling' proposal that Wilson had made: '[t]he British Government would use its influence in Warsaw to induce the Polish Government to cede to the German demands'.[10] When Dirksen asked Wilson how this could be squared with the British guarantee to Poland he replied that 'because Britain was giving Poland so much political backing she [Britain] was entitled to demand from the Polish concessions in order to avoid an entanglement with Germany'.[11] Poland was the prisoner of the guarantee and not Britain. Europe was set for a rerun of the Czechoslovakian crisis of the previous year.

This was explosive enough in itself and light years away from the bland account that Wilson had placed on file, but the extra aspects of Wilson's proposals that Dirksen mentioned in his other, far lengthier, accounts were almost equally astounding. The most extensive of these was a report that Dirksen made to the Auswärtiges Amt almost immediately.[12] It is consistent with what he told the Americans and his other written accounts: a memorandum he wrote for his own use during the war and his memoirs published in 1949. The whole project was to be accomplished through a formal non-aggression pact between Britain and 'greater' Germany. This was to be negotiated in secret talks to be held in Switzerland so as to protect the British Cabinet from 'indiscretions'. Such an agreement would automatically free Britain from its guarantee to Poland. Wilson confirmed that what he had said to Wohlthat still held good. Almost all the other inducements to Germany that Wilson had dangled before Wohlthat were on offer. Only the 'disarmament' loan offer was not repeated. Wilson accused Robert Hudson, the originator of the story, of having over-emphasised general discussions on how the financial disruption of disarmament might be coped with, and the idea was off the table. The more likely true explanation is that Chamberlain and Wilson had taken note of Hitler's claim to Lord Kemsley at Bayreuth that 'Germany was not after money', and knew how little the loan offer appealed to the Führer.[13] Wilson was explicit that he was making an official feeler on behalf of the British government, to which an answer was expected.

The answer took some while to come. Wilson had chosen to make his most blatant and cynical offer to desert Poland to the most poorly placed of all his intermediaries to Germany. When Dirksen returned to Germany – for good, as it proved – a few days later, he tried unsuccessfully to follow up his written report with a talk with Ribbentrop or even the Führer himself. As well as communicating Wilson's proposals, he wanted it to be made clear that he was convinced that Britain would indeed go to war to support the Polish guarantee. Dirksen began his campaign with Weizsäcker at the Auswärtiges Amt, who was entirely – and correctly – pessimistic. When Dirksen explained what he wanted, his professional boss could only shrug his shoulders and swipe his hand across the table as though the question had already been brushed aside.[14] Dirksen got no further. Ribbentrop pretended that he could spare no time to talk to the ambassador. This was clearly dishonest as he was spending hours in discussion with his own man in London, Fritz Hesse.[15] Dirksen concluded, probably accurately, that Ribbentrop 'didn't want to hear reports which did not fit in with his own ideas'.[16] He knew that Ribbentrop was a rabid enemy of Britain and less ready than Hitler to seek a peaceful solution to difficulties.[17] According to Dirksen's contacts, Ribbentrop was convinced that Britain would not fight to protect Poland.[18] This was driven home to Dirksen after he had spoken to the Italian ambassador to Berlin, Bernardo Attolico, who was an old friend from their time together in Moscow. Attolico complained that decisions were being taken in Berlin on the basis that Britain would not go to war, and Dirksen fully agreed with him that this was wrong. The conversation reached Ribbentrop's attention, probably through breaking into Italian diplomatic cyphers, and he instructed Dirksen via Weizsäcker to be more discreet in future. Ribbentrop was furious that Dirksen was saying anything that contradicted the advice that he was giving to the Führer. Dirksen was naturally anxious to learn what impression his report of the talk with Wilson had made in Berlin, but all he was told was that it was seen as another sign of British weakness.[19]

Wilson's last attempt to use back channels to make juicy offers to Hitler had failed utterly. He and Chamberlain had taken near-suicidal risks. Coming so soon after the leak of the Wohlthat talks, it could easily have doomed Chamberlain's premiership if anything of Wilson's proposals to Dirksen had been disclosed. Wilson was gambling that nothing would leak from the German side, as the mere fact of his conversation with Dirksen and the pantomime of secrecy around it would have been damagingly suspect in themselves. His minute of the conversation filed at the Foreign Office might just have stood up to scrutiny, but for Wilson's glaring failure to have taken the opportunity to deny the press reports of the Wohlthat talks.

# CHAPTER THIRTY-TWO

# PATHETIC LITTLE WORMS

*The enemy did not expect my determination. Our enemies*
*are pathetic little worms. I saw them at Munich.*
– ADOLF HITLER TO HIS GENERALS

After trouncing Churchill on the issue of the parliamentary recess, Chamberlain had been able to leave London in a state of happy confidence. His policy faced no serious challenge domestically, and there were two separate promising dialogues under way with Germany, either of which might defuse the crisis.

The British were left to wait a fortnight for an answer to the proposals that Chamberlain and Wilson had made via Kemsley. When it arrived, the talks between Germany and the Soviet Union were far advanced and the need to keep Britain in suspense had almost gone. It was a flat refusal to proceed. 'For as long as such confidence does not exist there can be no object in preparing for conversations of the kind which you have in mind. That is the Fuhrer's [*sic*] view also.'[1] The only consolation Chamberlain was given was Otto Dietrich's contribution for the never-to-be-published exchange of articles. Once more Downing Street had let itself be duped.

Dietrich's refusal to follow up the proposal ostensibly from Kemsley of the suggestion of further talks was rapidly followed by Ribbentrop's final contribution to the exchanges that Wohlthat had opened with Wilson and which had passed over to Dirksen. The bearer of the message was Fritz Hesse, who had been over in Germany for discussion with the foreign minister.* It took Hesse a few days to secure an appointment with Wilson, who had been on leave, otherwise the blows would have come almost simultaneously.[2] Even after Dietrich's refusal, Wilson took Hesse's message seriously enough to want to keep the meeting confidential and to see Hesse urgently. Their meeting was fixed on a Sunday, the first day available, and at Wilson's private flat in Kensington, where he had made his proposals to Dirksen. The answer Hesse brought was another flat rejection. The dispute between Germany and Poland could only be settled directly between the two countries. Only after the Danzig question had been dealt with would Hitler propose a general settlement to Britain that would meet its requirements.[3]

The risk that Wilson had taken in holding a furtive conversation with the German ambassador had been pointless. There is no sign that Wilson ever grasped that German foreign policy was the product of an even more chaotic process than his uneasy and underhand treatment of Halifax and the Foreign Office. The official diplomats of the Auswärtiges Amt had been almost entirely side-lined, and Dirksen was not even as close to the top of the Auswärtiges Amt as Erich Kordt, who was in the intimate circle of the Auswärtiges Amt boss, Ernst von Weizsäcker. There was never any real prospect that Wilson's proposal of abject surrender would be listened to seriously. It is an open question as to whether Hitler ever heard of it.

Wilson took the blow calmly, but made it clear to Hesse that he considered it serious. Both men, though, had strong interests in keeping the dialogue going and they continued to talk. Discussion turned to the possibility that a formula might be devised that would allow Danzig to be discussed at the same time as a general settlement. According to Wilson, this was at Hesse's instigation and vice versa. Given Wilson's well-established negotiating practice of edging his counter-party into taking the first step, it was probably a combination of the two. It really does not matter. If Wilson had agreed to see Hesse merely on the off-chance that he had something worthwhile to say, he need not have

---

* According to Hesse's memoirs, Wilson had sent him to Germany with proposals for a settlement, but there is no other evidence for this.

wasted more time. What matters is that Wilson, as the senior party to the conversation by far, believed that there was some prospect that the Hesse channel might still serve a useful purpose.

Hesse also fuelled Wilson's long-standing obsessive fear of the supposed risk of provoking Hitler, which had led him to his policy that the British government should be as unchallenging as possible in its public utterances. Hesse urged that Britain should not insist publicly on its guarantee to Poland; in his version because this was simply useless, in Wilson's because it would upset Hitler. When he reported the conversation, Wilson endorsed this argument and gave it further weight by claiming – quite incorrectly – that Hesse was a long-term and close follower of Hitler. This was the first time that Wilson had disclosed a contact with Hesse in any way formally, or to the Foreign Office, so he had grounds for exaggerating Hesse's importance and to justify the attention that he was lavishing on an obscure figure, who was not even an accredited diplomat or official. There are two likely sources for Wilson's erroneous view of Hesse: deliberate invention by Hesse's imaginative brain or accidental confusion between Hesse and Walther Hewel, who did meet Wilson's description. Either way, it is proof of the weakness in Wilson's back-channel diplomacy that he had failed to brief himself adequately (or at all) on the credentials of his intermediary. The previous year when he had met Hewel at the Berghof during Chamberlain's first journey to Germany, Wilson had known no more of him than the only very partially accurate description of him as Ribbentrop's private secretary.

Nothing could have been further from the truth than Chamberlain's belief that Hitler had put Danzig into cold storage. Nor was Chamberlain remotely correct in thinking that Hitler knew that Britain meant business. The British guarantee to Poland and all the other moves that Chamberlain had put in hand might as well never have existed. Even before the Ribbentrop–Molotov Pact was signed, Hitler was bent on war with Poland and two days after Hesse's visit to Wilson's flat, his military commanders were summoned to the Berghof to be briefed on Case White, the military plan to invade Poland. No formal record was kept of the meeting and the attendees were told strictly that they should not record what they were told, but sufficient officers disobeyed to allow a clear account to be prepared.[4] All recorded that Hitler was confident that Britain and France would not intervene to help Poland. The British Empire was too weak to oppose Germany. He explained his confidence by his experiences the previous year. He had seen his opponents at Munich and they were 'pathetic little worms' (*'armseligen Würmchen'*).

Downing Street had barely had time to digest the failure of its back-channel pursuit of friendship when it found itself confronted with the excessive success of its diplomacy towards the Soviet Union. Chamberlain and Wilson seem to have hoped that it would be possible to keep Stalin hanging on a string indefinitely. The Soviet dictator had other ideas and was far more open to the brutal and cynical power politics deal that the Germans were willing to offer him. Under the misleading title of a non-aggression pact they secretly carved up eastern Europe between them, partitioning Poland along a more-or-less arbitrary line. Hitler's history of anti-Bolshevik rhetoric and the supposed eternal struggle between fascism and communism counted for nothing when two ruthless dictators decided that their interests lay in cooperation rather than conflict. In the word of one Foreign Office wit, it was 'the day all the isms became wasms'. Hitler was so proud of his coup that he expected that the shock of the Ribbentrop–Molotov Pact would provoke the immediate fall of the British and French governments, and spent the morning that it was announced awaiting the news.[5] The pact certainly demonstrated the diplomatic incompetence of British foreign policy as set by Downing Street, but the British system of politics is not designed to punish governments for failure. Hitler's miscalculation here may explain why the Kemsley and Dirksen channels had been closed down.

The British were now in a corner, and the first avenue for saving face was to stage a rerun of the Czechoslovakia crisis, bullying the Poles into surrendering to the Germans. But this time there were far fewer tools at hand for Downing Street. The German claim was much weaker on Poland. There had been no repetition of the charade of the Runciman mission, which had given the appeasers the excuse to portray Prague as obdurate and unyielding. Warsaw, of course, had the Anglo-French guarantee in its pocket; it could be far tougher with Berlin than Prague could be.

After years of patronising and ignoring the United States, Wilson bit the bullet and tried to recruit them to bring the Poles to their senses. On 23 August he set off for another journey to a figurative Canossa, although the physical distance was far shorter than his four journeys to Germany in 1938. He took a taxi from Downing Street to the US embassy on Grosvenor Square to see the ambassador, Joseph Kennedy, which he followed up by a number of phone calls.[6] He had a stark message that Kennedy reported to Washington in equally stark terms:

> Sir Horace Wilson called me this morning and told me he saw no hope of avoiding war unless the Poles were willing to negotiate with the Germans. As things stand now that is the place to apply pressure. The British are in no position to press the Poles strongly, but if anything is to be accomplished action must be taken at once, as the Prime Minister feels the blow is fairly near.[7]

Kennedy, despite his resentment at months of being cold-shouldered by Wilson, whose dislike of the USA was all too evident, went into action to support this drive at appeasement. He phoned Washington and 'planted the idea of getting the Poles to talk', but the President was not due back from his holidays until later in the day.[8] Wilson wanted an answer rapidly and pestered Kennedy all day until he got through to the White House. Washington, though, could easily read what was afoot and had no inclination to get sucked into Wilson's scheme. In the words of the head of the State Department Western European Division, 'The British wanted one thing of us, and one thing only – namely, that we put pressure on the Poles. They felt that they could not, given their obligations, but that we could. As we saw it here, it merely meant that they wanted us to assume responsibility of a new Munich and to do their dirty work for them.'[9] No diplomatic offensive was unleashed to pressurise the Poles into surrender. Instead Roosevelt wrote open letters to Germany and Poland calling on them to settle their differences by negotiation, which were to be published at ten o'clock the following morning. This was precisely the kind of high-minded and unspecific approach to diplomacy that Wilson had vigorously derided in the past, but he had to be thankful for what was on offer. When Kennedy phoned the text of the letters through, he thanked him with a 'God bless you'.

With the danger of Soviet intervention entirely laid to rest by the Ribbentrop–Molotov Pact, Hitler knew that the last stage of the Polish crisis had arrived. He called Goebbels, his most valued and trusted partner, to his side for the crucial days that were to come. Goebbels had been languishing in semi-disgrace for some while, because his adulterous affair with the Czech film star Lída Baarová had threatened to torpedo his marriage and provoke a scandalously public proof that Nazi claims to higher sexual morality were nonsense. Such considerations now paled into insignificance against what was afoot, and Hitler set out his analysis of the diplomatic situation in greater detail:

> Poland's situation is hopeless. We will attack it at the first best opportunity. The Polish state must be smashed just as the Czechoslovakian state was. It is a more difficult question whether the West will intervene. At this moment one could not say yet. It depends on circumstances. London is more firmly positioned than in September 1938. So we must operate very cleverly. Just now London certainly does not want war. But it must save its face.[10]

Once more Downing Street had let itself be duped into believing that Hitler would accept a peaceful settlement. Wilson's attempts to convince Hitler that Britain was totally committed to standing by the Polish guarantee through his sundry emissaries had failed utterly. Whatever scripts they might have been working to, it was not what Wilson's emissaries said that had mattered to Hitler. The mere fact that they had been despatched meant that Britain wanted, above all, to avoid war. All Wilson had succeeded in doing was to make it certain to Hitler beyond doubt that Downing Street wanted peace and was desperate to be let off the hook of its commitment; Germany just had to help Chamberlain and Wilson wriggle off successfully.

The (to Hitler) mysterious survival of the Chamberlain government provoked a flurry of official and unofficial activity aimed at keeping Britain in play. Hitler recognised that the British were feeble, but knew that they would need a little help to fold. The day before the German armies were scheduled to move Nevile Henderson was summoned to see Hitler at the Reichskanzlei. He was treated to a bombastic interview and handed a letter offering Britain a guarantee of the Empire in exchange for a settlement over Poland. Quite how seriously Hitler meant this is an open question, but before he could discover whether the British would nibble at his bait, he was given pause for more thought. Almost unintentionally the British repaid the Germans for the shock of the Ribbentrop–Molotov Pact and briefly undid the damage that Wilson had wrought on Hitler's perception of their readiness to oppose him. Negotiations with the Poles on the detailed terms to embody the guarantee had been pursuing a leisurely course, but had finally reached a conclusion and a formal treaty was signed.

Wilson hoped to use Hesse's fictitious closeness to the Führer to make sure that Hitler did not fail to appreciate just what the news signified. Through George Steward, he passed on to the German half-journalist a gloss on the text of the treaty that was to be spread around the highest circles in Berlin – the Führer, Ribbentrop, Goebbels and Rudolf Hess – where he imagined that Hesse would be listened to. '[L]ike Odysseus Chamberlain had bound himself to the mast and was deaf to any further approaches.'[11] Who injected the classical flourish is an open question, but there is no sign that any of the intended recipients came to hear of it. Wilson was working off a wild exaggeration of Hesse's importance.

The Polish treaty was one of two shocks that hit Hitler on the afternoon of 25 August. A letter from Mussolini confirmed what many had suspected for some while: that the 'Pact of Steel' with Italy was made of a considerably more malleable material. Italy would not go to war alongside Germany. In the face of these new uncertainties Hitler decided to hold his hand and the final military orders for the invasion of Poland were not issued. There is no certainty which of the two pieces of news might have been decisive for Hitler, but most historians attach more importance to the Italian aspect.[12] An Italian attack on France would have practically eliminated any chance that the French army would attack the *Westwall*. The Polish treaty was a setback for Hitler, but it did not have the finality that Wilson tried to attach to it. The events of the next few days showed that Hitler still believed that Britain might not intervene, if handled correctly.

The first move was to bring into play yet another unofficial intermediary. Birger Dahlerus was an important Swedish businessman with strong ties to Goering, who took direct charge of his mission. The Swede's principal qualification was that he was entirely outside Ribbentrop's sphere of influence. In effect he replaced Wohlthat as Goering's man in back-channel contacts with Britain after Wohlthat had been eliminated by the public leak. Even at this late stage of the crisis, the rivalry between Goering and Ribbentrop was still an ever-present feature of German foreign policy. When Ernst von Weizsäcker had hijacked the dialogue with Wilson that Helmut Wohlthat had opened, Goering had been side-lined from any kind of diplomacy with Britain. If the British could be persuaded to back down through an approach in Goering's hands, it would help restore the balance that the Ribbentrop–Molotov Pact had swung in his rival's favour.

Whilst the German foreign policy machine remained severely fractured, its British counterpart was pulling together. Indeed the pattern of its operations reversed. It was the formal foreign policy machine that handled Dahlerus's unofficial approach, and it did so in a correct and structured way, light years removed from Wilson's furtive dealings with Wohlthat and Dirksen. When Dahlerus reached London he was met by Lord Halifax and Sir Alec Cadogan, with Wilson only aware and in the background. All he got to take back to Berlin was 'a platitudinous message' from Halifax, but Hitler had become so convinced of British weakness that he managed to read into it the hope that they would back down. Ribbentrop was loudly advising the Führer that the British would never intervene so he would also be proved wrong. Ribbentrop's confidence was fed by his man in London, Hesse: 'My information is that if Germany invades Poland there is no fear of British intervention. Sir Samuel Hoare has the ear of Neville Chamberlain. He is of the opinion that if Poland is attacked, Britain can always fulfil the letter of a declaration of war without going all out.'[13]

Whilst the Foreign Office was seeing Dahlerus, Wilson was left to deal with Hitler's formal diplomacy in the form of the letter that he had handed to Henderson. Cadogan had drafted a reply that was so direct in pointing out the gaps and vaguenesses of Hitler's letter and the incitement to Britain to break its word to Poland that it was tantamount to a rejection. Cadogan's professional colleagues supported the text, but it may have been too blunt for Halifax, who refused to approve it.[14] The job of drafting a more acceptable text was passed on to Wilson and his pro-appeasement ministerial acolyte, Rab Butler, to the dismay of Cadogan ('*What* a party') and his assistant, Oliver Harvey ('What a pair!').[15] Their efforts showed that the pure spirit of craven appeasement still ruled in certain quarters. Cadogan and Harvey were equally unimpressed by the product, describing it as '*quite* awful. I corrected worst errors' and '*very* flabby'. Even after Cadogan's attentions, the Cabinet found the reply 'too deferential' and rejected it, initiating a protracted process of redrafts which occupy a very thick file. Amongst the passages eliminated along the way were an expression of the British government's willingness to use its influence on Poland (shades of 'entitled to demand concessions'), *de facto* endorsement of Goebbels's stories of atrocities supposedly being perpetrated on Germans in the Polish corridor, a relativisation of British obligations to Poland that verged on trivialisation and a declaration that it would a 'tragedy' if no settlement were reached, together with sundry echoes of the dream of a world where Germany and Britain worked in happy harmony.[16] At almost the final stage, Wilson shoehorned into the reply a reference to Chamberlain's cherished goal of arms limitation in an imaginary 'transition from preparation for war to the normal activities of peaceful trade'.[17] Wilson was so over-wrought that he thought that Poland was still a monarchy. The last true Kingdom of Poland had been extinguished by another Germano-Russian partition in 1795.

Wilson and Butler formed a distinct peace party in London, whilst most of the professionals at the Foreign Office strove for firmness, 'terrified of another attempt at a Munich and selling out on the Poles.

Horace Wilson and R. A. Butler are working like beavers for this.'[18] The push for appeasement was supported ineffectually by Henderson, who was still in London. 'N.H.'s very presence here is a danger as he infects the Cabinet with his gibber.'

Neither the efforts of Dahlerus nor the formal diplomacy between Britain and Germany that continued until the last moment achieved anything. They served no purpose, though Chamberlain believed that 'the communications with Hitler and Goering looked promising at one time'.[19] At noon on 1 September Hitler issued the formal orders to attack Poland the following morning. He believed that Britain would not intervene.[20] Amazingly, even as German tanks rolled across the frontier, Chamberlain held back. The ultra-appeasing French foreign minister, Georges Bonnet, blocked a declaration of war, in the hope that Italian attempts to set up a new Munich would succeed. Innocently or otherwise, Chamberlain played along. When Chamberlain delivered a statement to the House of Commons at about 8 p.m., there was no mention of a time limit being imposed on Germany to withdraw from Poland, still less of a formal ultimatum. The Italian proposals were still under consideration. The House was furious and when the deputy Labour leader, Arthur Greenwood, rose to speak, Leo Amery shouted at him from the government benches, 'Speak for England.' The Cabinet staged a full-scale revolt, led by Sir John Simon, in a remarkable change from his habitual supine behaviour. By a supreme irony the one minister who had also been in the Cabinet that had declared war on the Kaiser in 1914 – and opposed it then – forced Chamberlain into war in 1939. Frantic attempts were made to persuade the French to move and in the midst of an apocalyptic thunderstorm the Cabinet met at 11.30 p.m. and decided to issue an ultimatum to Germany.

The Germans had one last shot left in the locker to try to head Britain away from standing by the Polish guarantee, and its direct target was Wilson, the weak spot in the British armour. Hesse, Ribbentrop's long-standing link-man to Wilson, was sent back to London with a new and, to the Germans at least, appealing proposal. The move was aimed not just at weakening Britain's resolve, it also insured Ribbentrop's standing vis-à-vis Goering against the possibility of a last-minute collapse in British willingness to defend Poland. Goering had led hands down in the diplomatic stakes ahead of Case White with Dahlerus's frantic shuttle diplomacy, but Ribbentrop had a route into the true heart of British foreign policy-making that could bypass the professional diplomats and political doubters, who had shown a depressing inclination to treat the proposals reaching them via the Swede with the caution and scepticism they deserved.

Hesse was sent to Wilson with a proposal redolent of Munich on the evening of 2 September, just as Chamberlain was fighting his rearguard action against the Cabinet's attempt to stop him reneging on the decision to impose a definite time limit on Germany. The proposal he brought had uncanny echoes of the Czechoslovakia crisis the year before. In September 1938 Chamberlain had escaped from the consequences of a Cabinet revolt against the Bad Godesberg terms by sending Wilson to Berlin. Ostensibly intended to flag British determination, Wilson had signalled to the Führer the weakness and irresolution behind the posture. The Germans were casting him in this role once again and Wilson was well cast for it. In the run-up to Prague, Wilson had invited himself to Berlin; Ribbentrop had refused to see him then, but six months later, he could make use of him. In his report on the conversation, Wilson claims to have turned the idea down flat unless Germany withdrew its forces from Poland, but in Hesse's heavily embellished and unreliable account, Wilson was willing to consider Hesse's proposal until a messenger brought him word that the Cabinet was already in session and deciding to send the ultimatum. Even if Wilson's version is entirely true and there was no such hesitation on his part, it is still astonishing that he wasted any time and effort on the remote and fantastic possibility that the Wehrmacht would pull out of Poland. It was a fitting final move in his inglorious career as Chamberlain's back-channel to Hitler.

The scales fell only gradually from Hitler's eyes. Franz von Sonnleithner, the Auswärtiges Amt liaison officer to the Reichskanzlei, described the scene when he brought a report which stated unequivocally that Britain and France were not bluffing to Hitler, Ribbentrop and Goering. None of the three had expected it and Goering clearly relished his rival's discomfiture.

Hitler and Göring read the text from the page together. Hitler was manifestly affected [*betroffen*] and said – it seemed to me in a reproachful tone – 'What now, Ribbentrop?' Göring cut in with a distinct challenge, 'You've got it now, Ribbentrop!' I was standing next to Ribbentrop and saw how he clenched his teeth in anger so his jaw stuck forward. '*Nun erst recht, mein Führer*'* was his answer.[21]

The decision by the western powers to declare war on Germany came as a shock to Hitler and, even more so, to Ribbentrop. The scene that Sonnleithner had witnessed between the Nazi leaders was replayed with even greater intensity. It fell to Paul Schmidt to translate the telegram that Henderson delivered with the British ultimatum to Hitler and Ribbentrop. He described Hitler looking as though he had been turned to stone until he turned to Ribbentrop, who appeared to have frozen too.[22] With a furious expression he asked, 'What now?' Schmidt interpreted Hitler's expression as an accusation that Ribbentrop had misinformed him of the British reaction. All Ribbentrop could manage by way of an answer was that he expected France to deliver a similar ultimatum in the next few hours.

---

\* A Nazi slogan, 'Now all the more'.

# CHAPTER THIRTY-THREE

# A POTATO WAR

*That is what Winston & Co never seem to realise. You don't need offensive forces sufficient to win a smashing victory. What you want are defensive forces sufficiently strong to make it impossible for the other side to win except at such a cost as to make it not worth while. That is what we are doing and though at present the German feeling is it is not worth while yet, they will presently come to realise that it never will be worth while. Then we can talk.*
– Neville Chamberlain to his sister

Throughout 1939 Hitler had misread the willingness of Britain and France to declare war over Poland, but he did see very clearly how little appetite Chamberlain had to impose a military solution on Germany. He foresaw unerringly what came later to be called the Phoney War when France lurked behind the supposed safety of the Maginot Line with no thought of assaulting the *Westwall* and the Royal Air Force was forbidden to bomb Germany as private property might be damaged. The shock of the ultimata and declarations of war did not make him doubt his judgement on this vital point. On the second day of the war with Britain he set out his analysis of the military situation to Goebbels: in the west there would only be a 'potato war'.[1] The original Potato War (more formally the War of Bavarian Succession of 1778–79) had become a byword for a futile, half-hearted war. The Prussian army of Frederick the Great in his last campaign and that of the Hapsburg monarchy manoeuvred inconclusively against each other, without fighting a single major battle, sustaining such casualties as they did from eating under-ripe potatoes direct from the fields.

Chamberlain, too, had thought about the nature of the war into which he might have to lead Britain. He had dreamed up an illusory picture of modern warfare to match the illusory picture of diplomacy towards fascist dictators that drove his policy in peacetime. It was loaded with the self-righteous, smug conviction that anything that ran counter to Churchill's opinions was correct.

That is what Winston & Co never seem to realise. You don't need offensive forces sufficient to win a smashing victory. What you want are defensive forces sufficiently strong to make it impossible for the other side to win except at such a cost as to make it not worth while. That is what we are doing and though at present the German feeling is it is not worth while yet, they will presently come to realise that it never will be worth while. Then we can talk.[2]

Provided that the Luftwaffe was stopped from destroying London, Britain only needed to sit it out. Chamberlain never seriously believed that Hitler would launch a full-scale attack in the west until it happened in May 1940. He pooh-poohed perceptive and accurate predictions amongst the generals that Hitler would. Chamberlain fell into the trap of imagining that Hitler thought in his terms. He projected onto Hitler his own horror at the huge casualties an assault on the Maginot Line would entail, together with a rational calculation of the costs and benefits of such an operation. Weirdly Chamberlain believed that Hitler would be deterred from attacking through Belgium and the Netherlands, as the generals again correctly expected, by 'political reactions [to] a breach in neutrality so flagrant and unscrupulous' and unspecified 'disastrous risks' if anything went wrong.[3] Even after Germany had opened its campaign in the west with the invasion of Scandinavia in April 1940 Chamberlain disregarded strong intelligence of a German build-up, to pour scorn on the notion of an attack through the Low Countries. Chamberlain's apologists often portray him as a leader who scrupulously attended to the opinions of his military advisers. His blindness towards Case Yellow, the German attack on France, shows that when they disagreed with his prejudices, he ignored them.

He had also learned little about Hitler. In Chamberlain's mind all Britain and France needed to do was to sit tight and continue to rearm, and ultimately Germany would give in with Hitler being deposed. A near-bloodless victory was possible.[4]

Chamberlain's notion of war with Germany seemed uncannily like a form of armed appeasement, but war had formally been declared. Simple politics demanded that Chamberlain open his government to a broader range of factions than the narrow grouping of loyalists through which he had ruled. Half-heartedly he invited the Labour Party into a coalition, but he was turned down flat. Labour had no incentive to join, quite apart from the bitter legacy of Chamberlain's openly expressed personal contempt for its leaders. He and his established allies would have been by far the dominant parties. In the words of Hugh Dalton:

> Having regard to our frequently expressed views of the PM and Simon, we could not enter a Cabinet in which these two were Numbers 1 and 2. Moreover, we should require the influence of Sir Horace Wilson to be eliminated. If we read that he had been appointed Governor of the Windward Islands and had already left England in order to take up this most respected position, we should be favourably impressed. ([Rab Butler] asked whether we really attached so much importance to Wilson as this. I say, 'Yes, certainly, and I have so told a member of the War Cabinet, and one of my colleagues has so told another.')[5]

It would have been politically impossible to keep Churchill out of government and he was made First Lord of the Admiralty; the Royal Navy was the only one of the three fighting services to be waging anything like active operations against Germany. It was similarly inevitable that Churchill become a member of the War Cabinet, although his relative standing was almost instantly diluted. The original idea had been for him to be the only service minister in the War Cabinet, but this failed because of the jealousy of the two who would have been excluded. All three service ministers became members, thus rather inflating numbers in an already unwieldy body. Anthony Eden was also brought back into the government as Dominions Secretary, with no seat in the War

Cabinet but an assurance that he would be asked to attend frequently. It was a clear sign that Eden had been brought back at a grade below the one at which he had left in 1938.

From the start the War Cabinet also featured a strong bureaucratic dimension. Its shape was deeply influenced by the experience of the First World War and Maurice Hankey, now Lord Hankey, had been called in to brief Chamberlain in detail in the last days of peace.[6] Wilson had already ear-marked Hankey for a major role, setting aside their disagreement over Hankey's succession as Cabinet Secretary the previous year.[7] Hankey was asked to join the War Cabinet even before war was declared and thus before Churchill was approached.[8] The appointment was driven by a desire to balance Churchill. 'As far as I can make out,' Hankey said, 'my main job is to keep an eye on Winston!'[9]

The composition of the War Cabinet was at best only a qualified recognition that the anti-appeasers were now fit to return to mainstream politics. It also gave Chamberlain an opportunity to place Wilson at the top level of the councils of state. With a handful of exceptions, he attended every one of the War Cabinet's meetings wearing his hat as the permanent secretary to the Treasury, which he had worn officially since September 1939, albeit listed as 'also present'. This was little remarked on at the time, but it did attract the disapproval of the Cabinet Secretary, Edward Bridges, even though he had been hand-picked by Wilson. Bridges was acutely aware of the bad reputation that Wilson had gained for 'seeking to exercise more influence or power ... than was right for a Civil Servant'.[10] After the war Bridges was promoted to be head of the Civil Service whilst remaining Cabinet Secretary, the first civil servant to combine the jobs. Part of his task was to establish a workable long-term structure for the top level of the Civil Service to rationalise the cumulative effect of a series of unplanned and ill-thought-out phases: the capricious autocracy of Sir Warren Fisher, Hankey's muddle of political and military planning, Wilson's unhealthy fusion of politics with bureaucracy and Churchill's wartime expedients. Bridges argued that the head of the Civil Service should not be Cabinet Secretary as well and quoted the example of Wilson's regular presence at Chamberlain's War Cabinets as a dangerous precedent. It was only as 'a temporary measure, to meet the special circumstances of the war' that Bridges accepted the dual jobs for a few months.[11]

Whatever the formal structure of the War Cabinet might have been, Churchill had no intention of being restricted by its processes. He bombarded Chamberlain with a stream of minutes on a wide range of subjects to the horrified frustration of Wilson, whose desk they crossed. Chamberlain shrugged this off at first with the cynical assessment that they were largely written to provide material for 'The Book' that he had no doubt that Churchill would write afterwards.[12] Finally, Chamberlain's patience ran out too and Churchill was summoned to Downing Street to be told that he should raise complaints directly with the ministers concerned or formally at the War Cabinet, as Chamberlain explained afterwards to Wilson.[13] The consolation prize for Churchill came in the shape of an informal dinner at the Admiralty with Chamberlain and their respective wives, a response to his complaint that his only contact with the Prime Minister was at War Cabinet meetings.

Wilson's standing with Chamberlain was unhurt by the catastrophic failure of the one aspect of war preparations of which he had been practically in sole charge. Wilson had sedulously worked to prevent the Ministry of Information (MoI) rising above the level of a desk planning exercise in peacetime. Anything more would have been a provocation to the Nazis and a playground for dangerously ambitious bureaucrats or politicians. The MoI proved to be a failure of gigantic proportions, both in terms of failing in its various missions and by deeply embarrassing the government. Practically all the ministry's structural flaws can be laid at the door of the way that Wilson had organised it. A measure of inefficiency is inevitable in any large organisation that comes into being in a brief period, but the MoI exceeded anything imaginable.

The MoI was responsible for both censorship and issuing news, but the balance between propaganda and keeping military secrets out of the news had not been worked out. The war was only days old when a muddle between the two tasks brought the MoI into public ridicule from which it never properly recovered. The news that the British Expeditionary Force (BEF) had arrived in France was cleared for publication – it had already been mentioned on French radio – but the generals then decided it was actually too sensitive to disclose. This decision was implemented with such grotesque heavy-handedness that it completely eclipsed any compromise of security from the original story. The police went around newspaper offices and distributors confiscating copies of editions that carried the story. Commuters were startled to find policemen tearing copies of their newspapers from their hands.

The festival of mockery this provoked received further fodder when it became public that the MoI had precisely 999 employees on its books. This gave an inescapably risible edge to public and parliamentary questions as to what they were all doing. This uncannily precise figure was mentioned twelve times in a derisive House of Commons debate on the ministry, as opponents of the government picked up this tempting numerical cudgel. Many MoI staff had been transferred from other branches of the Civil Service, which begged the question as to why they were qualified for work usually quite alien to their previous occupations. The presence of a number of former museum staff opened up another rich vein of ribaldry: 'I could not help thinking when I looked at this list that it was as though Lord Beaverbrook sacked his staff and then went round to the British Museum and carried back to Fleet Street all the mummies on which he could lay his hands.'[14] More seriously, the Labour opposition could also question the political impartiality of the MoI given the presence of Conservative Party figures such as Sir Joseph Ball in its ranks.

The MoI's problems went beyond the tension between news and censorship. It was over-manned, with an extensive set of provincial operations, designed to cope with the dislocation caused by the massive bombing of London that never came. Propaganda abroad was another unresolved nightmare. Sir Campbell Stuart, whom Wilson had built up as a counter-weight to Sir Stephen Tallents when he was cutting the ministry down to size in the wake of Munich, ran his covert foreign propaganda operation as an entirely private fiefdom, fighting off Foreign Office attempts to find out what it was up to and to bring it under a measure of control.

Wilson's personnel policy for the MoI was a serious weakness and left it struggling to cope with these problems. After the awful warning of

Tallents's vaulting plans for the ministry, he had picked people precisely because he thought they were biddable, unfamiliar with propaganda and unlikely to be tempted to use the MoI as a career stepping stone. The first out of the door was Lord Perth, the former appeasing ambassador to Rome, who was more interested in his pay than his work. Perth was so glaringly unfit that Wilson sacked him within days under pressure from Sir Samuel Hoare. Perth's immediate successor as director general was a professional senior civil servant, who recognised a career death trap when he saw one and bailed out after a couple of weeks. Wilson's choice as Minister of Information, the Scottish judge Lord Macmillan, almost immediately proved to be hopelessly out of his depth and was soon desperately seeking for a pretext to resign. In despair Wilson brought in Sir Walter Monckton, who had loyally and astutely helped Wilson and Stanley Baldwin's government in the frantic days of the abdication crisis, but was as ignorant of propaganda as any of his colleagues. Monckton's charm and patience helped rebuild relations with the Fleet Street editors, which had been sorely tested, but could do nothing to resolve the structural challenges that the MoI faced. Wilson tried to bolster the ministry by parachuting into it in an entirely nebulous capacity – albeit enjoying considerable high-level support – a Conservative MP, Tommy Dugdale, who was a friend of long standing and another key ally during the abdication crisis.[15] Dugdale had been parliamentary private secretary to Baldwin and had worked in close partnership with Wilson in directing the covert intelligence operations against Edward VIII and his allies, notably Winston Churchill.

Wars are not, of course, lost by bad propaganda or bad censorship, but the debacle of the MoI triggered the most severe criticism that Chamberlain's government had to face in open session in Parliament and thus in the public eye. Hoare doubtless relished the discomfiture of Wilson, who had sharply cut him out of the planning for the MoI in peacetime, when he spoke in a House of Commons debate. He confessed that 'the public has, I am afraid, lost confidence in the Ministry as originally organised' and gratuitously reminded Parliament of the hideous muddle over the BEF in France. Even Chamberlain admitted that the appointment of Macmillan to the ministry was 'my one failure and I am not sure that the best plan would not be to abolish the Ministry altogether'.[16] The failure of the MoI was emblematic of the policy of a government that did not really want to be fighting a war at all.

In the early weeks of the Second World War, there were moves to bring the war to an end rapidly from both ends of the political spectrum. On the far left, the Communist Party of Great Britain obeyed the instructions of its masters in Moscow to campaign for peace. Worryingly for Downing Street, on the right there was a peace initiative that came from circles dangerously close to both the Prime Minister himself and Wilson's own back-channel diplomacy. The Duke of Westminster, Chamberlain's host in Scotland a few weeks before, called together a group of what he saw as like-minded individuals at his house in London to launch a campaign.[17] The guests included the Duke of Buccleuch, who had travelled to Berlin for Hitler's birthday celebrations just after Prague, and Lord Rushcliffe, signatory of the letter to *The Times* appealing for one last attempt at negotiation, of which a number of people had thought the true author was Wilson. The group was treated to Westminster reading out a long pacifist and defeatist memorandum composed by Henry Drummond Wolff, one of the unofficial intermediaries between London and Germany in back-channel appeasement, who was also present. The memorandum assailed '[t]he newspapers – especially those controlled by the Left and the Jews' for insisting on the destruction of Nazism.[18]

Word of what was afoot almost immediately spread around government circles. Churchill wrote Westminster a letter of anguished complaint as 'one of your oldest friends'.[19] It warned him that a number of other members of the Cabinet were aware and that this kind of behaviour would lead the duke 'into measureless odium and vexation', citing the struggles that those who had opposed the Boer War and the First World War had faced to rebuild their careers, men of the left such as David Lloyd George and Ramsay MacDonald. This acted as a red rag to Westminster, who believed that his defeatist instincts were closer to the Prime Minister's true thinking than Churchill. In an apparent complaint at the severity of his criticism, he forwarded Churchill's letter to Chamberlain.[20] He also sent Chamberlain a copy of Drummond

Wolff's memorandum for comment, clearly regarding it as a legitimate, if not unexceptionable, document, capable of swinging the Prime Minister in favour of an early deal with Hitler.

Westminster had correctly judged that he was still in favour at Downing Street or, at least, too closely linked to the Prime Minister to be ignored or squashed firmly. Wilson and Ball were tasked with defusing this delicate situation tactfully, although Chamberlain was willing to intervene directly with the duke if Ball thought it would help.[21] It was Ball who spoke to Westminster, but whatever he said to him was not forceful enough to prevent the duke lending his house for another, this time larger, pro-negotiation cabal a fortnight afterwards, which attracted a number of MPs. Ball was not concerned that Westminster was peddling defeatist sentiment; his real concern was that the duke might end up actually undermining the prospects for an agreement with Hitler. Ball feared that Churchill might exploit his knowledge of Westminster's proposals that Britain should abandon eastern Europe to the Germans to steer government policy away from a negotiated settlement, to 'press hard for [the] immediate and categorical rejection' of the duke's proposals, which would have closed off an avenue for resuming appeasement once Poland was completely overrun.

Chamberlain had become sufficiently disillusioned with Hitler to entertain the notion that he might be challenged domestically. After the rebuffs administered to representatives of German dissidents – Theodor Kordt during the Czech crisis and Colonel von Schwerin during the Polish crisis – he took entirely seriously a far less well-attested approach from German generals reported by MI6. There was to be 'a new Government, with a complete change of policy' albeit with the possiblity 'Herr Hitler might be kept in an ornamental position'.[22] The matter was put to the Cabinet, where Churchill expressed reservations about the 'informal' handling and 'thought it was extremely perilous to contemplate anything which might be regarded as making terms with a regime with a Hitler façade'. Fired by the prospect of removing Hitler from effective power, Chamberlain overrode Churchill's objections and told the Cabinet 'that it would be unwise to take any action which might result in damping down the movement from which the present approach started'. A message was sent to keep the conversations going. Chamberlain began to nurse fantasies of Hitler having to 'die or go to St. Helena or become a real public works architect, preferably in a "home"'.[23] These dreams were soon rudely shattered when the MI6 officers sent to meet a supposed representative of the dissident generals at Venlo on the border between Germany and the Netherlands were kidnapped after a shoot-out by German forces commanded by Walter Schellenberg, the SS foreign intelligence officer, who had staged the fake plot as a trap for the British all along.[24]

Churchill's opinion of what Britain's war aims should be came when he made a radio broadcast on 12 November that was implacably hostile to the Nazi regime and personally abusive of its leader:

> You may take it absolutely for certain that either all that Britain and France stand for in the modern world will go down, or that Hitler, the Nazi régime and the recurring German or Prussian menace to Europe will be broken and destroyed ...
>
> Field Marshal Goering – who is one of the few Germans who have been having a pretty good time for the last few years ... [Hitler's] bad adviser, Herr von Ribbentrop, that prodigious contortionist ... [of Hitler] the frenzy of a cornered maniac ... the seething mass of criminality and corruption constituted by the Nazi party machine.[25]

This had a bad effect at Downing Street and Chamberlain rather endorsed the view that Churchill 'had descended to the level of the gutter, that he had let down the good name of England'.[26] Rab Butler thought it 'beyond words vulgar' and told the Italian ambassador that the broadcast's 'intransigently warlike thinking' was at odds with the views of the government and the Foreign Office.[27] The government would not reject and the country would accept negotiations and a deal, provided that they were lasting.

\*    \*    \*

Wilson's *de facto* membership of the War Cabinet remained hidden from the public gaze but his close ties to the Prime Minister were an inescapable fact. The public were forcibly reminded of it when Harold Nicolson, the MP who had first attacked the value of Wilson's advice to Chamberlain in the aftermath of Munich, returned to the attack with a highly successful short book published by Penguin under the title *Why Britain Is at War*. Chamberlain was blamed squarely for failing to understand the forces with which he was confronted:

> No sane person can doubt the purity of the Prime Minister's intentions. The only thing that was lacking was an understanding of the true nature of the Nazi movement. Mr Chamberlain imagined that he was dealing with a national revival; he was really dealing with a world revolution, led by an almost demented fanatic. He and his adviser, Sir Horace Wilson, stepped into diplomacy with the bright faithfulness of two curates entering a pub for the first time; they did not observe the difference between a social gathering and a rough house; nor did they realise that the tough guys therein assembled did not either speak or understand their language. They imagined that they were as decent and honourable as themselves.[28]

Of course, Chamberlain and Wilson were not quite so naive, but the image of a dialogue of the deaf between Nazis and appeasers, together with the pairing of the politician and the civil servant as sharers of the same illusions, still holds good today.

# CHAPTER THIRTY-FOUR

# A CIVIL SERVANT WITH A POLITICAL SENSE

*You might think it worthwhile to have a chat with him [Wilson]*
*sometime, for he is one of that very rare company of Civil Servants*
*who have also a political sense.*
– NEVILLE CHAMBERLAIN TO SIR JOSEPH BALL

One of the strongest aspects of Wilson's appeal to Chamberlain was that he was not a professional politician, so Chamberlain could trust him not to allow personal considerations of political ambition or alliance to taint the advice that he gave. Chamberlain relied on Wilson's advice on every possible topic and politics was no exception. John Colville, who went to Downing Street as Chamberlain's private secretary at the start of the Second World War, could observe closely the comings and goings within the government, notably a ministerial reshuffle in January 1940, and took the view that Wilson had 'commanding influence on political appointments'.[1] There is no reason to suppose that this had not been the case since early in Chamberlain's premiership. Colville's longer-serving and more senior colleague at Downing Street, Arthur Rucker, thought that Wilson 'intervened too much in politics'.[2] For better or worse Wilson was a political force in his own right.

On his deathbed Chamberlain wrote a letter to Sir Joseph Ball which was as near as he came to a political testament.[3] In common with almost anything Chamberlain wrote about the future, it proved to be wrong in almost every respect. With a final bout of unwarranted optimism he imagined that history would endorse his foreign policy. He advised Ball against launching an all-out attack on Labour, recognising it would be futile. He foresaw that the Conservative Party would find a new leader who would restore it to past glories. The process would be speeded on because 'the women of this country are by instinct and temperament Conservative in the main'. The notion that Churchill would lead the Conservative Party for the next fifteen years did not seem to have occurred to him. Chamberlain closed his letter by advising Ball to seek the advice of Wilson, 'for he is one of that very rare company of civil servants who have also a political sense'.

Insiders certainly saw Wilson as a major force in shaping the government. Ministers believed that their careers would suffer if they crossed him. The ministers involved in two of the more striking departures from Chamberlain's government held Wilson responsible for their removal. Eden, who had clashed directly with him, blamed Wilson for his departure from the Foreign Office.[4] Sir Thomas Inskip spread the net of accusation rather wider for his dismissal as Minister for Defence Coordination in January 1939 to catch the combined efforts of Wilson, Robert Hudson and David Margesson, the chief whip, who ruthlessly enforced obedience to Chamberlain amongst MPs.[5] Lord Swinton, the Air Secretary sacked in the wake of the disastrous House of Commons debate on the Royal Air Force, only blamed Chamberlain by name for his dismissal but the indictment of his critics who thought 'it all ought to be much easier' surely embraces the men behind the quick-fix schemes to produce aircraft that the RAF did not want: Sir Charles Bruce-Gardner and his patron, Wilson.

Wilson's influence worked in both directions. He was also a very valuable patron for a politician of whom he approved. Rab Butler claimed that it was Wilson, rather than the Prime Minister, who moved him to the Ministry of Labour in the spring of 1937, soon after Chamberlain's accession.[6] Butler and Wilson became close allies in the last phases of appeasement, working in far closer harmony than Wilson and Butler's ministerial senior, Halifax. Butler was practically the only minister who worked closely with Wilson on a day-to-day basis.

The high point of Wilson's influence on political appointments came with a reshuffle of the government in January 1940. The changes began to take shape with a discussion between Wilson and his ally Montagu Norman of the Bank of England, just before Christmas.[7] They talked about a number of ministers over whom question marks were hanging. There was no pressing need to reshape the whole government, but there was acute concern about Leslie Hore-Belisha, the War Secretary, who had been put in office by Chamberlain explicitly to counter the con-servatism of the military establishment in peacetime, but had ended up clashing with the generals outright in wartime. Here at least, Wilson was working in a grey area between objective fact-finding and political decision. Wilson had taken soundings of General Henry Pownall, the director of military operations, as to Hore-Belisha's standing with the Army in November 1939 and had been given a frank account of the difficulties that the minister was causing.[8] Together with the Cabinet Secretary, Edward Bridges, Wilson reported to the Prime Minister on these.[9] The conflict was so bitter that it could only be resolved by the removal of one party or the other; a mass sacking of generals would have been immensely controversial.

Chamberlain seems to have been against dismissing his one-time protégé from government entirely. Removing Hore-Belisha from the War Office appeared to provide an elegant solution to another urgent problem. Lord Macmillan was completely out of his depth as Minis-ter of Information and a political liability to the government. He was desperate to leave the job and so Hore-Belisha could have been moved sideways with relatively little loss of face. However, Wilson lobbied against Hore-Belisha being moved to the Ministry of Information, al-though the decisive intervention against the proposal came from the Foreign Office, which was concerned at the reaction to a Jew being put in charge of British propaganda.[10] The countries of south-eastern Europe were still neutral at that point and had long-standing anti-Semitic atti-tudes, so this was a brutal but realistic judgement. The campaign against Hore-Belisha that followed, however, was loathsome and a disgrace to all involved. Sir Joseph Ball's *Truth* ran a series of venomously anti-Semitic articles accusing him of involvement in dubious company promotions.[11] Chamberlain made no attempt to defend his former minister.

The veto on Hore-Belisha provided an opening for Wilson's long-standing client Sir John Reith, who had been sitting on the sidelines awaiting preferment for some months.[12] Wilson had recalled Reith from holiday in Canada when war was inevitable with the intention of giving his old and loyal follower a major job, but had been blocked. According to Reith, '[Wilson] had suggested various things such as Information and Supply Ministries that I should be minister of – but "they" wouldn't have it.'[13] A few months later, Wilson was powerful enough to override Reith's unknown opponents and he was appointed.

All of Wilson's previous involvement in ministerial appointments paled into comparison with the last and most dramatic move that he and Norman debated in the dark of the shortest day of 1939. Hore-Belisha was very small beer compared to another minister whom they decided to remove: Sir John Simon, the Chancellor of the Exchequer. Simon had been one of the most reliable pillars of Chamberlain's government, deploying his legalistic skills to put down any criticism of the government in Parliament, but Wilson disliked and feared his political ambitions, which aroused his deeply protective instincts towards Chamberlain, his patron and friend. With his remarkable lack of discretion about ministerial personalities he told a business contact, '[W]hen Chamberlain was ill in summer [1938] Sam Hoare and Simon, both with ambitions to succeed him, hovered round like vultures, anxious to be in at the kill and suspicious of each other. They impeded his recovery.'[14] Simon's notorious indecisiveness was a rather more valid drawback, although it hardly justified considering his removal. Wilson cursed him for taking 'an hour over things that didn't need more than ten minutes'.[15]

Simon's behaviour on the last day of peace offered another and more potent reason for Downing Street to turn against him. He had, for once, in fact shown himself to be very decisive indeed after the German invasion of Poland. He led a group of senior ministers who had gone to Downing Street on 2 September to demand that Britain declare war on Germany forthwith. Chamberlain was pleading that it was necessary to declare war at the same time as France, which was producing various supposedly practical reasons to postpone the move. Fairly or otherwise, it was suspected that Chamberlain hoped that something would save him from having to take the final step. Chamberlain was hustled into issuing an ultimatum to Germany. This was almost the last straw for Chamberlain, who complained afterwards, 'To crown all, a certain number of my colleagues in the Govt, who always behave badly when there is any trouble about, took this opportunity to declare that they were being flouted & neglected and tried to get up a sort of mutiny.'[16]

Simon had been one of the two key senior members of Chamberlain's team, but he was now castigated as someone who had never been reliable. Simon's willingness to take Britain into the Second World War stands in striking contrast to his actions in 1914, when he was one of only two Cabinet ministers to vote against declaring war on Germany.

Simon had another enemy, who was on very good terms with Wilson. In Jock Colville's words, 'Nobody surpassed the Governor of the Bank of England, in hostility to Sir John.'[17] Norman remained a regular visitor to 10 Downing Street well into wartime.[18] He was deeply dissatisfied with what he saw as Simon's lethargic handling of the war economy. According to a well-informed historian of the Bank of England, '[W]aging war with Germany called for a much more vigorous mobilisation of the nation's economic resources. Norman ... was tireless in his calls upon Ministers and the Treasury to get moving with an adequate economic policy. He went far beyond any normal bounds for a central banker.'[19] More debatably, Simon had recently proved to be far less helpful to Norman over the next chapter in the saga of the Czech gold reserves. Even after the public scandal in May 1939 and the outbreak of war, Norman had wanted the Bank for International Settlements (BIS) to continue passing the Czech gold over to the Germans, but by then, the worm had turned. Norman was instructed to tell the BIS not to continue these transfers after a 'long, controversial meeting' in October 1939 that included Halifax, the Foreign Secretary, and Simon, who had been complicit in the first set of transfers and had defended Norman in the House of Commons in May. If Simon had tried to protect Norman again in October, he had failed.

These were the only reasons why Simon should be dismissed. The government had not faced any serious challenge over the economic or financial handling of the war up to that point. When a group of junior ministers led by Robert Hudson had staged a short-lived and ineffectual protest against the handling of the war in December, Simon was not on their list of ministers who had failed to contribute and whose dismissal they demanded. Nonetheless Wilson and Norman concluded that there was 'an urgent necessity for a change'[20] and set the ball rolling for an intrigue to remove Simon from office. With an air of great mystery Norman, wrapped in a long cloak 'with his short beard, closely resembling Mephistopheles', was admitted to Downing Street by the back garden gate by one of the Prime Minister's private secretaries and told Chamberlain of his concerns.[21] The affair was so secret that Norman's visits had to be concealed from the ordinary messengers at Downing Street.

The Prime Minister decided to sack his Chancellor of the Exchequer.[22] With his customary capacity for self-dramatisation and vanity, this became a 'daring project' and the man who was intended to replace Simon was cast in 'the hero's role'.[23] Chamberlain and Wilson had already decided whom they wanted to replace Simon, but had omitted to tell Norman the identity of this hero; it is possible that he might have had second thoughts about the scheme if they had. Their choice had fallen on Josiah Stamp, who had recently been raised to the peerage, and he was anything but a conventional candidate for the job. In common with many other beneficiaries of Wilson's patronage for political office, he was not in any way a politician. He was a largely self-taught statistician and economist whose formal schooling had ended at the age of sixteen. He had risen through the ranks of the Inland Revenue before switching into the private sector through a directorship of the Bank of England under the patronage of Norman and becoming president of the executive of one of the big four railway companies, London, Midland and Scottish Railways. He became involved in numerous public bodies and his public service culminated when Chamberlain made him a part-time adviser to the government on economic affairs during wartime, although this did not stop him keeping his railway job. Here he argued for a relatively conservative approach that protected the value of sterling, held down inflation and sustained Britain's place in world trade rather than a 'heroic' move to an all-out war economy.[24]

The only obstacle that Chamberlain and Wilson could identify to appointing Stamp was that he was a peer and thus unable to sit in the House of Commons. At that time, peers could not simply resign their peerages. After detailed examination of the problem by the government law officers, it was concluded that it would be possible to 'dispeer' Stamp by Act of Parliament. The relevant correspondence was conducted in hand-written letters, obviating the need for typists to be alerted to what was going on.

Downing Street appears to have overlooked the fact that there was another, far more potent argument against promoting Stamp to Britain's second-highest political office. He was the highest-placed figure amongst a number of individuals who had publicly worked for friendly relations between Britain and Nazi Germany, later christened the 'fellow travellers of the right'. Curiously Stamp has escaped the attention of most writers on this topic, even though he was an early member of the Anglo-German Fellowship. Stamp was far closer to the heart of the Whitehall establishment than the retired military officers, backwoods peers, misguided idealists and outright crackpots who accounted for most of these fellow travellers. Stamp had made high-profile visits to Germany where he met Hitler and returned full of praise for the social measures that the Führer claimed to have undertaken.

Wilson had hoped to use Stamp as an intermediary with Hitler when he attended the Nuremberg Rally at the height of the Czech crisis, but Ribbentrop's insistence that Lord Brocket should have the place of honour at his tea party, seated next to the Führer, frustrated the plan.[25] When Wilson was considering a high-profile figure who might act as a direct contact with Hitler in the middle of 1939 as war approached, Stamp is the most likely candidate to have been the 'outstanding person in the British business world' whom Wilson had in mind.[26]

Stamp sympathised with some of the most controversial Nazi policies. He supported 'reasonable counteraction of Jewish domination'.[27] He had written to *The Times* arguing against a boycott by British academics of celebrations of the 550th anniversary of the University of Heidelberg because it had just sacked forty Jewish lecturers in obedience to Nazi law.[28] In the January edition of *Der Vierjahresplan,* the monthly journal of Goering's economics plan, he had praised Nazi autarky, arguing that the world would be split soon into countries with similar policies and those of more conservative bent like Britain. The only risk was that the rest of the world would lose access to 'the fruits of German progress'.

> Nobody will object to the successful execution of the Four-Year Plan provided that it does not rob the world of the benefit of Germany's gifted collaboration in social progress, science, and industry ... If one nation draws the line at a different point from ourselves we need not regard it as an act of injustice or enmity.[29]

He did not mention that the true reason for Nazi autarky was that it allowed the massive build-up of the German armed forces. Classing Nazi policy as an abstract choice between economic systems was a useful contribution to the blindness towards motivation and goals that underpinned appeasement.

With the question of his peerage overcome, Stamp was summoned to Downing Street by Chamberlain to be told of this new call on his services. Stamp expressed his willingness to serve in principle, but did raise a wide range of practical difficulties. These did not include his Nazi sympathies, but did include the 'point of honour' that he had spearheaded the railway companies in fraught negotiations with the Treasury and could not abandon them. It would have created a major conflict of interest. Wilson ruefully admitted, 'I *hadn't* thought of the Railway position. That is a snag.'[30] When Stamp sought the advice of Norman, the Bank governor was surprised that he was the candidate and recognised clearly the absurdity of the idea. He advised Stamp to turn down the offer firmly, even though this meant leaving the hated Simon in place. Chamberlain had to accept Stamp's arguments and 'thanked him warmly for the way I had considered it' but privately fumed at Stamp's 'very unheroic trepidation at the prospect that I saw he would be hissed off stage'.[31] Stamp was blamed for the collapse of a scheme that Chamberlain and Wilson had been colossally unwise to consider in the first place.

The Stamp episode shows how far out of contact with reality Chamberlain and Wilson had drifted. It provides a useful side-light on

Chamberlain's faith in Wilson's 'political sense'. In Wilson's world of politics, a leading minister could be fired on the joint initiative of a civil servant and a central banker. It did not matter that this was partly an act of political revenge for jostling the Prime Minister into making a move that was practically inevitable. Or that he was to be replaced by someone with no political and only slight technical qualification for the job, who was also burdened by a clear financial conflict of interest and a track record of sympathy for Nazi Germany.

*    *    *

One common thread running through most of the ministerial appointments in which the hand of Wilson can be detected, including the choice of Stamp, is his preference for non-politicians. Like his patron Sir Warren Fisher, who saw ministers as 'megalomaniac', Wilson appears to have taken a dim view of professional politicians and he treated their antics as those of fundamentally inferior creatures, which he would describe contemptuously to those he trusted.[32] Inskip had been replaced as Minister for Defence Coordination by a former First Sea Lord, Lord Chatfield. Chatfield had the added merit of having been resolutely defeatist and pro-appeasement. Wilson was especially proud of Chatfield's appointment because it was proof to him that Chamberlain was above politics: 'It should show everybody that we have a PM who does not let ordinary political influences affect his day-to-day conduct of affairs.'[33] In Wilson's eyes, Chamberlain had the laudable instincts of a civil servant and not the trivial instincts of a politician. It was the mirror image of Chamberlain's praise for Wilson as a politically alert civil servant.

The influence of established politicians over defence preparation was further diluted at the same moment by making Sir John Anderson Lord Privy Seal, with the key job of superintending air raid precautions. Anderson's entire career had been in the Civil Service, where he was regarded as a near superman. Both of Wilson's picks as Minister of Information fulfilled his goal of keeping the job out of the hands of a politician. Wilson made no bones about challenging a senior minister,

Sir Samuel Hoare, over the Ministry of Information, and defeated him easily. Another beneficiary of the January 1940 reshuffle was Andrew Duncan, who was given the Board of Trade. Duncan was appointed even though he had no political experience whatever. His entire career had been in business and he remained chairman of the Iron and Steel Federation even after he joined the Cabinet. He came from the same stable of industrialists clustered around Norman at the Bank of England as Charles Bruce-Gardner, Wilson's aircraft industry czar. Like Butler a couple of years before, Duncan received the news of his promotion direct from Wilson himself.[34]

Another minister whose fate had been discussed by Wilson and Norman was William 'Shakes' Morrison, who was seen as having failed as Minister of Food. He survived the January reshuffle but was demoted in April 1940 in favour of another friend and supporter of Wilson's, Lord Woolton. Woolton's chief occupation was the Lewis's department store empire and his deep knowledge of the textile industry had qualified him to advise the government on making preparations to clothe the armed forces when they would be expanded in wartime. Finding a suitable title for him when he was given a peerage in mid-1939 had proved a harder problem. He was born Frederick Marquis so his surname would have given him the confusing impression of his holding a higher grade of peerage than he actually did. The suggestion that he become Lord Windermere was supposedly vetoed by his wife, who objected to the Wildean allusion.[35] His eventual title came from the name of a Liverpool suburb, but the name went into popular culture from the 'Woolton pie', a meatless confection which became a much-hated symbol of wartime rationing, which he had promoted.

Wilson and David Margesson were also blamed for one appointment that erred far in the other direction.[36] Sir John Gilmour, Baronet, had been appointed to the Ministry of Shipping when it was created on the outbreak of war with neither political nor technical qualifications for the job. Gilmour was a Scottish grandee who had withdrawn from front-rank politics when Baldwin became Prime Minister for the final time in 1935. Chamberlain had regretted his departure then and he had practically no enemies, but as Chamberlain was being criticised for an elderly and uninspiring government team, it is hard to see why he should have been brought back in. Even Halifax found it in his discreet heart to cite the choice of Gilmour as an example of Chamberlain's bad judgement of people.[37] After six months, Chamberlain came to accept that as Minister of Shipping Gilmour had been a political problem.[38]

It is likely that Chamberlain played as much a part as Wilson, if not considerably more, in the choice of Gilmour. His penchant for bringing otherwise untalented aristocrats into government had already been noticeable in the appointments of Lord Winterton as *de facto* deputy Air Secretary in March 1938 and Lord Stanhope as First Lord of the Admiralty in October 1938. Perhaps Wilson thought that aristocrats were an improvement on professional career politicians as well.

Wilson's involvement in media management has already been discussed at length, but this was not the limit of what he would do to obtain a favourable reception to appeasement. The Lewis's department stores staged a highly successful boycott of German goods in protest at the *Anschluß* in March 1938. Worse, Woolton told his sales managers that the company would not give any more business to German manufacturers whilst the German government continued to persecute Jews. Wilson was a personal friend of Woolton, but this did not stop him summoning the retailer to Downing Street to be told in no uncertain terms that 'the Prime Minister disapproved of my action and that I had no right to interfere in this manner in the foreign policy of the country'.[39]

Stanley Baldwin, Chamberlain's predecessor, watched with dismay as much of his open style of government and friendly rapport with the Labour leaders was abandoned. As far as possible Baldwin had aimed to take foreign affairs out of party politics, but Chamberlain's abrasive reaction to Labour criticisms was making appeasement look like a purely Conservative policy. Baldwin had been concerned when Eden resigned. He never contemplated a return to politics or intrigued against Chamberlain, but to many his public silence was telling. Wilson visited Baldwin and tried to persuade him to speak publicly in favour of Chamberlain, but Baldwin brushed him off with the mischievous suggestion that the Prime Minister was already getting healthy support from Lord Beaverbrook.[40]

# CHAPTER THIRTY-FIVE

# MINISTER TO ICELAND

*Winston was furious, and exploded. Turning to Bracken who was with him, he said: 'Tell that man if that room is not cleared by 2 p.m. I will make him Minister to Iceland.'*

– Hugh Dalton memoirs

At the very end of the Phoney War the secret channel between London and Rome reopened for one final time. It was a fittingly symmetrical finale for Chamberlain's policy of appeasement, which had opened with the secret channel being used to bypass an unhelpful Foreign Secretary at a hostile Foreign Office and finally closed with the last, desperate grasp at the faintest hope of peace imaginable.

Sir Joseph Ball had kept up his good relations with Fascist Italy, which had become exceptionally close as he promoted Italy's side in its dispute with France. *Truth* ran stories so uncritically favourable to Italy as to be considered outright propaganda.[1] Chamberlain's work to improve relations between Britain and Italy was praised lavishly.

The last dialogue via the secret channel coincided roughly with a peace mission that President Roosevelt was despatching to Berlin and London in the person of Sumner Welles and may have been designed to pre-empt this. Chamberlain and Wilson were no keener on US help than they had been when they cold-shouldered Roosevelt's initiative in February 1938, which had helped to trigger Anthony Eden's resignation. London also had been given faint grounds for hope that Mussolini was becoming more pliant when Italy bowed to British demands to cease imports of coal from Germany and had asked for this to be publicised on the day of a visit to Rome by Ribbentrop, to Chamberlain's delight.[2] This had been enough for Cadogan to muse, 'There may be something in appeasement yet!!'[3] With his habitual over-optimism Chamberlain was growing in confidence that Britain's military strength had reached a point from which it could face Germany down.

All the familiar features of the secret channel played out again. Once again, Ball arranged for Adrian Dingli to visit Count Galeazzo Ciano in Rome and, just as had happened at the start of Chamberlain's campaign to undermine Eden, Dingli claimed to be bearing a message directly from Chamberlain.[4] By then Dingli had caught the eye of Britain's security service, MI5, and Guy Liddell, a senior MI5 investigator, wanted to find out what he was up to. Dingli still had friends in very high places and Liddell was warned off by the head of the Secret Intelligence Service (MI6), who knew that Dingli was working under top-level protection:

> Dingli is apparently off to Italy again on some hush-hush mission for Downing Street. We started to interrogate him on his business at the War Office but got a warning from Stewart Menzies that we had better not probe too deeply. It seems entirely wrong that this kind of thing should be going on without our knowledge.[5]

Dingli's task was twofold: to discuss a practical question of Italian ships detained by the British in the Downs and to convey the message that Chamberlain still believed that 'there was room for friendly understanding between England and Italy'.[6] Once again the Italian ambassador in London, now Giuseppe Bastianini, endorsed this claim to Ciano and urged him to receive Dingli. In Bastianini's words, Chamberlain was convinced that Mussolini shared his goal of a durable peace in Europe, and that *il Duce*'s assistance was vital to achieve his goal of rebuilding Europe. Dingli was to find out how Mussolini and Ciano could help in this quest.

Unlike in the secret channel's glory days when Downing Street had been united in its favour, Wilson had reservations this time. A three-cornered shadow fight ensued in which Wilson had the advantage of being able to speak to Chamberlain easily but Ball knew that his schemes fell in with Chamberlain's instinct. Chamberlain might even have sanctioned them explicitly. Ball could also trot out Rab Butler as someone already well in the know about the secret channel as a potential ally. When Dingli returned to London, Ball briefed Chamberlain on what had happened. According to Ball, Mussolini had risen to the bait and had let it be known that he was ready to broker a deal, possibly Ball's goal all along.

> [Mussolini] was willing to see if negotiations could be begun between England and Germany and would be willing to put proposals to Hitler as his own, but before doing so he wished D. to ascertain from the PM what were the British terms so that he would be sure of his ground in putting anything forward.

Chamberlain passed this on to Wilson, who was by then highly dubious about the whole arrangement. His memorandum of the conversation makes clear that he wanted to cover both his own back and that of the Prime Minister. He recorded that the Prime Minister had claimed he had told Ball he was surprised any such conversations had taken place and that there was 'nothing doing on the lines proposed'.[7] If nothing else, Germany had invaded Denmark and Norway since Dingli had been sent to Rome. '[I]t was probably no more than another specimen of the "feelers" that various people had thought they had observed since the war began.'

If Wilson had hoped that this would kill off the plan with a suitably sceptical memo lodged in the files, he was mistaken. Chamberlain was not going to fall in with Wilson's instincts and distance himself entirely from the scheme, even if Ball had started by acting completely on his own initiative. The Prime Minister was willing to reach out for any chance of a negotiated settlement, however weak, and sent Wilson back to Ball to find out 'what was happening'. Either Chamberlain had cleared Ball to send Dingli to Rome in the first place, or he clung to the hope that Mussolini might once again save his bacon. Wilson was now caught; the Prime Minister wanted to go ahead but he himself saw no prospect of success. Ball was insisting that Dingli's conversations were worth following up but Wilson was privately sure that the 'idea was preposterous'.[8] Wilson was charitable enough to dismiss Italian willingness to mediate as 'an exaggeration of Dinglys [*sic*]' but struggled to find some way of kicking the notion into the long grass with minimal fuss.

Ball endorsed the supposed claim of the Italian side that Mussolini's 'message' (Wilson's quotation marks) demanded a written reply and that it would be a mistake not to send one.[9] He and Wilson batted competing drafts for a letter to Mussolini back and forth. To the end Ball tried to convince Wilson that a letter should be sent to Mussolini over Chamberlain's own signature but Wilson finally persuaded Chamberlain to veto a letter of any kind. Ball was to accept that communication with the Italians should go through the regular channel of the ambassador to Rome, who fortuitously happened to be in London and available for briefing.[10] Ball knew he was beaten and Dingli was left to his own devices. He was reduced to sending an apologetic letter to Ciano pleading the effect of the German attack on Scandinavia for the delay in giving him a final answer from the London end of the dialogue. Dingli sent a copy direct to Wilson, perhaps recognising the direction in which the balance of power had now swung.

The secret channel was finally closed. Chamberlain's winnable war was also vanishing into the dreamworld from which it emerged as the German invasion of Denmark then Norway on 9 April 1940 demonstrated that the balance of military force and ability lay with Germany. It also set in train the events that removed Chamberlain from the premiership and Wilson from his seat of power in Downing Street. Wilson's perfunctory hand-written acknowledgement of Dingli's letter from his internal exile at Treasury Chambers was the obituary of both appeasement and his own days as the power behind the British government. Mussolini would soon leap on German success by declaring war on Britain and France in the hope of some pickings from the carcasses.

Hitler's failure to follow Chamberlain's script by remaining eternally passive in the west wrote the death warrant of Chamberlain's government. The attack on Scandinavia caught the British leadership entirely unawares, despite ample intelligence of German preparations. The military response was extempore, badly organised and ineffective. British forces landed at Namsos and Åndalsnes in the south of Norway to block the Germans, but found themselves on the defensive almost immediately and were pushed back remorselessly. The Germans enjoyed near-total air superiority. Only a fortnight after landing, the British were forced to evacuate. They had greater success with a landing in the north of Norway at Narvik, designed to deprive Germany of access to the crucial Swedish iron ore from Luleå in the winter months when the Baltic was frozen. This was a project that Churchill had long cherished. The Royal Navy inflicted serious damage on the Kriegsmarine in two battles, which left it in a severely weakened state and almost unable to give effective support to a German invasion of Britain. The land campaign at Narvik was far from perfectly handled, but did succeed in dominating the German forces until the British and French collapse in France forced them to evacuate.

Wilson organised a traditional Whitehall response to the British failure to anticipate the German invasion of Scandinavia. The Joint Intelligence Committee (JIC) was put in the frame to take the blame by having failed to give emphatic and unambiguous warning.[11] After unhurried discussion it was decided that the JIC should simply be told to make a great fuss of anything that it thought was really exciting.[12]

Whilst Wilson was trying to bolt bureaucratic stable doors, the fate of Chamberlain's government and Wilson's own domination of Whitehall was finally being decided by the politicians. A debate was called in the House of Commons. Churchill was directly in the firing line because the Royal Navy was heavily engaged in the Norwegian operations and he bore responsibility for British failure. But the true topic of the debate went far deeper than the military minutiae of a single campaign. A large Conservative majority, and ruthless measures by the whips, had prevented any serious challenge to Chamberlain since he became Prime Minister, but this masked growing doubt and suspicion amongst his MPs as to whether he was truly committed to opposing Hitler's Germany. Like steam building up in a pressure cooker, this concern was set to explode. For as long as there had been no open revolt, Downing Street could fool itself that it was truly in charge of the situation and that everyone who mattered knew that its analyses and policies were correct.

As the debate got under way, it was soon clear that Chamberlain would be forced into a major change in his government if he was to survive. It was notably bad-tempered as the opposition repaid Chamberlain for his years of contemptuously belittling them. Wilson was shocked to observe, 'The hatred written on their faces astonished him: it was the pent-up bitterness and personal animosity of years.'[13] The debate was enlivened by spectacles such as one of Chamberlain's opponents, Roger Keyes, the hero of the Zeebrugge raid in the First World War, turning up in the full dress uniform of an admiral of the fleet with four rows of medals. Chamberlain made a crucial tactical blunder when he claimed that 'I still have some friends in this House – to support the government tonight in the lobby', which gave him the air of someone speaking in personal and party interests. Churchill loyally supported the government without truly coming to Chamberlain's assistance.

Even at this late stage Chamberlain was only dimly aware of the cause of discontent with his government. When he spoke to a potential waverer amongst Conservative MPs, Victor Cazalet, he was unaware that there was any hostility to Wilson, or to Sir Samuel Hoare or Sir John Simon. Cazalet put him straight on the point with a detailed list of Wilson's bad choices of ministers and his interference in politics:

- Gilmour – Joke
- Reith – v. bad
- H. Nicolson – not being allowed to broadcast
- Young men – whom Whips and Party treated as traitors because they had voted against Munich.[14]

Chamberlain was far on the back foot and panic measures were put in hand to try to save him. He was willing to sacrifice his unpopular ministers to remain in power. Lord Dunglass, Chamberlain's parliamentary private secretary, tried to buy off Paul Emrys-Evans, one of the most tenacious dissidents:

[Dunglass] asked me whether my friends would vote for the government on the understanding that we should see the PM the following morning and place any demands we wished to make before him. He implied that the PM was prepared to carry out a dramatic reconstruction of the government. I told him that it was too late. I said that the Government could have been reconstructed at the beginning of the War or even as late as Christmas; we were thoroughly dissatisfied with such ministers as Simon and Hoare and with Sir Horace Wilson and his intolerable interference in politics and his evil influence on Policy. I also explained that the attitude of the Whips Office had been disastrous and that we did not think the PM had the right temperament for a Head of Government in wartime.[15]

Even in this desperate parliamentary crisis Chamberlain still had time for the press proprietor Lord Camrose. After the conversation with Cazalet Chamberlain had grasped who his critics objected to.[16] Revealingly, the one of Emrys-Evans's three targets he defended at all vigorously was Wilson. Apart from puzzlement at the hostility to Simon, he did not query why the two ministers should be in the firing line.

Even as Chamberlain braced himself to sacrifice Simon and Hoare, he kept his faith in Wilson. In the final crisis of the Chamberlain government, Wilson threw himself openly into action as its political supporter, throwing off the mask of political neutrality. He was one of the figures trying to buy off government opponents with schemes for reconstruction. Leo Amery, another long-standing dissident, learned to his disgust that Wilson was proposing to offer him a job. 'This is truly typical of the Horace Wilson methods and of the kind of opinion Neville's advisers have held as to the motives which inspired criticism and opposition.'[17] Behind Chamberlain's pretensions to high-mindedness lay a contemptuous belief that the only reason to oppose him was blackmail to obtain some advantage.

Chamberlain was even prepared to contemplate an alliance with Labour to keep his position, inspiring the contemptuous remark by one of their leaders that he was 'determined himself to stick on – like a dirty old piece of chewing gum on the leg of a chair'.[18] The Labour leaders were called in to speak to Chamberlain, Halifax and Churchill. Initially the party leader, Clement Attlee, was taken aback at the approach and appeared reserved, but his deputy, Arthur Greenwood, forthrightly poured cold water on the proposal.[19] They left a final decision to the party executive, which was meeting the following day. Greenwood's reservations went further than Chamberlain or his ministers, as was all too obvious when Greenwood told the story of the fall of Chamberlain's government in a moment of drink-fuelled exuberance a few days afterwards. As Bruce Lockhart reported,

> Greenwood hates Sir Horace Wilson ... thinks it is more important to get rid of him than Chamberlain. Labour wanted to get rid of him altogether. Winston couldn't (can't) do anything. But Greenwood has pledge from Winston that Wilson's claws cut for war. Greenwood referred to him (Wilson) the whole time as Sir Horace Quisling.*[20]

The result of the vote was terminal for Chamberlain. The government won by 281 to 200, but the huge defection of its supporters delivered a fatal blow. By normal standards it was a comfortable majority, but compared to the ones of over 200 that the government could normally command it was tantamount to a vote of no confidence. Only a handful believed that Chamberlain could survive; a massive reconstruction was a foregone conclusion. Wilson was also directly in the firing line. It was not just Labour who were deeply discontented with him. Even the most powerful body of mainstream Conservative parliamentary thinking, the 1922 Committee, had 'shown great animosity against Horace Wilson and he will probably have to retire upstairs in any case'.[21]

Chamberlain resigned but wanted to prevent Churchill taking over. He would have preferred Halifax, as did many mainstream Conservatives and King George VI. The two potential successors were summoned to Downing Street. Before the meeting Brendan Bracken begged Churchill to hold his tongue, dreading that however eloquent he might be, silence was the stronger strategy. Halifax knew that he was not the right man for the job and did not rise to the implicit challenge.

---

\* Vidkun Quisling, a Norwegian fascist, had become the country's puppet leader after the German invasion and his name became a generic term for a collaborationist politician.

Chamberlain had no choice but to give the ultimate prize to the man he had tried to hold back for so long. Churchill became Prime Minister on 10 May 1940.

There was never the slightest prospect that Churchill would keep Wilson on in his position as favoured and intimate adviser, but Wilson under-estimated how brutal his fall would be. Since his first arrival at Downing Street under Baldwin five years before, the symbol and source of his power had been the strategically placed office next to the Cabinet Room. When he first entered it, he had been fully aware that he did so through an informal arrangement that depended on the goodwill of the Prime Minister, but since then long years of power, coupled with the formal status as head of the Civil Service, had created a misleading air of permanence and entitlement. The grand room in Treasury Chambers was Wilson's by right as permanent secretary to the Treasury, but his office at Downing Street was at the discretion of the Prime Minister.

On Churchill's first day as Prime Minister, Wilson was instructed to vacate his office at Downing Street. There are a number of stories of precisely how this occurred, all equally colourful, all equally proof of the relish with which his fall from grace was received outside the narrow world of Chamberlain and his supporters.[22] There is no doubt that he was removed from Downing Street swiftly. According to one version of the tale,

> [Churchill] found Wilson still installed. He greeted him very courteously, said he was making changes and asked Wilson if he could vacate his room by 2 p.m. Apparently, Wilson did not quite realise the extent of his disgrace and, having many papers to clear, sent a message to ask if he could have till 6 p.m.
>
> Winston was furious, and exploded. Turning to Bracken who was with him, he said, 'Tell that man if that room is not cleared by 2 p.m. I will make him Minister* to Iceland.' Brendan went off on his errand and, according to Harold [Nicolson], delivered the message textually.[23]

---

* Diplomatic representative, ranking below a full ambassador.

There were most certainly many papers to clear and Churchill's remorselessness was a gift to future historians. The Downing Street files were in practice Wilson's working files and it is possible to trace the path by which Wilson handled many major issues through the way they were assembled. Doubtless Cabinet Office weeders suppressed egregious specimens of Wilson's work before the files became publicly available at the National Archives, but enough remains to see how he worked.[24]

It was an uncomplicated task to throw Wilson out of Downing Street, but his official position was a far more daunting fortress to attack. It was practically unheard of for senior civil servants to be 'asked to resign', except for serious breaches of ethics. The solution of banishing Wilson to an insignificant appointment overseas, which feature in every version of the tale of his removal from Downing Street, was actively, but inconclusively, canvassed.[25] As the military crisis that culminated in the Battle of Britain unfolded, the government had far more important matters to deal with. Wilson remained as head of the Civil Service and permanent secretary to the Treasury.

Wilson had kept a grand title and a theoretically influential job, but only a couple of months after his fall, he lost any protection he could have expected at the top of government. Political expediency dictated that Churchill keep Chamberlain on in a senior position, Lord President of the Council with a seat in the War Cabinet, however little sympathy there was between them. Churchill was Prime Minister and hugely popular with the public, but mainstream Conservative opinion was far more cautious, if not downright hostile.[26] Chamberlain was a touchstone of solid Conservative instincts that Churchill could not dispose of, but he was stricken by terminal stomach cancer, which forced him to resign at the end of September 1940. He survived a few weeks and died on 9 November.

The respect due to a former Prime Minister allowed Chamberlain the honour of a memorial service at Westminster Abbey but it was not publicised for fear that the Germans might try to exploit the occasion of Britain's top political leadership being concentrated in a single target for an opportunistic air raid. The service was sparsely attended in freezing temperatures, but Wilson was faithful to the last. Chips Channon heard that 'after everyone had left the Abbey, poor Horace Wilson, the once all-powerful eminence grise of the Chamberlain regime, was seen alone, his face contracted with grief, praying for his dead friend'.[27]

Wilson's fall was a professional humiliation and a personal tragedy.

# CHAPTER THIRTY-SIX

# A GUILTY MAN IN THE
# REALM OF KING ZOG

*Sir Horace Wilson established an ascendancy over Mr Chamberlain which
will take its place in history ... things came to a point when no major
decision of any kind was taken by the British Government
before Sir Horace was consulted.*
– CATO, *GUILTY MEN*

Churchill's circle swiftly extended the punishment of Wilson well
beyond simple professional demotion to something considerably
uglier and more menacing. A few weeks after Churchill became Prime
Minister a short book was published that went on to become a colossal success. In the words of one of its authors, *Guilty Men* sold 'like a
pornographic classic', reaching over 200,000 copies.[1] It was the first
and possibly the most ferocious attack on the appeasement regime,
and opened the battle over the rights and wrongs of British external
policy in the 1930s that rages still. *Guilty Men* was a savage assault on
a cast of fifteen men that it blamed for Britain's predicament in the
wake of Dunkirk, militarily isolated and fighting for its survival against
Hitler's immense military superiority. The cast was headed by Neville
Chamberlain and they were all politicians except for Wilson, who was
probably the first British civil servant to suffer this level of attack.

One of its twenty-four chapters was entitled 'What's There behind
the Arras?' and consisted of a remorseless attack on Wilson. It did not
question his patriotism or integrity but sniffed at the modesty of his

early career beginnings. The authors went beyond portraying him as the second most powerful man in the country and presented him as the true author of Chamberlain's policies. *Guilty Men* pointed out that his influence lingered on as head of the Civil Service, such that '[t]he dead hand of bureaucracy strangles with red tape all those who desire to take determined and drastic action'.[2]

*Guilty Men* was churned out in the space of a few days so shows plenty of signs of unevenness. It was not only venomous, it was shot through with dishonourable political agendas. Behind the pseudonym of Cato, the book was written by three journalists from across the political spectrum: Michael Foot on the far left, Frank Owen, a Lloyd George Liberal, and Peter Howard on the right. They all worked for Churchill's old crony Lord Beaverbrook. Beaverbrook made no bones about his attachment to *Guilty Men*.[3] The criticism of Wilson comes uncannily close to Attlee's and echoes the Labour leaders' frustration that they were not able to have him sacked entirely. Perhaps more important are the potential targets that *Guilty Men* spared. It left the newspapermen unscathed, even Geoffrey Dawson, the arch-propagandist of appeasement through *The Times*. Naturally Beaverbrook's remorseless advocacy of peace was not mentioned. Nor was the Labour Party's long-standing hostility to rearmament. The cast-list of politicians attacked included distinctly insignificant and short-lived figures from Chamberlain's government, as well as the more obviously important such as Sir John Simon, Sir Samuel Hoare, Lord Halifax and chief whip David Margesson.

*Guilty Men* expressed rancour if not hatred of the old regime, but a combination of practical politics and Churchill's instincts meant that there was no drastic purge of its targets. Hoare was exiled to Madrid as ambassador, although this was a crucial and responsible task, but the other senior politicians were moved to high-level political jobs. Churchill could not afford to alienate the Conservative Party and had no reason to put himself too deeply in the hands of Labour. The spirit of the Other Club dictated that political grudges should not be given excessive weight. Tolerance extended far down the line. Jock Colville, who had been a junior secretary to Chamberlain and an admirer of Wilson, kept his job and went on to become a key insider of Churchill's

governments. In his words, attitudes were marked by the 'general forgiveness he [Churchill] has bestowed on the Men of Munich'.⁴ It was
all in marked contrast to the vendettas that Chamberlain and Wilson
pursued against the opponents of appeasement and far closer in spirit
to Baldwin's progressive rehabilitation of the coalitionists after the Carlton House coup.

One of the most remarkable acts of forgiveness was what happened
to Sir Joseph Ball. He was removed from the Ministry of Information,
but given a senior security job despite MI5's knowledge of the secret
channel to the Italians. He was made deputy chairman of the Security
Executive, which oversaw the severe measures against all Axis nationals that Churchill ordered to combat a practically non-existent fifth
column.⁵

Wilson was a notable exception to this forgiveness. He was outside
the magic circle of power and was told very firmly to stay outside. His
job was grand and his workload was great, but he was a pariah. His
wife complained to Tommy Dugdale's wife Nancy, 'H. is always getting
ill mannered messages from W.C. to the effect that he is only to do
what he is told & to keep his place etc.'⁶ Churchill positively advertised
his continuing hostility to him. When Wilson sent the Prime Minister
a note covering a letter 'the PM may be interested to see', Churchill
put a red circle round the word 'interested' and wrote at the bottom,
'Why?'⁷ Personal conversations with the Prime Minister were rare and
unpleasant.⁸

The change of government also handed power to a new opponent
of Wilson. Clement Attlee, the Labour leader, became *de facto* deputy
Prime Minister. He quickly discovered – and resented – Wilson's web
of power across Whitehall committees: 'He ran everything. Dominated
the show. We pushed him off the whole lot of them and started afresh.'⁹

Wilson was deeply out of sympathy with the new regime. He referred
to Churchill as King Zog, after the deposed monarch of Albania who
smoked some 200 cigarettes a day and lived in exile at the Ritz Hotel.¹⁰
He complained at the new government's disorderly and capricious
working methods, which were in total contrast to the ordered, hierarchical pattern he had evolved under Chamberlain. He lamented that

Churchill did not understand the purpose of committees, doubtless mourning the wholesale destruction of the network to which Attlee had objected.[11] He darkly foresaw the danger of 'confusion in the "higher" regions (not an easy job in present circumstances)'.[12] Churchill's late-night, brandy-fuelled colloquies with his own cronies provided a sad contrast with the intense after-hours conversations between Chamberlain and Wilson that had been the rock of Wilson's power.

Wilson had to recognise that Churchill's position was practically unassailable, but his position as head of the Civil Service did give him one opportunity to savour the final fruits of revenge against one of Churchill's inner circle. Bob Boothby had escaped from the full wrath of Wilson in the summer of 1939, when the evidence against him had been relatively weak, but the appeasers had continued to stalk him. Boothby had continued to press for settlement of the Czech claims, in part because of the financial pressure of his own debts.[13] When he became a junior food minister in the new Churchill government, he fell under suspicion on a quite different score. He had become a shareholder in the British subsidiary of the Swiss Hoffmann-La Roche company, which benefited enormously from the Food Ministry's decision to mandate the addition of vitamin supplements to bread.

Shortly afterwards Richard Weininger, Boothby's Czech friend and business partner, fell under MI5 suspicion in one of the murkiest episodes in the whole affair. The MI5 files reveal an appalling picture of prejudice and guilt by association. MI5 took Weininger's contacts with two German spies as proof that he himself was a spy, and reasoned from his influential contacts in Britain that 'if he is engaged in espionage, he is a very dangerous spy'.[14] The search did find evidence that Weininger used the debts that influential individuals had incurred to him as a tool to manipulate them. From this MI5 extrapolated that Weininger was probably blackmailing his victims on behalf of German intelligence. Xenophobia and anti-Semitism were also at work: 'Since the international [euphemism for Jewish] element is marked in him, it is likely, [words missing] that if he is a spy he is a double cross agent and willing to sell himself to the highest bidder.' Weininger was treated remarkably severely, arrested at Boothby's flat where he was staying and detained in Brixton prison as a common criminal. MI5 might even have been using the espionage angle as a pretext. The Treasury solicitor gathered 'in casual conversation that MI5 have imprisoned Weininger because he is a crook financier. They hardly seem to be the best judges of this...'[15] The government was alert to the danger that Boothby might say publicly that the true motive for the operation against Weininger was to unearth incriminating evidence against him.[16] No worthwhile evidence of either espionage or blackmail emerged and Weininger was ultimately released. Spy mania was rife at the time but it is hard not to suspect that the true target of the operation was indeed Boothby and that Sir Joseph Ball might have played some part from his strategic position at the Security Executive.

The search of Weininger's papers in the flat did provide Boothby's enemies with one priceless item: clear proof that Boothby had forged the documents that supported his claim to compensation for Czech assets. When they were shown to a criminal barrister, he pronounced that they were 'conceived in fraud and brought forth in iniquity'.[17] The papers made their way up to Wilson because they concerned the Czech claims, which were being handled by the Treasury, and he began to draw the net around Boothby, briefing a former subordinate still at Downing Street on the investigation.[18] The moment had arrived to spring the trap and he called together the government's highest law officers. Together they concluded that the affair was too serious for Boothby simply to be offered the opportunity to resign quietly.[19] Wilson homed in on the 'forgery & intent to deceive' aspects.[20] He insisted that the papers be referred to the Director of Public Prosecutions 'as to the apparent forgery', ostensibly for his and the law officers' own protection (presumably from accusations of leniency) and because it would be difficult to decide on whether to pay the claim otherwise.[21] More likely, Wilson hoped that Boothby might be prosecuted. The letter to Boothby they drafted for the Prime Minister to sign focused on Boothby's false claim in August 1939 that he had no financial interest in Weininger's claim and stated that it was concerned only with the 'ministerial and Parliamentary aspects' but referred darkly to 'other matters' that were 'being inquired into'.[22]

Churchill was not satisfied with Boothby's confused response to the letter, which failed to squarely address the accusation of giving a misleading account, and demanded he resign as a minister. The subsequent parliamentary inquiry into Boothby's conduct was chaired by Sir John Gretton, a Conservative traditionalist and right-winger. Its conclusions were deeply critical of Boothby, practically endorsing the claim that he had lied. These conclusions were considered at the time (and still are) to have been severely biased against him, but he was not compelled to stand down as an MP. The sums involved were tiny compared to the value of the Czech gold handed over to the Nazis in 1939, but the two affairs became vaguely confused in the public mind. The spectacular and public denouement to the Boothby affair probably helped the Czech gold scandal to fade into near oblivion.

Thoughts of sacking Wilson re-emerged in 1941. Churchill proposed that he should be replaced by P. J. Grigg, whom Sir Warren Fisher had tried to bring in as his own successor in 1938, until overruled by Chamberlain in Wilson's favour. Churchill observed that Wilson 'has a very bad record and is the object of widespread mistrust'.[23] Sir Kingsley Wood, the Chancellor of the Exchequer and thus the minister responsible, advised against the move in a hand-written letter marked 'Secret', which gives an indication of the sensitivity of the question. There was almost nothing to fault in the Treasury's wartime performance and there were strong political reasons to retain Wilson: sacking him would appear as a '"Munich" victimisation by many members of the Conservative Party' and 'an affront to the Civil Service'. 'The people who would be most pleased ... would be the Socialists.'[24] There was also the practical consideration that in a year's time he could be retired on grounds of age.

Wilson's Civil Service post gave him another angle from which to harry the government. He chaired the committee responsible for approving honours and exploited this to load the dice in favour of established civil servants and against the outsiders who had been brought in as part of the war effort.[25] This led to a ferocious passage of arms when Churchill wanted to reward the Secret Service scientist Dr R. V. Jones for his extremely valuable work in helping to defeat the systems used by the Luftwaffe to bomb British cities, with a CB (Commander of the Bath).[26] Jones was rather a favourite of Churchill. James was confronted by Wilson's violent objection to such an honour for someone who was 'merely a Scientific Officer and ... could not possibly have done work of such merit in my lowly position. The most that would have been justified would have been an MBE or OBE [the two lowest decorations available].' The CB was certainly a distinguished accolade; under the old regime the diplomats William Strang and Frank Ashton-Gwatkin had received it for their work on Chamberlain's journeys to Germany and the Runciman mission respectively. Jones was told that Wilson had threatened to resign, but finally accepted that he should receive a CBE, which lay somewhere between the two decorations in status.

Operating from inside the Civil Service, Wilson could work to manipulate the official record of appeasement. In September 1941, his old Foreign Office adversary, Oliver Harvey, was complaining to Eden, once again the Foreign Secretary, about Wilson's 'attempts to stifle and bowdlerize the [British Diplomatic] Documents ... These particular conversations are the most convincing and graphic of the Munich period. Why should Wilson's papers receive a different treatment from those of our Ambassadors and Ministers?'[27] A year later, the haggling continued with 'the infamous Horace Wilson record of Munich' at the centre of the discussion.[28] Wilson had composed a sixty-page narrative of Munich and the events leading up to it, which was one-sided and inaccurate and aimed to demonstrate that appeasement was the only realistic policy.[29] Amongst its distortions was to present Churchill's Grand Alliance scheme as being focused on smaller eastern European states. The attempt to appease Hitler with colonies could not be avoided, but it was trivialised.

Wilson's official standing gave him the opportunity to influence the record in an even less creditable fashion, when evidence surfaced of his dubious interference in politics. Lord Stamp, whom Wilson and Montagu Norman had plotted to replace Sir John Simon as Chancellor of the Exchequer, wrote an incriminating record of the episode. In 1941 he was killed when a German bomb destroyed his house. Amongst the debris blown into the street was this record, and it was found by an air raid warden, who spotted that it was a highly sensitive document.[30] He took it to Downing Street and into the hands of Jock Colville, who happened to be on duty. Colville found it in his conscience not to tell the Prime Minister, but to pass the document to Wilson, then still permanent secretary to the Treasury. Predictably, no trace of this copy has ever been found, but Wilson and Colville reckoned without Stamp's compulsive hoarding of material and another copy survived in his files.

In 1942 Wilson reached the retirement age of sixty. There was never any prospect that he might be kept on and he left public service. Churchill allowed himself another gesture at Wilson's expense. He was replaced as permanent secretary to the Treasury by Sir Richard Hopkins, who was actually two years older than Wilson, thus well past the retirement age. In his previous capacity as head of the Inland Revenue Hopkins had shown himself to be very cooperative by approving Churchill's tax avoidance schemes whilst he was still in the wilderness.[31]

# CHAPTER THIRTY-SEVEN

# HE HAS RETURNED TO BOURNEMOUTH

*He came from Bournemouth and destroyed the British Empire
and has now returned to Bournemouth.*[1]
– SIR ORME SARGENT OF THE FOREIGN OFFICE
ON SIR HORACE WILSON

Churchill took final revenge on Wilson after his retirement, when word was passed around the higher reaches of the establishment that he was not to be employed. Even Wilson's old comrade in arms Montagu Norman of the Bank of England, who wanted to find him some lucrative and prestigious board position in the City, obeyed. He tried to place Wilson at the Hudson's Bay Company and a major steel firm, but when he took soundings he was firmly headed off and had to tell Wilson '[s]orrowfully and indignantly' that he had been urged 'not to proceed'.[2] The only interruption of his enforced idleness was the decidedly minor task of chairing the National Joint Council of Local Authorities' administrative, professional, technical and clerical services from 1944 to 1951.

Wilson cut a sadly diminished figure to those who had known him in his days of power. Chips Channon glimpsed him a couple of years after his retirement: [I]n the Green Park I ran into poor Sir Horace Wilson who often wanders about there, aimlessly and idly. He looked sad and *désœuvré* ... he who was once the eminence grise of England!'[3] The personal stress was magnified as Wilson's wife was confronted by the fickleness of humanity, as people who had sought her company in her husband's days of power now ignored her.[4]

Everywhere in London Wilson was confronted by the consequences of the failure of appeasement. The war that he and Chamberlain had tried so hard to prevent had brought the devastation from the air that he had feared when he first went to Downing Street in 1935. He found some consolation in helping Chamberlain's widow find a supportive biographer for her late husband. Their choice lighted on Oxford historian Keith Feiling, who produced a sturdy but not resounding defence of Chamberlain's reputation, which was written during the war though not published until 1946.[5] Moreover, Feiling acknowledged that 'an honest history will not pass over' the fact that the Foreign Office felt that 'the Prime Minister preferred the amateur advice of Sir Horace Wilson … to their own expert counsel' and that '[t]his impeachment must be admitted'.[6] By contrast, Sir Joseph Ball and his secret channel to Rome did not feature at all, and the clash with Eden was more or less glossed over.

Ball did not escape unscathed and in the post-war chaos produced a side-light on Chamberlain's appeasement of Italy. Grandi's report to Rome of the 'fighting cocks' conversation with Chamberlain and Eden, in which Ball featured prominently, came to light and was published in 1948.[7] Ball moved swiftly and mendaciously to protect his own reputation. He successfully applied legal pressure to prevent his name being mentioned in the British edition and he was described merely as Chamberlain's agent.[8] Privately he lied outright that his contacts with the Italian ambassador Grandi had been trivial (he never mentioned Grandi's successor, Bastianini) and falsely claimed that he had run his intermediary, Adrian Dingli, as a double agent against the Italians.[9] He was particularly anxious to rebut any suggestion that he and Grandi had conducted a discussion in the back of a taxi. One of his comments lends some credence to speculation that he had Dingli done away with: 'I arranged for M.I.5. to look after him in the usual way. He eventually shot himself when he was on the eve of being arrested by Scotland Yard for, I believe, some Company frauds.'[10] By the same token, it might be another instance of Ball's tendency to play up his ties to the secret world as a source of covert power. The risk of legal action and commercial pressure shielded Ball from being named as Chamberlain's intermediary by the historian and wartime intelligence officer Hugh Trevor-Roper.[11]

Wilson returned to his native Bournemouth to live the quiet life of a retired civil servant, with occasional visits to London. He joined the local Conservative Party, which brought him very briefly back into the public eye, as well as giving him the opportunity for a small act of revenge against his first *bête noire* amongst government ministers. Anthony Eden had gone on to reap the rewards of his early falling out with Chamberlain, serving as Churchill's deputy Prime Minister and finally rising to the top job in 1955. Obsessed with the vision of Colonel Nasser, the new nationalist ruler of Egypt, as a new Hitler, Eden threw the country into the debacle of the Suez crisis. In the aftermath of Suez, the senior figures of the Conservative Party showed exactly the same kind of solidarity that they and their predecessors had shown to Chamberlain during appeasement. Amongst the few rebels to criticise Eden openly was Nigel Nicolson, the son of Wilson's tormentor, Harold Nicolson, author of the 'two curates' crack about him and Chamberlain. The younger Nicolson was the Conservative MP for Bournemouth East and there was a powerful movement in the constituency association to deselect him, led by its chairman, a former Indian Army major, a stock figure of backwoods Conservativism of the era.[12] Wilson supported Nigel Nicolson in his troubles and chaired one of the meetings that he was permitted, where he could present his case. Nicolson lost by a narrow margin and was replaced by John Cordle, an impeccably respectable evangelical Christian, who promoted rigidly reactionary views on a wide range of social topics such as a campaign against 'pregnant' dolls and other toy figures with a lifelike flesh quality. He served as MP for Bournemouth East for eighteen years until it emerged that he was on the payroll of the corrupt architect and property developer John Poulson.

The historical battle over appeasement had got well under way in the first years after the end of the war.[13] It was fought by professional historians, broadcasters and individuals involved in the process who wanted to present their side of the case, politicians and diplomats. Fortunately for later historians, Wilson was firmly convinced that Chamberlain and he had pursued the correct policy, and he never missed an opportunity to present his (and Chamberlain's) case. He made no distinction between well-disposed writers and those with less kindly intent. Some of what he said was remarkably indiscreet. He never wavered from a direct and open argument that appeasement had been the only practical policy.

One of his early correspondents was Sir Samuel Hoare, who was already an established writer and, more importantly, wanted to get his own version of appeasement into print. Wilson's reward was a thoroughly dishonest whitewash in Hoare's *Nine Troubled Years*: 'Horace Wilson was in every respect the orthodox, conscientious and efficient civil servant. The partisan attacks upon him, on the ground that he was Chamberlain's éminence grise, who intrigued himself into a position of great political influence, are totally untrue.'[14]

Wilson was frank about the policy of appeasement, but less than honest about his own part in it. When asked about his secret back-channel diplomacy he lied outright: '[E]very conversation at any time that he had with anyone connected with Foreign Affairs, was reported by him in full, according to the usual custom, to the Foreign Office.'[15] He was only slightly more truthful when a historian at the Foreign Office began to take an interest in his furtive contacts with Helmut Wohlthat.[16] He admitted to only a single meeting with Wohlthat, which he claimed was intended solely to send the message of Halifax's Chatham House speech to Hitler via Goering. He practically denied meeting Wohlthat a second time in July and did not mention the telephone conversations with him once the story of his meeting broke publicly.[17] Of Dirksen's attempt to follow up the Wohlthat contacts and the proposals that Wilson made to him, he said not a word.

Apologists for appeasement developed the self-serving argument that the Munich agreements were entirely pragmatic moves, calculated to buy Britain the year's breathing space that it needed to bring rearmament to a point where military defeat by Germany would not be inevitable. The argument remains one of the most popular aspects to the case presented in favour of appeasement today, but Wilson himself supplied the proof that it was false. 'The aim of our appeasement was to avoid war altogether, for all time.'[18]

Sir Horace Wilson died on 19 May 1972 at the age of eighty-nine.

# ENDNOTES

## PREFACE

1. Templewood papers, XIX Wilson to Hoare, 10 July 1952
2. Robert Self, *Neville Chamberlain: A Biography* (Aldershot: Ashgate, 2006), p. 292
3. Rodney Lowe and Richard Roberts, 'Sir Horace Wilson 1930–1935: The Making of a Mandarin', *Historical Journal*, vol. 30, no. 3 (1987), pp. 641–2; G. C. Peden, 'Sir Horace Wilson and Appeasement', *Historical Journal*, vol. 53, no. 4 (2010), pp. 983–1014
4. Andrew Roberts, *The Holy Fox: A Life of Lord Halifax* (London: Papermac, 1992), p. 52; David Dutton, *Neville Chamberlain* (London: Arnold, 2001), p. 203

## PROLOGUE: A MAN I CAN DO BUSINESS WITH

1. John Wheeler-Bennett, *Munich: Prologue to Tragedy* (London: Macmillan, 1948), p. 108, fn 2; Leonard Mosley, *On Borrowed Time: How World War II Began* (London: Weidenfeld & Nicolson, 1969), p. 36; their information almost certainly came from Strang, whom Mosley interviewed
2. NA CAB 24/279 The prime minister's visit to Germany
3. NA CAB 24/279 The prime minister's visit to Germany
4. NA CAB 24/279 The prime minister's visit to Germany
5. Self, *Neville Chamberlain*, p. 314
6. Neville Chamberlain papers, NC18/1/1069 Chamberlain to Ida 19 September 1938
7. NA CAB 23/95 Meeting of 17 September 1938
8. NA CAB 23/95/6
9. Lord Strang, *Home and Abroad* (London: André Deutsch, 1956), p. 147
10. Neville Chamberlain papers, NC18/1/1070 Chamberlain to Hilda 2 October 1938
11. Strang, *Home and Abroad*, p. 147
12. Lord Home, *The Way the Wind Blows: An Autobiography* (London: Collins, 1976), p. 64
13. Paul Schmidt, *Statist auf Diplomatischer Bühne 1923–45* (Bonn: Athenäum, 1949), p. 417
14. Chamberlain speech at Heston aerodrome, quoted in Neville Chamberlain, *In Search of Peace: Speeches (1937–1938)*, ed. Arthur Bryant (London: Hutchinson, 1939), p. 302
15. Ivone Kirkpatrick, *The Inner Circle: Memoirs of Ivone Kirkpatrick* (London: Macmillan, 1959), pp. 121f
16. Joseph Goebbels, *Die Tagebücher von Joseph Goebbels: sämtliche Fragmente*, ed. Elke Fröhlich (Munich: K. G. Saur, 1987), 18 September 1938
17. Ernst von Weizsäcker, *Memoirs of Ernst von Weizsäcker* (London: Victor Gollancz, 1951), p. 150
18. Fritz Hesse, *Das Spiel um Deutschland* (Munich: List, 1953), p. 151

## CHAPTER ONE: PERSONAL DISCOURTESY IS HIS CHIEF WEAPON

1. Richard Toye, *Lloyd George & Churchill: Rivals for Greatness* (London: Macmillan, 2007), passim

2. Charles Hobhouse, *Inside Asquith's Cabinet: From the Diaries of Charles Hobhouse*, ed. Edward David (London: John Murray, 1977), 27 July 1908
3. Hudson Ewbanke Kearley, *The Travelled Road: Some Memories of a Busy Life* (privately published, 1935), p. 147
4. Baldwin papers, Windham Baldwin 3/3/12 Talk with Sir Horace Wilson 14 March 1954
5. Alan Bullock, *The Life and Times of Ernest Bevin, Vol. 1: Trade Union Leader 1881–1940* (London: Heinemann, 1960), p. 120
6. Churchill papers, 22/117 Coal committee minutes quoted in Gilbert, p. 207
7. Fred Glueckstein, 'Churchill as Bricklayer', *Finest Hour*, Winter 2012–13, p. 34
8. Churchill papers, CHAR 1/201/301 Churchill to Wilson 11 September 1928
9. Churchill papers, CHAR 1/201/301 Wilson to Churchill 14 September 1928
10. Graham Stewart, *Burying Caesar: Churchill, Chamberlain and the Battle for the Tory Party* (London: Weidenfeld & Nicolson, 1999), pp. 195, 105fn
11. Stewart, *Burying Caesar*, Chapter 7 and p. 181
12. Neville Chamberlain papers, NC18/1/951 Chamberlain to Ida 14 March 1936
13. NA T199/50b
14. Thomas Jones papers, P3/68 Notes of conversation with Sir Horace Wilson 16 July 1942
15. Lord Donoughue email to author, 14 February 2006
16. Sir Raymond Streat, *Lancashire and Whitehall: The Diaries of Sir Raymond Streat*, ed. Margaret Dupree, 2 vols (Manchester: Manchester University Press, 1987), 26 July 1935

CHAPTER TWO: WINSTON'S POWER FOR MISCHIEF
1. Phillips, Adrian, *The King Who Had to Go: Edward VIII, Mrs Simpson and the Hidden Politics of the Abdication Crisis* (London: Biteback, 2016), p. 134
2. Lord Reith, *The Reith Diaries*, ed. Charles Stuart (London: Collins, 1975), 8 April 1936
3. Phillips, *The King Who Had to Go*, p. 67
4. NA KV 4/1
5. Phillips, *The King Who Had to Go*, p. 93f
6. Duff Cooper, *The Duff Cooper Diaries 1915–1951*, ed. John Julius Norwich (London: Weidenfeld & Nicolson, 2005), 20 January 1936
7. Beaverbrook papers, BBK G/6/27 Draft memoirs
8. Crathorne (Dugdale) papers; Nancy Dugdale diaries
9. Sir Henry Channon, *'Chips': The Diaries of Sir Henry Channon*, ed. Robert Rhodes James (London: Weidenfeld & Nicolson, 1967), 22 November 1936
10. Reith diaries, 6 December 1936
11. Phillips, *The King Who Had to Go*, pp. 131f
12. Baldwin papers, Buchan to Baldwin 12 December 1936

CHAPTER THREE: MY MASTER IS LONELY JUST NOW
1. Quoted in Self, *Neville Chamberlain*, p. 128; the episode is described in detail at pp. 120–33
2. Neville Chamberlain papers, NC18/1/908 Chamberlain to Hilda 9 March 1935
3. Neville Chamberlain papers, NC18/1/989 Chamberlain to Hilda 13 December 1936
4. Neville Chamberlain papers, NC18/1/1024 Chamberlain to Ida 16 October 1937
5. Phillips, *The King Who Had to Go*, passim
6. Quoted in Self, *Neville Chamberlain*, p. 9
7. Neville Chamberlain papers, NC18/1/1023 Chamberlain to Hilda 9 October 1937
8. Phillips, *The King Who Had to Go*, pp. 240–43
9. Earl of Woolton, *The Memoirs of the Rt. Hon. the Earl of Woolton* (London: Cassell, 1959), p. 140
10. Neville Chamberlain papers, NC18/1/985 Chamberlain to Hilda 14 November 1936
11. Neville Chamberlain papers, NC18/1/1003 Chamberlain to Hilda 25 April 1937
12. NA CAB 127/157 Munich 1938; Martin Gilbert notes of first interview with Sir Horace Wilson (in author's possession)

13. Avon papers, Avon AP 7/24/81 J. P. L. Thomas memorandum
14. Streat diaries, 26 July 1935
15. W. J. Brown, *So Far* (London: Allen & Unwin, 1943), pp. 221f
16. Reith diaries, p. 220
17. Butler papers, RAB G10 Character study, F79/93 Butler to Brabourne 17 February 1939
18. Woolton memoirs, p. 140
19. Harold Nicolson, *Diaries and Letters 1930–39*, ed. Nigel Nicolson (London: Collins, 1967), 18 December 1939
20. Butler papers, RAB G10 Character study; Oliver Harvey, *The Diplomatic Diaries of Oliver Harvey 1937–1940*, ed. John Harvey (London: Collins, 1970), 29 January 1939
21. John Colville, *The Fringes of Power: Downing Street Diaries 1939–1955* (London: Hodder & Stoughton, 1985), 31 October 1939
22. John Colville, *Footprints in Time* (London: Victor Gollancz, 1976), p. 72
23. Cadogan, Sir Alexander, *The Diaries of Sir Alexander Cadogan OM 1938–1945*, ed. David Dilks (London: Cassell, 1971), p. 53
24. Kenneth Clark, *Another Part of the Wood: A Self-Portrait* (London: John Murray, 1974), p. 271
25. Templewood papers, XIX (B)5 Notes of conversation with Sir A. Rucker 24 October 1951, Cambridge University Library
26. Phillips, *The King Who Had to Go*, pp. 93f
27. Clark, *Another Part of the Wood*, p. 271
28. DGFP D II 382
29. Woolton memoirs, p. 140
30. Butler papers, RAB G10 Character study
31. Colville diaries, p. 19
32. Home, *The Way the Wind Blows*, p. 67
33. Woolton memoirs, p. 140
34. J. C. C. Davidson, *Memoirs of a Conservative: J. C. C. Davidson's Memoirs and Papers 1910–37*, ed. Robert Rhodes James (London: Weidenfeld & Nicolson, 1939), p. 272
35. Tom Bower, *Tiny Rowland: A Rebel Tycoon* (London: Heinemann, 1993), pp. 51–3, 58–65
36. Davidson, *Memoirs of a Conservative*, p. 272
37. Ian Colvin, *Vansittart in Office: An Historical Survey of the Origins of the Second World War Based on the Papers of Sir Robert Vansittart, Permanent Under-Secretary of State for Foreign Affairs, 1930–38* (London: Victor Gollancz, 1965), p. 191
38. Neville Chamberlain papers, NC18/1/949a Chamberlain to Ida 16 February 1936
39. Channon diaries, 27 April 1939
40. Neville Chamberlain papers, NC18/1/963 Chamberlain to Hilda 1 June 1936
41. Mander papers, B/4 Draft memoirs, Wightwick Manor; incorrectly dated 1938; Reith diaries, 6 May 1938
42. NA CAB 127/157 Munich 1938

## CHAPTER FOUR: TAKING PERSONAL CHARGE

1. Self, *Neville Chamberlain*, p. 266
2. DDI 8s VII 85 (author's translation)
3. Neville Chamberlain papers, NC18/1/1014 Chamberlain to Hilda 1 August 1937
4. Neville Chamberlain papers, NC18/1/1024 Chamberlain to Ida 16 October 1937
5. Patrick Cosgrave, *R. A. Butler: An English Life* (London: Quartet, 1981), p. 12
6. Martin Gilbert, 'Horace Wilson: Man of Munich?', *History Today*, October 1982
7. Neville Chamberlain papers, NC18/1/1031 Chamberlain to Ida 12 December 1937
8. Goebbels diaries, 4 January 1938
9. Phipps MSS, Phipps to Hankey 9 January 1938
10. Avon papers, AP 7/24/81
11. Neville Chamberlain papers, NC18/1/1020 Chamberlain to Hilda 12 September 1937 and NC18/1/1025 24 October 1937

12. Neville Chamberlain papers, NC18/1/1024 Chamberlain to Ida 16 October 1938
13. Neville Chamberlain papers, NC18/1/1031 Chamberlain to Ida 12 December 1937
14. Giorgio Peresso, 'Major Adrian Dingli, éminence grise of Anglo-Italian diplomacy in 1930', *Times of Malta*, 30 September 2012
15. DDI 8s VII 57, 85
16. NA PREM 1/276 Vansittart to Eden 26 July 1937, Eden to Chamberlain same date
17. NA PREM 1/276 Wilson to Chamberlain 26 July 1937
18. DDI 8s VII 127, NA PREM 1/276 Chamberlain memorandum 27 July 1937
19. Avon papers, AP 7/24/81
20. Neville Chamberlain papers, NC18/1/1014 Chamberlain to Hilda 1 August 1937
21. Neville Chamberlain papers, NC18/1/1015 Chamberlain to Ida 8 August 1937
22. NA PREM 1/276 Chamberlain to Halifax 7 August 1937
23. NA PREM 1/276 Vansittart to Chamberlain
24. Neville Chamberlain papers, NC18/1/1021 Chamberlain to Ida 19 September 1937
25. DDI 8s VII 438
26. F. H. Hinsley et al., *British Intelligence in the Second World War: Its Influence on Strategy and Operations, Vol. 1* (London: HMSO, 1979), pp. 53f
27. DDI 8s VII 571, 577
28. Harvey diaries, 19 January 1938
29. Templewood papers, XIX Cadogan to Hoare 26 October 1951

CHAPTER FIVE: WOOLLY RUBBISH
1. Neville Chamberlain papers, NC18/1/1038 Chamberlain to Hilda 6 February 1938
2. Avon papers, AP 7/24/81 J. P. L. Thomas memorandum
3. Grigg papers, Wilson to Grigg 31 January 1938
4. Templewood papers, XIX Cadogan to Hoare 26 October 1951
5. Cadogan diaries, 15 January 1938
6. Anthony Eden, *The Eden Memoirs: Facing the Dictators* (London: Cassell, 1960), p. 554
7. Eden memoirs, p. 556
8. Templewood papers, XIX Unsigned undated document from Foreign Office Library
9. Neville Chamberlain papers, NC18/1/1034 Chamberlain to Hilda 9 January 1938
10. DDI 8s VIII 29
11. DDI 8s VIII 60 n3
12. DDI 8s VIII 192
13. DDI 8s VIII 192 n1
14. Eden memoirs, p. 592
15. Eden memoirs, p. 592
16. Avon papers, AP 7/24/81
17. Neville Chamberlain papers, NC18/1/1039 Chamberlain to Ida 13 February 1938
18. Earl of Swinton, with James D. Margach, *Sixty Years of Power: Some Memories of the Men Who Wielded It* (London: Hutchinson, 1966), p. 115
19. Neville Chamberlain papers, NC11/1/616 Wilson to Anne Chamberlain 5 April 1944
20. Nicolson diaries, 6 January 1940, p. 56
21. Lord Moran, *Winston Churchill: The Struggle for Survival 1940–1965* (London: Constable, 1966), p. 323
22. Channon diaries, 3 June 1940
23. Channon diaries, 13 April 1939
24. Butler papers, RAB G10 Character sketch
25. Earl of Birkenhead, *Halifax: The Life of Lord Halifax* (London: Hamish Hamilton, 1965), p. 425
26. Templewood papers, XIX Cadogan to Hoare 26 October 1951
27. Lord Strang, *Britain in World Affairs: A Survey of the Fluctuations in Power and Influence, Henry VIII to Elizabeth II* (London: Faber & Faber / André Deutsch, 1961), p. 321fn

28. Earl of Halifax, *Fulness of Days* (London: Collins, 1957), p. 231
29. Templewood papers, XIX Conversation with Lord Halifax 8 July 1952
30. Templewood papers, XIX Conversation with Lord Halifax 5 December 1951
31. Templewood papers, XIX Between the Wars, Edward Halifax 15 June 1948

CHAPTER SIX: GETTING ON TERMS WITH THE GERMANS
1. Richard Griffiths, *Fellow Travellers of the Right: British Enthusiasts for Nazi Germany 1933–39* (London: Constable, 1980), pp. 146–8
2. A. L. Kennedy, *The Times and Appeasement: The Journals of A. L. Kennedy 1932–1939*, ed. Gordon Martel (Cambridge: Cambridge University Press, 2000), 7 November 1937
3. Kennedy journals, 20 October 1937
4. NA PREM 1/330 Henderson to Wilson 10 November 1939
5. Halifax, *Fulness of Days*, p. 185
6. Kirkpatrick, *The Inner Circle*, pp. 93–9; Schmidt, *Statist auf Diplomatischer Bühne*, pp. 377–9
7. Henrik Eberle and Matthias Uhl, *The Hitler Book: The Secret Dossier Prepared for Stalin* (London: John Murray, 2005), p. 25
8. Eberle and Uhl, *The Hitler Book*, p. 25
9. Goebbels diaries, 12 May 1937
10. Schmidt, *Statist auf Diplomatischer Bühne*, p. 379
11. NA PREM 1/330 Halifax diaries of visit to Germany
12. Cadogan diaries, 26 January 1938
13. Templewood papers, XIX Cadogan to Hoare 26 October 1951
14. Templewood papers, XIX Notes on conversation with Sir Alexander Cadogan 4 July 1951
15. Cadogan diaries, 8 March 1938
16. NA PREM 1/330 Wilson to Cadogan 14 January 1938
17. NA PREM 1/330 Wilson to Chamberlain 23 January 1938

CHAPTER SEVEN: A NEW CHAPTER IN THE
HISTORY OF AFRICAN COLONIAL DEVELOPMENT
1. NA PREM 1/330 Halifax diaries of visit to Germany
2. Neville Chamberlain papers, NC18/1/1030a Chamberlain to Hilda 5 December 1937
3. Neville Chamberlain papers, NC18/1/1036 Chamberlain to Ida 23 January 1938
4. NA CAB 27/623 Minutes of meeting 24 January 1938
5. NA CAB 27/623 Minutes of meeting 24 January 1938
6. NA PREM 1/247 Unsigned and undated memorandum 'The search for a solution of the colonial problem in Tropical Africa'
7. NA PREM 1/247 Unsigned and undated memorandum 'The search for a solution of the colonial problem in Tropical Africa'
8. Cadogan diaries, 24 January 1938
9. Harvey diaries, 5 March 1938
10. Leo Amery, *The Empire at Bay: The Leo Amery Diaries 1929–1945*, ed. John Barnes and David Nicolson (London: Hutchinson, 1988), p. 461
11. NA PREM 1/247 Eden to Henderson 12 February 1938
12. NA PREM 1/247 Halifax to Henderson 3 March 1938
13. DGFP D I 112; Goebbels diaries, 21 February 1938
14. DGFP D I 228
15. NA PREM 1/247 Henderson to Halifax 5 March 1938
16. Sir Nevile Henderson, *Failure of a Mission: Berlin 1937–1939* (London: Hodder & Stoughton, 1940), p. 115
17. Schmidt, *Statist auf Diplomatischer Bühne*, p. 391
18. NA PREM 1/247 Henderson to Halifax 5 March 1938
19. Goebbels diaries, 7 March 1938
20. DDI 8s VIII 329

21. Channon diaries, 3 January 1940
22. NA CAB 127/157 Munich 1938

## CHAPTER EIGHT: ALL THAT IS WELL SEWN UP

1. Anthony Adamthwaite, 'The British Government and the Media', *Journal of Contemporary History*, vol. 18, no. 2 (1983), pp. 281–97
2. 'Steward, George Frederick (8 February 1884–6 July 1952)', *Who's Who and Who Was Who* (Oxford: Oxford University Press, 2007)
3. James Margach, *The Abuse of Power: The War between Downing Street and the Media from Lloyd George to Callaghan* (London: W. H. Allen, 1978), p. 50
4. Neville Chamberlain papers, NC18/1/1014 Chamberlain to Hilda 1 August 1937
5. NA PREM 1/330 Notes of conversation between Hitler and Halifax
6. DGFP D II doc 138
7. Alfred Stirling, *Lord Bruce: The London Years* (Melbourne: Hawthorn Press, 1974), p. 92; David Low, *Low's Autobiography* (London: Michael Joseph, 1956), p. 279
8. DGFP D II doc 148
9. Dawson papers, diaries, 14 September 1938
10. Martin Gilbert, *Prophet of Truth: Winston S. Churchill 1922–1939* (London: Minerva, 1990), p. 928
11. Richard Cockett, *Twilight of Truth: Chamberlain, appeasement and the manipulation of the press* (London: Weidenfeld & Nicolson, 1989), Chapter 1
12. Hesse, *Das Spiel um Deutschland*, p. 36
13. DDI 8s VII 85
14. Anthony Adamthwaite, 'The British Government and the Media', p. 282
15. Reith diaries, 1 July 1937
16. Reith diaries, 11 May 1938
17. Churchill papers, 2/312, Churchill to Lord Davies, 13 January 1937
18. Cockett, *Twilight of Truth*, p. 193
19. Anthony Adamthwaite, 'The British Government and the Media', p. 287
20. Harvey diaries, 5 March 1938
21. Reith diaries, 10 March 1938
22. Thomas Jones papers, W/20/140 Wilson to Jones 10 June 1938
23. Asa Briggs, *The History of Broadcasting in the United Kingdom, Vol. 2: The Golden Age of Wireless* (London and Oxford: Oxford University Press, 1961–95), p. 637

## CHAPTER NINE: THE CENTRAL WEAKNESS

1. Hansard, 10 November 1932
2. Hansard, 23 November 1932
3. Hansard, 8 March 1934
4. Hansard, 23 November 1934
5. Wesley K. Wark, *The Ultimate Enemy: British Intelligence and Nazi Germany 1933–1939* (London: I. B. Tauris, 1985), pp. 37–41
6. Swinton, *Sixty Years of Power*, p. 118
7. Streat diaries, 26 July 1935
8. Quoted in Montgomery H. Hyde, *British Air Policy between the Wars 1918–1939* (London: Heinemann, 1976), p. 409
9. Wark, *The Ultimate Enemy*, pp. 59ff
10. Martin Gilbert (ed.), *The Churchill Documents, Vol. 13: The Coming of War 1936–1939* (Hillsdale, MI: Hillsdale College), Churchill to Hankey 16 October 1937
11. Maclean memorandum, Churchill papers, 2/304
12. Bruce-Gardner memorandum, c. 1954, Chamberlain papers
13. Wilson to Andrew Boyle, quoted in Andrew Boyle, *Montagu Norman: A Biography* (London: Cassell, 1967), p. 250, and NA PREM 1/224 Wilson to Chamberlain 25 June 1939

14. Boyle, *Montagu Norman*, p. 250
15. Chamberlain papers, NC11/12/1 Bruce-Gardner undated memorandum; NA PREM 1/236 Bruce-Gardner Statement on Aircraft Production 20 April 1938
16. NA PREM 1/236 Wilson to Chamberlain undated but c. 22 April 1938
17. Mosley, *On Borrowed Time*, p. 221fn; Mosley confuses Bruce-Gardner with Lord Crewe, who was not involved in air rearmament
18. Templewood papers, XIX Wilson to Hoare 18 September 1946; Chamberlain papers, NC11/1/92 Wilson to Anne Chamberlain 8 November 1952
19. NA PREM 1/238 Cleverley to Chamberlain 11 January 1938
20. NA PREM 1/238 Syers memorandum 29 January 1938
21. NA PREM 1/238 Wilson minute 11 February 1938
22. NA PREM 1/238 Wilson minute 10 March 1938
23. NA PREM 1/238 Wilson minute 10 March 1938
24. NA PREM 1/251 Hankey to Wilson 12 March 1938
25. NA PREM 1/217 Speed to Chegwidden 1 May 1936 and NA PREM 1/218 Wilson minutes of 9 and 18 February 1937
26. NA PREM 1/251 Wilson to Chamberlain 21 March 1938
27. NA PREM 1/251 Wilson to Chamberlain notes for meeting with TUC General Council 23 March 1938
28. NA PREM 1/252 Wilson to Chamberlain 25 March 1938
29. NA PREM 1/251 Wilson to Swinton 29 March 1938
30. NA PREM 1/251 Weir to Wilson 30 March 1938, Wilson to Weir 31 March 1938
31. NA PREM 1/251 Joseph Ball memorandum undated but probably 30 May 1938
32. NA PREM 1/251 Wilson memorandum 27 June 1938
33. NA PREM 1/238 Churchill memorandum on aircraft types 12 March 1938
34. NA PREM 1/237 Churchill to Chamberlain 18 April 1938
35. NA PREM 1/237 Chamberlain to Churchill 26 April 1938
36. NA PREM 1/236 Fisher to Chamberlain 5 April 1938

CHAPTER TEN: EVERY EFFORT TO BRING ABOUT APPEASEMENT

1. Anthony Howard, *Rab: The Life of R. A. Butler* (London: Jonathan Cape, 1987), p. 68
2. Private information
3. Lord Butler, *The Art of the Possible: The Memoirs of Lord Butler* (London: Hamish Hamilton, 1971), p. 76
4. Paul Stafford, 'Political Autobiography and the Art of the Plausible: R. A. Butler at the Foreign Office 1938–1939', *Historical Journal*, vol. 28, no. 4 (1985), pp. 901–22
5. DGFP D I 128
6. DGFP D I 148
7. Hansard, 14 March 1938
8. *The Times*, 15 March 1938
9. Templewood papers, XIX Talk with Halifax 10 June 1952
10. NA FO800/311 Phipps to Halifax
11. Neville Chamberlain papers, NC18/1/1042 Chamberlain to Ida 20 March 1938
12. Cadogan diaries, 14 March 1938
13. Neville Chamberlain papers, NC18/1/1043 Chamberlain to Hilda 27 March 1938
14. Neville Chamberlain papers, NC18/1/1043 Chamberlain to Hilda 27 March 1938
15. Hansard, 24 March 1938
16. DGFP D II 104
17. Ivan Maisky, *The Maisky Diaries: Red Ambassador to the Court of St James 1932–1943*, ed. Gabriel Gorodetsky (New Haven, CT: Yale University Press, 2015), 10 May 1938
18. Maisky diaries, 31 August 1938
19. R. A. C. Parker, *Churchill and Appeasement* (London: Macmillan, 2000), p. 160

20. DGFP D II 247; Hesse, *Das Spiel um Deutschland*, p. 122
21. Conversation between Dr Eva Hesse and author
22. Hesse, *Das Spiel um Deutschland*, p. 126
23. Hesse, *Das Spiel um Deutschland*, p. 129
24. NA PREM 1/330 Wilson to Chamberlain 12 July 1938
25. NA PREM 1/330 Wilson to Chamberlain 12 July 1938
26. DGFP D II 279
27. NA PREM 1/330 Wilson to Chamberlain 12 July 1938
28. DGFP D I 794
29. NA PREM 1/330 Wilson memorandum 22 July 1938
30. DDI 8s VIII 380
31. DDI 8s IX 116 n1
32. Cadogan diaries, 23 June 1938
33. Neville Chamberlain papers, NC18/1/1057 Chamberlain to Hilda 25 June 1938
34. Hansard, 23 June 1938
35. Duff Hart-Davis *Man of War: The Secret Life of Captain Alan Hillgarth – Officer, Adventurer, Agent* (London: Century, 2012), Chapter 8
36. Neville Chamberlain papers, NC18/1/1057 Chamberlain to Hilda 25 June 1938
37. DDI 8s IX 259
38. DDI 8s IX 264
39. NA FO 371/22689 Perth telegram 3 July 1939
40. Neville Chamberlain papers, NC18/1/1060 Chamberlain to Ida 16 July 1938
41. NA PREM 1/283 Hoare to Chamberlain 26 July 1938

CHAPTER ELEVEN: A NICE FRAUDULENT BALANCE SHEET
1. NA PREM 1/236 Wilson to Bruce-Gardner 18 March 1938
2. NA PREM 1236 Bruce-Gardner to Wilson 17 March 1938
3. NA PREM 1/236 Wilson to Bruce-Gardner 18 March 1938
4. NA PREM 1/236 Bruce-Gardner to Swinton 14 April 1938
5. 'MP criticises Air Ministry's policy', *Daily Telegraph*, 22 April 1938
6. NA AVIA 46/93 Minutes of Special Progress Meeting 25 April 1938
7. Wilson to Chamberlain undated but c. 24 April
8. NA PREM 1/236 Wilson to Chamberlain undated (but after 14 April 1938)
9. NA CAB 23/93/8
10. Swinton, *Sixty Years of Power*, p. 119
11. Amery diaries, 17 May 1938
12. Hyde, *British Air Policy Between the Wars*, pp. 370–75
13. Leo McKinistry, *Spitfire: Portrait of a Legend* (London: John Murray, 2007), p. 90f
14. Quoted in Sebastian Ritchie, *Industry and Air Power: The Expansion of British Aircraft Production 1935–41* (London: Frank Cass, 1997), p. 51
15. NA PREM 1/253 Churchill to Wood 9 June 1938
16. Churchill papers, 2/304 Hankey to Churchill 19 October 1937
17. NA PREM 1/253 Hankey to Chamberlain 24 June 1938
18. NA PREM 1/253 Chamberlain annotation dated 26 June on Hankey to Chamberlain 24 June 1938
19. Churchill papers, 25/14 Churchill to Wood 28 July 1938

CHAPTER TWELVE: A WISE BRITISH SUBJECT
1. NA CAB 23/94 Meeting of 22 June 1938
2. Harvey diaries, 6 September 1938
3. Templewood papers, XIX Talk with Lord Home 12 March 1952
4. NA PREM 1/265 Wilson to Halifax 22 June 1938
5. Cadogan diaries, 16 July 1938

6. NA PREM 1/265 Wilson to Halifax 22 June 1938
7. 'Mediation in Prague', *The Times*, 30 July 1938
8. Cadogan diaries, 26 and 27 July 1938
9. Sir Robert Bruce Lockhart, *The Diaries of Sir Robert Bruce Lockhart, Vol. I: 1915–1938*, ed. Kenneth Young (London: Macmillan, 1973), 17 October 1938
10. Bruce Lockhart diaries, 17 October 1938
11. Mosley, *On Borrowed Time*, p. 24
12. Mosley, *On Borrowed Time*, p. 23
13. Gilbert, 'Horace Wilson: Man of Munich?'
14. *The Times*, 3 September 1938
15. DGFP D II 382
16. NA PREM 1/265 Wilson to Chamberlain 25 August 1938
17. NA FO 800/304 Ashton-Gwatkin diaries 25 August 1938
18. Neville Chamberlain papers, NC18/1/1065 Chamberlain to Hilda 27 August 1938
19. Colvin, *Vansittart in Office*, p. 232
20. Maisky diaries, 31 August 1938
21. NA PREM 1/265 fol 116 Wilson to Chamberlain (1) 31 August 1938
22. NA PREM 1/265 fols 117–19 Wilson to Chamberlain (2) 31 August 1938
23. NA PREM 1/265 fols 89–93 Wilson to Chamberlain (1) fols 1 September 1938
24. NA PREM 1/265 Wilson to Chamberlain 1 September 1938
25. NA PREM 1/265 fols 85–88 Wilson to Chamberlain (2) fols 1 September 1938
26. NA PREM 1/265 fols 89–93 Wilson to Chamberlain (1) fols 1 September 1938
27. NA PREM 1/265 Message from Wilson to Chamberlain 1 September 1938
28. NA PREM 1/265 Wilson to Chamberlain 5 September 1938
29. NA PREM 1/265 Halifax to Chamberlain 5 September 1938
30. Colvin, *Vansittart in Office*, p. 235

CHAPTER THIRTEEN: THE BEST THE ENGLISH CAN DO

1. Cadogan diaries, 8 September 1938
2. NA T273/404 Wilson to Strang 11 September 1938
3. Self, *Neville Chamberlain*, p. 310
4. NA CAB 27/646
5. Colville diaries, 29 August 1942
6. Mosley, *On Borrowed Time*, p. 46
7. Goebbels diaries, 20 September 1938
8. NA CAB 27/646
9. NA CAB 27/646
10. NA CAB 23/95/6, p. 179
11. DGFP D II 579
12. Cadogan diaries, 24 September 1938
13. NA CAB 27/646
14. Harvey diaries, 24 September 1938
15. Harvey diaries, 25 September 1938
16. Strang, *Home and Abroad*, pp. 141f
17. NA CAB 23/95/6
18. Strang, *Home and Abroad*, pp. 142f
19. DGFP D II 610
20. NA CAB 127/157 Chamberlain to Hitler 26 September 1938
21. Goebbels diaries, 26 September 1938
22. Cadogan diaries, p. 106
23. Birkenhead, *Halifax*, pp. 424f
24. Schmidt, *Statist auf Diplomatischer Bühne*, p. 407

25. NA CAB 127/157 Munich 1938
26. Hesse, *Das Spiel um Deutschland*, pp. 213, 185
27. Kirkpatrick, *The Inner Circle*, p. 123
28. NA CAB 127/157 Munich 1938
29. Goebbels diaries, 27 September 1938
30. NA T273/406 Wilson telegram 27 September received 1.20 p.m.
31. Goebbels diaries, 27 September 1938
32. DGFP D II 618
33. NA CAB 127/157 Munich 1938
34. Goebbels diaries, 27 September 1938
35. Goebbels diaries, 2 October 1938
36. NA CAB 127/157 Munich 1938
37. DGFP D II 634
38. USSR Docs Vol I Lipski for Beck 27 September 1938
39. Goebbels diaries, 28 September 1938
40. DGFP D II 634
41. Goebbels diaries, 28 September 1938 (author's translation)
42. DGFP D II 634

CHAPTER FOURTEEN: THEIR JUST DEMANDS HAD BEEN FAIRLY MET
1. Reinhard Spitzy, *How We Squandered the Reich* (Wilby, Norfolk: Michael Russell, 1997), p. 246; DGFP D II 635
2. NA CAB 27/646
3. 'To the nation and Empire', *The Times*, 28 September 1938
4. NA CAB 23/95/10
5. DGFP D II 635
6. Hesse, *Das Spiel um Deutschland*, pp. 140ff
7. Hesse, *Das Spiel um Deutschland*, pp. 142–5
8. DGFP D II 657
9. Goebbels diaries, 29 September 1938
10. NA T273/407 Masaryk memorandum
11. DBFP 3/II
12. NA PREM 1/265 Chamberlain to Wilson 2 September 1938
13. NA CAB 127/157 Munich 1938
14. D. R. Thorpe, *Alec Douglas-Home* (London: Sinclair-Stevenson, 1996), p. 83; Colvin, *Vansittart in Office*, p. 276
15. Colville diaries, 15 February 1940
16. NA CAB 24/279; Strang, *Home and Abroad*, p. 148
17. NA T273/407 Wilson memorandum (almost certainly for Chamberlain) undated but after 5 October 1938
18. Colvin, *Vansittart in Office*, p. 276

CHAPTER FIFTEEN: CLEARLY MARKED OUT FOR THE POST
1. Stephen Roskill, *Hankey: Man of Secrets, Vol. 3: 1931–63* (London: Collins, 1974), pp. 279, 334
2. Churchill papers, 2/304 Hankey to Churchill 19 October 1937
3. Roskill, *Hankey: Man of Secrets*, p. 356
4. NA PREM T273/405 Fisher to Wilson 17 September 1938
5. NA T273/148 Fisher to Grigg 18 November 1938
6. Boyle, *Montagu Norman*, p. 316

CHAPTER SIXTEEN: THE APPALLING SUMS IT IS PROPOSED TO SPEND
1. NA PREM 1/236 Wood memorandum undated but November 1938
2. NA PREM 1/236 Wood to Chamberlain 9 December 1938

3. NA PREM 1/236 Wilson to Chamberlain 13 December 1938
4. NA PREM 1/236 Wilson memorandum 14 December 1938
5. Thomas Jones, *A Diary with Letters, 1931–1950* (London: Oxford University Press, 1954), pp. 421f
6. NA AVIA 46/93 Bruce-Gardner to Wilson 2 and 8 October and 4 November 1938
7. NA AVIA 46/93 Bruce-Gardner to Freeman 9 January 1939
8. NA AVIA 46/93 Bruce-Gardner to Wilson 3 April 1939
9. Mosley, *On Borrowed Time*, p. 221fn; Mosley confuses Bruce-Gardner with Lord Crewe, who was not involved in air rearmament
10. Norman papers, diaries, 30 August 1939
11. Swinton, *Sixty Years of Power*, p. 119
12. Wark, *The Ultimate Enemy*, p. 111
13. Wark, *The Ultimate Enemy*, p. 111
14. Admiral Karl Doenitz, *Memoirs: Ten Years and Twenty Days* (London: Cassell, 1990), p. 31 (author's calculation)
15. McKinistry, *Spitfire*, p. 151

CHAPTER SEVENTEEN: WELL ANCHORED
1. NA PREM 1/272 Wilson to Chamberlain 18 January 1938
2. NA PREM 1/272 Wilson to Chamberlain 18 January 1938
3. NA PREM 1/388 Bridges to Wilson 2 September 1938, Syers to Chamberlain 8 September 1938
4. NA PREM 1/388 Bridges to Wilson 2 September 1938
5. Neville Chamberlain papers, NC 7/11/31 Wilson to Chamberlain 18 October 1938
6. NA PREM 1/374 Stuart memorandum 16 March 1939
7. NA CAB 16/127 Tallents memoranda 7 November 1938
8. NA PREM 1/388 Wilson to Fisher 20 October 1939
9. NA CAB 16/127 Tallents memoranda 7 November 1938 and Willcox 'Projection or Publicity'
10. NA PREM 1/388 Wilson to Bridges 7 November 1938
11. NA CAB 104/88 Memorandum by Wilson 2 December 1938
12. NA CAB 104/88 Minute by Ryan undated but 2–6 December 1938
13. Tallents papers, memorandum undated but after 1940
14. Tallents papers, manuscript note undated but after 20 December 1938
15. Tallents papers, undated memorandum Ministry of Information
16. Sir Campbell Stuart, *Opportunity Knocks Once* (London: Collins, 1952), p. 185
17. Neville Chamberlain papers, NCL add. 14 Memorandum by G. W. of Special Broadcasting Arrangements

CHAPTER EIGHTEEN: ABANDONMENT AND RUIN
1. Stewart, *Burying Caesar*, pp. 320–23
2. Churchill press statement in Gilbert, *The Churchill Documents*, p. 1171
3. Nicolson diaries, 22 September 1938
4. Churchill to Orme Sargent 23 July 1947 in Gilbert, *The Churchill Documents*, p. 1181; Shiela Grant Duff in Gilbert, *The Churchill Documents*, p. 1183
5. Gilbert, *The Churchill Documents*, p. 1189; Colin R. Coote, *Editorial: The Memoirs of Colin R. Coote* (London: Eyre & Spottiswoode, 1965), pp. 173f
6. Parker, *Churchill and Appeasement*, p. 185
7. Hansard, 6 October 1938
8. Neville Chamberlain papers, NC18/1/1071 Chamberlain to Ida 9 October 1938
9. Norman Rose, *Harold Nicolson* (London: Jonathan Cape, 2005), p. 219
10. Hugh Dalton, *The Political Diaries of Hugh Dalton, 1918–39, 1945–60*, ed. Ben Pimlott (London: Jonathan Cape, 1986), 8 January 1941, p. 140; Halifax, *Fulness of Days*, p. 231
11. Neville Chamberlain papers, NC18/1/1072 Chamberlain to Hilda 15 October 1938
12. Hoare to Chamberlain 6 October 1938 in Gilbert, *The Churchill Documents*, p. 1202

13. Neville Chamberlain papers, NC18/1/1074 Chamberlain to Ida 24 October 1938
14. Churchill papers, 9/132 Winston S. Churchill broadcast to the United States
15. Neville Chamberlain papers, NC18/1/1075 Chamberlain to Hilda 6 November 1938
16. Parker, *Churchill and Appeasement*, p. 193f
17. Colin Thornton-Kemsley, *Through Wind and Tides* (Montrose: Standard Press, 1974), p. 92
18. Churchill papers, 7/56 Churchill to Hacking 18 March 1939 Gilbert p. 1035
19. Churchill papers, 2/333 Churchill to Duchess of Atholl 12 December 1938
20. Spencer Churchill papers, Churchill to Clemmie 29 December 1938; James Stuart, *Within the Fringe: An Autobiography* (London: Bodley Head, 1967), p. 95

## CHAPTER NINETEEN: RIDING THE TIGER

1. Neville Chamberlain papers, NC18/1/1071 Chamberlain to Ida 9 October 1938
2. Keith Jeffery, *MI6: The History of the Secret Intelligence Service, 1909–1949* (London: Bloomsbury, 2010), p. 317
3. Phillips, *The King Who Had to Go*, pp. 236f
4. Sir Percy Harris, *Forty Years in and out of Parliament* (London: Andrew Melrose, 1947), p. 149
5. Ronald Tree, *When the Moon Was High: Memoirs of Peace and War 1897–1942* (London: Macmillan, 1975), p. 76
6. Neville Chamberlain papers, NC18/1/1070 Chamberlain to Hilda 2 October 1938
7. DGFP D IV 251
8. Templewood papers, XIX Conversation with Halifax 5 December 1951
9. *The Times*, 10 October 1938
10. Mosley, *On Borrowed Time*, pp. 94f
11. Templewood papers, XIX Conversation with Halifax 5 December 1951
12. John Curry, *The Security Service 1908–1945: The Official History* (Kew: Public Record Office, 1999), pp. 121f
13. Christopher Andrew, *Defence of the Realm: The Authorized History of MI5* (London: Allen Lane, 2009), p. 205
14. Curry, *The Security Service*, pp. 121f
15. Templewood papers, XIX Conversation with Halifax 5 December 1951, Conversation with Sir Alexander Cadogan 14 November 1951
16. Bruce Lockhart diaries, 18 October 1938, p. 403
17. Neville Chamberlain papers, NC18/1/1075 Chamberlain to Hilda 6 November 1938
18. Neville Chamberlain papers, NC18/1/1077 Chamberlain to Hilda 27 November 1939
19. Cadogan diaries, 15 November 1938; NA CAB 27/624
20. NA CAB 27/624; C. A. MacDonald, 'Economic Appeasement and the German "Moderates" 1937–1939: An Introductory Essay', *Past & Present*, August 1972, pp. 105–13
21. NACAB 27/624 Meeting of 21 November 1938
22. Hesse, *Das Spiel um Deutschland*, p. 154
23. NA FO 1093/107 Hesse to Ribbentrop 25 November 1938
24. NA FO 1093/107; Hesse, *Das Spiel um Deutschland*, p. 156
25. NA FO 1093/107 Cadogan memorandum 29 November 1938
26. NA FO 1093/107 Cadogan memorandum pencil addendum 29 November 1938
27. Cadogan diaries, p. 127

## CHAPTER TWENTY: THE RIGHT LINE ABOUT THINGS

1. Quoted in T. P. Conwell-Evans, *None So Blind: A Study of the Crisis Years 1930–1939* (London: Harrison, 1947), pp. 172f
2. *The Times*, 7 November 1938
3. *The Times*, 9 November 1938
4. Reichs Propaganda Ministry circular of 28 October 1938 quoted in Conwell-Evans, *None So Blind*, pp. 172f
5. DGFP D IV 258 and 264

6. Neville Chamberlain papers, NC18/1/1076 Chamberlain to Ida 13 November 1938
7. NA PREM 1/247 Wilson to Chamberlain 6 December 1938
8. Colin Cross, *Adolf Hitler: 1936–1945* (Hodder & Stoughton, 1973), p. 322fn
9. Neville Chamberlain papers, NC18/1/1110 Chamberlain to Hilda 30 July 1939
10. Neville Chamberlain papers, NC18/1/1101 Chamberlain to Hilda 28 May 1939
11. Goebbels diaries, February 1938
12. Reuters archive, Wilson to Jones 17 July 1938
13. Reuters archive, Jones to von Ribbentrop 9 June 1938
14. Reuters archive, Young to Jones 19 September 1938
15. Goebbels diaries, 13 November 1938
16. Goebbels diaries, 15 November 1938

CHAPTER TWENTY-ONE: ADVICE FROM THE DEVIL
1. Neville Chamberlain papers, NC18/1/1074 Chamberlain to Ida 24 October 1938
2. Lord Ismay, *The Memoirs of General the Lord Ismay* (London: Heinemann, 1960), pp. 83f
3. Neville Chamberlain papers, NC18/1/1074 Chamberlain to Ida 24 October 1938
4. Hansard, 28 May 1938
5. Hansard, 17 November 1938
6. Nicolson diaries, 24 November 1938
7. NA CAB 4/29 Memorandum by the Minister for the Coordination of Defence 1505B 18 January 1939
8. Bruce Lockhart diaries, 17 October 1938; Jones, *A Diary with Letters*, p. 428
9. Inskip papers, INK P2 Sir Thomas Inskip diaries, 17 January 1939
10. NA CAB 24/283/6 Inskip memorandum to Cabinet 28 January 1939
11. NA CAB 4/29 Minutes of CID meeting of 26 January 1939
12. Roskill, *Hankey: Man of Secrets*, p. 395

CHAPTER TWENTY-TWO: THE MOUNTEBANK
1. NA PREM 1/265 Wilson to Chamberlain 2 September 1938
2. Boyle, *Montagu Norman*, p. 250
3. David Kynaston, *Till Time's Last Sand: A History of the Bank of England 1694–2013* (London: Bloomsbury, 2017), pp. 366–71, 383
4. Norman papers, diaries, 25 and 28 November 1938
5. NA CAB 23/96/9
6. 'Dr Schacht in London', *The Times*, 15 December 1938
7. Harvey diaries, 4 December 1938
8. Norman papers, diaries, 14–16 December 1938
9. Cadogan diaries, 15 December 1938
10. NA PREM 1/315 Extract from note of a conversation between PM and Dr Schacht on 15 December 1938
11. NA T188/227 Ashton Gwatkin memorandum 15 December 1938
12. Harvey diaries, 2 January 1939
13. Cadogan diaries, 3 January 1939
14. Norman papers, diaries, 4 January 1939
15. Cadogan diaries, 4 January 1939
16. Norman papers, diaries, 12 January 1939
17. Neville Chamberlain papers, NC18/1/1083 Chamberlain to Ida 28 January 1939
18. Cadogan diaries, 30 January 1939
19. Neville Chamberlain papers, NC18/1/1084 Chamberlain to Hilda 5 February 1939
20. Neville Chamberlain papers, NC18/1/1085 Chamberlain to Ida 12 February 1939
21. Norman papers, diaries, 18 January 1939
22. DGFP D IV 317
23. NA T273/408 Ashton Gwatkin report 5 March 1939

CHAPTER TWENTY-THREE: COMBATING HOARE'S HERESIES

1. NA PREM 1/368 Hoare to Chamberlain 27 February 1938
2. J. C. W. Reith, *Into the Wind* (London: Hodder & Stoughton, 1949), p. 341–2
3. NA CAB 104/88 Ryan to Davies 9 June 1939
4. NA PREM 1/368 Wilson to Chamberlain 2 March 1939
5. NA HO 45/23627 Alexander memorandum 7 March 1939
6. NA CAB 16/209 Minute of meeting 6 April 1939
7. NA CAB 104/90 Minutes of meetings 12 and 18 April 1939
8. NA PREM 1/388 Fisher to Hoare 12 April 1939
9. NA PREM 1/388 Wilson to Hoare 12 April 1939
10. NA PREM 1/388 Fisher to Hoare 12 April 1939
11. NA PREM 1/388 Waterfield to Fisher 20 April 1938
12. PRO, CAB 104/88, Rae to Fass, 19 April 1939; *The World's Press News*, 20 April 1939
13. NA PREM 1/374 Wilson to Chamberlain 9 May 1939
14. NA PREM 1/374 Wilson to Vansittart 10 May 1939
15. NA PREM 1/388 Wilson to Simon c. 3–6 September 1939
16. NA PREM 1/388 Wilson to Macmillan 7 September 1939

CHAPTER TWENTY-FOUR: THE END OF THE RAINBOW

1. Neville Chamberlain papers, NC18/1/1085 Chamberlain to Ida 12 February 1939
2. Hansard, 21 February 1939
3. Phipps MSS, PHPP 3/5 Wilson to Phipps 2 February 1939, Churchill Archive Centre, Cambridge
4. *The Times*, 10 March 1939
5. Cadogan diaries, 10 March 1939
6. Halifax to Chamberlain 10 March 1939, quoted in Keith Feiling, *The Life of Neville Chamberlain* (London: Macmillan, 1946), pp. 396ff
7. Halifax, *Fulness of Days*, p. 332
8. Neville Chamberlain papers, NC18/1/1089 Chamberlain to Ida 12 March 1939
9. Neville Chamberlain papers, NC18/1/1089 Chamberlain to Ida 12 March 1939
10. Templewood papers, XIX Cadogan to Hoare 10 January 1953; Gladwyn, Lord (Jebb), *The Memoirs of Lord Gladwyn* (London: Weidenfeld & Nicolson, 1972), pp. 86f
11. NA T273/408 Ashton Gwatkin report 5 March 1939
12. Cadogan diaries, p. 155
13. Cadogan diaries, 11 March 1939
14. Templewood papers, XIX Interview with Ball, 28 December 1951
15. NA PREM 1/332 Wilson amendment to draft article by Arthur Bryant
16. NA CAB 23/98/1
17. Mosley, *On Borrowed Time*, p. 177
18. Cadogan diaries, 15 March 1939
19. Neville Chamberlain papers, NC18/1/1090 Chamberlain to Hilda 19 March 1939
20. Neville Chamberlain papers, NC18/1/1090 Chamberlain to Hilda 19 March 1939
21. Neville Chamberlain papers, NC18/1/1090 Chamberlain to Hilda 19 March 1939
22. Harvey diaries, 21 March 1939
23. Mosley, *On Borrowed Time*, p. 208
24. Strang, G. Bruce, 'Once More unto the Breach: Britain's Guarantee to Poland, March 1939', *Journal of Contemporary History*, vol. 31, no. 4 (1996), pp. 721–52
25. Martin Gilbert, notes of second interview with Sir Horace Wilson (in author's possession)
26. 'A stand for ordered diplomacy', *The Times*, 1 April 1939; Iverach McDonald, *A Man of The Times: Talks and Travels in a Disrupted World* (London: Hamish Hamilton, 1976), p. 60
27. Kennedy journals, 4 April 1939
28. Neville Chamberlain papers, NC18/1/1092 Chamberlain to Hilda undated but probably 1–2 April 1939
29. Hansard, 3 April 1939

30. Neville Chamberlain papers, NC18/1/1093 Chamberlain to Ida 9 April 1939
31. Mosley, *On Borrowed Time*, p. 214
32. Self, *Neville Chamberlain*, p. 359
33. Neville Chamberlain papers, NC18/1/1094 Chamberlain to Hilda 15 April 1939
34. Neville Chamberlain papers, NC18/1/1094 Chamberlain to Hilda 15 April 1939
35. Neville Chamberlain papers, NC18/1/1095 Chamberlain to Ida 23 April 1939
36. James Lees-Milne, *Ancestral Voices* (London: Chatto & Windus, 1975), p. 69
37. Sir Alan Lascelles, *King's Counsellor: Abdication and War – the Diaries of Sir Alan Lascelles*, ed. Duff Hart-Davis (London: Weidenfeld & Nicolson, 2006), 25 September 1942
38. NA FO 800/315 Brocket memorandum 24 April 1939
39. Neville Chamberlain papers, NC18/1/1095 Chamberlain to Ida 23 April 1939
40. Goebbels diaries, 24 April 1939
41. NA FO 800/315 Brocket memorandum 24 April 1939
42. De Witt C. Poole interrogation of von Dirksen, Drummond Wolff papers, confidential note 26 June 1939
43. Butler papers, G10 Character study
44. Andrew, *Defence of the Realm*, p. 227

## CHAPTER TWENTY-FIVE: PAY WHATEVER PRICE MAY BE NECESSARY

1. Neville Chamberlain papers, NC18/1/1081 Chamberlain to Ida 8 January 1939
2. Neville Chamberlain papers, NC18/1/1082 Chamberlain to Hilda 15 January 1939
3. André François-Poncet, *Au Palais Farnèse: souvenirs d'une ambassade à Rome 1938–1940* (Paris: Fayard, 1961), p. 45 (author's translation)
4. Neville Chamberlain papers, NC18/1/1082 Chamberlain to Hilda 15 January 1939
5. Galeazzo Ciano, *Diaries 1937–1943* (London: Phoenix, 2002), p. 10
6. NA T273/410 Ball note dated 24 March 1939
7. NA T273/410 Ball to Wilson 4 April 1939
8. Neville Chamberlain papers, NC18/1/1093 Chamberlain to Ida 9 April 1939
9. NA T273/410 Wilson memorandum 17 April 1939
10. NA T273/410 Private secretary to Manenti 15 April 1939
11. NA 273/410 Chamberlain manuscript note on above
12. NA T273/410 Wilson to Cadogan 20 April 1939
13. NA T273/410 Wilson to Cadogan 1 May 1939
14. NA T273/410 Wilson to Cadogan 1 May 1939
15. NA 273/410 Ball memorandum 3 May 1939
16. NA T273/410 Ball to Wilson 5 June 1939
17. NA PREM 1/329 Wilson to Chamberlain 3 March 1939
18. NA PREM 1/329 Wilson draft undated but c. 6 June 1939
19. NA PREM 1/329 Wilson to Chamberlain 6 June 1939
20. NA PREM 1/329 Chamberlain to Daladier 13 July 1939
21. NA PREM 1/329 Daladier to Chamberlain 24 July 1939
22. NA T273/410 Ball to Wilson 5 June 1939

## CHAPTER TWENTY-SIX: CATCHING THE MUGWUMPS

1. Neville Chamberlain papers, NC18/1/1091 Chamberlain to Ida 26 March 1939
2. NA PREM 1/296 Wilson to Halifax 28 March 1939
3. NA PREM 1/296 Wilson memorandum 29 March 1939
4. NA PREM 1/296 Treasury memorandum
5. Sir Henry Pownall, *Chief of Staff: The Diaries of Lieutenant General Sir Henry Pownall, Vol 1: 1933–40*, ed. Brian Bond (Hamden, CT: Archon, 1973), 3 April 1939
6. Nicolson diaries, 20 April 1939
7. Nicolson diaries, 20 April 1939
8. Harvey diaries, 20 April 1939

9. Cadogan diaries, p. 175
10. Pownall diaries, 28 March 1939
11. Butler papers, RAB G10
12. Harvey diaries, 26 April 1939
13. NA PREM 1/387 'Meeting between Prime Minister and Trades Union Congress on introduction of Conscription', listed as missing and unavailable
14. Neville Chamberlain papers, NC18/1/1096 Chamberlain to Hilda 29 April 1939
15. Harvey diaries, 20 April 1939
16. DGFP D VI 272
17. Nicolson diaries, 26 April 1939
18. Neville Chamberlain papers, NC18/1/1092 Chamberlain to Hilda undated but 1–2 April 1939
19. Nicolson diaries, 3 April 1939
20. Channon diaries, 3 April 1939
21. Neville Chamberlain papers, NC18/1/1043 Chamberlain to Ida 20 March 1938
22. Neville Chamberlain papers, NC18/1/1093 Chamberlain to Ida 9 April 1939
23. Channon diaries, 19 May 1939
24. Neville Chamberlain papers, NC18/1/1091 Chamberlain to Ida 26 March 1939
25. Neville Chamberlain papers, NC18/1/1093 Chamberlain to Ida 9 April 1939
26. Neville Chamberlain papers, NC18/1/1100 Chamberlain to Ida 21 May 1939
27. Mosley, *On Borrowed Time*, p. 223
28. Channon diaries, 19 May 1939
29. Neville Chamberlain papers, NC18/1/1101 Chamberlain to Ida 28 May 1939
30. Neville Chamberlain papers, NC18/1/1101 Chamberlain to Hilda 28 May 1939
31. Maisky diaries, 30 May 1939
32. Self, *Neville Chamberlain*, p. 368
33. Neville Chamberlain papers, NC18/1/1107 Chamberlain to Hilda 15 July 1939
34. Neville Chamberlain papers, NC18/1/11105 Chamberlain to Hilda 2 July 1939; Neville Chamberlain papers, NC18/1/1108 Chamberlain to Ida 23 July 1939
35. Sir Edmund Ironside, *The Ironside Diaries 1937–1940*, ed. Roderick Macleod and Denis Kelly (London: Constable, 1962), 25 July 1939

## CHAPTER TWENTY-SEVEN: TALKING APPEASEMENT AGAIN

1. Nicolson diaries, 20 April 1939
2. 'The Reichstag speech', letter from Lord Rushcliffe, *The Times*, 3 May 1939
3. Harvey diaries, 3 May 1939
4. Cadogan diaries, 3 May 1939
5. Martin Pugh, *'Hurrah for the Blackshirts!': Fascists and Fascism in Britain between the Wars* (London: Jonathan Cape, 2005), p. 148
6. Drummond Wolff papers, Drummond Wolff to Ball 20 March 1939
7. Drummond Wolff papers, personal notes August 1969
8. Drummond Wolff papers, manuscript memorandum undated
9. Drummond Wolff papers, personal notes August 1969
10. Drummond Wolff papers, short notes of an interview… 27 January 1939
11. Drummond Wolff papers, report of a visit to Berlin 25 February–2 March 1939
12. Drummond Wolff papers, Drummond Wolff to Ball 20 and 24 March 1939
13. Drummond Wolff papers, letter Drummond Wolff to Ball 4 April 1939
14. DGFP D VI 368
15. Drummond Wolff papers, manuscript memorandum undated
16. DGFP D VI 380
17. Drummond Wolff papers, Drummond Wolff to Ball 19 May 1939
18. Drummond Wolff papers, manuscript memorandum undated
19. Drummond Wolff papers, Ball to Drummond Wolff 2 June 1939

20. Drummond Wolff papers, Hyde to Drummond Wolff 13 March and 30 September 1939
21. Leslie Field, *Bendor: The Golden Duke of Westminister* (London: Weidenfeld & Nicolson, 1983), p. 244; Paula Byrne, *Mad World: Evelyn Waugh and the Secrets of Brideshead* (London: HarperPress, 2009), pp. 133–40
22. Drummond Wolff papers, manuscript memorandum undated
23. Drummond Wolff papers, confidential note 26 June 1939
24. Drummond Wolff papers, Ball to Drummond Wolff 30 June 1939
25. Cadogan diaries, 29 June 1939
26. Harvey diaries, 1 July 1939
27. 'The choice for Germany', *The Times*, 30 June 1939
28. Dawson papers, diaries, 29 June 1939
29. Halifax, *Fulness of Days*, p. 208
30. Goebbels diaries, 1 July 1939
31. Goebbels diaries, 2 August 1939

## CHAPTER TWENTY-EIGHT: MORE WAYS OF KILLING A CAT

1. Drummond Wolff papers, manuscript memorandum undated
2. Neville Chamberlain papers, NC18/1/1106 Chamberlain to Ida 8 July 1939
3. Neville Chamberlain papers, NC18/1/1106 Chamberlain to Ida 8 July 1939
4. Maisky diaries, 5 July 1939
5. Neville Chamberlain papers, NC18/1/1107 Chamberlain to Hilda 15 July 1939
6. Neville Chamberlain papers, NC18/1/1108 Chamberlain to Ida 23 July 1939
7. Nicolson diaries, quoted in Gilbert, *The Churchill Documents*, p. 1561
8. Nicolson diaries, 19 July 1939
9. Ball papers, Luke to Ball 5 October 1940
10. R. B. Cockett, 'Ball, Chamberlain and *Truth*', *Historical Journal*, vol. 33, no. 1 (1990), pp. 131–42
11. *Truth*, 7 July 1939
12. Neville Chamberlain papers, NC18/1/1108 Chamberlain to Ida 23 July 1939
13. Neville Chamberlain papers, NC18/1/1105 Chamberlain to Hilda 2 July 1939
14. Andrew Roberts, *Eminent Churchillians* (London: Weidenfeld & Nicolson, 1994), pp. 287–303
15. Neville Chamberlain papers, NC18/1/1086 Chamberlain to Hilda 19 February 1939
16. Chamberlain, *In Search of Peace* (ed. Arthur Bryant), p. 207
17. Chamberlain, *In Search of Peace* (ed. Arthur Bryant), p. 217
18. Chamberlain, *In Search of Peace* (ed. Arthur Bryant), p. 103
19. Chamberlain, *In Search of Peace* (ed. Arthur Bryant), p. 155
20. Chamberlain, *In Search of Peace* (ed. Arthur Bryant), p. 7
21. NA PREM 1/335 Rucker memorandum 4 July 1939
22. NA PREM 1/335 Bryant memorandum 13 July 1939
23. DGFP D VI 716
24. Mosley, *On Borrowed Time*, p. 262
25. Mosley, *On Borrowed Time*, p. 262
26. Nachlaß Hesse, 1322/19 HW to FH 22/8/50
27. Neville Chamberlain papers, NC18/1/1108 Chamberlain to Ida 23 July 1939
28. Nachlaß Hesse, 1322/19 Wohlthat to Hesse 22/8/50
29. NA PREM 1/330 Wilson memorandum 19 July 1939
30. NA PREM 1/330 Wilson memorandum 19 July 1939
31. NA PREM 1/330 Wilson to Halifax 24 July 1939
32. Mosley, *On Borrowed Time*, p. 262

## CHAPTER TWENTY-NINE: MR BOOTHBY EXPECTS A RAKE-OFF

1. David Blaazer, 'Finance and the End of Appeasement: The Bank of England, the National Government and the Czech Gold', *Journal of Contemporary History*, vol. 40, no. 1 (2005), pp. 25–39

2. Hansard, 26 May 1939
3. NA T273/217 Waley to Wilson 3 August 1939
4. NA T273/217 Simon memorandum 3 August 1939
5. NA T273/217 Padmore (?) memorandum 5 August 1939
6. NA T273/217 Padmore (?) memorandum 5 August 1939
7. NA T273/217 Wilson memorandum 8 August 1939
8. NA T273/210 Manuscript note to Wilson memorandum 8 August 1939

CHAPTER THIRTY: TOO MANY PEOPLE AT THE JOB
1. Gladwyn (Jebb) memoirs, p. 93
2. Neville Chamberlain papers, NC18/1/1110 Chamberlain to Hilda 30 July 1939
3. Neville Chamberlain papers, NC18/1/1107 Chamberlain to Hilda 15 July 1939
4. NA PREM 1/335 Tennant to Chamberlain 4 July 1939
5. NA PREM 1/329 Wilson manuscript note 6 July on Rucker minute dated 4 July 1939
6. NA PREM 1/335 Wilson memorandum 10 July 1939
7. NA PREM 1/335 Tennant to Wilson 22 July 1939
8. NA PREM 1/335 Wilson memorandum 10 July 1939
9. NA PREM 1/335 Wilson memorandum 24 July 1939
10. NA PREM 1/335 Tennant to Ribbentrop 10 July 1939
11. NA PREM 1/335 Wilson memorandum 1 August 1939
12. Harold Hobson, Phillip Knightley and Leonard Russell, *The Pearl of Days: An Intimate Memoir of the Sunday Times 1822–1972* (London: Hamish Hamilton, 1972), pp. 211–15
13. NA PREM 1/322 Wilson to Chamberlain 25 July 1939 and NA PREM 1/322 Bryant draft article 'The British Point of View'
14. NA PREM 1/332 Wilson to Chamberlain 20 July 1939
15. NA PREM 1/332 Notes of the conversation with Herr Hitler 27 July 1939
16. Goebbels diaries, 12 July 1939
17. Otto Dietrich, *The Hitler I Knew* (London: Methuen, 1957), pp. 45f
18. Goebbels diaries, 28 July 1939
19. NA PREM 1/332 Wilson memorandum 31 July 1939
20. NA PREM 1/332 Wilson memorandum 1 August 1939
21. Henderson, *Failure of a Mission*, p. 231
22. Harvey diaries, 9 July 1939; Harvey to Halifax quoted on p. 435
23. Henderson, *Failure of a Mission*, p. 241
24. Brigitte Hamann, *Winifred Wagner: A Life at the Heart of Hitler's Bayreuth* (London: Granta, 2005), p. 305
25. James Marshall-Cornwall, *Wars and Rumours of Wars: A Memoir* (London: Leo Cooper, 1984), p. 125
26. NA FO 371/22974 Marshall-Cornwall to Halifax

CHAPTER THIRTY-ONE: ENTITLED TO DEMAND CONCESSIONS
1. Churchill papers, 2/367 Churchill to Lord Rothermere 19 July 1939
2. Edward L. Spears, *Assignment to Catastrophe*, 2 vols (London: Heinemann, 1954), p. 3
3. Neville Chamberlain papers, NC18/1/1110 Chamberlain to Hilda 30 July 1939
4. Neville Chamberlain papers, NC18/1/1110 Chamberlain to Hilda 30 July 1939
5. Neville Chamberlain papers, NC18/1/1111 Chamberlain to Ida 5 August 1939
6. DGFP D VI 743 n2
7. DGFP D VI 748
8. NA PREM 1/330 Butler to Wilson 2 August 1939
9. NA PREM 1/330 Wilson memorandum 3 August 1939
10. De Witt C. Poole interrogation of von Dirksen 12 and 14 September 1945
11. De Witt C. Poole interrogation of von Dirksen 12 and 14 September 1945, p. 25
12. Dirksen papers, p. 24
13. NA PREM 1/332 Note of Kemsley's conversation with Hitler 27 July 1939

14. Herbert von Dirksen, *Moskau, Tokio, London: Erinnerungen und Betrachtungen zu 20 Jahren deutscher Aussenpolitik 1919–1939* (Stuttgart: Kohlhammer, 1949), p. 256
15. Hesse, *Das Spiel um Deutschland*, pp. 182–6
16. De Witt C. Poole interrogation of von Dirksen 12 and 14 September 1945
17. De Witt C. Poole interrogation of von Dirksen 12 and 14 September 1945, p. 21
18. Dirksen memo quoted in Zachary Shore, *What Hitler Knew: The Battle for Information in Nazi Foreign Policy* (New York: Oxford University Press, 2003), p. 96
19. Dirksen memoirs, p. 256

## CHAPTER THIRTY-TWO: PATHETIC LITTLE WORMS

1. NA PREM 1/332 Dietrich to Kemsley 17 August 1939
2. Nachlaß Hesse, 1322/2 42 Hesse to JvR 22/8/1939
3. NA FO 371/22975 Wilson memorandum 20 August 1939
4. Winfried Baumgart, 'Zur Ansprache Hitlers vor den Führern der Wehrmacht am 22. August 1939. Eine quellenkritische Untersuchung', *Vierteljahrshefte für Zeitgeschichte*, vol. 16, no. 2 (1968), pp. 120–49
5. Goebbels diaries, 25 August 1939
6. Mosley, *On Borrowed Time*, p. 385
7. Kennedy to Sumner Welles 24 August 1939, quoted in Amanda Smith (ed.), *Hostage to Fortune: The Letters of Joseph P. Kennedy* (New York: Viking, 2001), p. 357
8. Smith, *Hostage to Fortune*, pp. 357f
9. Quoted in Mosley, *On Borrowed Time*, p. 385
10 Goebbels diaries, 24 August 1939 (author's translation)
11. Nachlaß Hesse, undated carbon copy also quoted in *Das Spiel um Deutschland*, p. 201
12. Donald Cameron Watt, *How War Came: the Immediate Origins of the Second World War 1938–1939* (London: Heinemann, 1989), Chapter 26; Sidney Aster, *1939: The Making of the Second World War* (London: André Deutsch, 1973), pp. 334–8
13. Hesse to Ribbentrop 26 August 1939, quoted in Mosley, *On Borrowed Time*, p. 408
14. NA PREM 1/331A Draft reply to message from German chancellor undated fols 454–5; Cadogan diaries, 26 August 1939
15. Harvey diaries, 27 August 1939
16. NA PREM 1/331A fol 359
17. NA PREM 1/331A fol 365 and DGFP D VII 384
18. Harvey diaries, 27 August 1939
19. Neville Chamberlain papers, NC18/1/1116 Chamberlain to Ida 10 September 1939
20. Goebbels diaries, 1 September 1939
21. Franz von Sonnleithner, *Als Diplomat im 'Führerhauptquartier'* (Munich: Langen Müller, 1989), p. 13 (author's translation)
22. Schmidt, *Statist auf Diplomatischer Bühne*, pp. 463f

## CHAPTER THIRTY-THREE: A POTATO WAR

1. Goebbels diaries, 4 September 1939
2. Neville Chamberlain papers, NC18/1/1108 Chamberlain to Ida 23 July 1939
3. Neville Chamberlain papers, NC18/1/1122 Chamberlain to Ida 23 September 1939
4. Neville Chamberlain papers, NC18/1/1122 Chamberlain to Ida 23 September 1939
5. Dalton diaries, 6 September 1939
6. Roskill, *Hankey: Man of Secrets*, p. 413
7. Roskill, *Hankey: Man of Secrets*, p. 416
8. Roskill, *Hankey: Man of Secrets*, p. 417
9. Roskill, *Hankey: Man of Secrets*, p. 419
10. NA T273/68 Bridges to Attlee 5 November 1946
11. John Winnifrith, 'Edward Ettingdean Bridges', *Biographical Memoirs of Fellows of the Royal Society*, vol. 16 (1970), pp. 38–56

12. Neville Chamberlain papers, NC18/1/1121 Chamberlain to Hilda 17 September 1939
13. Neville Chamberlain papers, NC7/9/63 Wilson minute 3 October 1939
14. Hansard, 11 October 1939
15. NA PREM 1/388 Wilson to Waterfield, 7 September for Dugdale's appointment
16. Neville Chamberlain papers, NC18/1/1126 Chamberlain to Ida 22 October 1939
17. NA PREM 1/379 Hankey memorandum 12 September 1939
18. NA PREM 1/329 Memorandum beginning 'At the present stage of the war...'
19. NA PREM 1/379 Churchill to Duke of Westminster 13 September 1939
20. NA PREM 1/379 Duke of Westminster to Chamberlain 15 September 1939
21. NA PREM 1/379 Chamberlain manuscript note on Wilson to Chamberlain 17 September 1939
22. NA CAB 65/56/4
23. Neville Chamberlain papers, NC18/1/1129 Chamberlain to Ida 5 November 1939
24. Schellenberg, Walter, *The Schellenberg Memoirs* (reprinted as *Schellenberg*) (London: Mayflower, 1965), pp. 30–44
25. Churchill broadcast, BBC written archives
26. Neville Chamberlain papers, NC18/1/1132 Chamberlain to Ida 19 November 1939
27. Colville diaries, 13 November 1939; DDI 9s II 218
28. Harold Nicolson, *Why Britain Is at War* (Harmondsworth: Penguin, 1939), p. 106

CHAPTER THIRTY-FOUR: A CIVIL SERVANT WITH A POLITICAL SENSE

1. Colville, *Footprints in Time*, p. 72; Colville diaries, p. 36
2. Templewood papers, XIX Notes on conversation with Sir A. Rucker 24 October 1951
3. Chamberlain papers, NC L add. 131 Chamberlain to Ball 28 October 1940
4. Nicolson diaries, 6 January 1940, p. 56
5. Quoted in Roskill, *Hankey: Man of Secrets*, p. 395
6. Lord Butler, *The Art of Memory: Friends in Perspective* (London: Hodder & Stoughton, 1982), p. 56
7. Norman papers, diaries, 20 December 1939
8. Pownall diaries, 28 November 1939, p. 259
9. Colville diaries, 13 December 1939
10. Colville diaries, 29 December 1939; Neville Chamberlain papers, NC18/1/1139 Chamberlain to Ida 20 January 1940
11. 'Belisha is no Loss', *Truth*, 19 January 1940; 'Belisha Once More', *Truth*, 19 January 1940; 'Our Fate in Our Hands', *Truth*, 19 January 1940; Cockett, *Twilight of Truth*, pp. 165–9; R. B. Cockett, 'Ball, Chamberlain and *Truth*'
12. Reith, *Into the Wind*, p. 346
13. Reith diaries, 13 September 1939, p. 230
14. Bruce Lockhart diaries, 18 October 1938, p. 403
15. Reith diaries, 7 June 1939, p. 229
16. Neville Chamberlain papers, NC18/1/1116 Chamberlain to Ida 10 September 1939
17. Colville, *Footprints in Time*, p. 73
18. R. S. Sayers, *The Bank of England 1891–1944*, 3 vols (Cambridge: Cambridge University Press, 1976), p. 646fn
19. Sayers, *The Bank of England*, p. 591
20. Stamp memorandum, quoted in J. Harry Jones, *Josiah Stamp, Public Servant: The Life of the First Baron Stamp of Shortlands* (London: Sir Isaac Pitman, 1964), pp. 337–40
21. Colville, *Footprints in Time*, p. 73
22. Neville Chamberlain papers, NC18/1/1139 Chamberlain to Ida 20 January 1940
23. Neville Chamberlain papers, NC18/1/1139 Chamberlain to Ida 20 January 1940
24. J. Harry Jones, *Josiah Stamp*
25. NA PREM 1/249 Wilson memorandum 12 September 1938
26. Dirksen papers, vol. II, p. 178

27. Lord Beveridge, 'Stamp, Josiah Charles, First Baron Stamp', Rev. Jose Harris, *Oxford Dictionary of National Biography* (Oxford: Oxford University Press, 2011)
28. Stamp letter to *The Times*, 10 February 1936
29. 'Nazi Four-Year Plan', *The Times*, 21 January 1938
30. Stamp memorandum, quoted in J. Harry Jones, *Josiah Stamp*, pp. 337–40
31. Stamp memorandum, quoted in J. Harry Jones, *Josiah Stamp*, pp. 337–40; Neville Chamberlain papers, NC18/1/1139 Chamberlain to Ida 20 January 1940
32. Reith diaries, 7 June 1939, p. 229
33. Phipps MSS, Wilson to Phipps 2 February 1939
34. Neville Chamberlain papers, NC18/1/1139 Chamberlain to Ida 20 January 1940
35. Michael D. Kandiah, 'Marquis, Frederick James, First Earl of Woolton', *Oxford Dictionary of National Biography* (Oxford: Oxford University Press, 2008)
36. Robert Rhodes James, *Victor Cazalet: A Portrait* (London: Hamish Hamilton, 1976), p. 227
37. Templewood papers, XIX Between the Wars, Edward Halifax 15 June 1948
38. Neville Chamberlain papers, NC18/1/1146 Chamberlain to Hilda 10 March 1940
39. Woolton memoirs, pp. 130–33
40. Harvey diaries, 7 June 1938

CHAPTER THIRTY-FIVE: MINISTER TO ICELAND
1. 'Through Italian Eyes', *Truth*, 22 December 1939
2. Neville Chamberlain papers, NC18/1/1146 Chamberlain to Hilda 10 March 1940
3. Cadogan diaries, 9 March 1940, p. 260
4. DDI 9s III 537
5. Guy Liddell, *The Guy Liddell Diaries: MI5's Director of Counter-Espionage in World War II*, ed. Nigel West, 2 vols (Abingdon: Routledge, 2005), 16 March 1940
6. NA T273/410 Wilson memorandum 20 April 1940
7. NA T273/410 Wilson memorandum 20 April 1940
8. NA T273/410 Wilson manuscript note undated
9. NA T273/410 Wilson memo 30 April 1940
10. NA T273/410 Wilson to Ball 2 May 1940
11. NA PREM 1/435 Wilson to Chamberlain 30 April 1940
12. NA PREM 1/435 Ismay to Wilson 5 May 1940
13. Colville diaries, 8 May 1940
14. Robert Rhodes James, *Victor Cazalet*, p. 227
15. Emrys-Evans papers, 58246 diaries transcript 8 May 1940
16. Camrose, Notes of a conversation with Mr Neville Chamberlain 9 May 1940 quoted in Gilbert, *The Churchill Documents*
17. Amery diaries, 9 May 1940
18. Dalton diaries, 9 May 1940
19. Amery diaries, 9 May 1940
20. Bruce Lockhart diaries, 15 May 1940
21. Colville diaries, 10 May 1940
22. Dalton diaries; Bruce Lockhart diaries; W. J. Brown, *So Far*, p. 222
23. Bruce Lockhart diaries, 14 March 1946
24. The most useful example of this are the successive drafts in NA PREM 1/466 of Wilson's account of the abdication crisis in preparing his 'official' account which reveal precisely points that he wished to keep quiet. This lies outside the scope of this book but see this author's *The King Who Had to Go: Edward VIII, Mrs Simpson and the Hidden Politics of the Abdication Crisis* (London: Biteback, 2016)
25. Bruce Lockhart diaries, 2 June 1940
26. Roberts, *Eminent Churchillians*, Chapter 3; Stewart, *Burying Caesar*, Epilogue; Self, *Neville Chamberlain*, pp. 434f
27. Channon diaries, 14 November 1940

CHAPTER THIRTY-SIX: A GUILTY MAN IN THE REALM OF KING ZOG

1. Michael Foot, *Aneurin Bevan: A Biography, Vol. 1: 1897–1945* (London: MacGibbon & Kee, 1962), p. 320
2. Cato, *Guilty Men* (London: Victor Gollancz, 1940), p. 90
3. A. J. P. Taylor, *Beaverbrook* (London: Hamish Hamilton, 1972), p. 563; Anne Chisholm and Michael Davie, *Lord Beaverbrook: A Life* (London: Hutchinson, 1992), pp. 379–83
4. Colville diaries, 19 August 1940
5. Andrew, *Defence of the Realm*, pp. 229f
6. Crathorne (Dugdale) papers, Nancy Dugdale to Tommy Dugdale 18 June 1940
7. Colville diaries, 19 August 1940
8. Crathorne (Dugdale) papers, Wilson to Nancy Dugdale 31 December 1940
9. Francis Williams, *A Prime Minister Remembers: The War and Post-War Memoirs of the Rt. Hon. Earl Attlee* (London: Heinemann, 1961), p. 40
10. Crathorne (Dugdale) papers, Wilson to Nancy Dugdale 25 October 1940
11. Colville diaries, 6 January 1941
12. Crathorne (Dugdale) papers, Wilson to Nancy Dugdale 26 June 1940
13. T273/218 Memorandum by Treasury Solicitor
14. NA KV2/2855 J. G. of MI5 to Home Office 26 August 1940
15. NA T273/218 Waley to Wilson 2 October 1940
16. NA T273/218 Unsigned undated memorandum prepared for Attorney General
17. NA T273/218 Wyatt to Wilson 1 October 1940
18. NA T273/218 Wilson manuscript memorandum 10 October 1940
19. NA T273/218 Wilson to Wood 10 October 1940
20. NA T273/218 Memorandum by Treasury Solicitor Wilson manuscript annotation
21. NA T273/218 Wilson to Wood 8 October 1940
22. NA T273/218 Draft letter to Boothby for Churchill
23. Churchill papers, CHAR 20/20 Churchill to Wood 26 July 1941
24. Churchill papers, CHAR 20/20 Wood to Churchill 27 July 1941
25. Dalton diaries, 20 March 1941
26. R. V. Jones, *Most Secret War* (London: Hamish Hamilton, 1978), p. 248
27. Oliver Harvey, *The War Diaries of Oliver Harvey 1941–1945*, ed. John Harvey (London: Collins, 1978), 19 September 1941
28. Harvey diaries, 28 August 1942
29. NA CAB 127/157 Munich 1938
30. Colville diaries, p. 41
31. David Lough, *No More Champagne: Churchill and His Money* (London: Head of Zeus, 2016), pp. 165f, 169f


CHAPTER THIRTY-SEVEN: HE HAS RETURNED TO BOURNEMOUTH

1. Emrys-Evans papers, 58247/41 Emrys-Evans to Julian Amery quoting Sir Orme Sargent of the Foreign Office
2. Boyle, *Montagu Norman*, p. 318
3. Channon diaries, 3 February 1944
4. Streat diaries, 3 April 1944
5. Dutton, *Neville Chamberlain*, p. 136f
6. Feiling, *The Life of Neville Chamberlain*, p. 327
7. Galeazzo Ciano, *L'Europa Verso la Catastrofe* (Milan: Mondadori, 1948), English translation published in Britain as *Ciano's Diplomatic Papers* ed. Malcom Muggeridge (London: Odhams, 1948)
8. Templewood papers, XIX Ball to Hoare 29 December 1948
9. Templewood papers, XIX Ball to Hoare 5 February 1952
10. Templewood papers, XIX Ball to Hoare 5 February 1952
11. Richard Davenport-Hines (ed.), *Letters from Oxford: Hugh Trevor-Roper to Bernard Berenson* (London: Orion Press, 2006), pp. 19f, 27f

12. Nigel Nicolson, *Long Life* (London: Weidenfeld & Nicolson, 1997), pp. 146, 175
13. Dutton, *Neville Chamberlain*, pp. 87–98; Self, *The Neville Chamberlain Diary Letters*, 4 vols (Aldershot: Ashgate, 2000–02), pp. 4–13; the historiography of appeasement has become almost a discipline in its own right
14. Hoare, Samuel, Viscount Templewood, *Nine Troubled Years* (London: Collins, 1954), p. 260
15. Neville Chamberlain papers, NC 11/1/813 Note on conversation with Wilson 17 July 1953
16. NA PREM 8/1130 Wilson to Bevir 1 October 1950
17. Nachlaß Hesse 1322/19; Wohlthat to Hesse 22 August 1950
18. Gilbert, 'Horace Wilson: Man of Munich?'

# SELECT BIBLIOGRAPHY

## ORIGINAL PAPERS

Avon Papers, Birmingham University Library
Baldwin Papers, University Library, Cambridge
Ball Papers, Bodleian Library, Oxford
Butler Papers, Trinity College, Cambridge
Cadogan Papers, Churchill Archives Centre, Cambridge
Neville Chamberlain Papers, Birmingham University Library
Churchill Papers, Churchill Archives Centre, Cambridge
Cilcennin (J. P. L. Thomas) Collection, Carmarthenshire Records Office, Carmarthen
Crathorne (Dugdale) Papers, private collection
Davison, J. C. C., House of Lords
Dawson MSS, Bodleian Library, Oxford
Emrys-Evans Papers, British Library, London
Fisher, Warren, private collection
Hankey Papers, Churchill Archives Centre, Cambridge
Hesse Papers (Nachlaß Hesse), Bundesarchiv, Koblenz
Inskip Papers, Churchill Archives Centre, Cambridge
Thomas Jones Papers, National Library of Wales, Aberystwyth
Kell Papers, Imperial War Museum, London
Mander MSS, Wightwick Manor, Wolverhampton
Monckton Deposit, Bodleian Library, Oxford
Norman Papers, Bank of England, London
Phipps MSS, Churchill Archives Centre, Cambridge

Reuters, Thomson Reuters
Swinton Papers, Churchill Archives Centre, Cambridge
Tallents, Stephen, private collection
Templewood Papers, University Library, Cambridge

## GOVERNMENT DOCUMENTS

Akten der Reichskanzlei
Documenti Diplomatici Italiani (DDI)
Documents & Materials Relating to the Eve of the Second World War
  (Dirksen papers)
Documents on German Foreign Policy 1918–1945 (DGFP)
National Archive (NA)
Trial of the Major War Criminals before the International Military Tri-
  bunal; Nuremberg, 14 November 1945–1 October 1946
US State Department, Interrogation Fritz Hesse 2 October 1947
US State Department, Dewitt Poole Mission 011887 – State Depart-
  ment Special Interrogation Mission – Interrogation of Ambassador
  Herbert von Dirksen

## PUBLISHED COLLECTIONS OF PRIVATE
## DOCUMENTS (LISTED BY EDITOR)

Baldwin, Stanley, *Baldwin Papers: A Conservative Statesman 1908–1947*,
  ed. Philip Williamson and Edward Baldwin (Cambridge: Cambridge
  University Press, 2004)
Bryant, Arthur (ed.), *In Search of Peace: Speeches (1937–1938)* [by Neville
  Chamberlain] (London: Hutchinson, 1939)
Ciano, Galeazzo, *L'Europa Verso la Catastrofe* (Milan: Mondadori,
  1948), English translation published in Britain as *Ciano's Diplomatic
  Papers* ed. Malcom Muggeridge (London: Odhams, 1948)
Davenport-Hines, Richard (ed.), *Letters from Oxford: Hugh Trevor-
  Roper to Bernard Berenson* (London: Orion Press, 2006)
Gilbert, Martin (ed.), *The Churchill Documents, Vol. 13: The Coming of
  War 1936–1939* (Hillsdale, MI: Hillsdale College)

Hunter, Ian (ed.), *Winston and Archie: The Collected Correspondence of Winston Churchill and Archibald Sinclair 1915–1960* (London: Politico's, 2005)

Minney, R. J. (ed.), *The Private Papers of Hore-Belisha* (London: Collins, 1960)

Self, Robert (ed.), *The Neville Chamberlain Diary Letters*, 4 vols (Aldershot: Ashgate, 2000–2002)

Smith, Amanda (ed.), *Hostage to Fortune: The Letters of Joseph P. Kennedy* (New York: Viking, 2001)

Soames, Mary (ed.), *Speaking for Themselves: The Private Letters of Winston and Clementine Churchill* (London: Doubleday, 1998)

## WORKS BY CONTEMPORARIES (OR BASED ESSENTIALLY ON CONTEMPORARY MATERIAL)

Birkenhead, Lord, *Walter Monckton: The Life of Viscount Monckton of Brenchley* (London: Weidenfeld & Nicolson, 1969)

Bridges, Lord, *The Treasury* (London: Allen & Unwin, 1964)

Cato, *Guilty Men* (London: Victor Gollancz, 1940)

*Clem Attlee: The Granada Historical Records Interview* (London: Panther, 1967)

Colvin, Ian, *The Chamberlain Cabinet: How the Meetings in 10 Downing Street, 1937–1939, Led to the Second World War – Told for the First Time from the Cabinet Papers* (London: Victor Gollancz, 1971)

Colvin, Ian, *Vansittart in Office: An Historical Survey of the Origins of the Second World War Based on the Papers of Sir Robert Vansittart, Permanent Under-Secretary of State for Foreign Affairs, 1930–38* (London: Victor Gollancz, 1965)

Conwell-Evans, T. P., *None So Blind: A Study of the Crisis Years 1930–1939* (London: Harrison, 1947)

Crozier, W. P., *Off the Record: Political Interviews 1933–1943* (London: Hutchinson, 1973)

Curry, John, *The Security Service 1908–1945: The Official History* (Kew: Public Record Office, 1999)

Dietrich, Otto, *The Hitler I Knew* (London: Methuen, 1957)

Feiling, Keith, *The Life of Neville Chamberlain* (London: Macmillan, 1946)

Gans zu Putlitz, Wolfgang, *The Putlitz Dossier* (London: Allen Wingate, 1957)

Gourlay, Logan (ed.), *The Beaverbrook I Knew* (London: Quartet, 1984)

Hyde, H. Montgomery, *British Air Policy between the Wars 1918–1939* (London: Heinemann, 1976)

James, Robert Rhodes, *Victor Cazalet: A Portrait* (London: Hamish Hamilton, 1976)

Jones, J. Harry, *Josiah Stamp, Public Servant: The Life of the First Baron Stamp of Shortlands* (London: Sir Isaac Pitman, 1964)

Low, David, *Low Again: A Pageant of Politics* (London: Cresset Press, 1938)

Low, David, *The World at War* (Harmondsworth: Penguin, 1942)

Margach, James, *The Abuse of Power: The War between Downing Street and the Media from Lloyd George to Callaghan* (London: W. H. Allen, 1978)

Nicolson, Harold, *Why Britain Is at War* (Harmondsworth: Penguin, 1939)

Roskill, Stephen, *Hankey: Man of Secrets, Vol. 3: 1931–63* (London: Collins, 1974)

Stirling, Alfred, *Lord Bruce: The London Years* (Melbourne: Hawthorn Press, 1974)

Strang, Lord, *Britain in World Affairs: A Survey of the Fluctuations in Power and Influence, Henry VIII to Elizabeth II* (London: Faber & Faber / André Deutsch, 1961)

Williams, Francis, *A Prime Minister Remembers: The War and Post-War Memoirs of the Rt. Hon. Earl Attlee* (London: Heinemann, 1961)

Wrench, John Evelyn, *Geoffrey Dawson and Our Times* (London: Hutchinson, 1955)

## PUBLISHED DIARIES

Amery, Leo, *The Empire at Bay: The Leo Amery Diaries 1929–1945*, ed. John Barnes and David Nicolson (London: Hutchinson, 1988)

Bernays, Robert, *The Diaries and Letters of Robert Bernays 1932–1939: An*

*Insider's Account of the House of Commons*, ed. Nick Smart (Lewiston, NY: Edwin Mellen Press, 1996)

Brooks, Collin, *Fleet Street, Press Barons and Politics: The Journals of Collin Brooks 1932–1940*, ed. Nicholas Crowson (Cambridge: Cambridge University Press, 1998)

Bruce Lockhart, Sir Robert, *The Diaries of Sir Robert Bruce Lockhart*, ed. Kenneth Young, 2 vols (London: Macmillan, 1973–80)

Cadogan, Sir Alexander, *The Diaries of Sir Alexander Cadogan OM 1938–1945*, ed. David Dilks (London: Cassell, 1971)

Channon, Sir Henry, *'Chips': The Diaries of Sir Henry Channon*, ed. Robert Rhodes James (London: Weidenfeld & Nicolson, 1967)

Ciano, Galeazzo, *Diaries 1937–1943* (London: Phoenix, 2002)

Colville, John, *The Fringes of Power: Downing Street Diaries 1939–1955* (London: Hodder & Stoughton, 1985)

Cooper, Duff, *The Duff Cooper Diaries 1915–1951*, ed. John Julius Norwich (London: Weidenfeld & Nicolson, 2005)

Dalton, Hugh, *The Second World War Diaries of Hugh Dalton 1940–45*, ed. Ben Pimlott (London: Jonathan Cape, 1985)

Dalton, Hugh, *The Political Diaries of Hugh Dalton 1918–40, 1945–60*, ed. Ben Pimlott (London: Jonathan Cape, 1986)

Dugdale, Blanche, *Baffy: The Diaries of Blanche Dugdale 1936–1947*, ed. N. A. Rose (London: Vallentine, Mitchell 1973)

Goebbels, Joseph, *Die Tagebücher von Joseph Goebbels: sämtliche Fragmente*, ed. Elke Fröhlich (Munich: K. G. Saur, 1987)

Halder, Franz, *Kriegstagebuch*, 3 vols (Stuttgart: Kohlhammer, 1962–64)

Harvey, Oliver, *The Diplomatic Diaries of Oliver Harvey 1937–1940*, ed. John Harvey (London: Collins, 1970)

Harvey, Oliver, *The War Diaries of Oliver Harvey 1941–1945*, ed. John Harvey (London: Collins, 1978)

Hobhouse, Charles, *Inside Asquith's Cabinet: From the Diaries of Charles Hobhouse*, ed. Edward David (London: John Murray, 1977)

Ironside, Sir Edmund, *The Ironside Diaries 1937–1940*, ed. Roderick Macleod and Denis Kelly (London: Constable, 1962)

Jones, Thomas, *Whitehall Diaries, Vol. 2: 1926–1930*, ed. Keith Middlemas (London: Oxford University Press, 1969)

Jones, Thomas, *A Diary with Letters, 1931–1950* (London: Oxford University Press, 1954)

Kennedy, A. L., *The Times and Appeasement: The Journals of A. L. Kennedy 1932–1939*, ed. Gordon Martel (Cambridge: Cambridge University Press, 2000)

Lascelles, Sir Alan, *King's Counsellor: Abdication and War – the Diaries of Sir Alan Lascelles*, ed. Duff Hart-Davis (London: Weidenfeld & Nicolson, 2006)

Liddell, Guy, *The Guy Liddell Diaries: MI5's Director of Counter-Espionage in World War II*, ed. Nigel West, 2 vols (Abingdon: Routledge, 2005)

Macmillan, Harold, *War Diaries: Politics and War in the Mediterranean, January 1943–May 1945* (London: Macmillan, 1984)

Maisky, Ivan, *The Maisky Diaries: Red Ambassador to the Court of St James 1932–1943*, ed. Gabriel Gorodetsky (New Haven, CT: Yale University Press, 2015)

Nicolson, Harold, *Diaries and Letters 1930–39*, ed. Nigel Nicolson (London: Collins, 1967)

Nicolson, Harold, *Diaries and Letters 1939–45*, ed. Nigel Nicolson (London: Collins, 1967)

Pownall, Sir Henry, *Chief of Staff: The Diaries of Lieutenant General Sir Henry Pownall, Vol 1: 1933–40*, ed. Brian Bond (Hamden, CT: Archon, 1973)

Reith, Lord, *The Reith Diaries*, ed. Charles Stuart (London: Collins, 1975)

Streat, Sir Raymond, *Lancashire and Whitehall: The Diaries of Sir Raymond Streat*, ed. Margaret Dupree, 2 vols (Manchester: Manchester University Press, 1987)

## MEMOIRS

Ashton-Gwatkin, Frank T., *The British Foreign Service: A Discussion of the Development and Function of the British Foreign Service* (Syracuse, NY: Syracuse University Press, 1950)

Attlee, C. R., *As It Happened* (London: William Heinemann, 1954)

Balfour, Harold, *Wings over Westminster* (London: Hutchinson, 1973)

Baxter, Beverley, *Men, Martyrs and Mountebanks: Beverley Baxter's Inner*

*Story of Personalities and Events behind the War* (London: Hutchinson, 1940)

Below, Nicolaus von, *At Hitler's Side: The Memoirs of Hitler's Luftwaffe Adjutant 1937–1945* (London: Greenhill, 2001)

Boothby, Bob, *Boothby: Recollections of a Rebel* (London: Hutchinson, 1978)

Brown, W. J., *So Far* (London: Allen & Unwin, 1943)

Bruce Lockhart, Sir Robert Hamilton, *Comes the Reckoning* (London: Putnam, 1947)

Bruce Lockhart, Sir Robert Hamilton, *Giants Cast Long Shadows* (London: Putnam, 1960)

Butler, Lord, *The Art of Memory: Friends in Perspective* (London: Hodder & Stoughton, 1982)

Butler, Lord, *The Art of the Possible: The Memoirs of Lord Butler* (London: Hamish Hamilton, 1971)

Cazalet-Keir, Thelma, *From the Wings: An Autobiography* (London: Bodley Head, 1967)

Chatfield, Lord, *The Navy and Defence: The Autobiography of Admiral of the Fleet Lord Chatfield*, 2 vols (London: Heinemann, 1942–47)

Citrine, Lord, *Men and Work: The Autobiography of Lord Citrine* (London: Hutchinson, 1964)

Clark, Kenneth, *Another Part of the Wood: A Self-Portrait* (London: John Murray, 1974)

Colville, John, *Footprints in Time* (London: Victor Gollancz, 1976)

Cooper, Duff, *Old Men Forget: The Autobiography of Duff Cooper* (London: Rupert Hart-Davis, 1953)

Coote, Colin R., *Editorial: The Memoirs of Colin R. Coote* (London: Eyre & Spottiswoode, 1965)

Davidson, J. C. C., *Memoirs of a Conservative: J. C. C. Davidson's Memoirs and Papers 1910–37*, ed. Robert Rhodes James (London: Weidenfeld & Nicolson, 1939)

Davies, Joseph, *The Prime Minister's Secretariat 1916–1920* (Newport, Monmouthshire: R. H. Johns, 1951)

Dirksen, Herbert von, *Moskau, Tokio, London: Erinnerungen und Betrachtungen zu 20 Jahren deutscher Aussenpolitik 1919–1939* (Stuttgart: Kohlhammer, 1949)

Doenitz, Admiral Karl, *Memoirs: Ten Years and Twenty Days* (London: Cassell, 1990)

Eden, Anthony, Earl of Avon, *The Eden Memoirs: Facing the Dictators* (London: Cassell, 1960)

Eden, Anthony, Earl of Avon, *The Eden Memoirs: The Reckoning* (London: Cassell, 1965)

Einzig, Paul, *In the Centre of Things: The Autobiography of Paul Einzig* (London: Hutchinson, 1960)

Engel, Gerhard, *Heeresadjutant bei Hitler 1938–1943: Aufzeichnungen des Majors Engel*, ed. Hildegard von Kotze (Stuttgart: Deutsche Verlags-Anstalt, 1974)

FitzRandolph, Sigsmund-Sizzo, *Der Frühstücks-Attaché aus London* (Stuttgart: Riegler, 1954)

François-Poncet, André, *Au Palais Farnèse: souvenirs d'une ambassade à Rome 1938–1940* (Paris: Fayard, 1961)

Geyr von Schweppenburg, General Baron, *The Critical Years* (London: Allan Wingate, 1952)

Gladwyn, Lord (Jebb), *The Memoirs of Lord Gladwyn* (London: Weidenfeld & Nicolson, 1972)

Gregory, J. D., *On the Edge of Diplomacy: Rambles and Reflections 1902–1928* (London: Hutchinson, 1929)

Grigg, P. J., *Prejudice and Judgement* (London: Jonathan Cape, 1948)

Halifax, Earl of, *Fulness of Days* (London: Collins, 1957)

Harris, Sir Percy, *Forty Years in and out of Parliament* (London: Andrew Melrose, 1947)

Harris, R. W., *Not So Humdrum: The Autobiography of a Civil Servant* (London: John Lane, 1939)

Henderson, Sir Nevile, *Failure of a Mission: Berlin 1937–1939* (London: Hodder & Stoughton, 1940)

Hesse, Fritz, *Das Spiel um Deutschland* (Munich: List, 1953)

Hesse, Fritz, *Das Vorspiel zum Kriege: Englandberichte und Erlebnisse eines Tatzeugen 1935–1945* (Leoni am Starnberger See: Druffel, 1979)

Hoare, Samuel, Viscount Templewood, *Nine Troubled Years* (London: Collins, 1954)

Home, Lord, *The Way the Wind Blows: An Autobiography* (London: Collins, 1976)

Ismay, Lord, *The Memoirs of General the Lord Ismay* (London: Heinemann, 1960)

Jones, R. V., *Most Secret War* (London: Hamish Hamilton, 1978)

Kearley, Hudson Ewbanke, *The Travelled Road: Some Memories of a Busy Life* (privately published, 1935)

Kirkpatrick, Ivone, *The Inner Circle: Memoirs of Ivone Kirkpatrick* (London: Macmillan, 1959)

Kordt, Erich, *Nicht aus den Akten* (Stuttgart: Union, 1950)

Kordt, Erich, *Wahn und Wirklichkeit* (Stuttgart: Union, 1947)

Leith-Ross, Frederick, *Money Talks: Fifty Years of International Finance* (London: Hutchinson, 1968)

Loßberg, Bernhard von, *Im Wehrmachtführungsstab: Bericht eines Generalstabsoffiziers* (Hamburg: Nölke, 1949)

Low, David, *Low's Autobiography* (London: Michael Joseph, 1956)

MacDonald, Malcolm, *People and Places: Random Reminiscences of the Rt. Hon. Malcolm MacDonald* (London: Collins, 1969)

Macfadyean, Sir Andrew, *Recollected in Tranquillity* (London: Pall Mall Press, 1964)

McKechnie, Samuel, *The Romance of the Civil Service* (London: Sampson Low, Marston, 1930)

Macmillan, Harold, *The Blast of War 1939–1945* (London: Macmillan, 1967)

Macmillan, Harold, *Winds of Change 1914–1939* (London: Macmillan, 1966)

Macmillan, Lord, *A Man of Law's Tale: The Reminiscences of the Rt. Hon. Lord Macmillan* (London: Macmillan, 1952)

Marshall-Cornwall, James, *Wars and Rumours of Wars: A Memoir* (London: Leo Cooper, 1984)

Massey, Vincent, *What's Past Is Prologue: The Memoirs of the Right Honourable Vincent Massey, CH* (London: Macmillan, 1963)

Maugham, Frederic Herbert, *At the End of the Day* (London: William Heinemann, 1954)

Moran, Lord, *The Anatomy of Courage* (London: Constable, 1945)

Nicolson, Nigel, *Long Life* (London: Weidenfeld & Nicolson, 1997)

Norman, Frank A., *Whitehall to West Indies* (London: Bodley Head, 1952)

Percy, Eustace, *Some Memories* (London: Eyre & Spottiswoode, 1958)

Reith, J. C. W., *Into the Wind* (London: Hodder & Stoughton, 1949)

Ribbentrop, Joachim von, *The Ribbentrop Memoirs* (London: Weidenfeld & Nicolson, 1954)

Ribbentrop, Rudolf von, *Mein Vater Joachim von Ribbentrop* (Graz: Ares, 2008)

Riley, Norman, *999 and All That* (London: Victor Gollancz, 1940)

Schellenberg, Walter, *The Schellenberg Memoirs* (reprinted as *Schellenberg*) (London: Mayflower, 1965)

Schmidt, Paul, *Statist auf Diplomatischer Bühne 1923–45* (Bonn: Athenäum, 1949)

Selby, Sir Walford, *Diplomatic Twilight 1930–1940* (London: John Murray, 1953)

Simon, Viscount, *Retrospect: The Memoirs of the Rt. Hon. Viscount Simon GCSI, GCVO* (London: Hutchinson, 1952)

Sonnleithner, Franz von, *Als Diplomat im 'Führerhauptquartier'* (Munich: Langen Müller, 1989)

Spears, Edward L., *Assignment to Catastrophe*, 2 vols (London: Heinemann, 1954)

Spitzy, Reinhard, *How We Squandered the Reich* (Wilby, Norfolk: Michael Russell, 1997)

Spitzy, Reinhard, *So haben wir das Reich verspielt: Bekenntnisse eines Illegalen* (Munich: Langen Müller, 1986)

Strang, Lord, *Home and Abroad* (London: André Deutsch, 1956)

Stuart, Sir Campbell, *Opportunity Knocks Once* (London: Collins, 1952)

Stuart, Sir Campbell, *Secrets of Crewe House: The Story of a Famous Campaign* (London: Hodder & Stoughton, 1920)

Stuart, James, *Within the Fringe: An Autobiography* (London: Bodley Head, 1967)

Swinton, Earl of, with James D. Margach, *Sixty Years of Power: Some Memories of the Men Who Wielded It* (London: Hutchinson, 1966)

Swinton, Viscount, *I Remember* (London: Hutchinson, 1948)

Tennant, Ernest W. D., *True Account* (London: Max Parrish, 1957)

Thornton-Kemsley, Colin, *Through Wind and Tides* (Montrose: Standard Press, 1974)

Tree, Ronald, *When the Moon Was High: Memoirs of Peace and War 1897–1942* (London: Macmillan, 1975)

Ustinov, Peter, *Dear Me* (London: Heinemann, 1977)

Vansittart, Lord, *The Mist Procession: The Autobiography of Lord Vansittart* (London: Hutchinson, 1958)

Weizsäcker, Ernst von, *Memoirs of Ernst von Weizsäcker* (London: Victor Gollancz, 1951)

Weizsäcker, Ernst von, *Erinnerungen* (Munich: P. List, 1950)

Westminster, Loelia, Duchess of, *Grace and Favour: The Memoirs of Loelia, Duchess of Westminster* (London: Weidenfeld & Nicolson, 1961)

Woolton, Earl of, *The Memoirs of the Rt. Hon. the Earl of Woolton* (London: Cassell, 1959)

## SECONDARY WORKS

Aldrich, Richard, and Rory Cormac, *The Black Door: Spies, Secret Intelligence and British Prime Ministers* (London: William Collins, 2016)

Andrew, Christopher, *Defence of the Realm: The Authorized History of MI5* (London: Allen Lane, 2009)

Aster, Sidney, *1939: The Making of the Second World War* (London: André Deutsch, 1973)

Beckett, Francis, *Clem Attlee* (London: Richard Cohen, 1997)

Bell, Peter, *Chamberlain, Germany and Japan 1933–34* (Basingstoke: Macmillan, 1996)

Bethell, Nicholas, *The War Hitler Won, September 1939* (London: Allen Lane, 1972)

Bialer, Uri, *The Shadow of the Bomber: The Fear of Air Attack and British Politics 1932–1939* (London: Royal Historical Society, 1980)

Birkenhead, Earl of, *Halifax: The Life of Lord Halifax* (London: Hamish Hamilton, 1965)

Birkenhead, Earl of, *The Prof in Two Worlds. The Official Life of Professor Frederick Lindemann, Viscount Cherwell* (London: Collins, 1961)

Bloch, Michael, *Ribbentrop* (London: Bantam Press, 1992)

Bosworth, R. J. B., *Mussolini* (London: Hodder Arnold, 2002)

Bourne, Richard, *Lords of Fleet Street: The Harmsworth Dynasty* (London: Unwin Hyman, 1990)

Bower, Tom, *Tiny Rowland: A Rebel Tycoon* (London: Heinemann, 1993)

Boyle, Andrew, *Montagu Norman: A Biography* (London: Cassell, 1967)

Bradford, Sarah, *George VI* (London: Fontana, 1991)

Brendon, Piers, *The Dark Valley: A Panorama of the 1930s* (London: Jonathan Cape, 2000)

Briggs, Asa, *Governing the BBC* (London: BBC, 1979)

Briggs, Asa, *The History of Broadcasting in the United Kingdom, Vol. 2: The Golden Age of Wireless* (London and Oxford: Oxford University Press, 1961–95)

Bryant, Arthur, *Stanley Baldwin: A Tribute* (London: Hamish Hamilton, 1937)

Bullock, Alan, *The Life and Times of Ernest Bevin, Vol. 1: Trade Union Leader 1881–1940* (London: Heinemann, 1960)

Byrne, Paula, *Mad World: Evelyn Waugh and the Secrets of Brideshead* (London: HarperPress, 2009)

Campbell, John, *Lloyd George: The Goat in the Wilderness 1922–1931* (London: Jonathan Cape, 1977)

Charmley, John, *Chamberlain and the Lost Peace* (London: Macmillan, 1991)

Charmley, John, *Churchill: An End to Glory – a Political Biography* (London: Hodder & Stoughton, 1993)

Charmley, John, *Lord Lloyd and the Decline of the British Empire* (London: Weidenfeld & Nicolson, 1987)

Chisholm, Anne and Michael Davie, *Lord Beaverbrook: A Life* (London: Hutchinson, 1992)

Churchill, Randolph S., *Winston S. Churchill, Vol. 2: Young Statesman 1901–1914* (London: Heinemann, 1967)

Cockett, Richard, *Twilight of Truth: Chamberlain, appeasement and the manipulation of the press* (London: Weidenfeld & Nicolson, 1989)

Coombs, David, with Minnie Churchill, *Sir Winston Churchill: His Life and His Paintings* (Dorset: Ware House, 2011)

Cosgrave, Patrick, *R. A. Butler: An English Life* (London: Quartet, 1981)

Cowling, Maurice, *The Impact of Hitler: British Politics and British Policy 1933–1940* (London: Cambridge University Press, 1975)

Cross, Colin, *Adolf Hitler: 1936–1945* (London: Coronet, 1974)

Cross, J. A., *Lord Swinton* (Oxford: Clarendon Press, 1982)

Cruickshank, Charles, *The Fourth Arm: Psychological Warfare 1938–1945* (London: Davis-Poynter, 1977)

Dale, H. E., *The Higher Civil Service of Great Britain* (London: Oxford University Press, 1941)

Dallek, Robert, *Franklin D. Roosevelt and American Foreign Policy 1932–1945* (New York: Oxford University Press, 1979)

Day, Peter, *The Bedbug: Klop Ustinov, Britain's Most Ingenious Spy* (London: Biteback, 2015)

Dinshaw, Minoo, *Outlandish Knight: The Byzantine life of Steven Runciman* (London: Allen Lane, 2016)

Dobbs, Michael, *Winston's War* (London: HarperCollins, 2002)

Dorril, Steven, *MI6: Inside the Covert World of Her Majesty's Secret Intelligence Service* (New York: Free Press, 2000)

Dutton, David, *Neville Chamberlain* (London: Arnold, 2001)

Dutton, David, *Simon: A Political Biography of Sir John Simon* (London: Aurum, 1992)

Eberle, Henrik, and Mathias Uhl, *The Hitler Book: The Secret Dossier Prepared for Stalin* (London: John Murray, 2005)

Evans, Sir Trevor Maldwyn, *Bevin* (London: George Allen & Unwin, 1946)

Faber, David, *Munich: The 1938 Appeasement Crisis* (London: Simon & Schuster, 2008)

Farman, Christopher, *The General Strike, May 1926* (London: Rupert Hart-Davis, 1972)

Field, Leslie, *Bendor: The Golden Duke of Westminister* (London: Weidenfeld & Nicolson, 1983)

Flaubert, Gustave, *Madame Bovary* (Paris: Gallimard, 1972)

Foot, Michael, *Aneurin Bevan: A Biography, Vol. 1: 1897–1945* (London: MacGibbon & Kee, 1962)

Foot, Michael, *Aneurin Bevan: A Biography, Vol. 2: 1945–1960* (London: Davis-Poynter, 1973)

Furse, Anthony, *Wilfrid Freeman: The Genius behind Allied Air Supremacy 1939–1945* (Staplehurst: Spellmount, 2000)

Gannon, Franklin Reid, *The British Press and Germany 1936–1939* (Oxford: Clarendon Press, 1971)

Garnett, David, *The Secret History of PWE: The Political Warfare Executive 1939–1945* (London: St Ermin's Press, 2002)

Gilbert, Martin, *Prophet of Truth: Winston S. Churchill 1922–1939* (London: Minerva, 1990)

Gilbert, Martin, and Richard Gott, *The Appeasers* (London: Weidenfeld & Nicolson, 1963)

Gladden, E. N., *The Civil Service: Its Problems and Future*, 2nd edition (London: Staples Press, 1948)

Gladden, E. N., *Civil Service or Bureaucracy?* (London: Staples Press, 1956)

Griffiths, Richard, *Fellow Travellers of the Right: British Enthusiasts for Nazi Germany 1933–39* (London: Constable, 1980)

Griffiths, Richard, *Patriotism Perverted: Captain Ramsay, the Right Club and British Anti-Semitism 1939–40* (London: Constable, 1998)

Hamann, Brigitte, *Winifred Wagner: A Life at the Heart of Hitler's Bayreuth* (London: Granta, 2005)

Harris, John, *Rudolf Hess: The British Illusion of Peace* (Northampton: Jena, 2010)

Harris, Kenneth, *Attlee* (London: Weidenfeld & Nicolson, 1984)

Hart-Davis, Duff, *The House the Berrys Built: Inside the Telegraph 1928–1986* (London: Hodder & Stoughton, 1990)

Hart-Davis, Duff, *Man of War: The Secret Life of Captain Alan Hillgarth – Officer, Adventurer, Agent* (London: Century, 2012)

Hennessy, Elizabeth, *A Domestic History of the Bank of England 1930–1960* (Cambridge: Cambridge University Press, 1992)

Hennessy, Peter, *Whitehall* (London: Secker & Warburg, 1989)

Hildebrand, Klaus, *The Foreign Policy of the Third Reich* (London: B. T. Batsford, 1973)

Hinsley, F. H., et al., *British Intelligence in the Second World War: Its Influence on Strategy and Operations, Vol. 1* (London: HMSO, 1979)

Hobson, Harold, Phillip Knightley and Leonard Russell, *The Pearl of Days: An Intimate Memoir of the Sunday Times 1822–1972* (London: Hamish Hamilton, 1972)

Howard, Anthony, *Rab: The Life of R. A. Butler* (London: Jonathan Cape, 1987)

Hyde, H. Montgomery, *Baldwin: The Unexpected Prime Minister* (London: Hart-Davis MacGibbon, 1973)

Irving, David, *The Rise and Fall of the Luftwaffe: The Life of Luftwaffe Marshal Erhard Milch* (London: Weidenfeld & Nicolson, 1973)

Jago, Michael, *Clement Attlee: The Inevitable Prime Minister* (London: Biteback, 2014)

James, Robert Rhodes, *A Spirit Undaunted: The Political Role of George VI* (London: Little, Brown, 1998)

Jeffery, Keith, *MI6: The History of the Secret Intelligence Service 1909–1949* (London: Bloomsbury, 2010)

Jenkins, Roy, *Churchill* (London: Macmillan, 2001)

Johnson, David, *Righteous Deception: German Officers against Hitler* (Westport, CT: Praeger, 2001)

Kavanagh, Dennis, and Anthony Seldon, *The Powers behind the Prime Minister: the Hidden Influence of Number Ten* (London: HarperCollins, 1999)

Kershaw, Ian, *Hitler 1936–1945: Nemesis* (London: Allen Lane, 2000)

Kershaw, Ian, *Making Friends with Hitler: Lord Londonderry and Britain's Road to War* (London: Allen Lane, 2004)

Koss, Stephen, *The Rise and Fall of the Political Press in Britain*, 2 vols (London: Hamish Hamilton, 1981–84)

Kynaston, David, *Till Time's Last Sand: A History of the Bank of England 1694–2013* (London: Bloomsbury, 2017)

Lees-Milne, James, *Ancestral Voices* (London: Chatto & Windus, 1975)

Longerich, Peter, *Goebbels: A Biography* (London: Bodley Head, 2015)

Lough, David, *No More Champagne: Churchill and His Money* (London: Head of Zeus, 2016)

Lowe, Rodney, *Adjusting To Democracy: The Role of the Ministry of Labour in British Politics 1916–1939* (Oxford: Clarendon Press, 1986)

McDonald, Iverach, *A Man of The Times: Talks and Travels in a Disrupted World* (London: Hamish Hamilton, 1976)

MacDonogh, Giles, *1938: Hitler's Gamble* (London: Constable, 2009)

McDonough, Frank, *Neville Chamberlain, Appeasement and the British Road to War* (Manchester: Manchester University Press, 1998)

McKinstry, Leo, *Spitfire: Portrait of a Legend* (London: John Murray, 2007)

McLaine, Ian, *Ministry of Morale: Home Front Morale and the Ministry of Information in World War II* (London: Allen & Unwin, 1979)

Macleod, Iain, *Neville Chamberlain* (London: Frederick Muller, 1961)

Madge, Charles, and Tom Harrisson, *Britain by Mass-Observation* (Harmondsworth: Penguin, 1939)

Maiolo, Joe, *Cry Havoc: The Arms Race and the Second World War 1931–41* (London: John Murray, 2010)

Middlemas, Keith, *Diplomacy of Illusion: The British Government and Germany 1937–39* (London: Weidenfeld & Nicolson, 1972)

Middlemas, Keith, and John Barnes, *Baldwin: A Biography* (London: Weidenfeld & Nicolson, 1969)

Moran, Lord, *Winston Churchill: The Struggle for Survival 1940–1965* (London: Constable, 1966)

Mosley, Leonard, *On Borrowed Time: How World War II Began* (London: Weidenfeld & Nicolson, 1969)

Murphy, J. T., *Labour's Big Three: A Biographical Study of Clement Attlee, Herbert Morrison and Ernest Bevin* (London: Bodley Head, 1948)

Murphy, Philip, *Alan Lennox-Boyd: A Biography* (London: I. B. Tauris, 1999)

Naylor, John F., *A Man and an Institution: Sir Maurice Hankey, the Cabinet Secretariat and the Custody of Cabinet Secrecy* (Cambridge: Cambridge University Press, 1984)

Neville, Peter, *Appeasing Hitler: The Diplomacy of Sir Nevile Henderson* (Basingstoke: Macmillan, 1999)

Newman, Simon, *March 1939: The British Guarantee to Poland – a Study in the Continuity of British Foreign Policy* (Oxford: Clarendon Press, 1976)

O'Halpin, Eunan, *Head of the Civil Service: A Study of Sir Warren Fisher* (London: Routledge, 1989)

Overy, Richard, *Goering: The 'Iron Man'* (London: Routledge & Kegan Paul, 1984)

Overy, Richard, *Interrogations: The Nazi Elite in Allied Hands 1945* (London: Allen Lane, 2001)

Padfield, Peter, *Hess, Hitler and Churchill: The Real Turning Point of the Second World War – a Secret History* (London: Icon, 2013)

Parker, R. A. C., *Chamberlain and Appeasement* (Basingstoke: Macmillan, 1993)

Parker, R. A. C., *Churchill and Appeasement* (London: Macmillan, 2000)

Peden, G. C., *Arms, Economics and British Strategy: From Dreadnoughts to Hydrogen Bombs* (Cambridge: Cambridge University Press, 2007)

Peden, G. C., *British Economic and Social Policy: Lloyd George to Margaret Thatcher* (Oxford: Philip Allan, 1995)

Peden, G. C., *British Rearmament and the Treasury 1932–1939* (Edinburgh: Scottish Academic Press, 1979)

Peden, G. C., *The Treasury and British Public Policy 1906–1959* (Oxford: Oxford University Press, 2000)

Perkins, Anne, *A Very British Strike: 3 May–12 May 1926* (London: Macmillan, 2006)

Phillips, Adrian, *The King Who Had to Go: Edward VIII, Mrs Simpson and the Hidden Politics of the Abdication Crisis* (London: Biteback, 2016)

Pile, Jonathan, *Churchill's Secret Enemy* (Createspace, 2012)

Pugh, Martin, *'Hurrah for the Blackshirts!': Fascists and Fascism in Britain between the Wars* (London: Jonathan Cape, 2005)

Quartararo, Rosaria, *Roma tra Londra e Berlino: la politica estera fascista dal 1930 al 1940* (Rome: Bonacci, 1980)

Ramsden, John, *The Age of Balfour and Baldwin 1902–1940* (London: Longman, 1978)

Read, Donald, *The Power of News: The History of Reuters*, 2nd ed. (Oxford: Oxford University Press, 1999)

Reader, W. J., *Architect of Air Power: The Life of The First Viscount Weir of Eastwood 1877–1959* (London: Collins, 1968)

Ritchie, Sebastian, *Industry and Air Power: The Expansion of British Aircraft Production 1935–41* (London: Frank Cass, 1997)

Roberts, Andrew, *Eminent Churchillians* (London: Weidenfeld & Nicolson, 1994)

Roberts, Andrew, *The Holy Fox: A Biography of Lord Halifax* (London: Papermac, 1992)

Rose, Norman, *Harold Nicolson* (London: Jonathan Cape, 2005)

Rose, Norman, *Vansittart: Study of a Diplomat* (London: Heinemann, 1978)

Roseveare, Henry, *The Treasury: The Evolution of a British Institution* (London: Allen Lane, 1969)

Ruggiero, John, *Neville Chamberlain and British Rearmament: Pride, Prejudice, and Politics* (Westport, CT: Greenwood Press, 1999)

Sayers, R. S., *The Bank of England 1891–1944*, 3 vols (Cambridge: Cambridge University Press, 1976)

Self, Robert, *Neville Chamberlain: A Biography* (Aldershot: Ashgate, 2006)

Seymour-Ure, Colin, *David Low* (London: Secker & Warburg, 1985)

Shay, Robert Paul Jr, *British Rearmament in the Thirties: Politics and Profits* (Princeton: Princeton University Press, 1977)

Shore, Zachary, *What Hitler Knew: The Battle for Information in Nazi Foreign Policy* (New York: Oxford University Press, 2003)

Smart, Nick, *Neville Chamberlain* (Abingdon: Routledge, 2009)

Smith, H. Llewellyn, *The Board of Trade* (London: G. P. Putnam's Sons, 1928)

Stafford, David, *Churchill and Secret Service* (London: John Murray, 1997)

Steiner, Zara, *The Triumph of the Dark: European International History 1933–1939* (Oxford: Oxford University Press, 2013)

Stewart, Graham, *Burying Caesar: Churchill, Chamberlain and the Battle for the Tory Party* (London: Weidenfeld & Nicolson, 1999)

Taylor, A. J. P., *Beaverbrook* (London: Hamish Hamilton, 1972)

Taylor, A. J. P., *The Origins of the Second World War* (London: Hamish Hamilton, 1961)

Taylor, S. J., *The Great Outsiders: Northcliffe, Rothermere and the Daily Mail* (London: Weidenfeld & Nicolson, 1996)

Taylor, Telford, *Munich: The Price of Peace* (London: Hodder & Stoughton, 1979)

Theakston, Kevin, *Leadership In Whitehall* (Basingstoke: Macmillan, 1999)

Thomas-Symonds, Nicklaus, *Attlee: A Life in Politics* (London: I. B. Tauris, 2010)

Thompson, J. Lee, *Politicians, the Press, and Propaganda: Lord Northcliffe and the Great War 1914–1919* (Kent, OH: Kent State University Press, 1999)

Thompson, Neville, *The Anti-Appeasers: Conservative Opposition to Appeasement in the 1930s* (Oxford: Clarendon Press, 1971)

Thorpe, D. R., *Alec Douglas-Home* (London: Sinclair-Stevenson, 1996)

Toye, Richard, *Lloyd George & Churchill: Rivals for Greatness* (London: Macmillan, 2007)

Trevor-Roper, H. R., *Historical Essays* (London: Macmillan, 1957)

Trevor-Roper, H. R., *The Last Days of Hitler* (London: Macmillan, 1947)

Turner, John, *Lloyd George's Secretariat* (Cambridge: Cambridge University Press, 1980)

Vyšný, Paul, *The Runciman Mission to Czechoslovakia 1938: Prelude to Munich* (Basingstoke: Palgrave Macmillan, 2003)

Wark, Wesley K., *The Ultimate Enemy: British Intelligence and Nazi Germany 1933–1939* (London: I. B. Tauris, 1985)

Watt, Donald Cameron, *How War Came: the Immediate Origins of the Second World War 1938–1939* (London: Heinemann, 1989)

Watt, Donald Cameron, *Personalities and Policies: Studies in the Formulation of British Foreign Policy in the Twentieth Century* (Notre Dame, IN: University of Notre Dame Press, 1965)

West, W. J., *Truth Betrayed* (London: Gerald Duckworth, 1987)

Wheeler-Bennett, John, *Munich: Prologue to Tragedy* (London: Macmillan, 1948)

Williams, Francis, *Ernest Bevin: Portrait of a Great Englishman* (London: Hutchinson, 1952)

Williamson, Philip, *Stanley Baldwin: Conservative Leadership and National Values* (Cambridge: Cambridge University Press, 1999)

Wilson, Thomas, *Churchill and the Prof* (London: Cassell, 1995)

Young, G. M., *Stanley Baldwin* (London: Rupert Hart-Davis, 1952)

Young, Kenneth, *Churchill and Beaverbrook: A Study in Friendship and Politics* (London: Eyre & Spottiswoode, 1966)


## JOURNAL ARTICLES

Adamthwaite, Anthony, 'The British Government and the Media', *Journal of Contemporary History*, vol. 18, no. 2 (1983), pp. 281–97

Blaazer, David, 'Finance and the End of Appeasement: The Bank of England, the National Government and the Czech Gold', *Journal of Contemporary History*, vol. 40, no. 1 (2005), pp. 25–39

Cockett, R. B., 'Ball, Chamberlain and *Truth*', *Historical Journal*, vol. 33, no. 1 (1990), pp. 131–42

Gilbert, Martin, 'Horace Wilson: Man of Munich?', *History Today*, October 1982

Glueckstein, Fred, 'Churchill as Bricklayer', *Finest Hour*, Winter 2012–13, p. 34

Henke, Josef, 'Hitler und England Mitte August 1939: Ein Dokument zur Rolle Fritz Hesses in den Deutschbritischen Beziehungen am Vorabend des Zweiten Weltkrieges', *Vierteljahrsshefte für Zeitgeschichte*, vol. 21, no. 2 (1973), pp. 231–42

Louis, W. Roger, 'Colonial Appeasement 1936–1938', *Revue belge de philologie et d'histoire*, vol. 49, no. 4 (1971), pp. 1175–91

Lowe, Rodney, and Richard Roberts, 'Sir Horace Wilson 1900–1935: The Making of a Mandarin', *Historical Journal*, vol. 30, no. 3 (1987), pp. 641–62

MacDonald, C. A., 'Economic Appeasement and the German "Moderates" 1937–1939: An Introductory Essay', *Past and Present*, vol. 56 (1972), pp. 105–35

Mills, William C., 'Sir Joseph Ball, Adrian Dingli, and Neville Chamberlain's "Secret Channel" to Italy 1937–1940', *International History Review*, vol. 24, no. 2 (2002), pp. 278–317

Parker, R. A. C., 'British Rearmament 1936–9: Treasury, Trade Unions and Skilled Labour', *English Historical Review*, vol. 96, no. 379 (1981), pp. 306–43

Peden, G. C., 'Sir Horace Wilson and Appeasement', *Historical Journal*, vol. 53, no. 4 (2010), pp. 983–1014

Phillips, Adrian, 'Chronicle of a Conspiracy Foretold: MI5, Churchill and the "King's Party" in the Abdication Crisis', *Conservative History Journal*, vol. 2, no. 5 (2017)

Stafford, Paul, 'Political Autobiography and the Art of the Plausible: R. A. Butler at the Foreign Office 1938–1939', *Historical Journal*, vol. 28, no. 4 (1985), pp. 901–22

Strang, G. Bruce, 'Once More unto the Breach: Britain's Guarantee to Poland, March 1939', *Journal of Contemporary History*, vol. 31, no. 4 (1996), pp. 721–52

Waddington, G. T., '"An Idyllic and Unruffled Atmosphere of Complete Anglo-German Misunderstanding": Aspects of the Operations of the Dienststelle Ribbentrop in Great Britain 1934–1938', *History*, vol. 82, no. 265 (1997), pp. 44–72

Willcox, Temple, 'Projection or Publicity? Rival Concepts in the Pre-War Planning of the British Ministry of Information', *Journal of Contemporary History*, vol. 18, no. 1 (1983), pp. 97–116

Winnifrith, John, 'Edward Ettingdean Bridges', *Biographical Memoirs of Fellows of the Royal Society*, vol. 16 (1970), pp. 38–56

## PERIODICALS

*Truth*
*The Times*

# ACKNOWLEDGEMENTS

This book has taken an unusually long time to write as it gradually evolved from my MPhil thesis on Sir Horace Wilson, which I wrote almost fifteen years ago. The list of people who have helped me along the way is correspondingly long.

Professor Nick Crowson of Birmingham University took me on as a graduate student and set me off on my long quest to track Sir Horace Wilson through legend and into history. The late Sir Martin Gilbert provided limitless inspiration and encouragement when I pursued my research into Sir Horace Wilson, encouraging me unfailingly to build on his pioneering work. He most kindly gave me a copy of the notes of his interviews with Wilson. Professor Eunan O'Halpin of Trinity College, Dublin, and Professor George Peden of Stirling University guided me through the higher reaches of the British Civil Service. My former colleague Bernard (Lord) Donoughue explained clearly the importance of power geography at 10 Downing Street. Associate Professor David Blaazer and Professor Neville Wylie each provided vital guidance on the Czech gold affair. Any errors in the book are of course my own.

Dr Eva Hesse was kind enough to spare the time to share with me her memories of her father and his time in London.

I am especially grateful to a number of individuals who have allowed me access to papers still in their personal possession as well as being immensely hospitable when I visited them: Lord and the late Lady Crathorne, at Yarm; Mrs Virginia Dessain kindly allowed me access to the personal papers of her grandfather Sir Stephen Tallents; Mrs Annie Pollock showed me the papers of her grandfather Sir Warren Fisher. The staff and volunteers at Wightwick Manor showed me another facet of the work of the National Trust.

My thanks go to everyone at the following archives who assisted me in my research: the Churchill Archives Centre, most especially Andrew Riley, who has been unstinting with his time, efforts and advice; the Cadbury Research Library's Special Collections at the University of Birmingham, in particular Martin Killeen; the Bank of England Archives, with special thanks to Margherita Orlando; John Entwisle, who opened the door to the treasure trove of the Reuters Archive at the National Archives at Kew; Bundesarchiv, Koblenz; Special Collections at Cambridge University Library; Trinity College, Cambridge; National Library of Wales, Aberystwyth; British Library, London; Special Collections at the Bodleian Library, Oxford. Dr John Boneham of the British Library gave me precious help in gaining access to crucial material.

A number of members and staff of the Flyfishers' Club sprang readily to my assistance in tracing the photograph of Chamberlain with Sir Joseph Ball and researching its origin: Emma Carter, Peter Hayes and Andrew Herd. Terry Mace delved into his treasure trove of aviation photos on my behalf. Colin Panter and everyone else at PA Images proved how a top-class research service makes a good archive great.

The Cadbury Research Library's Special Collections at the University of Birmingham has kindly granted me permission to quote from the Neville Chamberlain papers. Every effort has been made to trace copyright holders and to obtain their permission for the use of copyright material. I apologise for any errors or omissions in the above list and would be grateful if notified of any corrections that should be incorporated in future reprints or new editions of this book.

My brother David delved into his awesome knowledge of the early church to put Winston Churchill's allusions to St Anthony into perspective.

My agent, Robert Dudley, was an inexhaustible source of wise counsel and encouragement. Everyone at Biteback and Pegasus lent their enthusiasm and support all along the way, most especially Olivia Beattie and my editor, Jonathan Wadman, both of whose penetrating comments improved the manuscript throughout.

Lastly, this book would not have been possible without the help of my wife Sheila, whom I wish to thank for her advice, patience and support.

# INDEX

Amery, Leopold, 91, 277, 338, 371
Anderson, Sir John, 110, 217, 361
anti-Semitism,
  Chamberlain accuses ship-owner of
    profiteering, 144
  British public opinion on, 223
  *Kristallnacht* pogrom, 227–228
  Chamberlain and Wilson unsympathetic to
    Jews, 229
  Norman, 240
  alleviation of as cover for Schacht's visit to
    London, 241
  Chamberlain breaks taboo on criticising Nazi
    persecution, 258
  Drummond Wolff, 284–285
  Duke of Westminster, 287, 348
  *Truth*, 293
  Hitler believes Britain dominated by Jewish
    influence, 312
  *Truth* attacks on Hore-Belisha, 355
  Lord Stamp, 359
  Wilson criticises Woolton for campaign against,
    363
  MI5 suspects Weininger because of Jewishness,
    380
Ashton-Gwatkin, Frank,
  chosen for Runciman mission, 159
  false optimism on Czechoslovakia, 162
  refuses to discuss matters of substance with
    Czech observers at Munich, 185
  Schacht explains political reality of Germany
    to, 242
  supports German expansion in south-east
    Europe, 244
  proposes to Ribbentrop that Wilson visit him,
    245–246
  reports German plan to seize remainder of
    Czechoslovakia, 256
  mentioned, 160, 162, 185, 383
Atholl, Duchess of, 218
Attlee, Clement, 122, 371–2, 378, 379, 380

Baldwin, Stanley,
  in abdication crisis, 28–29, 35
  claims 'bomber will always get through', 114
  commits government to air 'parity' with
    Germany, 115
  declines to speak in favour of Chamberlain, 363
mentioned, 16, 17, 18, 21, 22, 23, 24, 27, 30, 31, 32,
    33, 34, 35, 37, 38, 39, 40, 41, 42, 43, 45, 46, 50,
    57, 58, 59, 61, 88, 97, 102, 104, 105, 107, 116, 117,
    128, 129, 153, 197, 200, 234, 236, 275, 294, 347,
    362, 373, 379
Ball, Sir Joseph,
  background, 51–53
  relationship with Chamberlain, 51–55
  opens secret channel to Italians, 62–63
  discloses British code-breaking success to
    Italians, 67
  helps arrange conversation between
    Chamberlain and Grandi, 72–74
  briefs Lobby correspondents, 102
  attempts to infiltrate Churchill's proposed visit
    to Czechoslovakia, 136–7
  proposes summit between Chamberlain and
    Mussolini, 143
  organises Chamberlain's broadcasts on Radio
    Luxemburg, 211–212
  boasts of tapping phones of anti-appeasement
    MPs, 220
  advises that France should concede to Italians,
    269–271
  new version of secret channel to Rome,
    269–270
  passes Italian flattery on to Chamberlain, 271
  dinner with Drummond Wolff, Wilson and
    Wohlthat, 287
  encourages Drummond Wolff's contacts, 287
  relationship with Duke of Westminster, 287
  bars Drummond Wolff from further
    involvement in German contacts, 288–289,
    291
  clumsy overtures to Wohlthat, 288
  controls *Truth*, 293, 355
  discloses planned date of general election to
    Wohlthat, 296–297

Ball, Sir Joseph, *cont.*
  fears Churchill might sabotage negotiated
    settlement, 349
  becomes very pro-Italian, 365
  sends Dingli to Rome, 366
  tries to persuade Chamberlain to reply to
    Italians, 368
  deputy chairman of Security Executive, 379
  lies about his secret channel to Italy, 386–387
  mentioned, xiv, 54, 55, 66, 68, 73, 74, 105, 124,
    136, 144, 212, 250, 252, 257, 264, 267, 270,
    272, 284, 309, 346, 354, 367, 381
Bastianini, Giuseppe, 366, 386
BBC,
  instructed not to comment on colonies scheme,
    91
  Ball believes government can control, 105
  and government, 105–106
  Reith and, 106–107
  content influenced by government, 108–110
  Wilson's role in picking new Director-General, 111
Beaverbrook, Lord,
  and King's Party, 32–33
  supports appeasement, 103
  gives Vickers management of Castle Bromwich
    factory, 202
  links to Hoare, 248, 250
  and *Guilty Men*, 378
  mentioned, 103, 247, 316, 346, 363
Beck, Józef, 279
Beneš, Edvard,
  obscene abuse of Chamberlain and Wilson,
    160, 172
  mentioned, 133, 161, 171, 178, 182, 186, 222
Bocchini, Arturo, 269
Bonnet, Georges,
  in London during Munich crisis, 172, 174–175,
    179
  works with Phipps to make Daladier appease
    Italy, 271–272
  mentioned, 180, 271, 272, 338
Boothby, Bob,
  Czech assets affair, 303–306
  forced to resign, 380–82
  mentioned, 215, 277, 301, 302, 306
Bracken, Brendan, 215, 235, 301, 302, 365, 372, 373
Bridges, Edward,
  new Cabinet Secretary, 193–194
  disapproves of Wilson in War Cabinet, 344–345
  mentioned, 147, 206, 207, 355
Brocket, Lord, 263, 264, 285, 288, 359
Bruce-Gardner, Sir Charles,
  given authority to troubleshoot delays
    in aircraft production, 120–21tense
    relationship with Lord Swinton, 147–151
  wants to boost production by ordering
    obsolescent aircraft, 149–150
  feeds Wilson arguments against ministry of
    Supply, 200

satisfied that aircraft production figures are
    increasing, 200–201
  close to Norman, 201
  mentioned, 124, 125, 152, 153, 154, 155, 199, 240,
    354, 362
Bruce-Lockhart, Robert,
  believes rejected for Runciman mission as too
    knowledgeable, 159–160
Bryant, Arthur,
  praise for Chamberlain, 294–295
  Hewel tells him Hitler in no hurry over Danzig,
    295
  mentioned, 296, 309, 313, 320
Buccleuch, Duke of, 263, 288, 348
Burgin, Leslie, 275
Butler, Richard 'Rab',
  background, 127–129
  ministerial career guided by Wilson, 128
  tells German embassy Britain wants friendship,
    129–130
  only minister to support Chamberlain's view of
    Soviets, 281
  drafts reply to Hitler's letter with Wilson, 337
  tells Italians that government's war aims
    different to Churchill's, 350
  Wilson sends to Ministry of Labour, 354
  mentioned, 47, 48, 50, 59, 76, 77, 131, 139, 277,
    309, 323, 338, 343, 362, 367

Cadogan, Sir Alexander 'Alec',
  replaces Vansittart, 60–61
  and Roosevelt initiative, 70
  pragmatic acquiescence in Wilson's position,
    84–86, 89
  Wilson tests his commitment to Chamberlain's
    policy, 86
  taken aback to find Wilson at Cabinet FPC
    meeting, 89
  believes Chamberlain hypnotised by Hitler, 174
  persuades Halifax to oppose Bad Godesberg
    terms, 174
  has evidence that Hitler saw Munich as
    humiliation, 224
  learns of Wilson's clandestine contacts, 226
  persuades Halifax to block political negotiations
    by Norman, 242–244
  evades calls to pressurise France on Italian
    demands, 270, 271
  confronts Wilson over covert appeasement,
    283–284
  handles Goering's intermediary, 336
  mentioned, 48, 68, 72, 77, 91, 104, 159, 166, 170,
    171, 182, 219, 223, 245, 253, 255, 258, 289,
    307, 316, 318, 337, 366
Camrose, Lord, 103, 291, 292, 312, 371
Castle Bromwich Spitfire factory,
  Wood awards project to Nuffield, 152–153
  crippled by production difficulties, 201
  Beaverbrook gives management to Vickers, 202

Chamberlain, Sir Austen, 58
Chamberlain, Ivy Lady, 68
Chamberlain, Neville,
  foreign policy goals, x–xi
  determined to conduct 'positive' foreign policy,
    xi, 41, 45
  Anglo-German Declaration, xi–xii, 7–8,
    186–187
  convinced he secured lasting peace at Munich,
    xi–xii, 189, 233–234
  opposed to Churchill's policy on Germany,
    xii–xiii
  partnership with Wilson, xiv–xv, 50–51
  first meeting with Hitler, 3–4
  misreads Hitler, 6, 173, 187, 222, 253, 257, 308, 320
  Hitler's true opinion of, 9, 10
  succeeds Baldwin as Prime Minister, 37
  background and early career, 37–38
  clashes with Churchill over rates reform, 38–39
  relishes Churchill's political difficulties, 40
  character, 41–43
  vanity, 42–43, 98–99, 211–212, 222–224, 268
  retains Wilson as advisor, 43–44
  task in foreign policy, 44–45
  balance of power in relationship with Wilson, 48
  trust between him and Wilson, 50–51
  relationship with Ball, 51–55
  takes personal charge of foreign policy, 57
  hostility to Foreign Office, 62, 65, 98, 259
  uses Ball's secret channel to make friendly
    overtures to Rome, 63–68
  opposes Roosevelt's initiative, 69–71
  determined to start formal talks with Italy,
    72–75
  recognises that Germany is more important
    than Italy, 79
  sees Halifax's invitation to Berlin as way of
    opening dialogue with Germany, 82
  enthusiasm for deal with Germany over
    colonies, 88–89
  colonies scheme grandiose and ill-thought-out,
    89–91
  and news management, 97–99
  and Wilson plan political response to criticism
    of air rearmament, 121–122, 124–125
  and Wilson believe Luftwaffe can destroy
    London, 123
  rejects Churchill's Grand Alliance, 134–135
  delighted at reception for his speech on
    Sudetenland, 135–136
  bombing of British ships puts under political
    pressure, 143–145
  relishes Churchill's misjudgement in Sandys
    affair, 145
  accepts Bruce-Gardner's claims for potential
    aircraft production, 150–51
  presents plan for British mediator in
    Czechoslovakia as fait accompli to Cabinet,
    157–158

  low opinion of Czechs, 161
  originates Plan Z, 169–170
  avoids discussing Daladier's three-power
    conference plan, 171
  insists Wilson accompanies him to Germany,
    171
  fears Luftwaffe attack on London, 173–174
  sees benefits of accepting Bad Godesberg terms,
    173–174
  sends Wilson to Berlin to outflank Cabinet,
    175–176
  recommends Czech capitulation, 182
  Hitler's letter brings hope to, 183
  announces to Parliament that Hitler has agreed
    to conference, 185
  challenges Wood on bomber strategy, 198–199
  uninterested in expert briefing on Luftwaffe, 200
  focus on narrow measure of military strength,
    201–202
  enthusiasm for broadcasts on Radio
    Luxemburg, 211–212
  angry exchange with Churchill during Munich
    debate, 214–215
  defends Wilson from criticism, 215–216
  unadventurous Cabinet reshuffle, 217
  sees Churchill's opposition to Munich as
    conspiracy, 219–220
  near to nervous breakdown, 220–21
  blames Churchill for Hitler's hostile speech, 222
  has no alternative to Halifax as Foreign
    Secretary, 223
  visit to Paris, 223–224
  believes German 'moderates' should be
    encouraged, 224
  sees Kristallnacht as obstacle to understanding
    between Britain and Germany, 229
  unsympathetic to Jews, 229
  opposed to creation of Ministry of Supply,
    233–236
  dismisses Inskip as Minister of Defence
    Coordination, 237
  secrecy over Schacht's visit to London, 241
  sees Schacht in London, 241–242
  believes economic problems will force Hitler to
    negotiate, 244–245, 253
  discusses curtailing Hoare's influence on
    propaganda with Wilson, 248
  accuses Churchill of war-mongering, 253
  in bubble of optimism, 253–255
  gives optimistic briefing on foreign affairs to
    press, 254–255
  blames effect of 'rainbow' briefing on
    journalists, 255
  unprepared for seizure of remainder of
    Czechoslovakia, 257
  initial reaction to Prague to continue with
    appeasement, 258
  insists he will go on with his policy despite
    Prague, 258

Chamberlain, Neville, *cont.*
  resists Halifax's call for resolute response to
    Prague, 258
  hardens his stance towards Hitler in
    Birmingham speech, 258–259
  proposes four-power declaration, 259
  endorses qualification of Polish guarantee by
    *The Times*, 260
  resists Churchill's call for Parliament to be
    recalled after Albania, 261
  self-confidence shaken by Prague and Albania,
    261–263
  spirits bolstered by reports from aristocratic
    visitors to Berlin, 263–264
  visits Rome with Halifax, 267–268
  snubs France's ambassador to Italy, 268
  delighted by reception of Italian crowds, 268
  political pressures on post-Prague, 273
  believes announcement of conscription well-
    timed, 276
  suspicions of Soviet Union, 278, 280–81, 282
  resists alliance with Soviet Union, 278–282
  determined to keep Churchill out of
    government, 292
  sees press campaign in favour of Churchill as
    Soviet conspiracy, 292
  relishes *Truth*'s attacks on Churchill, 293
  believes he has discreet channels to Germany,
    307
  overrules Wilson on sending Tennant to
    Germany, 309–310
  take charge of follow-up to Kemsley mission,
    316–317
  believes Hitler ready to back down over Danzig,
    320–21
  instructs Wilson to meet German intermediary,
    323
  risk taken in proposal to Dirksen, 327
  proposals made through Kemsley rejected, 329
  believes unofficial contacts hopeful, 338
  imagines war can be won without serious
    fighting, 342–343
  wartime government, 343–344
  calls Churchill to order, 345
  receptive to false overtures from Germany,
    349–350
  Nicolson criticises as naive, 350–51
  values Wilson's political advice, 353–354
  chooses Stamp to replace Simon, 358–359
  relishes diplomatic success with Italy, 366
  overrules Wilson on Dingli's 1940 mission,
    367–368
  and Norway debate, 369–370
  forced to resign, 372–373
  death of, 374
  mentioned, 1, 2, 5, 7, 9, 10, 21, 22, 25, 29, 30, 35,
    39, 45, 46, 47, 48, 49, 58, 60, 61, 76, 77, 80,
    81, 84, 85, 87, 90, 91, 93, 95, 96, 100, 101,
    102, 103, 104, 110, 111, 117, 118, 120, 127, 128,
    129, 130, 131, 137, 139, 141, 142, 147, 148, 152,
    154, 159, 160 162, 163, 164, 165, 166, 172, 177,
    178, 179, 181, 184, 186, 187, 188, 189, 191, 192,
    194, 195, 197, 204, 206, 207, 208, 209, 213,
    225, 226, 227, 228, 229, 232, 239, 240, 246,
    250, 256, 267, 268, 269, 270, 271, 272, 273,
    274, 275, 276, 277, 278, 279, 280, 281, 282,
    283, 285, 286, 289, 290, 291, 292, 293, 294,
    295, 296, 297, 298, 308, 311, 313, 314, 315, 318,
    325, 331, 332, 334, 335, 336, 339, 341, 344, 347,
    348, 355, 356, 357, 360, 361, 362, 363, 365,
    368, 370, 371, 373, 375, 377, 378, 379, 382,
    383, 386, 387, 388
Channon, Henry ('Chips'), 76, 277, 278, 280, 385
Chatfield, Admiral Lord, 237, 361
Churchill, Winston,
  clashes with Wilson at Board of Trade, xii, 13–14
  opposed to Chamberlain's policy on Germany,
    xii–xiii
  early career, 11–12
  as Chancellor of the Exchequer, 16–17
  attempts to join builders' union, 18–20
  opposition to India Bill takes him into political
    wilderness, 20–21
  reservations about Edward VIII's relationship
    with Mrs Simpson, 28
  seen by Wilson as dangerous leader of King's
    Party, 31–33
  damages his standing by support for Edward
    VIII, 33–35
  clashes with Chamberlain over rates reform,
    38–39
  political difficulties relished by Chamberlain, 40
  access to BBC restricted, 108
  adopts cause of air rearmament, 114–116
  criticises Baldwin's pessimism about air warfare,
    115
  recognises that Hitler is a danger, 115–116,
  member of Air Defence Research Committee,
    116
  confronts government with well-briefed
    criticism of air rearmament, 124–125
  promotes Grand Alliance to defend
    Czechoslovakia, 133–134
  proposed visit to Czechoslovakia, 136–137
  criticises government over bombing of British
    ships, 144
  and Sandys affair, 145
  bemoans slow progress of ADRC, 153–154
  recognises that bombers at disadvantage to
    modern fighters, 154–155
  passes on warnings from Germany of attack on
    Czechoslovakia, 162–163
  appoints Beaverbrook Minister of Aircraft
    Production, 202
  during Munich crisis, 213–214
  angry exchange with Chamberlain during
    Munich debate, 214–215
  abstains in Munich debate, 215

weakness of his support in Parliament, 215, 301
broadcast to US decrying Munich agreement,
    217
Conservative Party hostility to his views on
    Munich, 217–218
phone conversations tapped, 219–220
attacked by Germans, 227–229
Germans blame for shooting of German
    diplomat, 228
advocates creation of Ministry of Supply,
    234–235
sees *The Times* article on Polish guarantee as
    sinister, 260–61
calls for Parliament to be recalled after Albania,
    261
rejected as Minister of Supply, 275
understands importance of alliance with Soviet
    Union, 277
signs Eden's motion calling for true national
    government, 277
fails to catch Chamberlain out over Soviet
    Union, 280
accurate prediction of alliance with Soviet
    Union, 282
press campaign for his inclusion in government,
    291–293
attacked in *Truth*, 293
attacks government over Czech gold, 302
secret German emissary advises including him
    in government, 318
opposes long Parliamentary recess, 319–321
Chamberlain thinks he does not understand
    war, 342
standing in War Cabinet diluted, 343–344
minutes Chamberlain on numerous topics, 345
criticises Duke of Westminster's defeatist
    activities, 348
Ball fears Churchill might sabotage negotiated
    settlement, 349
objects to covert discussions with Germany, 349
abuses German leaders in broadcast, 350
accepts Labour call for curbs on Wilson, 372
becomes Prime Minister, 372–373
removes Wilson from Downing Street, 373
limited purge of Chamberlainites, 378–379
treatment of Wilson, 379
considers removing Wilson as head of the Civil
    Service, 382
veto on retirement jobs for Wilson, 385
mentioned, x, xii–xiii, 22, 25, 27, 28, 44, 45, 46,
    58, 61, 75, 76, 95, 97, 103, 104, 105, 120, 122,
    125, 131, 132, 135, 147, 150, 151, 152, 164, 173,
    194, 197, 200, 222, 233, 235, 236, 248, 253,
    262, 273, 278, 281, 294, 305, 321, 329, 347,
    354, 369, 370, 371, 374, 377, 380, 382, 383
Ciano, Count Galeazzo, 63, 67, 68, 73, 145, 267,
    269, 270, 366, 368
colonies scheme,
    inspired by Goering, 83,

background, 87–88
colonies scheme grandiose and ill-thought-out,
    89–91
ill-timed, 91–92
German reaction to, 92–95
appeasers try to trivialise, 95
importance in history of appeasement, 95–96
Colville, John 'Jock', 48, 206, 353, 357, 378, 384
Conwell-Evans, Philip,
    unofficial intermediary with Germany, 80–81
    Wilson jobs his advice against FO's, 85
    in Munich crisis, 183–184
    mentioned, 161, 284
Cooper, Alfred Duff, 163, 175, 182, 207, 215, 217,
    220, 227, 229, 277

Daladier, Édouard,
    attempts to organise three-power discussion on
        Czechoslovakia, 171
    in London during Munich crisis, 172, 174–175
    refuses to appease Italians, 272
    mentioned, 10, 180, 185, 213
Dalton, Hugh, 1, 343, 365
Davidson, J. C. C., 52, 53, 54
Dawson, Geoffrey,
    supports appeasement in *The Times*, 102–103
    relationship with Halifax, 102–103
    discusses wording of article on Polish guarantee
        in *The Times*, 260
    discusses article on Chatham House speech
        with Halifax, 290
    mentioned, 81, 105, 260, 378
Dietrich, Otto, 313, 314, 316, 317, 329, 330
Dingli, Adrian,
    relationship with Ball, 62–63
    warns Ribbentrop to seek alliance in Rome, 271
    mission to Rome in 1940, 366
    Balls claims was a double agent, 386
    mentioned, 72, 267, 268, 269, 367, 368
Dirksen, Herbert von,
    pessimistic despatch from London, 140
    understands importance of Wilson, 141
    discrepancies between his and Wilson's accounts
        of their conversation, 324
    surprised by Wilson's offer to abandon
        guarantee to Poland, 325
    tries to report Wilson's proposals to Ribbentrop,
        326
    mentioned, 4, 244, 264, 307, 319, 322, 323, 327,
        329, 330, 332, 336, 388
Dobbs, Michael, xiv
Drummond Wolff, Henry,
    background, 284–285
    exaggerates his role as intermediary with
        Germany, 285–286, 288
    hosts dinner for Ball, Wilson and Wohlthat, 287
    mentioned, 288, 289, 291, 296, 309, 348, 349
Dugdale, Tommy, 347, 379
Duncan, Andrew, 362

Dunglass, Lord (Alec),
  says Hitler signed Anglo-German Declaration
    perfunctorily, 8
  claims Anglo-German Declaration was astute
    manoeuvre, 187–188
  and Chamberlain's fight for survival, 370–71
  mentioned, 51, 54, 215

Eden, Anthony,
  Wilson portrays as originator of appeasement,
    ix–x
  background, 58
  resists Fisher's encroachments, 59
  clashes with Wilson over Roosevelt initiative,
    70–71
  resists formal talks over de jure recognition of
    Italian conquest of Ethiopia, 72–74
  forced into resignation, 74–75
  Parliamentary motion calling for true national
    government, 277
  limited role in Chamberlain's wartime
    government, 343–344
  blames Wilson for his dismissal, 354
  mentioned, ix–x, 46, 60, 61, 62, 63, 64, 65, 66,
    68, 69, 76, 77, 82, 84, 85, 91, 95, 98, 101,
    109, 127, 130, 142, 143, 144, 164, 173, 204,
    215, 216, 223, 227, 229, 273, 277, 363, 365,
    366, 383, 386, 387

Fass, Sir Ernest, 250, 251
Fisher, Sir Warren,
  ambitions, 22–23
  places Wilson at 10 Downing Street, 23–24
  and Wilson manipulate Chamberlain to take
    action against Edward VIII, 28–30
  tries to encroach on Foreign Office, 59–62
  criticises slow pace of air rearmament, 125
  and Wilson thwarts Hankey's plans for his own
    succession, 191–194
  fails to have Grigg appointed as his successor, 194
  vision of the head of Civil Service as chief
    adviser to Prime Minister achieved, 195
  mentioned, 30, 32, 35, 49, 107, 111, 155, 210, 240,
    247, 248, 250, 344, 361, 382
Freeman, Sir Wilfrid, 148, 153

Geyr von Schweppenburg, Leo, 264, 286
Gilbert, Sir Martin, xiv, 260
Goebbels, Josef,
  orders press attacks on Churchill and other
    opponents of appeasement, 227–229
  approves of Reuters interview with him about
    Kristallnacht, 232
  mentioned, 75, 83, 99, 185, 205, 230, 254, 290,
    316, 321, 334, 335, 337, 341
Goering, Hermann,
  bonds with Henderson, 80
  mentions colonies to Halifax, 88
  welcomes Drummond Wolff, 286

contrasting policy objectives towards Britain,
    308–309
  tries to rebuild position in unofficial contacts
    with Britain, 316
  taunts Ribbentrop, 321–322
  mentioned, 85, 87, 139, 140, 141, 142, 160, 185,
    225, 241, 245, 285, 287, 296, 323, 336, 338,
    339, 350, 360, 388
Grandi, Count Dino,
  won round to secret channel, 63
  conversation with Chamberlain, 64–65
  conversation with Chamberlain and Eden, 73
  praises Ball's assistance, 74
  mentioned, 57, 66, 67, 68, 72, 81, 145, 269, 271,
    272, 386
Greenwood, Arthur, 338, 372

Halifax, Lord,
  replaces Eden as Foreign Secretary, 76–77
  background, 77
  ambivalence of towards appeasement, 77, 290
  invited to hunting exhibition in Berlin, 82
  unsuccessful meeting with Hitler, 82–83
  visit to Germany, 82–84
  impressed by Goering, 83
  tries to stop press criticism of Hitler, 100–101
  relationship with Dawson, 102–103
  meets Wiedemann, 141
  proposed speech at Geneva, 164–166
  excluded from missions to Germany, 171, 185
  persuaded to oppose Bad Godesberg terms by
    Cadogan, 174
  acquiesces in Leeper's communique, 176
  briefs Churchill during Munich crisis, 213
  advises Chamberlain to broaden government, 216
  tells Chamberlain of Hitler's obscene comments
    on him, 222
  has evidence that Hitler saw Munich as
    humiliation, 224
  supports creation of Ministry of Supply, 237
  delays Ashton-Gwatkin's mission to Berlin, 244
  complains to Chamberlain about optimistic
    briefing on foreign affairs to press, 255
  calls for resolute response to Prague, 258
  drives through guarantees to Greece and
    Romania, 261
  visits Rome with Chamberlain, 267–268
  and doubling in size of Territorial Army, 274
  Chatham House speech, 289–290
  handles Goering's intermediary, 336
  mentioned, 3, 88, 94, 104, 110, 127, 135, 158, 159, 170,
    182, 185, 198, 214, 219, 221, 223, 226, 237, 243,
    244, 245, 263, 270, 299, 311, 314, 316, 318, 319,
    323, 330, 337, 354, 357, 363, 371, 372, 378, 388
Hankey, Sir Maurice,
  prepares political response to Churchill's
    criticisms on air, 154
  Wilson and Fisher thwart his succession plans,
    191–193

contingency plans for Ministry of Information, 205–206
counterweight to Churchill in War Cabinet, 344
mentioned, 120, 155, 194, 207, 210, 240

Harvey, Oliver, 239, 337, 383

Henderson, Sir Nevile,
appointed ambassador to Germany, 79–80
presents colonies scheme to Hitler and Ribbentrop, 92–94
despairing despatch to Halifax, 94
and Plan Z, 163, 169
opposes warning to Germans, 170
and Norman's mission to Berlin, 243–244
futile journey to Bayreuth, 317
mentioned, 3, 82, 90, 91, 95, 100, 101, 130, 166, 176, 179, 182, 205, 221, 227, 230, 232, 239, 256, 276, 335, 337, 338, 340

Henlein, Konrad,
leads Sudeten Germans, 132
visit to Hitler, 162
triggers crisis, 171
mentioned, 133, 141, 142

Hesse, Fritz,
allies with Steward against Leeper, 105
briefs Ribbentrop on importance of *The Times* article on Sudetenland, 137
seeks to present scheme for phased transfer of Sudeten districts, 183–184
sees Wilson's overture as evidence of British submissiveness, 225
tells Wilson proposals made through Dirksen rejected, 329–330
urges Wilson not to insist on guarantee to Poland, 331
brings last-ditch appeal to Wilson, 338
mentioned, 138, 140, 173, 185, 221, 226, 284, 298, 308, 326, 335, 336, 339

Hewel, Walther,
friend of Hitler, 5
falsely claims to Wilson that Hitler had been impressed by Chamberlain, 5
Wilson unaware of his true standing, 5, 331
falsely claims to Kirkpatrick that Hitler had been impressed by Chamberlain, 9
suggests that Britain sends German-speaker to talk to Hitler, 264
tells Bryant that Hitler in no hurry over Danzig, 295
gives Tennant mixed signals, 311–312
mentioned, 5, 10, 286, 296, 308, 311, 320

Hitler, Adolf,
first meeting with Chamberlain, 3–4
perfunctory attention to signature of Anglo-German declaration, 8
true opinion of Chamberlain, 9–10
ensures Halifax has more successful meeting with Goering, 83
and colonies scheme, 93–95

relishes hypocrisy of colonies scheme, 94
complains of press criticism in Britain, 100
feeds British anxiety about weakness in air power, 116
increases demands at Bad Godesberg, 172–173
furious in meeting with Wilson, 176–177
uses speech to keep door open to Chamberlain, 178–179
second meeting with Wilson convinces him that British are bluffing, 179
complains of criticism in British press, 184–185
confers with German leaders on options for Czechoslovakia, 186
complains about Vansittart's propaganda committee, 204–205
speech against British 'interference', 222
attacks Churchill, 228
determined to seize remainder of Czechoslovakia, 256–257
sees aristocratic visitors to Berlin as Chamberlain's emissaries, 264
contrasting policy objectives towards Britain, 308–309
believes Britain dominated by Jewish influence, 312
makes positive impression on Kemsley, 314–315
true motives in conversation with Kemsley, 315–316
tells military commanders of plan to attack Poland, 331–332
wants to help London save face, 334
offers guarantee of British Empire, 335
delays attack on Poland, 335–336
believes Britain might not intervene, 336
surprised at British declaration of war, 339–340
knows Britain will not attack, 341
attacks in West, 368
mentioned, x–xiv, xvi, 1, 2, 7, 35, 44, 45, 47, 73, 79, 81, 82, 83, 85, 87, 88, 91, 92, 96, 99, 101, 104, 109, 110, 115, 130, 131, 134, 137, 138, 140, 141, 142, 161, 162, 163, 165, 166, 167, 169, 170, 171, 172, 173, 174, 175, 176, 177, 178, 179, 180, 181, 182, 183, 186, 187, 188, 200, 209, 213, 214, 215, 218, 219, 224, 225, 227, 229, 230, 231, 232, 234, 239, 240, 242, 243, 244, 245, 253, 258, 259, 261, 262, 263, 269, 272, 273, 274, 278, 279, 282, 283, 285, 286, 288, 289, 291, 292, 293, 295, 296, 297, 298, 307, 310, 311, 313, 317, 318, 320, 321, 325, 326, 327, 329, 330, 337, 338, 342, 343, 348, 349, 350, 359, 367, 369, 377, 383, 387, 388

Hoare, Sir Samuel,
supports bringing Eden back into government, 216
ambitions in field of propaganda, 247–250
whitewashes Wilson, 388
mentioned, 58, 59, 76, 104, 128, 170, 223, 251, 252, 336, 347, 356, 362, 370, 371, 378

Hore-Belisha, Leslie,
    dismissed, 355
    rejected as Minister of Information because he
        was a Jew, 355
    anti-Semitic attacks on in *Truth*, 355
    mentioned, 32, 145, 233, 236, 237, 274, 356
Hudson, Rob,
    responsible for leak of Wohlthat talks, 297–298
    mentioned, 236, 237, 307, 310, 315, 325, 354,
        358, 385

Infield, Louis,
    Czech assets affair, 304–306
Inskip, Sir Thomas,
    appointed as Minister of Defence
        Coordination, 21
    influences air rearmament, 119
    swings round to favour a Ministry of Supply,
        236–237
    dismissed as Minister of Defence Coordination,
        237
    blames Wilson for his dismissal, 237, 354
    mentioned, 361

Jebb, Gladwyn, 307
Jones, Sir Roderick,
    agrees that Reuters should follow government
        guidance, 231
    offers Hitler Reuters interview, 231–232
    mentioned, 230

Kearley, Hudson, 13
Kemsley, Lord,
    mission to Hitler at Bayreuth, 312–316
    mentioned, 103, 217, 218, 317, 325, 329, 332
Kennedy, Joseph,
Kirkpatrick, Ivone, 333–334
    well briefed on Hitler's view of Chamberlain,
        8–9
    mentioned, 10, 177, 179
Kordt, Erich, 127, 130, 131, 330
Kordt, Theodor,
    passes phone intercepts to Downing Street, 160
    tells British that firm stance will trigger
        conspiracy against Hitler, 166–167
    mentioned, 161, 167, 172, 183, 318, 323, 324, 349

Leeper, Rex,
    conducts press campaign against appeasement,
        104–105
    proposes Bruce-Lockhart as Runciman's
        assistant, 159–160
    firm communique during Munich crisis, 176
    mentioned, 178, 214, 221
Lindemann, Professor Frederick, 116
Lloyd George, David, 11, 12, 13, 16, 23, 25, 37, 38, 81,
    154, 191, 192, 200, 217, 233, 234, 277, 278, 320,
    348, 378
Londonderry, Lord, 81, 116, 117

MacDonald, James Ramsay, 23, 39, 53, 82, 97, 117,
    128, 348
Macmillan, Lord, 159, 215, 235, 249, 250, 252, 301,
    347, 355
Maisky, Ivan, 136, 163, 277, 278, 292
Manenti, Mario, 269–270
Margesson, Captain David, 237, 354, 362, 378
Masaryk, Jan,
    obscene abuse of Chamberlain and Wilson,
        160, 172
    rejects Bad Godesberg terms, 174
    conversations with Churchill tapped, 219–220
    mentioned, 161, 222
MI5,
    abdication crisis, 29, 31
    Ball's career at, 51–52
    and Hitler's obscene abuse of Chamberlain, 222
    obtains copies of Hesse's letters to Ribbentrop,
        226
    warns of move on remainder of Czechoslovakia,
        256
    Wilson's oversight of, 265
    aware of Dingli's mission to Rome, 366
    suspicions of Weininger, 380–81
    mentioned, 53, 379
Milch, Erhard, 119, 154
Ministry of Information,
    Hankey's contingency plans for, 205–206
    missteps during Munich crisis, 208
    Hoare briefed on, 248
    Wilson constrains, 250–52, 345
    Hore-Belisha blocked as minister, 355
    wartime failure of, 345–348
    emblem of poor preparation for war, 347–348
    mentioned, 362, 379
Ministry of Supply,
    Churchill campaigns for, 200, 234–235
    emblem of commitment to full rearmament, 233
    Inskip and, 236–237
    attenuated version as concession to pressure,
        262, 274–275, 283
Molotov, Vyacheslav, 331–336
Morrison, William 'Shakes', 362
Mussolini, Benito,
    proposes four-power conference to settle
        Munich crisis, 6
    gains kudos by silencing propaganda to
        Palestine, 99
    importance to of news management and
        propaganda, 99
    acquiesces in *Anschluß*, 142
    seizes Albania, 261
    low opinion of Chamberlain and Halifax, 268
    reneges on agreement with Hitler, 335–336
    mentioned, x–xi, 44, 45, 59, 62, 63, 64, 66, 68,
        69, 75, 77, 81, 82, 88, 95, 98, 101, 143, 144,
        185, 204, 224, 234, 247, 251, 262, 267, 269,
        270, 271, 272, 279, 281, 282, 308, 365, 366,
        367, 368

Neurath, Konstantin von, 91, 92, 185
Nicolson, Harold,
    proposed talk censored by BBC, 109
    criticism of Wilson made public, 215
    appalled by choice of Burgin as Minister of
        Supply, 275
    dislikes Chamberlain, 276
    detects resurgence of covert appeasement, 283
    sees Chamberlain reinvigorated by resumption
        of appeasement, 293
    criticises Chamberlain and Wilson as naive, 350–51
    mentioned, 134, 292, 370, 373, 387
Nicolson, Nigel, 387
Norman, Montagu,
    background, 240–41
    secrecy over Schacht's visit to London, 241
    discusses ministerial reshuffle with Wilson,
        355, 356
    plans to remove Simon as Chancellor of the
        Exchequer, 356–357
    clashes with Simon over Czech gold, 357
    furtive visits to Downing Street, 358
    fails to get retirement jobs for Wilson, 385
    mentioned, 120, 201, 239, 242, 243, 244, 245,
        302, 360, 362, 383,
Nuffield, Lord, 152, 201

Petschek, Paul, 304–306
Phipps, Sir Eric, 61, 79, 80, 271, 272

Reith, Sir John,
    dominated by Wilson, 106–108, 110–11
    Wilson seeks appointment for, 356
    mentioned, 32, 47, 105, 109, 211, 247, 370
Reuters, 230–31
Ribbentrop, Joachim von,
    anti-British after failure of his embassy to
        London, 3, 81
    ambassador to London, 81–82
    and colonies scheme, 93–94
    uses Hesse as conduit, 225
    rejects proposal that Wilson should visit Berlin,
        245–246
    contrasting policy objectives towards Britain,
        308–309
    unreceptive to Tennant's overtures, 311–312
    demands information on Wohlthat talks, 322–323
    ignores Wilson's proposal on guarantee to
        Poland, 326
    surprised at British declaration of war, 339–340
    mentioned, 4, 5, 9, 85, 92, 110, 130, 131, 137, 138,
        139, 140, 176, 185, 221, 226, 264, 271, 284,
        285, 286, 289, 295, 310, 324, 329, 331, 332,
        334, 335, 336, 338, 350, 359, 366
Roosevelt, Franklin D.,
    proposes conference, 69–71, 74–74
    open letter to Germany and Poland asking
        them to settle differences, 333–334
    mentioned, 85, 91, 164, 186, 262, 365

Rootham, Jasper, 48
Rothermere, Lord, 103, 141, 319
Royal Air Force rearmament
    Wilson involved in xv
    Churchill calls for, 45–46, 114–115
    Wilson's sensitivity about, 108
    background, 113–114
    Baldwin pledges to maintain 'parity' with
        Luftwaffe 115–116,
    Churchill briefed on slow progress, 116, 124–125
    Swinton, 117–118
    outdistanced by Luftwaffe, 119–120
    politics of, 120–22
    administrative measures improve, 147–148
    delivery of 12,000 aircraft over two years
        approved, 150–51
    parity resurfaces as goal, 197–198
    heavy bomber strategy, 198–199
    obsolescent designs, 201
Runciman, Lord,
    Wilson's choice as mediator for Czechoslovakia,
        158–159
    seen as pro-Sudeten, 161
    mentioned, 103, 162, 164, 185, 217, 244, 319,
        332, 383

Schacht, Hjalmar Horace Greely, 88, 240, 241, 242,
    244, 245, 285
Schmidt, Paul, 4, 8, 177, 315, 340
Simon, Sir John,
    brutally cross-examines French ministers, 175,
        180
    weak performance over Czech gold debate, 302
    leads Cabinet revolt over declaration of war,
        338
    Wilson and Norman plot to replace, 356–358
    mentioned, 43, 58, 59, 76, 116, 164, 165, 170, 171,
        220, 223, 274, 302, 305, 306, 343, 360, 370,
        371, 378, 383
Sinclair, Sir Archibald, 151, 320
Spears, Edward, 136–137
Stalin, Josef,
    agrees non-aggression pact with Germany, 332
    mentioned, 278, 279
Stamp, Lord,
    Pro-Nazi, 359–360
    refuses Chancellorship, 360
    mentioned, 358, 361, 383, 384
Stanley, Oliver, 220, 245, 254, 257, 297
Steward, George,
    press officer at Downing Street, 97–98
    finds ally in Hesse, 105
    warns Hesse of Chamberlain's political
        vulnerability, 173
    aware of Hesse's standing with Ribbentrop,
        183–184
    tells Hesse Germans should only deal direct
        with Downing Street, 221–222
    mentioned, 97, 102, 109, 137, 178, 226, 243, 335

Strang, William,
    accompanies Chamberlain and Wilson to
        Germany, 2
    reservations about Anglo-German Declaration, 8
    drafts Anglo-German Declaration, 8, 187
    surprised at Halifax's acquiescence in
        Chamberlain's encroachments, 77
    instructed to list ways Munich agreement
        improved on Bad Godesberg terms, 188
    mentioned, ix, 3, 7, 175, 187, 383
Stuart, Sir Campbell,
    allies with Wilson and Fisher against Tallents,
        210–11
    runs activities in foreign propaganda as private
        fiefdom, 346
    mentioned, 251, 346
Stuart, James, 218, 318
Swinton, Lord,
    driving force in air rearmament, 117–119
    tense relationship with Bruce-Gardner, 147–151
    opposes Bruce-Gardner's support of obsolescent
        aircraft designs, 148–150
    bitterness at damage done by his removal,
        151–152, 201
    mentioned, 75, 120, 121, 122, 125, 153, 186, 189,
        200, 202, 354

Tallents, Sir Stephen,
    ambitions for Ministry of Information,
        207–209
    alienates Foreign Office, 209
    dismissed, 210
    mentioned, 211, 247, 249, 250, 346, 347
Tennant, Ernest,
    offers to act as intermediary to Ribbentrop, 309
    proposes offering Germany financial incentive
        to settle, 310
    pessimistic conversations with Ribbentrop and
        Hewel, 311–312
    mentioned, 307, 314
Thomas, J. P. L.,
    Fisher attempts to suborn, 61–62
    mentioned, 46, 69, 74, 75
Thomas, Jimmy, 22, 48, 61, 121, 240
Thornton-Kemsley, Colin, 217–218

Vansittart, Sir Robert,
    background, 60
    reasons for replacement as head of Foreign
        Office, 60
    opposes Plan Z, 170
    chairs committee on propaganda, 204–205
    mentioned, 3, 61, 62, 65, 66, 70, 84, 104, 165,
        223, 244, 284

Weininger, Richard, 301, 303, 304, 305, 306, 380, 381
Weizsäcker, Ernst von,
    gives Wilson positive account of Chamberlain's
        first talk with Hitler, 4–5

revives Wohlthat contact with Wilson, 323
    mentioned, 9, 140, 180, 181, 229, 263, 326, 330,
        336
Westminster, Duke of, 'Bendor',
    background, 287
    and defeatist meetings, 348–349
Wiedeman, Fritz, 140–41
Wilson, Sir Horace,
    portrays appeasement as Eden's policy, ix–x
    clashes with Churchill at Board of Trade, xii,
        13–14
    partnership with Chamberlain, xiv–xv, 50–51
    chosen to accompany Chamberlain to
        Germany, 2–3, 171
    uncritically passes German flattery on to
        Chamberlain, 4–6
    feeds Chamberlain's vanity, 5–6, 13–14, 239–240
    background, 13–14, 46
    rise to top of Civil Service, 15–16, 22–25, 43
    General Strike, 17–18
    and Churchill's attempt to join builders' union,
        19–20
    advocates firm action against Edward VIII,
        28–29
    and Fisher manipulate Chamberlain to take
        action against Edward VIII, 29–30
    sees Churchill and King's Party as danger, 31–32
    retained as advisor by Chamberlain, 43
    supports Chamberlain's focus on foreign policy,
        46
    personality and skills, 46–47, 49
    perceived as powerful, 47–49
    sees Churchill and King's Party as danger,
        47–49
    balance of power in relationship with
        Chamberlain, 48
    trust between him and Chamberlain, 50–51
    opposes Roosevelt's initiative, 69–72
    tests Cadogan's commitment to Chamberlain's
        policy, 85–86
    trivialises British press freedom, 101–102
    dominates Sir John Reith, 106–108
    drives search for successor to Reith at BBC, 111
    picks Sir Charles Bruce-Gardner to overcome
        aircraft delivery delays, 120–21
    and Chamberlain plan political response
        to criticism of air rearmament, 121–122,
        124–125
    tasked with negotiating trade union support for
        rearmament, 122–124
    and Chamberlain believe Luftwaffe can destroy
        London, 123
    guides Butler's ministerial career, 128–129
    assures Kordt Chamberlain and he are
        committed to appeasement, 130–31
    unperturbed by Anschluß, 136
    deprecates any sign of frigidity towards
        Germany, 138
    first contact with Wohlthat, 138–139

Wilson, Sir Horace, *cont.*
    briefs von Dirksen on British fall-back position
      on Sudetenland, 141
    supports Bruce-Gardner against Lord Swinton,
      148
    chooses mediator for Czechoslovakia and his
      chief assistant, 158–159
    briefed on Czech leaders' obscene comments on
      Chamberlain, 160
    questions right of Czechoslovakia to exist, 161,
      188–189
    tells Kordt Britain supports negotiations over
      Czechoslovakia, 161–162
    Ashton-Gwatkin feeds false optimism on
      Czechoslovakia, 162
    unsettled by developments in Czechoslovakia, 163
    alerts Chamberlain to danger that Halifax
      might not reject advice from Churchill, 164
    tries to make Halifax soften proposed speech in
      Geneva, 164–166
    sees Foreign Office as threat to peace, 166
    ignores Kordt's plea that Britain take firm
      stance, 166–167
    originates Plan Z, 169–171
    advocates plebiscite in Sudetenland, 170
    goes to Berlin as Chamberlain's emissary,
      176–180
    keeps first meeting with Hitler going, 177
    decides against delivering Chamberlain's oral
      message to Hitler, 178
    softens impact of Chamberlain's oral message,
      179–180
    assures Hitler he will 'make … Czechos
      sensible', 180
    does not answer when Hitler asks what Britain
      would do if France attacked, 180
    recommends Czech capitulation, 181–182
    reports conversations with Hitler to inner
      Cabinet, 181–182
    tells Hesse that form of German occupation of
      Sudetenland crucial, 184
    tells Czech observers at Munich their country's
      fate, 185–186
    possible role in origin of Anglo-German
      Declaration, 186
    distorted account of Anglo-German
      Declaration, 187–188
    believes Munich agreement just, 188–189
    prepares to defend Munich agreement, 188–189
    with Fisher thwarts Hankey's plans for his own
      succession, 191–194
    appointed as head of the Civil Service, 194–195
    thwarts Fisher's plans for his own succession,
      194–195
    deprecates Wood's revival of air parity target,
      197–198
    challenges Wood on bomber strategy, 198–199
    focus on narrow measure of military strength,
      201–202

hostility to propaganda, 203–204
given authority over propaganda, 206–207
chooses new Minister of Information designate,
    207
manoeuvres against Tallents, 208–211
first open criticism of, 215–216
advises against broadening government, 216
detects disloyalty to Chamberlain by senior
    ministers, 223
sounds Hesse on possible agreement to
    humanise warfare, 225
forbids references to *Kristallnacht*, 229
lack of sympathy for Jews, 229
arranges subsidy to Reuters, 230
fears outcry against sell out of Czechs, 232
and origins of economic appeasement, 239–240
relationship with Norman, 240
secrecy over Schacht's visit to London, 241
sees Schacht in London, 241–242
manoeuvres against Hoare's propaganda plans,
    248–252
selects Directors General for Ministry of
    Information, 250–51
praises Chamberlain's persistency, 253–254
admits it would have been politically impossible
    not to give Poland guarantee, 260
tells Chamberlain public need firm response to
    Albania, 261
advises Chamberlain on response to Prague and
    Albania, 262
responsible for handling IRA bombing
    campaign, 264–265
wants Foreign Office to pressurise France on
    Italian demands, 270
works through Bonnet to make Daladier
    negotiate with Italy, 271–272
and doubling in size of Territorial Army, 274
discusses conscription with unions, 275–276
ranks Poland above Soviet Union, 280
proposes scheme to nullify an alliance with
    Soviet Union, 281–282
dinner with Ball, Drummond Wolff and
    Wohlthat, 287
outlines possible settlement to Wohlthat, 296
inadequate disclosure of Wohlthat talks,
    298–299
targets Boothby in Czech assets affair, 303–306
superintends unofficial visitors to Germany,
    307–308
concerned at number of unofficial emissaries to
    Germany, 309
briefs Tennant for his mission, 310, 311
edits Bryant's article, 313
briefs Kemsley for his mission, 314
take charge of follow-up to Kemsley mission,
    316–317
tells Dirksen Britain willing to abandon
    guarantee of Poland, 324–325
risk taken in proposal to Dirksen, 327

Wilson, Sir Horace, *cont.*
  proposals made through Kemsley rejected, 329
  proposals made through Dirksen rejected, 329–330
  incorrectly believes Hesse to be influential with Hitler, 331
  asks Americans to pressure Poland to negotiate, 333
  fails to convince Hitler that Britain will stand by guarantee to Poland, 334
  tries to persuade Germans that Polish treaty proves British determination to stand by guarantee, 335
  drafts reply to Hitler's letter with Butler, 337
  claims he rejected Hesse's appeal, 339
  Labour wants his influence curbed, 343
  de facto member of War Cabinet, 344–345
  responsible for final shape of Ministry of Information, 345
  attempts to rescue Ministry of Information, 347
  Nicolson criticises as naive, 350–51
  influence on ministerial appointments, 353, 354, 361–363
  and dismissal of Hore-Belisha, 355
  discusses ministerial reshuffle with Norman, 355–356
  plans to remove Simon as Chancellor of the Exchequer, 356–357
  chooses Stamp to replace Simon, 358–359
  had not considered Stamp's conflict of interest, 360
  prefers non-politicians as ministers, 361–362
  asks Baldwin to speak in favour of Chamberlain, 363
  criticises Woolton's protest against Nazi anti-Semitism, 363
  reservations about Dingli's 1940 mission, 366–367
  changes to JIC practice, 369
  criticised for poor choice of ministers, 370
  abandons political neutrality, 371
  remains as head of Civil Service, 374
  weeps at Chamberlain's funeral, 375
  attacked in *Guilty Men*, 377–378
  unhappy with Churchill government, 379–380
  orchestrates hostile investigation into Boothby, 380–81
  opposes honour for Dr R. V. Jones, 382–383
  early attempts to influence history of appeasement, 383
  suppresses evidence of Stamp affair, 383–384
  retires as head of the Civil Service, 384
  helps Mrs. Chamberlain choose biographer for her late husband, 386
  and Bournemouth by-election, 387
  insists that he and Chamberlain pursued correct policy, 387–388
  insists that lasting peace was the goal of appeasement, 388

  death of, 388
  mentioned, 9, 10, 27, 34, 35, 37, 44, 54, 59, 60, 61, 62, 64, 65, 74, 75, 76, 77, 80, 82, 84, 89, 91, 95, 96, 97, 103, 104, 105, 109, 110, 113, 118, 127, 142, 145, 150, 151, 152, 155, 157, 172, 173, 174, 175 183, 205, 212, 213, 221, 222, 226, 228, 231 237, 243, 245, 246, 247, 255, 257, 258, 255, 267, 269, 283, 284, 285, 287, 288, 289, 292, 295, 297, 299, 301, 302, 312, 315, 318, 319, 320, 321, 323, 324, 325, 326, 332, 336, 338, 346, 348, 349, 365, 368, 373, 385, 386, 387
Winterton, Lord, 121, 122, 151, 363
Wohlthat, Helmut,
  and Goering's involvement in foreign policy, 138–139
  first visit to London, 138–139
  dinner with Ball, Drummond Wolff and Wilson, 287
  second mission to London in 1939, 295–299
  discuss response to leak of talks with Wilson, 298
  mentioned, 140, 141, 142, 285, 287, 288, 289, 307, 308, 310, 311, 315, 322, 323, 324, 325, 327, 329, 336, 388
Wood, Sir Kingsley,
  awards Castle Bromwich Spitfire factory project to Nuffield, 152–153
  conciliates Lord Nuffield, 152–153
  adopts RAF's bomber strategy, 198
  admits a Ministry of Supply would provoke Germany, 235
  advises against removing Wilson as head of the Civil Service, 382
  mentioned, 154, 155, 197, 199, 200, 201
Woolton, Lord, 37, 43, 44, 47, 49, 50, 51, 362, 363

Young, Gordon, 232